SECRETS, LIES, AND BETRAYALS AT THE SOFT DRINK

GIANT

by

Gregory A. Clark

Foreword

Courage is not the absence of fear, but rather the strength to act in spite of it. Gregory Allen Clark is a daily reminder of this to the "status quo" at The Coca-Cola Company. He discovered a pattern of injustice and inequality in the workplace at the soft drink conglomerate that challenged him to stand firm against years of racial discrimination and unfair promotion practices. Greg Clark remains focused on the goal of exposing the soft drink giant with what he calls, "the truth–not just facts," which he believes can be manipulated–and has been by The Coca-Cola Company.

This is a nonfiction account and a first-hand testimony to the inequalities, injustices, discrimination, open expressions of prejudice and even contempt fostered upon himself and other African Americans at Coca-Cola that led to a $192.5 million class action lawsuit involving over 2000 employees.

In Secrets, Lies, and Betrayals at the Soft Drink Giant, Clark chronicles his tenure as a Security Officer, a seven-year episode riddled with contradictions and frustrations. He recounts how he joined the company with all the hope and expectation of a talented new hire, only

3

to become the next victim of an ingrained racist culture in the workplace. As a Security Officer and one committed to the safety and justice of the corporate environment, he discovered his own civil rights being attacked by supervisors, who felt threatened by his level of educational preparedness, as well as his race. They repeatedly suppressed his opportunity to advance in a career where he clearly demonstrated a passion for law enforcement, had a healthy work ethic and possessed leadership qualities. Always displaying a professional posture, Clark had impeccable credentials. He genuinely felt he possessed the knowledge and attributes that would propel his career with The Coca-Cola Company. However, others at the Coca-Cola Company felt the need to place open and difficult barriers in his path.

While the book focuses mainly on the culture of deception at Coca-Cola, it offers a few glimpses into how he became the man he is today, sharing personal vignettes of his youth, his family and the source of his incredible inner strength–his enduring faith in God.

Born in Holly Hill, South Carolina, as one of four children to Minnie and James Clark, Jr., Greg learned the value of hard work early on from his father who had to move his family up and down the east coast in order to provide them with a good life. After graduating from

the University of South Carolina with a Bachelor's degree in Criminal

Justice in 1989, he settled in Atlanta. In 1997, he earned a Master's

degree in Management. With a background of several years working in

private sector security, healthcare and within the penal system, Greg

felt he was more than adequately prepared to be considered for

employment at the Coca-Cola Company where his career could

advance as part of the organization. However, following a series of

instances of questionable actions and responses from management,

Greg's investigative mind began to wonder. He could not understand

why he was repeatedly not being considered for promotion at The

Coca-Cola Company after first being hired in 1996. He had been

overlooked for over 30 positions in 7 years within the security

department for positions in which he was qualified. Secrets, Lies, and

Betrayals at the Soft Drink Giant chronicles the hurdles he faced within

his own department, human resources and ultimately in the courtroom.

Eventually, the baton of deception was passed along to the original

counsel in the case of Clark vs. The Coca-Cola Company originally

filed in December of 1998. Cyrus Mehri, one of the most powerful racial discrimination attorneys in the country was overheard speaking to fellow attorneys in a manner that left Greg with a very bad feeling about him. It was then that he was led to prominent attorney Mr. Willie Gary.

His story reminds African Americans and other minorities that as a people, while they have made significant strides, there are still frontiers to conquer, particularly in companies like Coca-Cola that hold steadfast to the 'Good Ole Boy' System. He recounts the sheer arrogance and inconsideration of the hiring and promotion practices, and moreover the endorsement of decisions of higher ups that supported the actions of subordinates thereby creating the culture of Coca-Cola. He shares with readers the experiences of other colleagues who confided in him with their own humiliating stories of poor treatment at Coca-Cola. Reminiscent of the civil rights struggles of the 60's, Secrets, Lies, and Betrayals at the Soft Drink Giant is an inspiring story of one man's struggle for justice and fair treatment that led to a class action suit and the world-wide image shattering and stock plummeting consequences associated with their actions. The company has now made a commitment to examine their internal make-up, to develop ways to be more sensitive to people of different backgrounds and truly create a more culturally diverse workforce for all. Yet, it remains a sad state of affairs that in the year 2003, it is an unfortunate reality that such blatantly unfair hiring protocol, promotional practices and ingrained corporate culture are so prevalent at one of America's most highly regarded companies.

Kris

Preface

This book is the manifestation of a response to the principles inbred in me to be a person of faith, courage, preparedness and character.

Acknowledgements

I salute the original plaintiffs who stepped out on faith with me initially, as well as the more than 2000 other employees who experienced racial discrimination and joined our quest for parity and equal opportunity in the workplace at The Coca-Cola Company.

I wish also to acknowledge the associates, who have exemplified true Christian character and have been an unwavering tower of courage in the face of opposition through this entire ordeal. For every prayer that was said on behalf of those that stepped out to say "no more" I thank you.

Table of Contents

Secrets, Lies, and Betrayals

Chapter 1

Great Expectations

All my life, I have waited and searched for an employer that would accept me equally and promote me accordingly. Thank you Lord for the doors you opened to allow me to enter such a prestigious company as The Coca-Cola Company. As a little boy growing up in Holly Hill, South Carolina, a small country town in Orangeburg County, I remember how important it was to have a good job and how necessary it was to work hard to keep it. I remember all of my father's hard work to ensure my two brothers, my sister and I would have an honest chance to being successful in life. My father is the hardest working man I know.

As a child I could not understand why he would always insist on doing everything flawlessly. One day my father snatched the rake out of my hands as I worked in the yard. He could see I wasn't doing a good job. He said to me, "Gregory, don't learn to be so 'shitten'. Boy, in this world no one will give you anything. You got to hustle and prepare yourself for whatever life may present." I always listened, for he spoke with such a loud demanding voice and with such enthusiasm I

11

was almost afraid not to look in his direction and take heed when he spoke.

My father graduated from Roberts High School in Holly Hill and later traveled the East Coast learning a profession I thought did not match his demeanor. At the age of 19, he was a chef in one of the largest hotels on the East Coast, The Breakers of West Palm Beach, Florida. I can remember traveling during my adolescent years to many of the finest hotels in this country. White Face Inn in Lake Placid, NY, The Essex Sussex Hotel in Spring Lake Beach, NJ and in Alexandria Bay, NY, were a few of them that were fortunate enough to have my father accept the position of chef.

There is an old saying that "behind every good man there is a strong woman." My mother epitomizes the very essence of a good woman and a loving mother. She is a God-fearing, Holy Ghost-filled woman who made sure when my father was away working all was well at home. I remember all the hot meals and the strong support she gave each of us. Even today, I do not think my father realizes how many miracles we received through my mother's prayers and faith.

My father felt in order for me to be successful in life, I needed to be educated and go further than he in school. I never understood why he insisted so strongly on my going to college and earning a Bachelor's degree. Nevertheless, I never questioned him. He always said, "I would never tell you anything wrong. Your trials and tribulations I've experienced a thousand times." He experienced trials, some of which I knew about, but I wish he would have shared more about racism in this country.

I wish I realized there would be people who would fear me because of my level of education and my ambition, and be uncomfortable because I was black. Because of my upbringing and moral belief, I believed all men and women were created and should be treated equally. In his own way, my father tried to tell me some might frown upon you because you are different than them, because you have a particular job title, or because you represent a threat to "business as usual."

I wish Chef told me I would be denied positions because I had more education than the hiring manager. I wish Chef told me that in corporate America, white males with high school diplomas, who clearly did not qualify for management positions, would be given the position

over minorities with relevant advanced degrees of learning.

But, as I think back I remember Chef always said, "Son, it is not

what you know, it's who you know." I now understand what he was

saying. This world does not always present a clear picture of its reality.

I thank the Lord for my parents and for all they taught me.

I will never forget my first day at The Coca-Cola Company. The

beautiful marble floors and all the giant glass windows brought the

morning sunlight beaming proudly into the corporate environment. The

aesthetics of the building fascinated and astounded me. I remember

how well dressed the associates were. Most of the men dressed in dark

suits in black, navy blue or dark brown. The women wore loud colors

and many seemed to prefer skirt suits with accenting scarves and heels.

The group I worked for was nothing short of sharp. I remember

meeting my manager, Keith Marks, for the first time. He was standing

in the administration office when another white male, assistant

supervisor Tom Majors, introduced us. Keith told a joke I thought was

terrible, but everyone else in the office laughed, so I did as well. I soon

would come to believe in corporate America, most managers and directors hired people who were willing to do whatever they were told regardless of how one personally felt about the issue or task. But, at the start, I was mesmerized by the idea of working for such a prestigious company.

When I arrived at The Coca-Cola Company, the city of Atlanta was preparing for the 1996 Summer Olympics, which were only a few weeks away. During this time, the security department in which I worked would be constantly challenged. It was not a secret the Olympics would make a mark on the city's history, and The Coca-Cola Company would be a part of that as the city's most recognizable trademark. Some seemed to think the city was awarded the Olympics because of Coca-Cola.

I was thrilled to be a part of the excitement. The electricity in the city as it counted down the days until the Olympics was unlike anything I'd ever witnessed. I knew the months in preparation and throughout the Olympics was a chance for me to shine in my job. I also knew there'd be many opportunities for advancement when the Olympics were over. So, I concentrated on giving my "all" at work every day to make my employer proud.

As The Games launched and after they finished, many positions in my department were opened and some new positions were also created. I started thinking, 'I have only been in the department for a few months; nevertheless, if something comes available I am interested in, surely I am going to apply.'

In June of 1996, I applied for a Security Specialist position in the Investigations Group. The job requirements were 1-2 years of investigations experience; however, according to the posting, a Bachelor's degree would be considered in place of the experience. My Bachelor's in Criminal Justice and Master's in Management, along with my many years of experience seemed to be more than enough foundation for me to excel in the position.

The location of this position was in the group that handled most of the reports on stolen items within the company and a few other things relating to security and investigations. The interview period for the job began and ended. I did not receive an interview, nor did I receive any notification from the staffing department stating I did not qualify for the position. The Coca-Cola Company chose the "target selection interview process" to select their candidates. This process was one I was familiar with and strongly disapproved of. It allows managers to choose less qualified candidates and never be questioned about their decision. In the target selection system, minority candidates with strong educational backgrounds and experience could be overlooked. In the end, the position was given to a candidate who clearly did not meet the qualifications on the job announcement.

To my astonishment, I learned that this had long since been a practice in the department, as well as the company. Many of the senior and older officers that were in the department for a number of years joked about the company's hiring process. I heard comments like, "It does not matter what the qualifications of a potential candidate are", and "The security managers will always select the person that threatens their job the least." I thought this was just an assumption shared by a few coworkers until I got a telephone call before departing work one day.

My team leader, Stephen Grooms, called to say he needed to see me. I responded, "I am on my way." Many things crossed my mind as I walked down the corridor leading from the USA Building to meet with him.

Stephen greeted me and began by acknowledging that he was aware that I had applied for the Security Specialist position. I responded, "Yes I did." He went on to ask if there was anything wrong with my resume. I laughed and said, "Well, the paper is not the most expensive you can buy." Stephen then told me the manager of the hiring group was uncomfortable with my education. I asked, *"What do you mean 'uncomfortable' with my education?"* Stephen replied, "In this company, it is not common to see a black male as young as you are with a Bachelor of Science degree in Criminal Justice from a school like the University of South Carolina and a Master's degree in Management from Mercer University."

I sat there for a few moments staring at Stephen. I thought to myself, 'Stephen was currently seeking his Bachelor's degree.' Stephen was a former military man and he shared my race. I should have been insulted but I felt nauseated, confused, disappointed, and then a little angry. I thought, 'How dare you all have the audacity to question the authenticity of my educational credentials!' Each school has a registrar's office that will gladly confirm the status of each student that has ever attended the school. Stephen then stood and lowered his head as I left the room.

I shared my concerns with a friend I met shortly after coming to the company. He stated out of all of the supervisors in the Security Department, none had a Bachelor's degree. Therefore, when someone like me entered the department, it led others to examine themselves. I left work that day truly hurt. The very same education I sacrificed for made a white man with a General Education Diploma (GED) uncomfortable. *What effect would this have on my advancement in the department?*

My wife is a southern lady. She had the privilege of being raised on a farm and was a hard worker. She is my backbone, my inspiration, as well as my joy. After I explained to her what happened, she told me to remain focused on my goals and to continue working to achieve them. For the next several months, I began to study the culture of The Coca-Cola Company through the eyes of an educated black man who happened to be a security officer. I was curious if my experience was an isolated incident or a practice of the culture.

The associates appeared to be so influenced by the titles others held in the company. A system existed where each associate of the company was issued an I.D. badge. The executives and company officers wore green badges, and were considered the big money earners of the company (e.g., vice presidents,-executives). Red badges were given to associates who received benefits and all the privileges that came with being an employee of the company. Black badges were given to contract employees. This group, I imagined, was important enough to be given a job temporarily, but not essential enough to be given benefits. It was interesting how the associates of the company would treat their fellow co-workers according to the color of their badges.

I also noticed that blacks mostly wore black badges. Whites normally wore the green badges. Company policy stated every associate was to wear an I.D. badge on company grounds, and it was the job of my department, security, to stop and ask those without one visible for their I.D.

I remember many times stopping a "green badge" whose badge was in their pocket or purse. Often times, I would get strange looks for asking an associate who happened to be a green badge for their I.D.

The looks varied but most often they were looks that suggested tenure, as if to say, 'I have been here for almost 25 years, how dare you stop me and ask for my I.D. badge.'

When standing post, I often observed many of the associates coming to work with very long faces and dragging in from the parking garages as if they really did not want to be at The Coca-Cola Company on Mondays. On the other hand, on Fridays many of the same associates would come in the building with large smiles on their faces and shout "Happy Friday" as they approached. I often said to myself, 'Those of you who do not realize what a blessing it is to rise and prepare to come to a job cannot possibly realize the joy in each and every day of having a job.' I got the feeling that maybe many of the associates of the company were a little spoiled and needed a reality check.

One day as I stood at a post the security department referred to as the "Tech Connector," I counted the number of whites and blacks I saw. To my astonishment, forty-five white people came by before I saw even one black person. The black person was a contract employee who worked in housekeeping. I played these games hours at a time on various posts and became more curious each time I did it. Here is a company that is a household name in almost every black home in the world, but it does not appear the company is practicing what it preaches.

I did not rush to any judgments. Instead, I promised myself I would stay focused in order to accomplish my goals. My goals were to earn a position that offered advancement, and to earn a position where my education and experience would be accepted and appreciated.

In January of 1997, I met with Keith Marks and Stephen Grooms, my manager and supervisor. I requested the meeting to ask if there were going to be any positions available where he felt I could better serve the department. Keith responded by stating there would be some driving patrols and console positions available, and everyone would be interviewed and the best candidates selected. Not once did Keith mention a supervisor position would be available.

The following month, I requested a meeting with the director of the security department. I met with the director, Jim Reeves, a white male in his late 40's. It was an eye-opener. At Jim's request, Keith attended the meeting also. Jim was very aware of my credentials and after a short discussion related to the department; we had a little small talk. I was shocked by one of his statements. He said there were many young professionals with advanced degrees who were not able to find jobs. While this may have been true, I wondered why he was telling me this. I was the <u>only</u> person in the security structure with an advanced degree. Even he did not have a Master's degree. *Why he was telling me this?* Surely, in his position, he must have realized the asset I could be to the department, if given the right opportunity.

As the conversation neared an end, it was apparent my director had already decided I would not be given a position in the department. It was also apparent my manager informed him of my concerns and of our past conversations. As we all stood to exit the room, Keith said, "Well Jim, I think we have found our next Team Leader." The Director, Jim, said nothing as Keith patted me on my back as if I was a slave that had done a surprisingly good job in the fields that day. I was very uncomfortable and angry. A handshake would have sufficed.

The next time I saw Keith, he went on and on about how well I behaved and how comfortable I appeared conversing with Jim. I knew from that statement there were expectations and a particular

unbecoming manner in which my manager had expected me to behave.
I began wondering. *If these two white men who are in decision-making
positions can be so narrow minded, how many more are there in the
company, and in what positions are they hiding? Does it stop at being
narrow-minded or are there more adjectives to better describe their
actions? Is it possible that the chairman of the company believes
educated blacks, also having a place in this company, a place that is
much lower than that of whites? Were other minorities treated this way
too?*

In March of 1997, a supervisor position became available. The job
required a Bachelor's degree in Criminal Justice or related field;
however, extensive varied professional experience would be considered
instead of the degree. The position required at least five years of
experience in security, law enforcement or related fields, including 2-3
years of security supervisory experience. I had all of those credentials.

I applied for the position through the company's staffing
department and again did not receive a response from the staffing or
security departments. One security officer passing my post asked if I
received an interview for the position. I responded, "Not yet." The

officer went on to explain the process of interviewing had already started and Tom Majors was the first person to be interviewed. Tom was a white male with neither the education nor experience the job description required, but the manager liked him. I wondered why I was not contacted like every other candidate who did not receive an interview.

While standing post, my Team Leader, Mr. Grooms, passed and I asked if the interview process started. Stephen replied, "Yes." I then expressed my concern that I did not get a response back from the staffing department about an interview. Stephen then said, "I am only interviewing the names that I have been given." That evening, I went about my usual routine – worked out, played some basketball at the gym, and then went home to unwind and prepare for the next day.

It was approximately 10:00 p.m. when the telephone rang. I answered and a voice on the other end said, "Is this Gregory Clark?" I replied, "Yes," and my mind immediately began working to figure out the familiar voice on the other end. "This is Stephen Grooms. I am calling to let you know that you will be interviewing for the supervisor position at 10:00 a.m. tomorrow."

Did he just say I have an interview in less than 12 hours? "That's great, but why am I just now being notified?" I asked him. "I don't know Greg, but just be prepared," he responded. I hung up the telephone feeling a bit of anticipation, but mostly angry. Angry that they felt I was not entitled to the same notice other candidates were given. I was angry it appeared I was being set up to fail by not being given sufficient time to prepare for such an important interview.

What was the urgency for my interview to be done on such short notice? Perhaps I was only given an interview to be appeased and I was never a serious candidate for the position. One would think management would want to establish a precedent of hiring the most qualified candidates for each position. Whatever the circumstances, I made up my mind to give it my best shot.

The interview process was divided into two parts. During the first part of the interview I met with my team leader, the evening shift team leader and the manager of the Investigations Group. The interview format was one I was very familiar with, the Situation Task Action Result (STAR) interview process. I had recently studied it during my graduate studies at Mercer University. I experienced and used this style several times in former management positions with my previous employers. My interview went extremely well. One interviewer later came back to me to say how much he enjoyed listening to me articulate my experiences.

The second part of the interview went so well that after the interview was over my manager stated what a joy it was for him to have interviewed me. Also present in this interview was the development coordinator for security, Lynn Baker. Lynn stated she found me very easy to talk with and said she truly enjoyed meeting me. After Lynn made that comment my manager stated, "Indeed, the interview went extremely well; however, there will be other positions coming available in the department."

I looked at one of the three interviewers, the third shift team leader. He was a black man and I wanted to assess his facial expression. But I could not; he lowered his head just as I looked in his direction, as if he was ashamed of the comment that was just made. I was shaken and stunned because my worst fears had been confirmed. My interview was a joke. Before I left the room, I knew the position had been filled before my interview process even began. Keith's comment also confirmed for me that I was only given the interview to be appeased. I was never viewed as a serious candidate for the position.

A few weeks passed and the debriefings for the position began. Lynn Baker and Keith Marks were responsible for the debriefings. When I arrived for my meeting, Lynn and Keith were sitting behind a desk with a single chair placed directly in front of them. Keith then cracked a joke; this let me know I did not get the position. I have studied behavior for a long time and was around Keith long enough to know he told jokes when not so pleasant news was forthcoming. He looked nervous and uncomfortable. He said the reason I was called at home at such a late hour informing me of the interview was because my resume had gotten lost in the system. I showed no emotion on my face but I thought to myself, 'what a liar.' Lynn sat next to Keith very quietly as if she knew I knew he was lying.

As Keith continued talking, I remembered a memorandum I received a few weeks prior from Lynn, before the interview process began. It stated that she (Lynn) received my resume and would continue to review it and search for a position that would best match my credentials. I sat and listened to why I did not receive a position that

I was more qualified for-than any other person in the department. Lynn stated, "I do not see where your past experience matches what we are looking for here at headquarters. Furthermore, I do not think that you believe your present job as a security officer is important". *When did she become a mind reader?* Yet, Keith Marks, who served as the hiring manager of the department, did not give me any reason why I did not receive the position. After all was said, I was given an opportunity to respond. I anticipated that I would not be getting that job so I was prepared to respond to whatever reasons were given as to why I did not get the position.

I asked Lynn and Keith if they had a copy of the job announcement with the requirements for the position. Both responded, "No! We do not." I promptly handed each of them a copy of the job description. The description asked for extensive and varied professional security/law enforcement experience. I then gave them each a copy of my resume with the exclusion of my Bachelor of Science in Criminal Justice and Master's degree in Management, I told them I had worked in the penal system, health care, private security sector and presently in corporate security. Lynn then had the audacity to ask me if I thought I was too ambitious.

I paused for a few moments, looked in her eyes and I wondered if I were a white male with the credentials that I possessed, would she have asked the same question. I responded to Lynn with a simple, "No! I do not." I find it hard to believe that Keith's and Lynn's efforts to dismiss my education and past experience would have been so blatant if I were white. The two grew quiet for several moments and then Keith, appearing to be angry, said "the decision has already been made and you did not get the position." Before exiting, I thanked the two for their time and consideration.

I left the room confused and disappointed. As I walked down the corridor to the elevators to return to my post, my heart grew heavy and so did the tears in my eyes. I could hear my father saying, "Boy, deal with these white folks. Only you can stop yourself from becoming successful." After I returned to my post, I realized for the first time in my life, I had experienced blatant racism. It was subtle, very professionally administered but indeed racism. *How could it be here at The Coca-Cola Company?* This company donates millions of dollars to black college foundations, and professes it treats and promotes people of all races equally.

That was it! Racism! It was there all along, but because of my naiveté and my unwillingness to accept that racism existed in The Coca-Cola Company, I had been reluctant to label the treatment I had experienced. But wait, no one called me a nigger. This type of racism was different from what I had previously experienced, heard of, or read about.

As I reflected on my experiences, it became clear to me that instead of calling me names and throwing rocks, sticks, and bottles or turning on fire hoses, these white folks designed and implemented a new attack. No name calling but they limited my earning ability. Nobody threw a stick at me but they blocked me from promotions. Instead of a physical attack, it was a financial and emotional attack.

Surely, they realized that men are normally considered the head of household. Surely, they knew that historically the male in the family was considered the breadwinner. Yet they denied me the chance to do those things well for my family. By limiting my opportunity for advancement in the workplace; they kept my salary limited. It appeared to me their attitude was: If we control the amount of money he is bringing into his family, we can directly control the neighborhoods he lives in and the schools his children will attend.

As my mind stretched to consider this sort of covert attack on blacks, I wondered if this type of racism was a common thread in the corporate structure. *Did it affect other races or people who were "different?"* I feared that if this kind of injustice could be prevalent at Coke, there may be other such major corporations with the same growing and festering racist plague.

Chapter 2

A Pattern of Being Passed Over

In April of 1997, Keith Marks announced Tom Majors was selected to fill the team leader's position. This was not a surprise to me. Keith had already selected Tom to act in the position until it was filled and he was the first person interviewed. Tom was given the position although he did not meet the educational or the experience requirements for the position. His credentials became general knowledge and small talk for many of the officers. This, I thought, was an excellent example of how whites took care of each other.

I asked one of the older black males, Mitch, who had been in the department for 15 years, "How could a person get a position that almost doubles their salary and clearly not be qualified?" Mitch looked at me with a fatherly concern and said, "The boy is white, Clark. White folks will always take care of their own. You have too much education for these 'Crackers.' Use them to get what you want and get the hell out of The Coca-Cola Company. This is no place for a young educated black male like you." I realized that Mitch was filled with bitterness, but his intentions were sincere.

Each day after departing, I would leave work and try to relieve daily stress by working out at the Run & Shoot Gym on Metropolitan Avenue just south of the city. However, this was not an easy thing for me to digest. I depended on and looked forward to hugging my wife when I returned home each day. She is the best thing that ever happened to me. To this day, I do not know what I did to deserve her, but I am thankful to have her by my side. She never once tried to persecute or ridicule me for the actions I took. When I made a decision that did not go as planned, she always remained positive.

Toward the latter part of March 1997, a lead officer position became available. This position was an assistant to the team leader's position. I applied for the position through the staffing department and was told during the first week of May that I did not qualify for the position. I asked Meena Swats, the talent acquisition person, for the reason and if she had personally looked at my resume. She replied "yes," and began thumbing through a pile of about thirty-five resumes. After I watched her look through the resumes, she finally reached mine at the very bottom of the pile and said, "I must get back with you on this decision after I further review your resume."

I knew that this was the first time Meena saw my education and experience. She appeared to realize how senseless it was to blurt out that I did not qualify for the position. I pressed and asked her, 'If I qualified for the position of team leader a few weeks ago and the lead officer reports to the team leader, how could I not qualify for this vacancy also?' Meena then stated, 'I did not say you did not qualify; I meant you were not chosen.' I asked, 'If professionalism, demeanor, and credentials did not figure into the selection process, what criteria were used?' Meena began to grow visibly agitated and said, "Sometimes they are hand-picked by Management." As I sat in an upright position, feet flat on the floor, with my back pressed against the back of the chair, I noticed this woman appeared to be more interested in my manicured nails than what I was saying.

After realizing that Meena obviously had not looked at my resume and that a conspiracy definitely revealed itself, I left the office. Before I left the room, Meena stated, "I will review your resume and get back with you." To date, I have not heard from her.

Here it was again, a different month, a different position, a different department, and a different white person delivering the racism, but it all stemmed from the same source. *I thought, 'How could she not select me for an interview with all I brought to the table?' What if my manager Keith Marks and Lynn the security coordinator deliberately overlooked me for the position?* If I had gotten the position, I would have been working with both of them.

I had applied for several positions and began to realize that the bright future that I hoped for at The Coca-Cola Company may not be bright at all. Keith and Lynn chose Henry Idom, a black, retired military male, to fill the position. I thought this was strange. A few weeks prior, Henry applied for the team leader position only to be told by Keith and Lynn he did not have the education required for the position. However, a few short weeks later he was given the position he also lacked educational credentials for. This indicated these managers simply placed a black male in the position for statistical purposes, not because it was the best fit.

Why were these people intent on holding me down? A manager or any person in a leadership or decision-making position should have been seeking the best-qualified person, regardless of color, for each position in their department.

Why did it seem these two older white people with the obvious upper hand, were seeking to kill the spirit and the ambition of this young black educated male?

Why did the management of my department fear me? Was it simply because I am a black male and the media has always depicted black males as being dead-beat fathers, on drugs or having being convicted of at least two serious crimes by the age of twenty-one... and I am none of those things? Or is it because I stand 6 feet and 4 inches tall, strong and clean-cut?

Could it be that when members of the predominantly white management team approached me, I looked them straight in the eyes as I answered their questions, and even had the audacity to ask questions of them?

In April of 1997, I was blown off my feet by the termination of an entire department with the exception of one associate. An incident occurred that embarrassed the upper management group of security. There were meetings held by management trying to decide how this delicate situation was going to be handled. Management first called a meeting to warn all of security, if any word of this leaked out of the department, the person accused would be terminated immediately. It was a scandal that originated in the Internal Investigations Department. This group was considered a step above the security officers and a step beneath the corporate security division.

There was obviously a collective agreement made by some of the members and the manager of the group. Apparently, the group had access to a private telephone line of one of the local radio stations. This radio station had a wide range of listeners and was popular because it rewarded money for being the correct numbered caller, selected by the station's disc jockey. Consequently, there were a few big winners who came out of the Investigations Group.

A member of the group won approximately $50,000, and chose to have his money delivered to the place from which he made the lucky telephone call, The Coca-Cola Company headquarters on North Avenue in Atlanta. Ironically, I was working the main gate when the truck entered looking for the gentleman. The radio station did an investigation of its own and found there were many big winners coming from the same number at The Coca-Cola Company. The radio station confronted Coca-Cola and the company properly dealt with the problem internally and confidentially.

This event embarrassed the security department, as well as the company; it could not possibly reach the public. Upper management quickly provided the only two black members of the group with an ultimatum. The two were given an opportunity to resign with a minimum severance pay of three months. Another gentleman, a white male was also given an ultimatum, but he sought legal representation and remained at the company for a few more weeks after the offer. The manager of the group was also removed. However, because of the sensitive nature of the situation, upper management decided to wait a few weeks after the dust had settled to remove the manager of the group. Security management wanted to make certain those who knew of the entire incident had forgotten or lost interest in the incident before the only manager of the group was also removed.

Management needed to try and find a way to make it look normal, that a white male in a management position, in his early thirties, with a GED and all the stock options that are given to white males in his position, could possibly decide to walk away from the company and pursue a career in the insurance industry. This did not go as smoothly as management expected. Many of the members of the security department had knowledge of the incidents and were openly discussing it. Most of the security officers knew that this was the company's way of gently removing a white person liked by upper management.

I was curious if there were laws the company disregarded in order to protect the whites that were knowingly committing unlawful acts? Who would question a company that has been looked upon as the most diverse company in the world? How often do we hear of a Black organization to which The Coca-Cola Company has donated thousands of dollars to, like the United Negro College Fund for instance? And, how often do we subscribe to black-owned magazines that are supposed to represent and depict universal equality for all, especially African Americans, and see one or two blacks The Coca-Cola Company uses as featured tokens in advertising? The blacks in the company, in my opinion, are used to continually win over and deceive other blacks into believing working for the company is the best thing that could ever happen to them.

Ultimately, by featuring one or two of the few blacks in management positions in black-owned magazines, the company succeeds in doing many things. First, it proclaims to the public it promotes and evaluates fairly, which undoubtedly is a lie. Please, let us not continue to be misled. The Coca-Cola Company knows many of these readers of the magazines are black professionals. Therefore, they strive to and have indeed made a commendable impression on those who care that blacks are being treated equally in corporate America. Because blacks perceive the company as one that treats them fairly, they will continue to purchase its products.

I can remember my father telling me that controversy is not all bad. He would also say that if there is a relationship, whether business or personal, where everything always appears to be peachy keen, if one looks deep enough something is drastically wrong. He was correct. Oftentimes, as humans we perceive a situation to be one particular way. Moreover, from that perception, an attitude is formed and from that attitude a behavior is acted out.

The country and the world have perceived The Coca-Cola Company as being a company that cares about the people of the world.

If the true reality of The Coca-Cola Company is in its goal to provide equal growth for all, why is there only one black executive vice president of the company? Statistically, the spending power of the minority is one of the most powerful and consistent moneymakers for shareholders worldwide. Therefore, the population that brings in the most money for the organization should be represented more fearlessly at all levels of the company. *On the other hand, how many of the Board members are black?*

Why is it that a black man or woman in a position where he or she is obviously a token minority, thanks and praises the organization instead of seeing that there are several other positions which should also be filled by minorities? Why are there so few blacks at the vice president, director and managerial levels? It is imperative to note that companies have placed "double minorities" in a few key positions in the hopes of winning favor but in reality have given them no power. A black female executive for instance is likely without the power to affect or contest the inequalities of the culture so often referred to as "The Good Ole Boy System."

Certainly, I am not saying that the black directors of the company or people at that level would actually do anything if the opportunity presented itself. However, it is fair to suggest that because of the dogmatic ways I have seen the company terminate and remove blacks in positions of power; it would be unwise if any of these carefully placed few were to begin a war that obviously they could not win.

I have witnessed on more than one occasion blacks with years of experience in the company, called to one of the vice president floors, terminated from employment and then escorted out of the building by security. Normally, the company chooses to list the reason for the termination as a violation of the "Code of Conduct." I quickly learned that the company feels it can legally protect itself if the termination is listed under these circumstances. I couldn't help but wonder if the position was initially filled with someone who was truly qualified then this termination might not have occurred.

I started thinking back to the comment that Stephen made when I applied for the security specialist position in his group. He told me that the reason I did not get the position was that one of the managers was uncomfortable with my education. It is amazing how some things work.

The same white managers that made sure a white male got the position, terminated the very same white male who did not qualify for the position.

I prayed God would give me strength to endure and persevere over all that was evil and not of Christ, and by His grace; mountains would begin to be moved. As I stood on my post, my white supervisors would pass me on their way to meetings and chuckle. I imagined maybe they were thinking, "He has all the experience and education, but look where he is and look where we are." At one point, I disliked everyone that was associated with holding me back from being promoted.

Not only were there many whites overlooking my credentials, but also a handful of blacks who were given positions representing the Equal Employment Opportunity Commission Group in the company. Coca-Cola really did a job putting this group together. The group consisted of very few blacks. The ones I knew of were an investigator of allegations and an administrative assistant. I remember e-mailing that particular investigator to request a meeting.

When I arrived in her office I realized she was one of the black women I would frequently see rushing in the corridors. She always seemed to be stressed. Her office was messy. There were papers and folders everywhere. She was a well-dressed, attractive woman and from the look of her office, one might think she was a very busy sister. I carefully shared my concerns with her and presented some documentation as well. During the first meeting, she appeared to be extremely interested in what I was saying.

Two months passed before we were able to review the findings of her investigation. When I returned to her office, I could sense the news I was about to hear was not pleasant as I sat down. Immediately she stated, "I found all of your allegations to be false." She went on to say each person in a supervisor's position qualified for his or her positions. As she continued to talk, I could no longer hear her voice.

I was looking at her but I saw all the white faces of my management team and heard the exact same words they said to me earlier. I knew then a proper investigation was not done; she simply went down to see my manager and listened to what he said. The investigator smiled and thanked me, for bringing many things The Coca-Cola Company was not aware of to the attention of the company.

I was not sure of what she meant until several weeks later. It was then I learned every supervisor and assistant supervisor had registered to begin working on a Bachelor's degree, including the manager, Keith, who continuously tried to ignore my Master's degree. Here we had a manager working with the EEOC representative of the company trying to cover up blatant racial discrimination. Apparently, in many organizations blacks are given positions where their primary function is to eliminate any person's idea they have been discriminated against. *Was that what these folks were doing too?*

The Coca-Cola Company handpicked each person that works in its EEOC Group. I once saw a member of this group walking down the corridor towards her office with a little black boy about ten years old. I imagined the handsome little fellow was her son. I grew sad, for I could not help but think that his mother may have a job in which she was forced to help perpetuate racism in corporate America. Didn't she realize that the very same games she is helping the culture of Coca-Cola play with my life and my family's lives might also be played against her precious little boy who will soon grow up to be a black man?

46

At that point, I felt no anger. I knew she thought she was doing what she must do to raise her child. I wondered how her heart would be saddened when she realized the system she was once a part of was the very same system that may prohibit her beloved son from making an honest living. On that day, I was reminded many of us do not see the true structure of society. I believed in my heart if she knew her son would someday experience racism as I had, her approach to her job would have been different.

The investigations department soon found itself with several vacancies. Two of the three positions were filled from outside of the company and a white male who was an administrative assistant for several years filled the other investigator's position. There were no interviews for the positions or any job postings. This was a case where the department manager (Keith) saw a need to fill a position and simply placed in the position another white male who he liked. The jobs required a Bachelor's degree in a related field and several years of experience in security and investigations, but once again, selected candidates did not meet the requirements. One candidate who received the job had worked side by side with me as an officer and had no problem sharing his work experience with me, so I knew without a

doubt he was hired without the required credentials.

Certainly, the company was aware of federal guidelines that

stipulate the number of minorities, which must be employed in the

company. Nevertheless, the company cushioned itself with attorneys

who were paid to protect its golden image. *Could the company find*

ways to manipulate statistics so they appeared to be within the

standards of the law? An example of this was the hiring of minorities.

If federal guidelines stipulate a number of minorities must be working

in the company, and does not stipulate the degree or salary level which

they should hold, the company may have very well hired a large

number of minorities and placed them in lower, salaried positions. That

was the case in my department where managers continued hiring whites

for the higher salaried positions and blacks for the lower.

By January of 1998, I counted more than twenty positions for

which I qualified. At this point it was obvious I would not be

considered for management or a higher salaried position in the

department, no matter what! I guessed management felt offended

because I had confronted my superiors in person and in writing. After researching many issues I found to be against company policy, and some against the law, my feeling was confirmed. I was not the only educated black male that experienced racism at this level. *Why was I so shocked?* Maybe asking these questions was for the purpose of making myself take a deeper look into the problem.

I remember being told by a colleague about an African American female who was out on stress leave because she had experienced racial discrimination at The Coca-Cola Company. I thought little of this situation until I spoke with the sister. I telephoned her and introduced myself. She quickly took over the conversation. Because of the relationship she had with a former coworker of mine who gave me her telephone number, she became instantly comfortable with me. The sister's name was 'Lady Two'. She was an associate at The Coca-Cola Company for nine years. She asked me how long had I been in the company and what my job was? I answered her questions and she continued sharing some of the experiences she had. She was very articulate and well versed on exactly what happened to her and why. After a short conversation, I invited her to a meeting that changed my life forever.

We met secretly to discuss some of the concerns both former and current black employees had about the culture of The Coca-Cola Company. Then, I decided to set up a second meeting. The meeting was held at one of the associate's homes that also had experienced racial discrimination.

For many months I'd been in close contact with Rev. JW, President of the Clayton County Chapter NAACP. Rev. Watts and two NAACP office holders were also in attendance. At this second meeting, Rev. Watts suggested we start the meeting with a prayer and then allow each person to introduce themselves and tell a little about their experiences at Coke. I sat, listened and observed. I heard things that I could hardly believe. I saw strong black men break down in tears as they shared their experiences at The Coca-Cola Company. I listened to people who were associates of this company for 15-20 years or more, share similar experiences about how they had been mistreated. I heard stories about white directors and managers referring to black associates as "buckwheat" and "nigger" even with the white person doing the name calling face to face. No one could bear to look at the other as experiences were shared in the room. Rev. Watts and his colleagues shook their heads in disbelief and buried their faces in humble hands.

The sadness in the room was unlike anything I had ever experienced. Each person bowed their heads as if they were ashamed of what they endured. They appeared to be blaming themselves for what The Coca-Cola Company put them through. I thought I had 'been through something,' but what I experienced paled in comparison to what was shared. The room appeared cold. As each associate shared his or her period of stress, the tears flowed as they spoke. I thought to myself, *"Why am I here? What is my purpose for coming to this gathering?"*

Then it was my turn to share my experiences. I did not know where to begin, so I began by telling them all to hold their heads up. "Not one of you is responsible for what has happened to you. You are only responsible if you leave this meeting after hearing what you have heard and do nothing." I said, "You are only responsible if you turn your heads and act as if all is well in The Coca-Cola Company, knowing your history has proven different." Before I knew it, my voice raised an octave and I sounded as though I was preaching. This wasn't my intention at all. All I wanted to share was it was not a coincidence African Americans are discriminated against. We live and work within a system that promotes and tolerates racial oppression.

I believe it is by design blacks are discriminated against. I am not suggesting that blacks are the only people who are discriminated against, nor am I suggesting that every black person has been discriminated against. However, I am a black male who has formed an opinion from my personal experiences. I realize others are discriminated against too because of the color of their skin, their stature or other reasons. However, on this particular day I spoke of my experience and how I was passed over in my department for promotion after promotion. I pointed out I first thought I needed to be in the department for a specific period of tenure to be promoted and how I later learned white males with less education and tenure were being promoted and I was not even given a chance to interview.

Lady Two, who became a lead plaintiff, contacted the soon-to-be lead counsel after she met Mrs. Roberts, a plaintiff of Roberts vs. Texaco at one of her book signings in Atlanta. She had an opportunity to speak freely with Mrs. Roberts and it was then she learned of a

52

courageous lawyer, Cyrus Mehri. Lady Two was excited to get in contact with this man. She was pleased with the interest Cyrus showed to her concerns. I was skeptical. I wondered why Cyrus was so interested in a person he knew absolutely nothing about. I became even more curious when I learned he was one of the most sought after discrimination lawyers in the country. Lady Two called me to share the conversation she had with Cyrus.

I was processing. I then decided to meet with a few people who I knew were having similar problems to see how they felt about possibly going forward with a lawsuit. A conference call with Cyrus was arranged and I contacted only a few people to participate. The call was informal but informative. We shared a few of our experiences at The Coca-Cola Company. The lawyer then shared a few general points about discrimination cases, especially those in the South. He spoke of the 'Good Ole Boy System' that ran The Coca-Cola Company.

The call lasted for a little over an hour and at the end Cyrus sounded extremely concerned, almost apologetic, about what we were experiencing at the company. During my psychology courses, I studied behavior. Drawing from that I could sense Cyrus seemed sad that he could not help us at that time. Not understanding his hesitation, I did not know if I could trust Cyrus. So, instead of giving him all that we had I only gave him enough information and detail to make him thirsty.

Before ending the call, Cyrus encouraged all of us to stay together and to be there for each other. The mood in the room was unfamiliar. We heard for the first time how lengthy, difficult and involved it would be to continue as a group trying to prove our concerns were valid. As I looked around the room I saw long faces; some showed signs of fear and others were blank. I, too, felt after this call we could not possibly win. We did not know what our next steps should be, but I was not willing to quit.

As I drove home I recalled one of my father's friends sharing with me how my father was forced to defend himself over the years. Chef grew up in the 50's and raised a family through the 60's and 70's. It is unrealistic to think as a black man with a position considered to be a white man's job; my father did not experience racism at its worst. Robert "Hash" Brown was my father's friend, he shared some of the situations my father faced, like the time my father had received the Chef's position at The Breakers Hotel in West Palm Beach, FL. In the late 60's and early 70's, it was unheard of for a black man to be the Chef at an establishment as large and as prosperous as The Breakers Hotel. Many of the white employees had a problem with reporting to a black man. Hash recounted to me many of the times my father had to defend himself physically against whites who were so prejudiced they wanted to harm him.

As I drove, my mind went a little deeper and focused on my future. I started thinking, *'I do not have any children yet, what if God chooses to bless me with a little one and that child confronts me one day with a situation that is racially motivated? How do I tell my son or daughter that they should turn their heads and walk away from blatant racism, without confronting it in some form or fashion? What kind of father would I be?* As I continued to think about the situation we were in, I knew I should press on, if for no other reason than for the sake of my unborn children. My father did not turn his head and hope that when he turned his head back, the racism would have taken care of itself. Instead, he stood his ground, picked his battles and fought with all of his might. And that is one of the reasons I am the man I am today.

There are many black fathers that have endured the pain and disrespect of being called names such as nigger, boy, and coon by racist whites. Nevertheless, through name calling and fighting, I imagine neither my father nor other black fathers lost focus of what was necessary and essential to raise their families. My father ignored being called a coon, nigger or boy, so that I could one day live to be a man. That reason alone was enough for me to find the strength to continue fighting for equality for all people. By continuing the fight our parents started, maybe our children won't have to fight as hard for what is rightfully theirs. At that point, I realized every member of the group might need to be reminded what the true struggle was really about.

I decided to strike up conversations with other black associates in the company just to see what, if any, concerns they had with the culture of The Coca-Cola Company. As I was standing one day in the USA Lobby, a focal point of all the traffic at headquarters, I spotted a black male to whom I often spoke. This brother had not been blinded as to what was really happening in the company. Ike had been at a manager's level for many years and was no stranger to the racism in the company. We often spoke of the number of blacks who were in his group and the number of black managers per white managers in the company. Ike and I talked about what it takes as a black man to be successful in The Coca-Cola Company. He believed for a black man in the company, there was no blueprint for success.

Ike worked in almost every major city in this country for Coke. His white managers told him it was necessary for him to move his family many times to acquire the experience needed to work at headquarters. However, when he finally arrived in Atlanta, he quickly learned he had far more experience and time in the field than any of his white managers. He also realized he could work both sides of the bottling business, as well as the marketing aspects of the company. After talking to the whites in his group, he learned many of them received transfers to Atlanta without any experience in the field. Ike spoke of a "glass ceiling." He used this expression to describe the level to which blacks were allowed to rise in his group.

Ike mentioned of about 200 people in his group, there was not one black director. Ike was normally a soft spoken person, but the more he spoke of the "glass ceiling" the more agitated he became. So I asked him, "Are there any other people that might have similar concerns?"

Ike responded, "Every black person that walks through the doors of The Coca-Cola Company as an employee has a concern. These concerns focus on the racist culture of The Coca-Cola Company; however, I am not sure just how open they will be to talk about what is going on. Most of the blacks are afraid to discuss the true reality of the company for fear of losing their jobs. Something needs to be done."

I then saw a black female to whom I often spoke. I asked her if she or any people she knew had concerns about the culture in The Coca-Cola Company. She smiled and glanced back over each of her shoulders before saying, "Why don't you call me and we can arrange some time to talk?"

I waited an hour before calling her. We agreed to meet in the basement of her building so no one would see us talking. When I met her, she thanked me for coming. This seemed strange because it was me that approached her. She then told me there were many blacks who were suddenly let go from the company. These people had been with The Coca-Cola Company for almost 25 years and overnight it seemed they were no longer qualified for their jobs. She went on to say The Coca-Cola Company had an ingenuous way of getting a person who had been terminated to sign a "Disclaimer Agreement." This was a contractual document designed to keep blacks or anyone that left The Coca-Cola Company from going to the public and speaking negatively about the company. The young lady, Jane, then spoke of how disappointed she was with the number of blacks in her department. She was an educated woman with an advanced degree in a technical field. Jane felt because she was a single mother of two, she was not in a position to speak out on the injustices in her department. However, she agreed to get in touch with the people she knew who were interested in discussing their experiences at The Coca-Cola Company.

As the days passed, I met more blacks who were concerned with the plight of African Americans in the company. Several of them had been with the company for many years and had very strong opinions of why things happened the way they did. I listened.

After carefully screening those that approached me, it was time to set another meeting with everyone. I was skeptical of every person I met. While I wanted every black to be with us, I knew that some might choose to warn the company about what was forthcoming.

Most of the people were so tired of the system they agreed to meet any time after work. It was essential to make sure those who said they were interested knew the importance of keeping the information exchanged confidential. I became increasingly concerned with protecting the livelihoods of those who were willing to meet. After a lot of careful thinking and planning, we decided to meet in a public place – a restaurant. I located a restaurant that would be convenient for everyone. Members of the NAACP were again present.

We met on Sunday afternoons and to my surprise, every person who said they would attend was there. I made a checklist of everyone I spoke with and scratched their names off as they entered. This meeting took off in a different direction than the first one. The same people who cried and were ashamed of their experiences now spoke with confidence. We knew this was going to be the most serious obstacle most of us had ever faced. Our goal was to let the entire world know that The Coca-Cola Company discriminates based on race.

Certainly, Coke had a strategically designed system to counter any attack on its integrity or image. If The Coca-Cola Company controlled and manipulated the media, it could promote and advocate corporate harmony as much as it liked without there being any system of evaluation or monitoring to determine if that which has been projected is an actual reality. Several of the NAACP members shared experiences of fighting discrimination within large, rich and powerful corporations. They spoke of the many ways a company would try to refute the allegations brought forth. They warned that many companies choose to begin marketing projects designed to counter such attacks or alleged charges. In others words, The Coca-Cola Company would probably begin advertising more fearlessly targeting the black population. In addition to marketing strategies, companies would also pay large sums of money to African Americans who were respected worldwide and have them market their products.

As these concerns were being shared, I looked around to see the expressions on everyone's face. All eyes and minds appeared to be focused. Throughout the meeting not once did I hear any negative comments as to what was about to take place. I left the meeting feeling proud, for I knew the group collectively decided to go forth no matter what. I could sense the group's mood transferred from one of pity and gloom, to that of a determined unified force.

A short time passed before Rev. Watts informed me of a letter he drafted and sent to Doug Ivester, Chairman of The Coca-Cola Company. Rev. Watts described the amount of time that passed without a response from The Coca-Cola Company as "lengthy." I asked if he thought the company took his letter seriously. He replied, "If they did not, maybe they will once they realize I am not going away."

I had a great deal of confidence and trust in Rev. Watts. I'd ask him questions trying to detect a sign of weakness or fear but I never saw him afraid. We often spoke at odd hours of the night to make sure we were always on the same page. After a few more weeks, Rev. Watts shared with me that he had heard from The Coca-Cola Company. He stated, "The lady in charge of the EEOC group called. She wanted to know what would be the best time to meet with a few of the vice presidents of the company." Rev. Watts went on to say, "It was not until I spoke of a protest march to another black male with close ties to senior management at The Coca-Cola Company that I was then granted this meeting."

On August 31, 1998, the NAACP met with the Vice President of Human Resources, Mitch Walker, and the Vice President of External

Affairs, Ingus James. The Sunday before the meeting, we met and discussed a few concerns the NAACP found alarming. There were more allegations of racial discrimination. In this meeting, Rev. Watts informed me The Coca-Cola Company agreed to have me present during the meeting. I told him not to believe that, and to expect something or someone to stand in the way of me attending the meeting.

The next day, I informed my supervisor of the meeting I was scheduled to attend and the time of that meeting. This supervisor, Tom, was the same unqualified white male my manager Keith Marks hand-picked. A few minutes after leaving the office, I received a telephone call from Tom. I could tell the call was on speakerphone. I realized my manager Keith was in the office listening to the conversation. Tom asked me some questions trying to see how much information I would volunteer about the meeting. He began asking questions as if he was genuinely concerned. After a few initial questions, he asked who I was meeting with. I told him that I was not exactly sure, but I was certain a few of the company's vice presidents would be there. Tom then burst out laughing as if he thought I was joking.

On the other hand, his laugh also implied that because of my position as a security officer, I could not possibly have had the power to arrange such a meeting. Keith then spoke up. He stated, "Ann (black female member of the diversity in the workplace group) informed him of a meeting. However, your name was not on the list as a participant and therefore you are not to leave your area to attend the meeting." Keith said repeatedly "Clark, your name is not on the list, so do not leave your area." I answered his insistent refrain with this response, "My not being present in the meeting was anticipated; furthermore, my absence will not have a bearing on the outcome of the meeting."

This controlling maneuver provided me with an excellent example of how some people crawl around to cover up all of their wrongdoings when a possible leak might surface. Keith and Tom were furious because of the dirty deeds they were currently doing would possibly reach the public. The two also realized the concerns of a black educated male they intentionally ignored had been heard by an organization that protests when minorities have been found to have been discriminated against. The last thing The Coca-Cola Company needed was to be boycotted by African Americans.

In the early 80's, Rev. Jesse Jackson and others boycotted when it was learned The Coca-Cola Company discriminated against blacks. Many management positions were given to blacks because of that boycott. However, if Rev. Jackson or any leader were to look at the numbers of minorities in management and other essential positions today, free from being bought, I am sure they would encourage another boycott. They would not be silent.

Many might ask what we must do as a people. Others may suggest things are not as they used to be, when blacks took to the streets marching and singing the familiar song "We Shall Overcome". *Is it wise to continue supporting an organization that has made billions of dollars off minorities, but will not hire, promote, evaluate and treat blacks properly because of the color of their skin? Have you ever stopped and wondered why large companies like The Coca-Cola Company and Texaco advertise so heavily, depicting black families as being joyful when they are using their products? Or why do large companies with one token black board member use black athletes who are considered role models to promote their products?* As black people we must take the time and carefully consider these things. We must consider where we spend our dollars and concentrate on keeping the black dollar in the black community.

In Corporate America, minorities have often been told it is not what you know, but who you know when seeking a promotion or new position. From my experiences, this is true. However, I find it more interesting that some whites have decided which African Americans are worthy to be promoted.

The game of life can be played with many different rules. Some of the rules are public knowledge; however, there are unspoken rules too. For instance, some whites think they are the only race that is privileged. Or, for those of us who work or have worked in large companies such as The Coca-Cola Company, look around or think back to the physical make-up of the black males that are working and have worked in corporate America. I do not think it is a coincidence that most black males in corporate America are normally a particular height and size. I have noticed there are few black males of a tall, muscular or slender build working at The Coca-Cola Company. I found it also interesting the majority of their personalities are humble, docile and non-threatening.

Often times, when a member of the security management team approached me, I would receive very little eye contact from the person who was speaking to me. I have learned that most white males have a problem when it comes to looking up at a black man and holding a conversation while making eye contact, especially when they know the person to whom they are speaking is educated and comfortable with whom he or she is.

My father taught me as a young man to look a person in the eyes when speaking to them. By doing this, he said you would accomplish several things. First, you let that person know you care enough to at least look at them when you are speaking. Secondly, he said, it quickly builds trust. People normally get good feelings and feel they can trust you since it is more difficult to be untruthful to a person who is looking you in your eyes. I imagine this may explain why many white males in corporate America would hesitate to hire a black person who appeared to be sure of himself and comfortable with his spirit. When people feel good about themselves, their spirit is as radiant as the morning sun, even on a cloudy day.

Chapter 3

I'm Not Alone

Each of us has someone whom we admire. I had the privilege of meeting Marvin Sam, a black man who had been working at The Coca-Cola Company for 14 years. This brother approached me as if he knew me and introduced himself. Marvin was a tall man and was very well dressed. He spoke with a uniqueness which was unfamiliar to me. His unusual and particular charm made all who came in contact with him feel welcomed. As we stood and chatted, many associates came by and spoke to him as if he was very well respected in The Coca-Cola Company. It seemed that all people went out of their way to acknowledge this individual. I was impressed, for it was rare to see a black man command such attention and respect at The Coca-Cola Company.

A few weeks passed before I saw Marvin again. However, I remember seeing him one day with a very concerned look about his face. I asked Marvin what was going on with his department. To my surprise Marvin responded, "Not a damn thing, these white people are crazy. They really think black people are ignorant." For the first time, I saw a man who was normally very calm become very angry. Marvin asked if I would have some free time later to come by his office and chat. I responded, "Certainly."

During lunch I could hardly eat because I was puzzled as to what Marvin could have possibly experienced that made him so angry. When I arrived at his office, Marvin was on the telephone and made a motion to let me know he would be off shortly. As I sat waiting, I looked around his office and was shocked by a book that was lying in clear sight on his desk. The title of the book was "Racism in Corporate America." I wondered if Marvin, at his level in The Coca-Cola Company, could be experiencing racism too.

Marvin hung up the telephone and his first words were "Brother, you don't have any idea what this company is truly about." Marvin then shared with me his recent annual performance evaluation. As I glanced over the document, I saw his final rating was listed as a "CE" (clearly exceeds). I became more curious as to why Marvin was angry after seeing his annual rating. I knew if I received a "CE" I would be pleased, for it is the highest rating a person can receive in The Coca-Cola Company. Marvin looked at me and said,

"I am sick of this shit. Yes, I received the highest rating one can receive, but for the past 14 years I have received ratings of CE and ME (meets and exceeds), but I have never been promoted during my tenure with the company while my white male counterparts, who started at the same time and even after me have been promoted. This is the same bullshit that brought Rev. Jackson here the first time."

Marvin went on to describe how Jesse came in the early 80's and formed a march in Atlanta on The Coca-Cola Company. Marvin smiled when he told me the theme of the march was "Don't Choke on Coke." He added The Coca-Cola Company had so few black people in management positions it was embarrassing to other blacks that worked in the company.

In fact, what Coca-Cola did was go out and hire two blacks to serve as spokespersons for The Coca-Cola Company. However, after a few blacks received management and other positions that were thought to have been only for whites, the two black spokespersons were ultimately given senior level positions in the company. Because of Marvin's position he was well aware of how blacks were 'prostituted' by the company to generate huge dividends for the shareholders and fool the public regarding the makeup of the company.

Ordinarily, Marvin would not have been so outspoken with me but we all have our breaking point, and now after proving himself for many years he realized, because he was a black man, he'd reached the "glass ceiling" and he would not be promoted any higher in the company. I sat in amazement wondering why or how things could have gotten so one-sided in the company. *How could whites hold almost every management position in The Coca-Cola Company and continuously make billions of dollars from so many minorities?* Marvin told me that I would be a fool to think these people were not aware of what they were doing, as he had watched the company use people in important public positions and even organizations to achieve the desired image.

If you are a minority, think back to if and when you were ever called in to see a white manager about a concern of yours or a problem he or she was having with you. When you arrived in the room, the seats were probably pre-arranged, regardless of the number of people who

71

were already in the room. The manager would be sitting behind a desk in a chair that sits higher than the chair that was given to you. Moreover, you likely thought absolutely nothing about this. This may seem petty but it is not. Sitting in the lower chair in such situations indicates a lack of power in relation to the others in the room. We must realize that every opportunity given to most whites is utilized to reign above blacks.

Unfortunately, we live in a society where every decision is based on color. As much as we would like to think of this as not being true, we are able to accept the truth when we begin to put things in a different perspective. After speaking with several black men at The Coca-Cola Company, it was interesting to learn who they felt were considered the least threatening to whites. If we carefully looked around and saw the number of black males in broader corporate America, it would be interesting the number of responses we would probably come up with regarding who would be considered the least threatening. At the headquarters of The Coca-Cola Company, there were a shockingly small number of black males in professional positions. We must realize that every decision made in this country has some reference to skin color.

In February of 1999, I remember calling a friend just to see how things were going. This has proven to be one of the most sickening days I had ever experienced on "The Plantation", more commonly known as The Coca-Cola Company. When my friend Dena answered the telephone, she was crying. I was shocked. I wondered what could be so devastating that she would be so upset at work. I asked her if all was well with her family. She responded, "Yes." I became more concerned, for I knew she had a very strong spirit, and she was surely aware of what had to be done to survive as a black person in The Coca Cola Company. I asked her again what was wrong and this time she responded, "I am tired of this shit. These damn slave drivers must be out of their minds to think all black people are crazy and will tolerate this bullshit."

This sister was one who always found humor in the many racist practices of the company. She continued sharing that she applied for a job in another department and went through a series of five interviews for the same position. "Obviously, Clark, they were interested in me,"

73

she stated. Earlier that day, she overheard her "hateful ass manager" answering the telephone and asking someone, "What job did she apply for?" She said her manager then made the statement, "Well, I don't see how she can do that job as she can't even do her present job. No! I don't have a copy of her last performance evaluation but I am currently doing her 1998 evaluation and I will gladly walk it over to Human Resources personally." Dena then said, "The heifer walked to the door and slammed it, and thirty minutes later called me in the office to review my annual evaluation."

Dena went on to describe how her manager intentionally made mountains out of issues that Dena had almost forgotten. For example, her manager would give her work to do just because she thought she was not working hard enough, but in actuality her advanced computer skills allowed her to find ways to quickly but accurately complete all assignments. Her manager, "that bitch" as she described her, said because of the speed in which she finished her assignments, she was not using her time wisely. Dena continued to vent and expressed that it was bad enough that she was the only black in the department, and that in her position of administrative assistant was certainly the lowest paid in her group. Nevertheless, she was on time every-day, and never gave "that bitch" a reason to evaluate her poorly.

Because she was crying so loudly and getting more upset, I asked her to come down to where I was sitting just to get away and gather herself. I explained to Dena there was never a reason or a time when a black person should allow the racist actions to bring them to tears. Dena then told me she could not leave her desk, and when asked why she shockingly replied, "My manager won't let me leave when I want to. I must ask her to leave my desk to go to the restroom or anywhere else. She told me if she is not in her office and I must leave, I should write a note telling her where I am going, what time I will be back and indicate the time that I left on the note." I was speechless.

I could not believe anyone would stoop so low as to insist another adult must ask for freedom to move about in their workplace. What in the hell was this woman thinking! Dena was a black woman who appeared to have as much pride and spirit as any other strong sister I knew in the company. I often heard Dena talk about how strong the man was she was dating. Yet, she told me she had never shared the horrible racist experiences with him. She was humiliated.

Personally, I'd rather work two full-time jobs and a part-time job if necessary to support my family rather than suffer that kind of abuse. One of the wonderful things about life is having someone special to share the good times as well as the bad times. Yet she was too ashamed to do that. I had an opportunity to share some of my concerns about her well-being in her work environment. After our conversation, Dena decided she needed to do something about her current position, and later decided it would be in her best interest if she resigned from the company.

Chapter 4
Can We Be One?

It was the second week of Black History Month in 1999, when three different black associates, approached me. I found it interesting the only connection between these men was their color. None of the three were aware of the other's position or decision to leave the company. I remember each of them being full of joy as they shared their news of departing the company. I even joked with each of them saying, "How dare you have the audacity to leave a company as powerful as this." I went on to tell them that black folks should be happy with just having a job in The Coca-Cola Company. Each of them laughed with a sigh of relief as if it acknowledged the familiar saying of "Yee-aah right!"

It was ironic, for when I spoke with the three separately; they all stated that as black men in this company they felt they could not go anywhere. The "glass ceiling" was much too prevalent and too low. Two of the three brothers worked in technical fields and the other in marketing. All three were well educated, focused young men who refused to continue working for a company whose culture promoted racial discrimination.

On February 22, 1999, an alarming call came into the security center. An individual reported the medical department was needed because an associate had collapsed at his desk. When security responded to the call, a black male was found slumped over at his desk. The first security officer on the scene was trained as a First Responder and immediately began searching for a heart rate. After no heartbeat was found, he began CPR to try to revive the man's heart. The company's medical staff arrived shortly after the ambulance. The paramedics, along with the other staff, tried to save the man's life, but they could not. The brother was only 35 years old and was a husband and proud father of two. I was curious as to what stress, if any, played a part in shortening the young brother's life.

On Friday March 5, 1999, at approximately 9:00 a.m., I met with Keith, the security manager, to discuss two documents I refused to sign. When I arrived at his office, the seating arrangement was exactly how I anticipated. Keith had already placed a chair that sat lower than his in front of his desk. Normally, when there were other white supervisors in the office, Keith would have brandished an antagonistic smile denoting a touch of arrogance. That had been his norm with me, but on this day, he had a face of stone. I knew from his appearance that he did not want to meet with me but it was a requirement of his position.

The first document he shared with me was my annual evaluation. My supervisor, Tom Majors, the 28-year old white male with a high school diploma who my manager conveniently placed in a leadership position, felt I "met" the requirements of a security officer. I explained to my manager that there were obviously some problems with educated blacks being promoted in the department. He responded by saying I was "aware of my salary and position before taking the position, and as far as he was concerned, the company does not have to promote me." This I felt was a racist statement.

I asked him, "Are you saying because I accepted a position in The Coca-Cola Company I shall and will not ever be promoted?" He again repeated his previous response. I then asked him, "If the chairman of The Coca-Cola Company was hired in his position, could he look forward to being promoted in this department?" He had no response and so I went on to ask, "Are you insinuating that because he is a white male and I am a black male; he deserves and has earned the right to be promoted, and I have not?"

I sat and thought to myself, here he was telling me I was not going to be promoted, but at night he was in school attending the exact university from which I received my graduate degree. In addition, every supervisor in the department was suddenly in school getting the education that was required prior to their obtaining their positions.

Earlier that week, the department distributed a new policy manual for the security department. I was not comfortable signing the document because at the top of the paper was the word "disclaimer." When my manager came to collect my signed disclaimer, I told him that my signature would relinquish my right to prosecute and use the material if it was learned I was discriminated against. My manager was very angry that I had the audacity to challenge the department's manual. I explained I learned from personal experiences it was not always good to go along with the majority when making decisions that would affect me personally.

Later that same afternoon, I received a call from my supervisor, Tom Majors. He said he needed to see me again as soon as possible. When I arrived at his office, he asked me if I was going to sign the disclaimer. I told him I'd not sign until I cleared it with a friend of mine. He then told me I would be terminated if I did not sign the disclaimer, and asked for my company identification badge. I told him I was leaving the office to make a telephone call. He followed me out of the office, and when I turned to him and stated I needed to make a telephone call, Tom turned red. Perspiration formed on his face as if he was the one that had just been told he was terminated. I wondered why I was being treated like a criminal or like I'd done something wrong.

I had not yet been terminated, nor was I previously viewed as a threat to anyone. Unlike negative media portrayals of black men, I was free from a criminal record and drugs. It was obvious his superiors were using this young white male to do a job they were reluctant to do, for they knew their actions were unjust. Nevertheless, I returned to the office after contacting my legal advisors. They felt that the manner in which I was being forced to sign the document was unfair; however, we agreed it was best I sign. So I did. I also told Tom I did not appreciate being treated like a criminal. I also stated I was aware that he did not issue the mandate to have me removed from the company if I would not sign the document.

As I shared my concerns with Tom, he listened. He sat like a small child listening to an older person they did not like, but respected. The next day I saw Kcith, the manager of security, who spoke as if he knew nothing about the situation in which I was placed the day before. My manager, Keith Marks was a man who apparently believed if he smiled when certain influential people were around, he would stand a good chance of winning them over. He was the typical white man who realized he had been given his position simply because he matched the fit the company prefers to acknowledge.

It took me two years of researching the company to realize what the staff in the HR department referred to as a "company fit" and that it was not a clear procedure or a particular written requirement. For the longest time, I would listen to other blacks say that they had been denied positions for years because they did not match the "fit" the company sought. I too had been told this on every position I had applied for. Yet, at first I was unwilling to accept The Coca-Cola Company discriminates against blacks, and I refused to believe that this large, powerful company could have possibly survived this long without having been boycotted by minorities. How is it that black people as a whole have been misled all these years?

It was sickening to know The Coca-Cola Company sponsored the National Association for the Advancement of Colored People (NAACP) National Convention held in Atlanta in the Summer/Fall of 1998. I was standing post when I saw a black male carrying a specially-made handbag with The Coca-Cola trademark in one corner and the NAACP's shield in the lower corner. I was concerned the company hid its racist ways, which had wounded so many. I was shocked to see all the leaders that embraced The Cola-Cola Company because of its financial pledges.

How was it that this company was continuously featured for its sponsorships throughout the world? *I wondered for a moment, 'had the company bought all the black leaders of our nation?'* I failed to believe that the president of the NAACP was on the payroll of any corporation. I had heard this great man speak on many different occasions and he did not appear to be a black man that had a price tag on his forehead.

How was it that The Coca-Cola Company could apparently deceive the entire world? Every executive officer of the company must have been fully aware of the ratio of blacks to whites in the company, as well as the number of black managers compared to whites. Nevertheless, no one cared enough to say, "sooner or later we are going to get caught."

What was it about the company that made everyone forget about what's right and focus on quenching their thirst? Why is it that countless numbers of blacks were fooled and misled by this organization daily? Did this not raise any issues in anyone's mind? Why didn't the media report negative information on a company this size? Surely, these must have been headlines that were locked behind the iron gates to protect the associates from public outcry.

Fathers, both black and white, have always had to leave their homes and families in pursuit of the almighty dollar. The dollar over the course of hundreds of years of black history has brought many of our leaders and people to shame for they have sold their souls. I often wonder what I can do to make sure money does not cause me to lose sight of what is important in life. I think it is best I thank God for the peace of mind that He has given me. In addition, as I begin to thank Him, I must focus "On Christ the solid rock I stand, all other ground is sinking sand." When we place things in their true perspectives, the right decision is much easier to make.

One might ask how or why have so many blacks lost their spirit in corporate America? Often times images can be created that are so vivid and realistic we prefer believing what appears to be what the majority accepts rather than what is morally correct and welcomed by the minority.

Please do not misunderstand what I am suggesting. There is nothing wrong with sacrificing, preparing, and planning for a great career, which may lead to a very enjoyable life. I am a firm believer that to fail to prepare is to prepare to fail. However, each one of us has prepared ourselves for the future; some of us more than others. Some make their choice by choosing to prepare nothing.

One of my concerns is for the many minority Americans who have strategically prepared for their future with companies like The Coca-Cola Company, only to be held back in some cases by the attitudes of white managers or even other blacks who have sold their souls to white America. Not every person, black or white who has a position in Human Resources or an Equal Employment Opportunity Commission

85

Group seeks to deprive minorities of quality positions, but I contest that a good many did at The Coca-Cola Company.

Yes, there are fair-minded people who strive to do a good job and who follow the letter of the law. But I am suggesting with the billions of dollars being spent on advertising and marketing each year by major corporations appealing to black Americans, very little of the profits transfer into creating a more diverse workforce or the elevation of qualified minorities. It is staggering to consider the number of black employees is still so small compared to the millions of dollars made by the company through marketing to the black community.

In the spring of 1999, some associates from the security department were leaving for other positions within The Coca-Cola Company. Most that transferred out were white. I thought this was very peculiar because over the past three years, several black males who sought other positions within the company were not successful in attaining them, or able to exit the department for another. One of the most racist procedures related to this fact was the policy that states that the manager of the department to which you are currently assigned must agree to release you to accept another position within the company. It should not be a surprise if the white managers were reluctant to release black associates from their groups. I believe it is an unfortunate reality that managers who were prejudiced against minorities with solid credentials did not want them to be challenged mentally and compensated accordingly as they might be elsewhere in the company.

I learned that when one spoke of the racism in a company such as Coke, it was a universally accepted practice, and moreover a culture. It was also no secret to the Executive Officers (Green badges) of The Coca-Cola Company that approximately 90% of the managers worldwide were white.

The concept behind racism is to control the actions, limit growth, demoralize, and-implant a feeling of inferiority to a particular race or races of people. As such, it should be easier to see how a manager with questionable education and experience could use such tactics as a way to exert power in his or her position. It became clear to me that many white associates of The Coca-Cola Company were allowed to transfer from department to department without any apparent interference from management; and how black associates seemingly "caught hell" trying to advance in the same manner. *Would a white person who did not fairly earn their position or salary advocate for a qualified black to*

obtain a salary of equal or greater value?

Many minorities working in corporate America accepted a position just to get through the doors of corporate America, just as I did. I accepted the security officer's job at Coke because I felt the company I heard so much about as a child would certainly see my ambition and allow me an equal opportunity to work and advance. Many of us were fooled by this perception.

Once on the inside of The Coca-Cola Company, I realized the equal opportunity perception was a far cry from the actual reality of the company. The "glass ceiling" doctrine runs rampant on "The Plantation". There is little room for advancement or even mobility. Not only were there "glass ceilings", but "glass walls" as well. *Again, I wondered, how it was possible for this company to have survived for so many years without being exposed.*

There was one sister whom I often spoke to about my concerns. Mary was a sister who was different from anyone else in the security department. She wasn't afraid to confess that Jesus Christ was her Lord and Savior. There were often times in the department when management would make hiring decisions that were clearly racially motivated, and other officers would be visibly angry. She too would get upset but the Holy Spirit would not allow her to lose her calmness. I remember her applying for a job in which she was clearly the only qualified candidate. I spoke to her shortly after I learned she was not chosen for the position. I began by apologizing because I wanted to let her know that many blacks shared her pain and frustration, and she was not alone. Mary looked at me in a very confident way, smiled and said, "My Jesus knows it all. He knows and sees all that is happening."

Her demeanor did not surprise me. I was more surprised with how easy and peacefully she spoke about those that made the decision. I knew how much Mary wanted the new job. After preparing for the interview, she shared with me her view that only if Jesus said it was to be; would it then be. I asked her how she had so much respect for those that knowingly did her wrong. She replied, "I love the Lord, it is in Him I find joy, not The Coca-Cola Company."

In security, there were several different types of training. While most of it was truly comprehensive and needed, there were times when some of the courses seemed to gloss over highly critical issues. These sessions were on topics such as diversity, race relations and employee-supervisor complaints, and were almost always conducted due to a mandated memo from upper management to address a particular issue or complaint. A poor job was done by the managers of the security department in relating the significance of this knee-jerk training to the department's daily operations.

I could tell by the way they presented the information they had no sincere intent to change policy, procedure or opinion. They addressed the issues with lip service but never intended to instigate healthy change. Instead of tackling real issues head on, we were forced to attend 2-3 day communication and telephone etiquette training classes. It was boring. The instructors were ill-prepared to facilitate the learning process and most of them had little or no previous experience in their designated block of instruction.

On the first day of one class, ideas for the mission statement were introduced. The first few statement ideas consisted of some of the duties of the officers and each example tended to be one very long paragraph. After seeing what the group came up with, it was then time for comments from the class, but only a few of the officers made comments on the mission statement. I shared with the class that a mission statement should be easily remembered and-recited instantaneously. I also shared that a few years prior the Ritz Carlton hotel won the prestigious Malcolm Baldridge Award for Quality, and their mission statement was as simple as "Men and Women, serving Men and Women." The instructor of the class grew visibly upset about the comments I made. She was angry but she obviously agreed with my assessment because she immediately shortened the mission statement and told the class that it would be fine to use the shorter version. As the day progressed, officers voiced many concerns about issues they thought were unfair business practices within the department.

In corporate America I learned that few managers who have climbed up the corporate ladder by doing "dirt" to others, answered questions specifically. Conversely, I chose to present facts and quote statistics when communicating with management. This caused my immediate management to develop a high level of hostility toward me. Consequently, many of my fellow colleagues would sometimes ask me how I could function in an environment that was so blatantly full of hate.

I grew tired of having associates who also worked in security walk so close to me they almost touched me without opening their mouths to say a word. I grew tired of having doors constantly slammed in my face when trying to enter a room or elevator. I grew tired of all the ugly, constant looks of hatred as I greeted the associates as they arrived for work. The hatred that my white management group possessed for me got so bad that many of my peers became afraid to converse with me in the presence of management. Yet, the question my colleagues never stopped asking me was "Just how do you continue to work under these disparate conditions?" My response was very simple but powerful and meaningful - "I pray."

I explained to one Christian brother at one point that I abhorred each white member of management. I'd begun to take everything personally, every glance, every memorandum, every decision...everything! As they would pass my post, I imagined them saying, "We have him just where we want him." If this was truly their thinking, then yes, they did have me where they wanted me. I was full of hatred, which is not in line with the word of Jesus Christ.

One day I started thinking about the other brothers and sisters who were all managed by the same group of people as me. I wondered how they were dealing with the racism and discrimination in their department. Brother Stover was a security officer who believed that indeed, The Coca-Cola Company discriminated against me. I had a great deal of respect for him because he was not afraid to stand up for what he believed. Stover looked at me and said, "God sees everything that happens in our department and in the company. It is He and only He who has the power to change the hearts of those in leadership positions. Do not allow yourself to become full of hate. God has a way of working everything out. He can make your enemies your footstool and give you peace in the midst of a world, or in this case, a company that is infested with evil unlike any you have ever experienced."

I am a living witness that God can remove all the hate and anger from your heart without leaving a scar. He performed surgery on my heart and never once used a surgical instrument. I remember speaking to one of my supervisors after I'd given this battle to the Lord. As he was walking away, I realized the ill feeling I usually had in my stomach was no longer there. The next day, my manager came by my post and tried to hold a conversation with me. Surprisingly, I was very

comfortable talking with him. I did not think about the many wrongs

that he'd intentionally committed against me. Instead, I was able to see

and was more concerned with the sadness and misery in his life. *I

wondered what horrors would make a person knowingly commit

unlawful and hateful acts towards another.*

I have learned that a person in a leadership capacity, who is not

God-fearing, is less likely to do the right thing. Some may ask, 'What is

the right thing when every situation is different?' The heart of the

person rendering the action will know before anyone else knows if the

decision made was the right one.

Occasionally, I would find myself searching my heart for the reason

that so many could possibly hate me. One day I was in the

Identification Office talking with one of the newly hired females on the

security team. We were just there having a bit of small talk when Keith,

my manager, passed by and saw us. She immediately left my presence

and followed him in the office. She just abruptly walked away, as if in

fear of reprimand or of losing her job.

Then I remembered, this woman had only been in the department for a few weeks, and already, she'd been given the opportunity to work in the administrative office. Here was a white female who had obviously been brought into the department as a stepping-stone to obtaining a position other than that of a security officer. Although the department was made up of more than 90% black officers, the decision makers did not care about the type of message it would send by giving this person advancement opportunities it took black officers years, if ever, to earn. I then realized this person's loyalty was to the manager, not to the security team. She knew she had been and would continue to be the recipient of unearned privileges so long as she continued doing whatever she was told. After being in the department for just a few months, she chose to accept another position. She barely knew me but she sided with her future-holders.

Chapter 5

Discrimination Case Gets National Media Attention

Sitting in the break area one day in deep thought, a young male who was a friend of mine, walked up to me with smoke coming out of his ears. This brother had been in the company for 7 years and had joined The Coca-Cola Company in London. He had tears coming from his eyes and was visibly angry. I asked, "Terrence, what's wrong?" He responded, "I cannot believe how we are treated in this company." He shared he was working on a project that would enable the company to know the amount of money each brand was making with a single keystroke.

He explained this was one of many projects needed but no one wanted to take responsibility of doing the job. He shared he successfully developed the method, but was not given credit for it. Terrence stated he traveled overseas with work several times for long periods of time. He paid his dues but his management team still felt they could treat him as if he was ignorant to the practices in the company. After venting for about twenty minutes, Terrence finally got to the nucleus of his problem.

Terrence stated he had been working on another project that was very involved and time consuming. Prior to beginning the project, his manager stated there would be a position created that would better suit the type of work he was assigned. Terrence explained he completed the project in one-third the time allotted. After presenting the completed project to his manager and hearing from his manager what a wonderful job he'd done, the bad news came.

His white manager told him they'd completed the job description for the new position and felt he was an excellent candidate. Terrence said he was given an opportunity to review the qualifications for the new position and to his surprise, it was the exact job description he was asked to write a few months ago with one exception. The pay grade for the proposed position was a pay grade lower than the one he had written. His manager was suggesting he accept a position that was a pay grade lower than the pay grade he was currently working in. This was certainly not acceptable! Terrence was livid.

He asked me, "If I were white, would my manager have the audacity to approach me with such an insult?" I responded, "No! I do not think so." Before Terrence walked away he mentioned one day these people were going to get exactly what they deserved.

I asked out of curiosity 'what could that possibly be?' Terrence shared that in the past seven years he hadn't been in a single meeting where the focus of the meeting was not "image-related." He continued by saying, "If the public actually knew what happened to African Americans behind the walls of The Coca-Cola Company, the company would fall as quickly as a tree cut in the forest." Little did Terrence know someone had already felt his pain and decided the public should not have to be given or fed false perceptions any longer.

How does one deal with an organization the size of The Coca-Cola Company that discriminates? How does one deal with any company that discriminates? The first and most important factor was to be able to identify that discrimination actually existed. I carefully replayed all the events that may qualify as discrimination to make certain that I was not just assuming or imagining there was a problem. In order to prove workforce disparities, there must be a paper trail. It is important to document any action that seems unfair, and to note the time, place and person committing the act.

I kept in mind the company had an Affirmative Action Department. The law requires them to do so but I questioned if the company had any real interest in equality! I also remembered the company probably paid each member of this group well. *Would any of their findings be based on truth?* They were a well-paid department and were as vested in towing the corporate line as anyone.

I stayed prayerful and remained focused for I knew a change was coming. It was the end of April 1999 and just a few days were left before the entire world would know that The Coca-Cola Company had been charged with racial discrimination. The mood of the company was nothing special, it was business as usual. Many associates were talking about how wonderful it was that the stock price rose the past week. Things looked good for the company.

I had many thoughts about what I knew was coming. I knew the group coming forward would be under an enormous amount of stress and pressure. I could not help but wonder what kind of father or man I would be if I focused only on myself. Two years of planning and sacrificing would soon be put to the test. I was not sure we could make a difference. I knew we were up against a giant. There was the possibility I could lose my life. I wasn't even sure if our claim would be taken seriously.

Nevertheless, I chose not to be focused on anyone but Jesus, as my faith was in God. I remember as a little boy growing up in The Greater Life Tabernacle when I first learned about God's greatness in Sunday school. I will never forget my Mother saying "If God is for you, the world can't do you any harm. And what God has for you, it is for you." God knew we were not lying, and He saw first-hand the dogmatic treatment blacks were forced to deal with in the company.

I recall one summer my father and I spent together in Spring Lake, New Jersey. My father was a very proud man who did all he could to hide the bad experiences he'd encountered in America. He was willing to work hard to provide for and educate his children. I remember coming into the Bath and Tennis Club in Spring Lake Beach, NJ, where he worked that summer. The temperature outside was well over 100 degrees. When I walked in the kitchen, he was working behind the range. He was working so hard. I stood there for a few moments before he noticed I was standing watching him. The sweat was rolling off of his face like someone had taken a bucket of water and poured it on his head. He looked directly into my eyes and for a moment, we stared at each other. I remember growing angry that he had to work so hard to earn a living for the family. But, Chef never once complained. He reached in his pocket, threw me the car keys and told me to go ahead; he would catch a ride home with Hash, his right-hand man in the kitchen.

I often thought of all Chef's hard work to ensure our family would have an honest chance in life. I knew it was necessary for me to go forward with the lawsuit. My father did not work for almost half a century for me to be denied an equal opportunity at life, nor did he raise a foolish child. He always told me, "There are too many ways in life to be a fool for one man to dodge them all. Once you realize your mistakes, learn from them and do not continue down the same path." I knew I would one day want my child to be as proud of me as I am of my father. The decision was made.

On the evening of April 22, 1999, years of hard work were presented to the Federal Court System. The following day, The *New York Times* ran an article stating four blacks filed a racial discrimination case in federal court against one of the largest beverage companies in the world. *I was not sure what the company would do.*

How they would respond? I knew I could not worry about the reaction

of those who created this degrading work environment.

It was about 9:00 a.m. when I first heard someone say the article

ran in *The New York Times. The Wall Street Journal* picked up the

story also. In the twinkling of an eye, the mood of the company

changed. I saw directors and vice presidents rushing from building to

building. It appeared that all of the managers were going in the same

direction. The word was out!

One of the black associates came to me and gave me a copy of the

article. The joy in the faces of the black colleagues was something I

would not soon forget. Normally, Fridays at the company were

considered beautiful days at headquarters because the weekend had

arrived, but not this one. Word of the article spread like wildfire

through the company. Before long almost everyone knew. Many

minorities were happy and walking around with smiles larger than I'd

ever seen. Many of the other associates, on the other hand, were

furious.

My feelings at that point were mixed. I was thrilled the public finally had an opportunity to hear what happened behind the walls of the company. But, I was still confused as to why things had to go this far. I was pleased the process to punish and correct the racist environment at The Coca-Cola Company had begun. As I stood in the Coca-Cola USA lobby, the focal point of the complex, I had an opportunity to see how an organization that intentionally deceived the public for many years, responded when the public heard how the company spat at and trampled upon some of its employees. All the big names in the legal department moved swiftly through the corridors. I knew this was just the beginning of a long hard battle that would leave many casualties. I soon remembered there had never been a war without casualties, so I knew I must remain focused on what truly mattered in this war -- uplifting the name of Jesus.

I scheduled a vacation for the following week. I knew when the facts behind the case went public it would not be wise for me to be at work. My research of the company revealed the harm done to blacks was intentional, not coincidental. I knew there were many whites in the company that were successful because they were able to hide the many

103

talents and skills of various minorities in the company. As long as the treatment of blacks could be kept behind the walls of The Coca-Cola Company the 'Good Ole Boy System' would remain in place and unchanged. But now the system was exposed, I was not afraid. I did not fear the company or the power of those in leadership positions.

I felt many had knowledge of the true culture of the company, and I imagined they thought the company was so powerful and so well-respected it would be impossible for negative publicity to influence consumers. I did not believe that all of the leaders of the company set out with negative intentions. However, good leaders making no decisions could be even more detrimental than bad leaders making bad decisions. Coke had plenty of this dubious neutral leadership style.

I did not work the weekend, but I heard almost the entire Human Resource Department, attorneys, executives and many other associates were at the complex as if it were a normal business day. I was curious just what was happening. Then the Chairman, Doug Ivester issued a statement to the media in an article which ran in the *Atlanta Journal Constitution* on Saturday, April 24, 1999. It stated "The Coca-Cola Company was built over time by people of all races, colors and creeds.

Discrimination at The Coca-Cola Company is not tolerated. If discrimination is alleged, we investigate it. If we find it, we act to stop it. Our goal is the fair, equitable and honest treatment of all of our associates. While we believe the lawsuit is without merit, we take the allegations seriously."

After the chairman, the number one man in the company, took such a powerful stance against the lawsuit, I again wondered why there was so much activity at the offices on a weekend. In one breath, the spokesman for the company stated the lawsuit was without merit and in the very next breath, stated they could not comment on the statistics for they had not had time to analyze them. *How could the lawsuit be without merit and the statistics, which were an essential part of the lawsuit, had not been researched before such a statement was made to the public?*

The same article which included Doug Ivester's statement to the public also listed the comparisons of black and white associates in the company. "The lawsuit says there was an average $19,211 gap between salaries of whites and African Americans at the company's corporate headquarters in 1995, and a $26,830 gap three years later." The lawsuit also stated, "The highest percentages of African American workers

were found in the lowest pay grades."

Pay Grade	White	Black
Grade 5 (Administrative)	58%	36.5%
Grade 11 (Professional/Managerial)	85%	7.8%
Grade 14 (Director)	87%	4.4%
Grade 15 (Vice President)	95%	1.5%

The article continued to say that, "Black senior managers are concentrated in the non-revenue-producing and less-powerful divisions.

	White	Black
Global Marketing	54	2
Information Systems	46	1
Office of the CFO	41	1
Product Integrity	42	0
Technical Operations	82	1
Corporate Affairs (PR)	16	3
Human Resources	37	10

These appalling statistics sent shock waves through the city often

referred to as being "too busy to hate." The entire lawsuit was posted

on the internet at

www.essential.org/action/spotlight/coke/complaint.html.

Source: *Atlanta Journal Constitution*, Saturday, April 24, 1999.

The company obviously had never experienced anything this powerful. Actions taken without careful consideration to the consequences were now revealed. The following week every associate in the United States received an e-mail from the chairman of the company stating the lawsuit was without merit; however, it was taken very seriously. I wondered how serious the leaders of the company had taken the plight of the African Americans. Not very seriously if you considered the number of African Americans in senior management positions, 1.5% - which constituted approximately fifteen people worldwide.

My timely week of vacation was spent working another job to keep my household in order. I received many calls from friends concerned about my well-being. It was gratifying to hear all the wonderful well wishes from those who realized how serious and committed we were to bringing change to The Coca-Cola Company. Despite well wishes from my friends, I could not help to wonder what it would be like when I returned to work. After release of the article in the *Atlanta Journal*

Constitution printed on Saturday, April 24, 1999, everyone had a pretty good idea of the role I played in formulating the group which ultimately brought charges against the company.

Many people were simply in a state of denial when they heard what was actually happening. Few people wanted to believe that the company that many regarded as the most diverse in the world, could be facing allegations such as these. Those who naturally assumed the best were forced to ask questions.

My first day back at work, a lot of people stared at my name on my security shield before looking angrily into my eyes. My co-workers told stories of white associates who would boldly walk up to them and ask if their name was Gregory Allen Clark. Some even said they felt threatened by the manner in which the white associates approached and spoke to them.

My first post was one that was in a high volume area which many associates would pass going to their offices. As I stood and secured that area, one of The Coca-Cola Company's few black attorneys walked by me and smiled as he made a comment that really put things in perspective. He said that he thought I would be posted on the corner of

North Avenue and Lucky Street directing traffic. As he walked away he insisted that I continue showing the entire world how The Coca-Cola Company treats black associates. His comments encouraged me and I welcomed his sense of humor as well, for it surely broke the ice.

As I stood on post I watched the white associates make efforts to see if I was the person they had recently read so much about in the newspapers. After many realized that I was "that person", many of them would go to their work areas and bring other associates back to whisper and point at me when they thought I was not looking. I felt uncomfortable, like an animal on display. As days passed, the looks and stares continued and many associates became more vocal. I remember being approached by a white female associate who asked if I was the person she saw in Sunday's paper. I told her I was not sure of what picture she was referring to; however, I had taken some photos for the *Atlanta Journal Constitution*. She then told me that she was surprised. I asked her why and she said, "I thought you had better sense than that." As she walked away I said to her, "God bless you."

In researching the company I felt it was important to know the faces of the members of the legal counsel in the company. White attorneys for the company were among those who stared at me as if I was

anything other than a focused, educated, black man. I often wondered

what was behind the long, glaring looks that I received. At first I was

not comfortable working around so many people that had obvious hate

for me. Upper management security group of The Coca-Cola Company

was lily white. By this time I think they realized that I was not going to

run away from the racist environment and treatment I had been

rendered.

In conversations with my management group, I raised concerns I

had about the culture of the department and of the company. Because of

my position and salary, I think managers making 3 to 4 times my salary

thought I would just go away. I made it a priority to speak at least twice

with every person that should have knowledge of the treatment I was

subjected to. I realized after several of these meetings that regardless of

who I spoke to, they all had the same story. The Coca-Cola Company

does not discriminate.

Two weeks before the article ran exposing racism at Coke in

newspapers like the *Wall Street Journal* and *New York Times,* I met

with my manager and told him I had concerns about my status in the department. He responded as he always did by reminding me I was aware of my salary and my position when I was hired and he, as a manager, did not have to promote me. In the past, each time he would respond to me in this manner I would accept his response and leave. That was before the lawsuit. Before going into the room this time, I decided when I heard his familiar refrain, I would share something that was simple but fitting for the occasion.

Sure enough, he mentioned I knew my salary and position before accepting the job. I responded to him that the chairman of The Coca-Cola Company also knew the position he was hired into before accepting a job in the company. He was not hired as the chairman of The Coca-Cola Company, but worked his way into the position. I then asked, *"Are you telling me that because he is white he has the opportunity to advance and because I am black I do not?"*

He got angry. His face and eyes turned red. He then stated this meeting was over because he was running late for another meeting. I remember him also telling me I could always leave the company if I was not happy. Such a comment was not appropriate for any manager to suggest to an employee, but when he got angry his true colors showed.

About ten minutes later I passed his office and there he sat. I remember sharing with him I was continuing my struggle in the company for personal reasons. Perhaps I made him think, for there he sat idle. Apparently the meeting that caused him to rush me out of the office was no longer important.

As I stood post and received dirty, unwanted looks and listened to mean, unnecessary comments, I became more and more focused on bringing change to The Coca-Cola Company. After two years of planning, anticipating and preparing for the heartache and pain, my preparation fell short of what I really needed to fight the company. It was hard. The only peace I could rely on was resting in the arms of Jesus.

Working around people that I knew hated me for opening the eyes of the world to the true reality of the company was extremely hard. As time passed I grew tired of hearing the comments from the white associates in the hallways. But never once did I feel like we had done anything wrong. Many of the white males that worked in security stopped speaking to me. This, I knew was an admission of guilt. The complaint was also posted on the Internet including a list of names and a little background information on many of the white associates that were given positions over me.

I read the complaint over and over but I could not find anything in it that was not truth. Some of the white associates that were listed in the complaint quickly found jobs in other departments or left the company. I realized that it was not the complaint that the white associates were having a problem with, but the accuracy of it. I learned to walk by those who refused to speak to me as if they were not silent. I walked by faith and not by sight.

The response from the black associates of The Coca-Cola Company was interesting. The chairman of The Coca-Cola Company sent a second e-mail to all of the US associates in which he again stated the lawsuit was without merit, for The Coca-Cola Company does not tolerate racial discrimination; if there is a complaint, the company investigates and immediately handles any situation found to be unjust. This was a joke to me. Yes, the company had people in place who were supposed to objectively investigate all complaints brought to the

113

group's attention. However, an objective investigation was hardly the case I had experienced. Investigators were all employees of The Coca-Cola Company. *I wondered, "How concerned to find truth could this group have been?"*

The investigators who took actual complaints from the associates also had open door policies to speak with managers and/or directors relating to the incidents. These investigators also received paychecks from the company, as well as stock options and also various special privileges for those of certain grades. I imagined when I met with my manager, human resources and the investigator they merely saw me as a "black security guard" who was simply angry because he was not able to progress through the corporate system. Because of the well-knit social relationships that most people in Human Resources/ Staffing Departments had in the company, it was difficult to keep conversations confidential. They probably thought they could treat me unfairly and I would have to deal with it. After all, I was a security guard in the company's lowest salary grade and black. I was someone who in many minds, was simply supposed to take orders and do as they were told.

114

A companywide gag order was placed on all Coke associates. The order stated that no one should be discussing the complaint, and prohibited discussion of the lawsuit with anyone. Because of the manner in which the chairman addressed the complaint to the associates, the Lead Counsel for the plaintiffs filed a motion with the courts stating that the company violated communication laws by sending these e-mails. The attorneys for the company responded by saying this was just a maneuver used by attorneys and that it was also without merit.

In preparing and researching, we expected the company to continue using the few token black associates in the company to try and win over public opinion. I believe that some of the blacks in senior management positions had been given positions with presumed authority, but with little or no power. It was not a coincidence that The Coca-Cola Company had channeled the majority of the black associates in senior management into non-revenue generating positions. It was also not a coincidence that most of these positions were highly visible to the public eye.

Where and when does it stop? As blacks, we need to be concerned with how some whites have obviously designed a system to prostitute our people. For several weeks, articles on the issue ran in hundreds of newspapers around the country. Most of the television stations reported stories that The Coca-Cola Company had a racial discrimination lawsuit filed against it, but also noted that few of its executives and supporters believed it was with merit.

As days passed, it was obvious the company could not maneuver its way out of this situation. It would not blow over. *So, what does a company do when the media is vocal and raises questions in the minds of the same public that was programmed to believe that the company is too diverse to discriminate?* The company was worth billions of dollars and money was used for leverage by giving charitably to the black community in an effort to protect the company's image to that community.

Knowing the influence and media muscle The Coca-Cola Company has, and having studied the culture of the company, I was not at all surprised when the tide turned. *The Wall Street Journal* ran an article on May 18, 1999, written by Nikhil Deogun which featured the opinions of several prominent black ministers and leaders in the Atlanta community. Reverend Timothy McDonald, President of Concerned Black Clergy, a renowned Atlanta activist organization, spoke on the complaint that was filed against the company. The article quoted the minister saying, "I don't think they'll get a lot of support." One reason, he added, was that "Coke deserves consideration, many black leaders say, because of its generosity. Coca-Cola is a regular contributor to national and community groups benefiting African Americans, contributing millions of dollars a year directly and through the Coca-Cola Foundation."

I respect ministers of the Gospel. However, I was curious to know if the Reverend had stopped for a moment just to consider giving the thousands of blacks that endured years of pain and frustration in the racist environment of The Coca-Cola Company any consideration. I failed to believe the minister asked God for guidance before he made his comments.

Another Black leader, Thomas Dortch, President of 100 Black Men of America, gave his opinion too. His organization is an Atlanta-based group that works to improve relational differences among America's youth as well as educational and economic opportunities. He stated, "A lot of companies make billions of dollars and do not reinvest in the community, but Coke does, so I'm a little more sympathetic and tolerant." It was obvious from the leader's statement, he felt that as long as a company shares a few dollars of the billions of dollars that African Americans contribute as consumers, it was okay to pay, promote, evaluate and terminate blacks and other minorities unfairly. Maybe he was thinking he could secure donations for his organization's next Annual Ball.

It is not unrealistic to believe that many of the so-called leaders in the black community were on several of the corporation's payrolls, in one way or another. Nevertheless, it was essential to be mindful that he was a single black man representing an organization. *So many others could not possibly have the same simple perception, or could they?*

An associate professor of political science at Clark Atlanta University saw through the financial smoke screen and stated that many of the organizations rely on Coke for support, so he imagined they'd be reluctant to criticize. Not all were quiet though. Joe Beasley, the director of the southern region for the Rev. Jesse Jackson's

Rainbow/P.U.S.H Coalition was concerned enough to state that he was disappointed with the legal response Coke filed, which was mostly a blanket denial of the various allegations. Beasley went on to say he recently received $10,000 from Coke for a conference he organized, but he does not take hush money. He lost the taste for Coke once before and he could quickly do it again.

He had not forgotten in 1981, Rev. Jesse Jackson led a boycott of Coca-Cola "Don't Choke On Coke," and chastised the company for not doing enough to hire and promote blacks. The ensuing boycott accused Coke of doing more to garnish its reputation with Atlanta's African American leadership by promoting two well-known black executives, who for years had been Coke's primary contact to community and civic leaders.

Carl Ware, a black male and former president of the Atlanta City Council, had risen to president of Coke's African American unit. Ingrid Saunders Jones, a former schoolteacher and City Hall member, was corporate vice president for External Affairs and also chaired The Coca-Cola Foundation. The article clearly stated that Coke enhanced its reputation by promoting two black people.

Atlanta was the city known to be a "Black Mecca." *How was it possible that out of all the blacks that were living and working in Atlanta for only two blacks to get promoted? Was the city naïve enough to believe that by this act, the company does not discriminate?* If there was ever any writing on the wall, there it was.

Coke did not use any fancy tactics to obtain their goals. With the publicity-motivated promotion of just two blacks, the black community should have been infuriated. Coca-Cola proved they needed just to promote two token blacks to gain favor from an entire community of black people. It was a small price to pay to bolster the company's reputation and keep blacks purchasing their products.

As time went by, newspapers were filled with articles which included some of the general details about the case. Many leaders from the black community were called upon to voice their concerns and opinions about the lawsuit. It was interesting that some of the leaders of the most recognized churches in the city chose not to go public with their opinions.

On May 20th, 1999, *The Wall Street Journal* ran another article that stated an internal report was presented to The Coca-Cola Company more than three years prior to the filing of our lawsuit. This report (Ware Report) recommended a number of initiatives to enhance diversity, including addressing "why there are so few African Americans in certain areas and levels of the business." The article stated this document, dated December 1995, was significant because it indicated that the Chairman, Doug Ivester, who was Coke's president at the time, was aware of the need for greater diversity including more senior black executives. The report also listed eight "preliminary recommendations." The author went on to say that while the report acknowledged Coca-Cola's efforts to improve diversity, it also appeared to address some of the same issues contained in the recent racial-discrimination lawsuit brought forth by four blacks against the company.

A key allegation was that blacks hit a "glass ceiling" at Coca-Cola. Few executives ever advanced to senior positions at the company. Also, the suit contended that black employees face "glass walls" that "virtually segregate the company into divisions where African American leadership is acceptable, and divisions where it is not," noting that black executives are usually channeled into "non-revenue generating areas," such as human resources, external affairs and community relations. High-level positions in marketing and finance, for instance, are almost all white, according to the suit.

As always, Coke denied the allegations. Although one of the recommendations in the document says Coke should "challenge the pattern the company has fallen into of placing African Americans into certain areas." Ironically, the very same and only black president in The Coca-Cola Company led the project which pointed out diversity issues. A management consulting firm, J.O. Rodgers & Associates, of Stone Mountain, GA, was retained to assist with that report. A spokesman from the firm stated that it did work with Coke on this project; however, they declined to speak publicly because it's a "very confidential engagement." The firm also suggested that for further inquires please contact Carl Ware, who was reported to be out of the country at that time.

Here was proof that the chairman of The Coca-Cola Company not only knew but was well informed of the fact that there were not enough blacks in key positions throughout the company. He chose to sit on this information rather than act. After the article ran in *The Wall Street*

Journal making this information on the report public knowledge, the chairman of the company decided to formulate a task force to enhance the diversity in the workplace at the company. Once again he chose the highest ranking African American in the company. This single black in the upper realm along with a white male president, co-chaired the group called the Diversity Council. The co-chair chosen was a man who made a noticeable attempt to speak on a first name basis to all the associates who crossed his path. He was selected because the leaders of the company felt he had a good rapport with the majority of the blacks and was somewhat trusted and respected by them.

The announcing of the Diversity Council and its co-chairs was indeed a predictable response by the company. *Why did the company now see a need now for diversity in the workplace? Was it because one of the most detailed lawsuits ever filed on behalf of African Americans in this country had landed on its doorstep? Why did the chairman not listen to the report presented more than three years earlier and act then?* Things had gotten worse not better in those three years, and the embarrassing statistics proved that blacks could not possibly have been considered as equals in The Coca-Cola Company.

A company once regarded as one of the most diverse companies in the world was guilty of racial discrimination. *Where could it hide? Furthermore, why would a chairman not listen to the highest-ranking black in the company, if he truly respected him? If there were never a problem, the Consulting Firm would have never been hired.* These facts indicated the leaders of the company knew many years before the lawsuit was filed that the number of blacks working in professional positions was a joke. But they were arrogant and felt they were untouchable, I imagine. Surely, no one would possibly think of challenging them, let alone a person that worked in the lowest salary grade in the company.

This article should have made black leaders who spoke out so proudly and gracefully just days prior in the Journal supporting The Coca-Cola Company feel absolutely foolish. I am confident that each black leader who acted as if it was insane for anyone to consider The Coca-Cola Company discriminated against blacks, felt betrayed. It was no secret that there was one black female strategically placed in a highly visible publicized position who was seeking the support of the Civil Rights Organizations on behalf of the company. No one likes to look like a fool, certainly not those chosen by various groups of blacks as leaders in their communities. Nevertheless, this article and the obvious lesson the reporter sought to display should have shown these black leaders, or any leader for that matter, that things are not always as they appear. Everything that glitters isn't gold.

After this article, there were no additional comments from the black community leaders swearing that The Coca-Cola Company could not possibly have been discriminating. It was as if they knew that after several months of the issue being public, The Coca-Cola Company presented absolutely no evidence to support its denial. The company long regarded as the most diverse in the world was obviously hiding something. All the money, all the arrogance, and all the power in the world could not help the company win this war.

I believed The Coca-Cola Company could not and would not win this war. They needed to confess their wrongdoings before the people who helped to make it what it was. It was in many ways a silent war, I thought. I learned that one minister who had been counseling one of the four plaintiffs for two years prior to the filing of the lawsuit chose to remain silently out of the mainstream on the issue. *Is it possible this pastor chose silence because he did not want to ruin his future*

contributions from The Coca-Cola Company?

Ironically, during the time The Coca-Cola Company faced this lawsuit, the city of Atlanta was also going through a historical movement. A white man of the Southern Leadership Education Development Program wanted to apparently turn back the timetable for African Americans. This gentleman was on a mission to do away with Affirmative Action in the City of Atlanta. At the time, Mayor Bill Campbell spoke with a very firm and still voice. He said that he would not allow the racists to turn back the timetable for blacks. This group alleged that blacks were receiving unfair advantages in receiving city contracts, among other things, because of Affirmative Action. Mayor Campbell held rallies at City Hall and also surrounded himself with many leaders in the community who shared his views. I was shocked that these political leaders were rallying against an organization that made no bones about what they wanted, yet few people were so attentive to what was happening in one of the city's largest employers – Coca Cola.

The Coca-Cola Company had been accused of doing the exact same thing this white man was attempting to do. No one had the courage to tell the company that until it made a public defense that was more impressive than simply saying the allegations were without merit, we will assume the allegations are true and blacks will boycott your products. It was disturbing to me as I realized that many blacks were willing to give up their right to be treated like an equal so long as they had a job, even one paying less than their white counterparts. I fail to see how being bought equates to being treated as an equal human being.

Why do we as minorities allow ourselves to be misled by the oppressive practices of Corporate America? It was no coincidence that The Coca-Cola Company's two highest ranking blacks were given their positions specifically for the purpose of keeping the black community thinking and behaving the way the company desired.

I am not saying that these two people were not qualified for their positions. Personal opinion doesn't matter and I do not have details of their particular job performance. I am speaking of the facts. The fact was that blacks were not present in the highest levels of management in

127

any other, less visible but more revenue-impacting, departments. It was a fact that in the very few senior management positions held by blacks in the company, the level of power, salary and privileges were not equal to that of a white person in the same position.

Many blacks believed that this was simply the way things were and the way they would always be. It will be a cold day in hell before I voluntarily give up my right to be treated as an equal, just because some believe history has named and placed boundaries on my future.

Remove personal opinion and think of the limitations that society has placed on blacks as a whole. Think what chance our children would have to be successful if we act as though our lives were not still being impacted and altered by racism and discrimination. When I first realized that The Coca-Cola Company had managers who were intentionally discriminating against me, I thought that the best thing for me to do was to leave the company. But, I knew I had a role to play. My parents worked hard for the opportunities I would have in education, vocation and life. I needed to soldier on to make it better still for the next generation and I couldn't walk away knowing the price my parents had already paid.

Chapter 6

The Coca-Cola Tap Dance Act

The Coca-Cola Company was a proud and arrogant company. An important mission of the company was to protect the image and integrity of Coca-Cola in the world marketplace. Their ultimate goal, of course, was to make a substantial profit for its shareholders. In doing so, it strives to place a Coca-Cola product within arm's reach of every human being on the face of this earth. These are goals that only the largest beverage company in the world could have.

My concern focused on how the company treats all of its black employees. It was fact that while The Coca-Cola Company had strategically designed marketing schemes to target African American dollars; it had not showed the same level of concern for its African American employees. This realization became more obvious as I considered the number of black board members and leaders in the company. This company had the power and finances to build major bottling companies throughout the world. It was smart and intentional in its operations.

129

How could the leaders of Coke fail to recognize the many talents of their various minority employees? I believed it was impossible for this to be done. I also believed that the hearts of the past and present leaders of The Coca-Cola Company must change to better its culture. For many years blacks at Coke had sought help from organizations created to investigate allegations and complaints of discrimination or other unlawful acts but few advances were made.

Instead, the company had done an excellent job over the years of suppressing or alleviating negative media before it reached the public. It was surprising that The Coca-Cola Company didn't manage to stop the negative publicity or news of this lawsuit from reaching the public. Black senior executives at Coke had knowledge of the lawsuit, and actually started asking questions early on about rumors of a class-action lawsuit. *Was it possible that the few blacks in senior management positions could or would have developed a sense of arrogance to think the lawsuit would not come to pass, or did they secretly wish for a lawsuit of this kind?*

Several months following the filing of the lawsuit, The Coca-Cola Company featured two black senior executives in a newspaper article in the *Atlanta Journal Constitution*. One of the company's vice presidents stated, "I myself am a good example, a proof that "glass walls" do not exist at The Coca-Cola Company." This, I thought, was unusual. Here was the only black president ever in the company saying he was proof that "glass ceilings" did not exist. If ever there was a person who had knowledge of discriminatory practices in the company, surely this man had it. *What would make a man lie before his people knowing that millions would hear his words?*

If that vice president didn't admit what was there, others did. Black males pulled me to the side to share how much they appreciated me stepping forward and speaking out against the racist environment of The Coca-Cola Company. These intelligent, hard-working, career-oriented fathers came to me with sincere looks in their eyes to share just how much they were thankful for what was done.

I told each of them I appreciated all their thoughts and prayers. But I couldn't help but wonder why none of these men had stepped forward to become a leader in this process. As a low ranking employee at Coke, most of these men were in positions higher than mine. *Why did it take the lowest ranking guy to speak up? Why was I the only black male*

131

willing to step forward and shout to the world what was obvious to

almost every black that was ever employed on "The Plantation"?

Many of the black men I spoke with answered my pondering. They

said they had children, mortgages and bills that kept them from

speaking out against racism in the company. *I wondered if the brothers*

stopped to think for one moment, could they really be "successful" in a

racist culture such as Coke's? What model of success were they

offering to their children? Did they not think I loved my family too?

Wasn't your family the best reason of all for one to speak up?

An article written by Sallye Salter in the *Atlanta Journal*

Constitution depicted other professionals, such as the black architects

of Atlanta, who felt the company had discriminated against them in the

issuing of projects. Perhaps a few small voices speaking up had caused

a ripple of noise through the community.

While the blacks considered raising their voices, many of the white

associates who once spoke and socialized with me now were silent.

Since the lawsuit, they made it known they wanted nothing more to do

with me. There was no more small talk; to put it bluntly, there was no talk at all. I quickly understood what needed to be done to survive in the company.

Let me explain. I did my undergraduate work at the University of South Carolina, home of the "Gamecocks." One of the company's white attorneys graduated from Clemson University, a rival of USC. Oftentimes, we would ask one another who we thought would win when a good team was competing against either of our schools. He, along with many other associates, now refused to acknowledge me, or enter into conversation or small talk as they had prior to the filing of the lawsuit. In fact, it appeared that many changed their route through the corridors to avoid having to communicate with me. I realized I was being ostracized; however, I remained professional and pleasant to everyone. I became so focused on changing the racist environment; I knew it was imperative for me to look beyond those who were simply angry because their beloved company had been exposed to the world.

Almost every day there were articles in the news across the country about the lawsuit. It was obvious the company wanted to protect its image in the media. When the lawsuit was first reported to the public, the general attitude was not very favorable at all towards the plaintiffs.

Many thought we were just a few blacks that were not able to progress in the company; so we decided to file a lawsuit. But as the initial shock, denial and time passed, it became evident that the lawsuit had merit. Many reporters started writing stories to depict a different side of the company.

Weeks and then months passed. The Coca-Cola Company had not yet rendered any proof stating why the lawsuit was without merit. The company instead filed a motion for dismissal stating the only thing the four plaintiffs had in common was their color. Personally, I thought it was absurd The Coca-Cola Company would try and challenge the legitimacy of the case with such a simple and obvious approach. Every person with knowledge of the case knew all the plaintiffs were black. Coke's attorneys argued that the plaintiffs all alleged they had been discriminated against in different ways. The defense attorneys wanted the judge to dismiss the case because they felt there was no commonality among the plaintiffs. The commonality was discrimination. The shock was the many forms and manners in which it existed.

How low will an organization stoop to hide? This argument was especially sickening to me for I knew the reason we presented four examples of discrimination was due to the overwhelming proof of discrimination of blacks in pay, promotions, evaluations and terminations. Our attorneys provided one case for each of the four areas of the law, although each litigant was discriminated against in multiple ways.

During the first 30 to 60 days after filing the complaint, Federal Judge Richard Story gave our attorneys broad freedom to talk with other African American employees in The Coca-Cola Company who felt they were discriminated against. He also ruled that the company must turn over its database of policies and procedures by the middle of June 1999. The day the database should have been delivered, our attorneys said that the company's attorneys called to say that their computers were down. We knew that The Coca-Cola Company was lying and trying to prolong the delivery of the data.

Why would an innocent company not follow the orders of the judge? Why would a company whose chairman boldly stated that the lawsuit was without merit, try to prolong the process of clearing its name? Would a company that has nothing to hide not honor the judge's orders? There were many excuses The Coca-Cola Company's attorneys continued using in reference to the database. It was obvious they realized its practices were not fair against blacks. The truth would soon be known.

In June of 1999, the company faced one of its largest scares in its history. Local and national news stations reported children of Belgium were complaining of dizziness, nausea and other symptoms after drinking Coke products. This should have caught the attention of senior management, but it did not affect them the way you might think it would.

Instead of going in person to see the conditions of the children, Doug Ivester, Chairman of the company, sent some members of senior management to analyze the situation and report back to him. A reporter later asked him why he did not have a second in command or the president of the company fly to Belgium. Mr. Ivester responded by saying he did not want to filter any information he would receive by sending one of the presidents of the company. He did not want to have any information filtered, yet he sent several senior management members into Belgium before arriving there himself. This incident in many ways depicted the coldness that senior management had developed for their consumers.

In the end, the company reported that scientists diagnosed the illness as being "Mass Sociogenic Illness" (MSI), which is described as a constellation of symptoms of an organic illness without identifiable cause and which occurs among 2 or 3 more persons who share beliefs related to those symptoms. In other words, they claimed the children were not really sick. Because of the many reports of illness, they said that the children merely thought they were sick in their minds but were not really physically ill. At the same time, the company admitted that some kind of chemical accidentally spilled on some of the containers of product which produced a foul smell that reportedly triggered the initial illness. *Well, which was it; an imaginary illness or one linked to a Coca-Cola product?*

I thought the response that the children were not really sick depicted the lack of sensitivity that is manifested in the way the company operates at world headquarters on a daily basis. The company was too proud to admit that maybe it did something wrong. Not until

137

the government prolonged the process of allowing the products to return to the shelves did The Coca-Cola Company admit that, yes, it did play a part in this unfortunate situation. The story had been public for a week before Doug Ivester finally flew to Belgium.

This delay should have sent a message to the world. When the number one beverage company in the world has a health or safety problem with one of its products, upper management feels that it is fine to respond verbally instead of in person. Furthermore, there was no hurry in making a personal, public appearance to address the matter to the world or people of a nation.

A week later, Mr. Ivester saw it necessary to personally take responsibility for the company's actions. In a ninety-second television commercial, he apologized for the company's role in Belgium and vowed that The Coca-Cola Company's products are safe and will remain safe to consume. A few days after the commercial aired, a report from Warsaw, Poland indicated evidence of E- coli found in the bottled water. Distribution of Coke branded products again froze. *How would the company respond this time?*

In a matter of days, this unusual situation presented itself for the company. By this time, The Coca-Cola Company must have known that someone was trying to get their attention. *Was anyone listening to what was being said? Did anyone care about who was speaking?* With the negativism that swept around the world, it became obvious that someone was trying to get the attention of many people and of a very large company.

Who could possibly be so courageous to attempt such a task? Who would command the attention of a company with such power and resources? Who'd want to limit or impair the sales and growth of an organization such as The Coca-Cola Company? Who had patience to work to gain its undivided attention?

On June 29, 1999, the *Atlanta Journal Constitution* ran an article informing its readers that Judge Richard Story would be holding a hearing on July 15, 1999. The decision would be crucial for both sides. If the judge ruled for Coke, only four plaintiffs could be represented in the suit. If he ruled for the plaintiffs, the attorneys for the plaintiffs could continue preparing documentation and interviewing other potential class members. I was not fearful the judge would not rule in our favor. I believe the early filing of the motion to dismiss was just a

tactic by Coke to try to keep the truth from reaching the public.

I never understood why a company claiming innocence as Coke did

would file for dismissal at the beginning of discovery. This was the

period of time when Coke's attorneys would have had the opportunity

to question the named plaintiffs. It was also the time when the two

opposing sides would share information with one another.

Nevertheless, without presenting any concrete evidence, The Coca-

Cola Company filed for the class action to be dismissed. *Was this*

another example of corporate arrogance? Would the judge dismiss the

class so early in discovery? Because of our innocence we did not fear

the company or the legal process. We were hoping the case would be

heard in court one day.

On July 1, 1999, Judge Richard Story ordered the company to

release their employment database. This placed the company directly

under the looking glass. This database was to include each employee's

salary, race, education, evaluation, position, as well as several other

essential items. This ruling sent a clear message that the judge would

not allow the company to tie this case up in the courts for years. He wanted information. I imagined the judge was saying, "If there is nothing to hide then by all means show your hand."

It appeared he was a judge that was not going to tolerate the company using the legal system as a vehicle to hide behind. As Coke continued trying to out-maneuver the justice system, our attorneys continued working diligently. In weekly conferences, the plaintiff's team informed us of any changes and what was forthcoming. As The Coca-Cola Company continued making excuses about producing requested evidence, the foreign market was continuing to decline. The company's stock was lower than I had seen it since arriving in the organization.

In an *Atlanta Journal Constitution* article of June 29, 1999, there was mention of a letter that Lead Counsel for the plaintiffs received anonymously. The letter was very detailed in outlining that The Coca-Cola Company had set up a room called the Learning Center. In this room, the letter stated there were fax machines, computers, cameras and shredders. The article also described how Judge Story asked Coke's attorneys about the room. The attorneys admitted that the room existed. However, their position was that the only purpose of the room was to have a place where the company's attorneys could work without being disturbed. What was it? Was it a learning center or a war room where the lawyers were free to shred and dispose of any negative records, if they desired?

I propose it was the latter of the two. Many associates in that building talked of the shredding machines in that room. *Why so many shredders? What was being destroyed and disposed of?* One associate told me he had overheard a conversation about the room and that no one was to know its purpose. That explained why the windows were darkened on the inside of the room so that passersby couldn't see inside. Several associates stated they did see shredders in the room.

At this point, I wished someone would come forward and tell the judge what they saw in the room. Because of the fear of losing our jobs and of whites, I knew it was unlikely that anyone would speak out. Encouraged as usual though, I walked by faith and not by sight. I depended on God and held on to His unchanging hand. I had little confidence in man, for the let downs were continuous.

July 15, 1999, the date of Judge Story's decision and hearing was finally here. The speculation in the media had again surfaced. The local news stations reported on the importance of the decision. The possibility of what black's experienced at The Coca-Cola Company would finally be heard in a court of law. Everyone knew what this ruling would mean.

When I arrived at work on this day, there were signs posted throughout the company stating that the Chairman, Doug Ivester would be available for a Face-to-Face Chat at 2:30 p.m. in the auditorium. I was so filled with joy that it was very hard to concentrate on my job. I was not at all worried. I am a strong believer that if one is to worry then they should not pray; on the other hand, if one is to pray then they should not worry. I knew that Jesus had not brought us this far to leave us.

Most of the black associates in the company were ecstatic. They believed that when Judge Story finally ruled, many of their pains and frustrations would be momentarily soothed. Years of tears shed and heartache would soon be heard by a nation.

Simply boycotting Coca-Cola products would not make the difference. Throughout the struggle, I learned the quickest way to get a leader's attention was to find ways to impact their own personal bottom lines of the money they made. The last thing the company and the shareholders wanted was a national boycott by African Americans.

I still wondered why a company that markets itself to blacks and prides itself on gaining the black dollar would willfully deceive an entire nation of people. The lawsuit had been public knowledge for almost three months and The Coca-Cola Company had yet to render one piece of evidence either supporting or disputing the allegations brought forth. I wondered what the leaders of the company were thinking. Surely, they knew that the company's name alone would not get them through such serious charges. I prayed the judge would look beyond the defendant's mighty name and into the law when he made his ruling.

The weeks prior to the hearing and more specifically, the week of the hearing, many of the executives would go out of their way to make eye contact with me and speak. This I found intriguing. For more than three years, I walked the halls of The Coca-Cola Company clothed in the same navy blue, polyester uniform. Few people cared to speak to me, certainly not any executives, for I was just a black security guard.

Their usual silence was accepted behavior in the company. Only those people thought to be of help to others were frequently spoken to.

As soon as the lawsuit was filed, I became 'someone' behind the racist walls of The Coca-Cola Company. To the blacks, I was someone who saw a wrong being done to my people and refused to allow it to be done any longer. On the other hand, many whites thought of me as the educated negro who was not pleased with just being a security guard at The Coca-Cola Company. Some might have gone as far as to think that 'this negro guard thinks he is better than all the rest of them. Regardless of his education, he is still a negro.'

In a matter of days, most white associates who passed me began calling me Mr. Clark. Some executives who had never spoken to me before now felt comfortable enough to call me by my first name, Greg. I thought these people must really think I am a fool or that all blacks are ignorant to the games played.

I refused to let The Coca-Cola Company or any person for that matter play with my life. I took my career and my responsibilities as a husband very seriously. I was not shocked by the attention that I received after the lawsuit was filed. Having studied the culture of the company, I had a good idea how the white associates would respond to a black male after they realized that someone had identified a problem that plagued blacks and other minorities since the company was established. I never focused on what people thought of me.

Regardless of what had happened, I knew most white associates would despise me for my actions. I decided I'd simply respond to them by sharing an old gospel song that my great grandparents sang as they labored in the fields. The song is titled "May the work I've done speak for me." The words of this song reach the very depths of our hearts. My response to the associates who questioned my identity was made clear through these words.

I was playing basketball at Run & Shoot on Metropolitan Avenue when I realized that the court hearing should have been over. After a pick-up game of basketball, I decided to check my telephone. This proved to be one of the most exciting days in the gym. I had several messages waiting for me. I knew that Judge Story had made a decision and clearly someone was excited about sharing the news with me.

After checking all the messages, it was confirmed that Judge Story ruled in our favor. Judge Story ruled that The Coca-Cola Company presented no evidence indicating that the motion class action status should be dismissed. I had been praying for a long time and I knew this was the work of the Lord.

Amid my faith walk, there was no doubt in my mind this battle was won before it began. I'd studied and followed Jesus for a long time, and knew Him as many things, including a lawyer who had never lost a case. Rejoicing on a conference call with the three courageous women who had come forward with me, we praised God. We thanked God for all that He had done and all that He was going to do.

I could not wait until I got home to share the news with my beautiful wife. She had been by my side every step of the way and was thrilled to hear the good news. As I shared the news with her, a large smile came upon her face and she too began praising and thanking God in her own way.

The day after the verdict, the atmosphere at headquarters was interesting. Most of the white associates had previously acted as if there had not been a racial discrimination lawsuit filed against The Coca-Cola Company. Many flaunted attitudes that suggested that The Coca-Cola Company could get out of anything at any time. The ruling on

July 15th sent a shockwave throughout the company and the arrogance many of the whites had before the ruling seemed to have vanished.

I remember how pleasant and confident many of the white executives and associates appeared the days before the ruling. However, the Friday after the ruling their confident air was nowhere to be found. The balloon of arrogance they'd once waved in my face was deflating. They now realized this was not just another case of a few upset employees filing a lawsuit. The tension in the company the day thereafter was horrendous.

The company was definitely divided. Black associates were openly talking about the suit, while many of the white associates would act as if they could not hear, or did not know what all the talk and praise was really about. I thanked God for the many sisters and brothers who open-heartily claimed the victory against The Coca-Cola Company. Prayer changes things.

Ironically, the very same day the court hearing was preceding downtown, The Coca-Cola Company was having a company-wide talk with the chairman. These meetings were held at headquarters. A number of unusual questions came out during this meeting. A white male stood and asked the chairman to what cause did he attribute the loss of so many qualified, talented associates who had recently left the company. He also wanted to know what the chairman intended to do about the morale in the company.

The chairman responded by saying something to the effect that all associates must find individual ways to motivate themselves. A few other questions were asked, before a black female associate stood and asked the chairman, *"Why must I stand while or when I am speaking to you?"* The auditorium exploded with laughter, but she didn't smile. I think the chairman sensed that she was indeed very serious. He responded by saying that it would give him an opportunity to see who he was speaking to.

The chairman appeared to be visually shaken by several of the questions, but none as much as when a white female associate asked him about the racial discrimination lawsuit filed against the company. He stated he would allow one of his assistants to respond to that particular question. His assistant, a white male, stated that company representatives are in court as we speak and are fighting because we believe the case does not merit class action status. The auditorium was so quiet you could hear the person 10 feet away swallow.

The lawsuit was on everyone's mind but no one felt it was appropriate to talk about it. Many wanted to believe it was impossible for anyone to accuse a company perceived as being one of the most diverse in the world, of discriminating against an entire race of people. Many of the whites were unsure what the lawsuit actually entailed. There was a lot of division in The Coca-Cola Company.

This was not the only issue threatening the image of the company. There were many issues in Europe that got out of hand. The European governments somehow developed a dislike for the business style of the company and its leaders. Billion dollar deals crashed because of the company's delivery mechanism to the decision-makers in Europe.

A few months passed and Atlanta, "the city too busy to hate", was silent about the lawsuit. For several months there were only a few articles printed about the case. It was as if everyone was hoping that the next time any news broke it would be news that the company could use as a solid defense against the case, but to no avail.

In September, the *Atlanta Journal Constitution* wrote an article stating that the plaintiffs' attorneys filed a motion accusing The Coca-Cola Company of withholding crucial documents. The documents, the article described, allegedly contained proof that the company was well aware of the ratio of blacks to whites in the company and had refused to acknowledge and/or address the problem. The article further stated that the report which the top African American male submitted to Doug Ivester and which was completed by a local consulting firm; documented several areas where the company lacked adequate representation of African Americans.

In July of 1999, *Fortune* magazine wrote an article on Doug Ivester and The Coca-Cola Company entitled "Crunch Time." The article was very well written and addressed many realistic issues. There was only one thing that investors and stockholders truly cared about according to the article -- making money. That had been my experience working in the company. Nothing else really mattered but the bottom line and profit in The Coca-Cola Company. The article also spoke of the chairman as being a victim of bad timing. It also referred to Mr.

Goizueta, the former chairman of Coke, as being a "God," and certainly

having "God watching over him."

In sixteen years, Mr. Goizueta transformed a laggard into

America's most admired company. He died of lung cancer in October

1997 as the dollar was strengthening and economic plague just striking

Asia. Unlike Mr. Goizueta, his successor, Doug Ivester favored an

aggressive approach that people were unsure of. Many felt his "bulldog

leadership style" was definitely not what The Coca-Cola Company

needed during these trying times.

Where did The Coca-Cola Company go wrong? Fortune describes

the company's basic problem as follows:

> Ivester and his acquisition team saw themselves as beneficent
> foreign investors ("We demonstrate how we're good for the
> economy"), while regulators view them as ugly Americans bent
> on Coca-Cola-nizing the planet." It added that the deal to buy
> Orangina from Paris-based Pernod Ricard, announced a short
> time ago has been rebuffed by French authorities--no surprise,
> considering that the government had fined Coke for anti-
> competitive practices earlier that year. Although the Schweppes
> buyout was a done deal in more than 100 countries, regulators
> in Mexico and Australia, where Coke's market shares exceed
> 50%, have blocked it. Australian antitrust chief Allan Fels
> stated if The Coca-Cola Company had consulted local officials
> early on, "it would have faced severe problems." Coke CFO
> Chestnut, the company's point man on Schweppes, recently met
> with Fels in Australia. Fels liked the modest Scot.

Nevertheless, he said, "all proposals are rejected. End of story." But still this was not enough, Ivester revised plan B, C, and D in France, Australia, and Mexico. But with Schweppes in Europe, he was routed. Coke had structured the Acquisition in such a way that the company would be able to circumvent approval from the European Union, a strategy that seemed clever until it turned out to be stupid. At an April press conference in Brussels, the EU competition commissioner, Karel Van Miert, blasted Coke management: "They thought they could pull the wool over our eyes. They should learn to respect the rules along with everyone else."

In May of 1999, facing likely vetoes from other antitrust officials, Ivester cut most of the European continent out of the Schweppes purchase agreement and reduced the price from $1.85 billion to $1.1 billion. "I could foresee a protracted dialogue, he stated. "It didn't seem worth the effort." Van Miert didn't hesitate to claim victory: "They thought we would be too naive or not determined enough to stop them," he crows. "They were overconfident and a bit arrogant."

The article went on to suggest that Ivester might do well to apply a similar strategy to his problems closer to home. Some people think he should have solicited black leaders who were friendly to Coke, such as Jesse Jackson and Nelson Mandela, to speak up for the company when four current and former employees filed racial discrimination suits in any form.

Ivester said that he couldn't discuss any details of the case because the judge warned Coke not to try the case in the press. There was no reason to think Coke was vulnerable, except that Ivester might have been in another situation where reason didn't prevail: It's cheap to sue. It's expensive to defend. And, if the lawsuit reaches the courtroom, a jury decides.

Even the reporter felt that if Coke could get a leader from the black community to speak out on its behalf it would substantially help its situation. I was curious if the author ever considered that no prominent black personality was volunteering to speak up to help the company. Perhaps likely candidates remained silent because they felt there was merit to the lawsuit.

The September 1999 issue of *Fortune* magazine printed another article that reinforced the accusation in the lawsuit. The article began by acknowledging that Fortune and the Council on Economic Priorities (CEP), a non-profit research firm, enhanced the second annual list of America's Best Companies for minorities by trying to assess the true impact of a company's overall diversity efforts. To do that, they asked companies whether they have diversity programs, such as sensitivity training for executives and minority-recruiting initiatives. They also asked just how many employees were directly affected by the programs. An example was the number of managers' bonuses that are tied to fulfilling diversity goals in their departments. Likewise, they ascertained just how companies that routinely visited historically black colleges hired many minority graduates. The data gathered enabled the team to better determine whether a company was truly making diversity work or simply paying lip service to the idea. The results were factored into each company's final score and ranking.

The survey was separated into twelve categories. These included measuring minority representations on the company's board of directors, among corporate officers, the twenty-five highest-salaried employees, and for middle management, the total work force and hires made in the past year. In addition to the previously noted new data, there were two other categories listed which attempted to measure whether companies put their money where their mouth was in terms of diversity: the percentage of dollars spent with outside suppliers went to minority-owned firms, and the percentage of underwriting business flowed to minority-owned investment banks? Companies were also asked what percentage of charitable contributions was given to programs that primarily benefit minorities. Each category was assigned a measured percentage, varying in value according to importance.

155

Every company was then scored by statistically comparing its

performance with those of its peers in the survey. In other words,

companies were graded on a curve. *Was it any surprise why Coke was*

not in the top percentages of the companies? Not to me.

Chapter 7

Is There Any Substance to The Lawsuit Against Coke?

The media attention the lawsuit carried should have generated some mention or action from the very organizations whose purpose and mission was to uphold racial equality. However, in this instance their silence and inactivity puzzled me. The civil rights organizations were silent on the issues at hand.

Many months later, this group with its very influential position in the black community had not made one comment of any kind in support of the plaintiffs and their lawsuit against The Coca-Cola Company. Large corporations use tactics to silence such organizations, I discovered. Was it coincidence or had the organization been silenced?

If this was not a mere coincidence, and the organization was bought for a price, then who'd remain to call a racist a racist? Is any form of discrimination to one in four blacks not an injustice to the entire race? Who will tell the white leaders that they can't toss us pennies to placate us while they poison the minds of our children? If we continue allowing corporations to prostitute our people, is it unrealistic to believe that our children will be the ones who are ultimately being hurt? If we have been playing without a playbook, it is high time to document the plays and teach our children how to play.

The city remained so quiet that even the interest of a reporter from *The Atlanta Inquirer* received little attention. The author began his article by asking, "Is there any substance to the lawsuit against Coke?" The article continued to ask, "Who do you know that's speaking out about it?" The author suggested that all blacks should be interested in the Coke saga and that studies have shown that blacks consume nearly 10% more soft drinks than the population as a whole and they are important consumers of the Cola Flavor segment.

The article carried on to say, "Filed in Atlanta on April 22, 1999, the suit claimed Coke pays blacks less, fires them at a higher rate than other employees, and gives them lower evaluation scores. According to the filing it added, the average salary for a black Coke management employee is $45,215, compared with $72,045 for other employees. The reporter then asked, what do black Americans think of the suit and the situation? Although the national black community has given little support to the employees, the case is reminiscent of the one at Texaco Inc. settled in 1996 for $176 million at the threat of a Jesse Jackson led civil-rights boycott that blemished the oil company's brand name. Coca-Cola has much more of a philanthropic presence and image among African Americans than did Texaco. Blacks spend over $3 billion a year on soft drinks and represent a market Coke covets. The article added that Coca-Cola has been visible in the black community for decades and has been even more visible since the April suit.

On the same day that U.S. District Judge Richard Story was to hold a hearing on the suit, Tom Joyner, host of the nation's most popular morning radio show targeting African Americans, held a concert in Charlotte, N.C. and asked all guests to bring Coke bottle caps to help the United Negro College Fund. This occurred subsequent to the suit filing and after Ingrid Sanders Jones, head of the Coke's Community Affairs and Foundation, had appeared on the show to donate $25,000 to the fund. The families of Martin Luther King Jr., who've been regular recipients of Coke's foundation funds, are boycotting South Carolina for flying the Confederate flag.

Donald McHenry, former U.S. Ambassador to the United Nations and a member of the company's board of directors, and J. Bruce Llewellyn, a black who owns the Philadelphia Coca-Cola Bottling

Company were asked: Is there any substance to the suit? As yet, no black group had threatened a boycott. Such a move could cost Coca-Cola as much as 2 percent of its gross revenues. Coca-Cola generated $19 billion in revenues in 1998 and could be hit with a fine of as much as $450 million if they pursued the case in court. To avoid this, the company may seek to settle the case for $50 to $100 million.

After several months of hearing nothing about the suit, this reporter saw it necessary to report on what was still a delicate topic. It was refreshing to know that someone was thinking about the four plaintiffs and wanted to let the city know that this case is serious, ugly, and very much alive, but I wondered why the report was spoken now after such a lengthy media silence.

Despite a quiet in the media, there were still many associates who were furious with me. At times, it seemed there was no longer a need to wear my name badge. Those who disliked me knew me by sight and had no problem letting me know that they wanted nothing to do with me. It had been common courtesy to meet and greet people with a friendly hello once they arrived at work.

I started watching whites as they approached me from a distance. More and more would look at me from afar but as soon as they were close enough to speak to me, they'd quickly turned their heads. Nevertheless, I continued to speak my greetings.

I did not want to believe that such a large number of people hated me. The looks were so cold; I sometimes put on a face of stone in an effort to let them know I was not afraid. I never once feared any associate, leader, nor anyone else in the company.

It was a discomfort to step on an elevator only to be recognized by a white associate who would then quickly exit so they'd not be enclosed in the space with me. If they stayed, many stood so close to the door they risked losing their noses! I had to find different ways to motivate myself in this hostile environment.

Although I could not see exactly what changes were going on in the company, I knew from the many reports that black associates were being promoted to management and director level positions on a weekly basis. *I would smile and ask myself, why now?* I tried to focus on the good that we were doing to deal with the hatred that was so obvious. I knew the results and the reactions from others would be ugly, but I also knew someone had to step up to the plate, stand tall and not strike out.

I remember from going to church as a boy at Greater Life Tabernacle, and in my mother's wise words that God never gives us more than we can handle. These were comforting words at a time when I thought I was alone. She also told me that no matter how hard or long my struggle may appear to be, Jesus is never late. I'd visualize her smiling and saying, "when you least expect Him; He is right on time."

God-fearing Christian brothers and sisters played an enormous role of helping me cope with the racist attitudes I faced each day. The Learning Center was a security post where I found it very relaxing to work and get away from most of the attitudes in the company. At least I thought it was a retreat until one day while I was sitting there doing some work on the computer. I realized that there were many associates who would turn their heads and look at the wall when I addressed them with a "Good Morning" or "Hello." Other white associates appeared angry or had strained expressions as they passed.

There was not a single post where I could go and not receive the looks of hatred and anger. One day for some reason, the hard stares and ugly looks really got to me. Before I knew it there were tears running down my face. I didn't have time to call to be relieved, so everyone who came by and glanced at me knew something was wrong. I could think of no other name to call, but that of Jesus. I began praying and said to God, "You are the one that made me and prepared me for this challenge; if I ever needed you Lord, I sure need you now."

In a matter of seconds, a brother came by and said, "My brother, I see you smiling each and every day, speaking and greeting these people, but you must be going through something." It was just as if, through his words, Jesus said, "I would never leave you, nor forsake you." As I began to respond to this brother, I felt a burst of energy come over me unlike anything I'd ever felt. It was warm and made me feel a little lighter. It was almost as if I had lost weight in a matter of seconds.

The brother continued by thanking and praising God for the four plaintiffs having enough courage to come forward and fight the fight that so many other blacks refused. In a matter of minutes, I'd forgotten why the tears were running down my face and began concentrating on the greatness of God.

163

I was always reluctant about calling my wife at work to let her know when I was upset and having a difficult day. Keeping my feelings hidden, I thought, was the best way to protect her. I was wrong. A Christian brother who had prayed with me in my struggle shared with me that God gave me a wife with whom to share deep feelings. He added even when I thought I was protecting her; she already knew when something was not right with her husband. He was right. Not only did I feel better when I spoke openly with my wife, but she told me that she always knew when something was wrong. I thanked God for allowing someone to open my eyes so that I might see another one of the many blessings of having a loving and supportive wife.

More time passed and still there was little being reported in the media and newspapers. Many black associates would ask me if we had settled the case quietly. "No," was my reply of course. This case was not about a quick settlement, nor was it about money. Many of the blacks that were discriminated against by the company had left the company or either gone to be with our Lord and Savior, Jesus Christ. I was not going anywhere.

It was time for the company to accept and publicly acknowledge their wrongdoings to the world. The company then could begin building an environment that truly promoted equality. Nothing else would be accepted. That was my goal.

Throughout the summer of 1999, things were quiet in the media but not behind the walls of the company. In July, I was placed on the executive level floors in the North Avenue Tower. This was a new post that the security management team thought was essential to enhance the protection of the executives.

My very first day working the post gave me a true insight of how the lawsuit affected the leaders. At about 7:30 a.m., I came face to face with the chairman of the company. Although I saw him often, these circumstances were different. The area that was allotted for the security officer to sit was in a hallway. I sat at that post when I heard someone walking in my direction. I looked up and as the chairman of the company passed the doorway, he said "Good Morning." He looked at me strangely, almost as if he was trying to figure out where he had seen my face. A few minutes later, he passed again and this time he took a longer look at me. He did not look as though he was trying to place my face this time. It appeared he recognized that I was the security officer that initiated the racial discrimination lawsuit against the company.

For the first time in person, I witnessed how uncomfortable he appeared. A few minutes later, one of the major financial officers passed, and he too looked as if he had seen a ghost and was not pleased. Despite their reactions, I remained focused and did my job. As one might expect, I was rarely placed on the executive floors after this.

The more time that passed, the more white associates began showing their frustration or acting out their anger towards me. Comments and pointed fingers continued by many as they passed by me. One Saturday morning I was posted at an entrance gate. A white manager who normally spoke to me had become silent in recent weeks and on this day, he entered the gate slowly. I had not yet raised the gate arm and this manager still moved forward slowly towards the closed gate, stared into the booth until our eyes met and he gave me 'the finger.' Now, that was a new type of finger pointing!

I wasn't angry. Instead I thought how childish and senseless his action was. I knew he was expressing what many others felt. I did not react to that manager but I did call my console operator and shared the experience with him. The operator was a black male and I asked him, *"Does it mean the same thing when a white person gives you the finger as it does when a black person does?"* He said, "Well Clark, I always thought that the finger was universal...yes, it does."

While I didn't become angry, he did. He asked if I wanted him to place me somewhere else. I responded by telling him, "that there was no place to escape the racism in the company." The action this manager took was an example of the sick mentality in The Coca-Cola Company. Insults were hardly a real man or real company's answer to such a serious issue, but it was as though they didn't know how to respond otherwise.

It was soon time for the annual job evaluation process to begin. The entire company had adopted a new evaluation process called "Maximizing Performance." In this system, employees had the opportunity to first evaluate themselves and then compare their notes to those of their supervisors. I understood the system explicitly and saw it as just another way of holding blacks back in the company. After all, the final rating would still come from the supervisor, which had not changed. Employee ratings were not input but rather a sign of all-too-familiar lip service.

I recalled the positive things I'd done as a security officer that past year and decided to mention just a few of the situations I'd encountered since the lawsuit was filed. I told of the finger gesture encounter, proud that I had remained calm and sure that this would let my supervisor catch a glimpse of what I encountered day to day.

Upon reading my report, my supervisor called me in and demanded that I tell him who it was. I told him that I had already confronted the person and I would not give him a name. In return he stated that he must let his supervisor know because this type of behavior is not tolerated at The Coca-Cola Company. I smiled and thought to myself that was the exact line that the chairman used when he made his very first response to the media in reference to the lawsuit, and by now we all knew that was a lie.

A few hours had passed when I ran into the manager of the security department. I wonder what he thought when my supervisor shared the finger gesture incident with him. Since the filing of the lawsuit, he had been virtually unseen. He used to be much more present in the department but not so these days. I think he realized that if it were not for his racist attitude there would not be a racial discrimination lawsuit in process.

As if I believed the line about a finger gesture not being tolerated. I knew the company was lying again. I also knew they had established a new War Room from which to battle the lawsuit. The original room, established in May of 1999 in the Learning Center was known for its blackened windows and shredding machines. Unlike the initial room, the new room, room #7, had a door which led to the outside of the building. A privileged associate shared with me that the group wanted to use this second room because it would be easier to get the shredded documents from the building, sight unseen.

As a security guard, I was able to move frequently from building to building and gained a substantial amount of knowledge as to how offices were moved and setup inside of the company. Coke used outside contractors for many of their services such as vending, mail, and some catering. Consequently, the group that was tasked with the role of moving departments was the security department. I figured someone in our department must have been in 'the room' in

169

conjunction with its setup or move from the first location to the second.

I hoped it might be someone who wasn't afraid to talk about what they saw there.

I started with asking the guys that I would casually come in contact with while patrolling and securing the complex. As I asked each person, I'd stare into their eyes to gauge their initial reaction before their verbal response. Often the eyes will tell the truth, before it has been altered or deviated from and certainly before the mouth has opened.

The men I asked were big and strong. They looked like they could move not just the contents, but a building itself. They were the right guys to ask for they'd helped set-up the room, yet they said they did not remember what type of equipment they'd placed in the room. That's what they said with their lips but their eyes told me something else – they showed fear. I realized that if I wanted to hear the truth, I had to get the timing and questions to the right person. One of the conquerors of fear is anger. I needed to find one of the guys who helped with the move and also who the company had made angry enough to tell the truth.

A few days later, I saw one of the brothers who often entered that complex. My instincts told me that in the right situation, he would be the one to break the silence. Two days later, I had opportunity to chat with this brother, and he too appeared to be afraid initially. However, the more we started talking about music, sports, etc., the more he began to open up. I waited until I thought the right moment presented itself, and I asked, "Have you ever been in room #7 in the Learning Center?"

He responded, "Yes, I have." I then asked if he helped set the room up. He responded, "No, I did not." So, I changed the subject and asked him about his future plans. He spoke of plans to go into business for himself. He went on to say that he was not very far from stepping out of the company and into his own venture.

Here was my chance. I asked him, "Did you see any shredding machines while you were in room #7?" He replied, "Yes, I did." I could tell that he was now comfortable talking to me, so I asked him if he was willing to talk to some people (my attorneys) about what he saw in the room. He replied, "If I can find the time, I will."

I respected this brother. He may have been just as afraid as any other worker in the company to speak up; however, he was not willing to let fear deter him from doing what he felt was right. He also shared with me the response of a white male coworker who was in charge of setting up the room when he had asked him about the shredders. The white man said, "Listen buddy, you don't want to know what is going on in that room. Everything in that room is top secret, buddy, top secret. Everything that comes out of those computers goes straight in those shredders."

The black brother laughed as he told me this story, for he believed that one had to know his co-worker in order to understand what was so funny. I didn't know that white co-worker of his but I knew a multitude just like him.

Affirming information filed in my mind, I once again thought about the faith walk I was on. A faith walk means not taking the easy road. A faith walk means not being silent. Faith walking is about long-term integrity not short-term comfort or satisfaction.

So I continued showing up for work, focused on the long-term effect of how our efforts would reflect upon, and hopefully change, the company. Media silence continued and news reached me of blacks being promoted within The Coca Cola Company. I wondered if the

172

blacks receiving these positions felt they'd earned their position, or if they thought they were simply given a position because of the lawsuit. While I was pleased that a few of the brothers and sisters received positions that would help them better take care of their families, I knew this was not enough. To me, it was too little, too late.

The company since its inception realized that there were no blacks in key positions. How could you not notice a virtually all-white leadership elite? Instead of correcting the problem, each of the company's leaders focused on increasing their shareholders' value in the company. The strength of Coca Cola stock was what mattered.

The number of blacks who were intentionally held back from receiving promotions or key positions did not matter. *Why?* Because such facts or statistics were not part of an investor's or shareholder's knowledge when they considered the value equation for Coca Cola stock.

Until now, few thought to ask perhaps of the company's racial makeup. *When an investigating agency asked, would it get real and accurate figures or post shredder feedback? Was The Coca Cola*

173

Company a corporation worth being modeled after, or was it hiding

deep, dark secrets?

Chapter 8

Depositions: Personal Accounts for the World to Hear

While the media was quiet, behind the scenes our attorneys and those hired to represent the company were hard at work. For months the company continued making lame excuses about why it was not releasing any data or information. I read a newspaper article stating that the company had released hundreds of papers that Judge Story had ordered them to produce. They had released papers alright – just not anything legible. The papers released were written in so many codes that the experts for the plaintiffs were unable to decipher what the codes represented.

It was another intentional move that the company decided to make to prolong the true facts from being known. And still the company seemed to thrive on claiming to be one of the most diverse in the world. If this is a fact, why were the attorneys representing The Coca-Cola Company stamping each piece of the database confidential instead of sharing them with the public? If the company were fair and diverse, then it had nothing to hide and no reason to withhold documents.

If I was in the power position of the company, and I had done absolutely nothing wrong; I would gladly surrender my records to the accusing party so they'd see how proud and committed to equality and diversity the company actually was. On the other hand, if I was guilty and had enough money to hire an army of attorneys, it would be easy to withhold documents, stall for time, and search for a legal loophole to end the case.

Regardless of what one may feel, I realized there was no doubt that the company knew it was wrong. It had been caught with its pants down, and was now running to hide while the world watched and waited for its comment. It was not about a company's embarrassment though, it was a battle that was not mine or the company's alone, it was the Lord's and I was not worried.

During the week of November 8, 1999, The Tom Joyner Radio Show in Atlanta celebrated its anniversary. There were many events planned throughout the city and even a lunch engagement was held in the Central Reception Building (CRB) at Coke's Headquarters. I was posted in the CRB that day and was afforded the opportunity to observe the atmosphere and people who attended the luncheon.

There was a small greeting committee standing at the entrance of the building, smiling and happy when Mr. Joyner walked in. Mr. Joyner was jovial and greeted the ladies with a hug before he was escorted upstairs to lunch. As I stood watch, I saw a few black associates of the company going upstairs to participate and meet Mr. Joyner and his crew. I smiled inwardly as I wondered: *Why would The Tom Joyner Show be at The Coca-Cola Company in the middle of a highly publicized racial discrimination lawsuit?*

Why would the company be interested in the most popular radio voice in this country among African Americans? As I stood casually looking over the rotunda, I made eye contact with the one black female who was probably responsible for having Mr. Joyner at the company. When she saw me she looked as if she had seen a ghost. Her eyes stretched and she had a very disappointing look on her face. She appeared to be upset that I was standing in the area. I greeted her and she, in return, spoke quickly as if trying to appear that my presence did not concern her. It was too late. Her eyes had already expressed what she truly felt about my presence.

I knew who this woman was. I often passed her in the corridors and she would smile as if I did not know that she was the driving force behind all the money thrown out to the black leaders and organizations in the community. While many of the black pastors and leaders were afraid to speak out on behalf of our lawsuit or on whatever they felt was the truth, there were a handful of leaders who had the courage to do just that.

Rev. JW and I remained close through this period. When we spoke, I would always greet him with the same question. "Hey Reverend, are you still fighting the battle or has Coke bought you too?" Each time he'd reply with, "Bought who? There is not enough money for Coke to buy my soul." All the times I would address him that way he never once became angry or upset. He knew what I meant.

In contrast, when a person has been confronted with the truth and it is something they are not comfortable with or not proud of; anger or defensiveness often shows itself. Rev. Watts was never angry or defensive. He was a man who stood on the same solid ground throughout our time journeying together. I knew that in spite of his knowledge and speculation that other NAACP groups were probably bought by Coke, he chose to stand for what he believed was right. His right hand man, Mr. GS, was another black man I never had to wonder about. They stood firm on their beliefs and were willing to tell the world how they felt about the racist culture of the company.

One weekday, near midnight, I received a page from Rev. Watts. Not a man to normally contact me so late, I knew something was up. I returned the page only to learn a little more about how the company tried to flex its power to hide the racism that was by now public knowledge. The Reverend told me that two of Atlanta's most prominent blacks, an insurance man and a former mayor, had been calling him at home and work. They wanted to arrange a time to meet with him, and amid Rev. Watts' busy schedule, they settled on meeting for dinner that night.

Rev. Watts shared with me that the conversation during dinner was mostly about the lawsuit and The Coca-Cola Company. This insurance man explained that the former mayor was out of town and could not make the dinner; however, their concerns and viewpoints were similar. He then wanted to know what the reverend felt about the lawsuit and if asked by the courts, what would he say.

179

Rev. Watts stated that he told him, "I was going to tell the truth about all that I know." Rev. Watts said this prominent businessman grew quiet and thoughtful. After a few moments passed, he asked Rev. Watts what sort of things did he like? Rev. Watts then asked, "What do you mean?" The man further elaborated and said, "You know, like cars and so forth."

I could hear anger rising in Rev. Watts' voice as he recounted the discussion to me. He answered the insurance man with, "I have a car. No! Thank you." The businessman offered to pay for dinner but Rev. Watts was not a fool to the ways of the lost, and paid for his own meal.

The anger in his voice only made me feel proud for I knew he was one black man that would not be won over by the dollar. It was clear to Rev. Watts and I that someone at The Coca-Cola Company felt the need to put a cap on the NAACP leader that helped initiate the lawsuit. Thus this man was sent to try and buy his silence.

Why would there be a need for late night telephone calls and dinner invitations by black men that were well known and politically connected in the communities?

I was not at all surprised by the rage expressed by Rev. Watts or by his experience with this man. I understood that the reason why so many whites at the company behave the way they did was because many of them viewed blacks as being out of rhythm, uncultured, and afraid to stand up for what they believe. And for those willing to take a stand, many were also easily willing to take a payoff because they were really still fearful underneath. "Selling out" is a term that is widely used when one refers to a black who apparently takes the side of a white person even though he/she knows the truth and what is morally right before making the wrong decision. With this understanding of the term, many might suggest that a number of our black leaders have sold out to large corporate empires.

An example of "selling out" could be an instance where a group of people make public accusations about an organization, and the one and only highest ranking black in the organization steps up and states that all the allegations are false for he or she was able to rise to a top position in the company. While that token person probably feels that he or she is doing what is best for themselves and for the company, they are really enslaved to the company. I imagine it must be a terrible feeling to know the right thing to do, but be afraid to do it.

I found comfort in believing that an action is considered justified if it creates the greatest amount of good for the largest number of people. While it may seem very difficult in the beginning without a view of the outcome, it is a noble cause because it is in the interest of the greater good. I found it important to focus on justice, and consider the beginning as my ending. My happiness, joy, peace and livelihood should not rest in the arms of any organization. My focus was on Christ the solid rock on which I stood for all other ground was sinking sand.

As I thought of all that Jesus had brought me through, my eyes became full. In life, sometimes the road we are given seems unfair, difficult and hard to bear. Nobody said that life would always be what we expected it to be, but my Jesus said that as long as I keep my hand in His hand, He would never leave me nor forsake me. Forget dwelling on sellouts, my thoughts began and ended with completing the work that My Lord and Savior had placed before me.

The *New York Times* published an article on November 8, 1999 stating that Carl Ware, the highest-ranking black in The Coca-Cola

Company had resigned from his position because of the new organizational structure designed by Chairman, Doug Ivester. The article stated that Mr. Ware was initially to step down from his position in late 2000; however with Mr. Ivester's announcement of a new structure led him to step down sooner. Mr. Ware was embarrassed and infuriated that he, the top African American in the company would now report to someone who been his peer for many years. The newspaper added that a good friend of Mr. Ware's stated he had been frustrated for many years about the way he has been treated in the company, and viewed this final shuffle as a slap in the face.

Why would the chairman of any organization surround himself with six white males in the middle of a racial discrimination lawsuit? Could he be a racist? The chairman had an opportunity to keep the highest-ranking black one step away from him, but he chose to do exactly what we alleged for the past six months. Surely, the chairman and the board of directors of the company realized how the public would perceive this. If they realized what public perception would be, they didn't seem to care.

During the month of October, I learned how and why a company that was seemingly on top of the world could suffer a decline in morale, profits and perception. Overall make-up of the company and marketing strategies had not changed drastically, but the top layer of the company had changed in this powerful company. Leaders at this top level, operating based on their personal beliefs could be dangerous.

For instance, a white leader that was raised in a small southern town with few blacks and even fewer in significant jobs might not consider blacks as equal. Likewise, a black leader raised with the opposite set of circumstances might also have a slanted view. It is usually ignorance and arrogance that cause leaders to make decisions rooted in discrimination. The danger increases if that leader has a large ego and a view of being larger than human. Decisions made from these positions are seldom wise or fair.

On Friday, November 19, 1999, there was a hearing that would decide many of the issues in discussion for the past six months. Judge Story appointed another magistrate to assist him in deciding many of the issues in the case. Cokes' initial argument was that it did not have enough time to collect the requested data.

Both sides were given the opportunity to be heard, and Judge Story then ordered The Coca-Cola Company to turn over all documents that were relevant to the case. He added that this court order was handed down five months ago and if the company felt that it could not meet the deadline, it should have asked for more time. He then stated, "The company did not request more time; therefore, I am ordering no later than December 16, 1999, that all of the documents be turned over to the plaintiff's attorneys."

I wondered how the attorneys for the company felt when they realized their stall tactic had failed. Although this was the first time this particular Judge had ruled on any of the motions, I felt he knew that something was going on that the company was trying to hide. Company insistence that its records were confidential, and that the public did not have a right to see the breakdown by race of employees seemed like diversions for the purpose of hiding the truth.

The arguments the attorneys for Coke presented were extremely weak, which made the Judge's decision easy. I was pleased to see that the presiding judges had a passion for the law and were not concerned or willing to be misled by the wealth of The Coca-Cola Company. It

185

appeared that attorneys for the company could not use bullying tactics to win. The judges were concerned with facts and they, unlike many of the black leaders, were not concerned with the company's worth or the amount the company contributed to the community. I felt sure they knew the significance of the case and was aware of the tricks that could be played. At this point, the only side rendering tricks was The Coca-Cola Company.

After six months of being in the public eye, no black leader would step up and demand Coke to come clean. Instead, as time passed and the case grew older, more money continued to be funneled through to the black community. The company campaigned to get certain Civil Rights Organizations to offer awards in the company's name and to give some even to the company itself. However, we learned these new manipulative 'requests' were denied.

One afternoon there was a meeting for the attorneys working on the case and the lead plaintiffs. In this meeting one of the lead plaintiffs stressed her concern that with all the negative publicity and the ridiculous way the company has responded to the lawsuit, not one black group was willing to tell the Icon to put up or shut up. One of my co-plaintiffs was so burdened because she felt that no one was behind us. I sat and listened quietly as the other sisters tried to calm her. I knew exactly how the sister felt and what her concerns were.

After listening, one of the attorneys pondered for a moment then said that he was not at all displeased with the way the black community has responded – often with silence - to the case. His comment really hit home with me. What it said to me was that in his 20 plus years of experience in dealing with Civil Rights groups he has come to the realization that blacks will fight among themselves before they unite and fight those that have done an injustice to their people.

While he was willing to accept the fact that it was okay that the leaders of these organizations were afraid of The Coca-Cola Company, I could not. The longer I listened to the attorneys, the clearer the picture became. In not so many words, they were saying they expected the black leaders to run, hide and accept gifts from the company.

Please do not misunderstand what I am suggesting. I am thankful for each and every attorney who accepted the task of representing the group. They all were well-researched and came highly recommended. However, I feel it a travesty to not expound upon the perceived

187

perception of these brave men and women who came forward to file the suit. Each of them became a part of the case believing in their hearts that the case was with merit, myself included. As a black man that was raised by a strong black man, my tolerance for the continued excuse-making by our attorneys on behalf of black organizations came quickly to an end. I was no longer willing to listen to whites make excuses for African Americans to African Americans about an issue that is as clear as crystal.

To date, the company had not presented one piece of data to refute the numbers that were printed in the *Atlanta Journal Constitution* on April 23, 1999. Instead, the company conducted business as usual, spreading buy-out money throughout the black community. This was an archaic way of thinking; nevertheless, I understood what the company was hoping to accomplish. The corporation wanted to buy the support of the black community and to silence those who would normally speak out against racism.

As money was spent, I didn't worry. I knew that the more money the company spent, the more prayers were being prayed. And, I knew that money is no match for prayers. The company could not understand

and did not want to understand that this movement was about righteousness. It was not an auction, nor was it a time to ignore the blacks who had faithfully dedicated their lives to bringing change to the company. The company believed that money changes things but it does not.

While I leaned on the power of prayer and Coke leaned on its buying power, I knew that I had the key to change and they didn't. No one could buy his or her wrong into a right, for the Creator had seen, heard and reviewed all the evidence and already ruled. He has tried every case that has ever been presented in a court of law and ruled accordingly.

When I thought of all that He has done for me, my soul cried out, 'Thank you Lord. Oh thank you God for saving me.' Regardless of the number of times I felt like running and hiding from the many unwanted looks, gestures and rudeness, I knew that I could not. For comfort, I called on the most powerful name I knew, Jesus. Never once did He fail me.

Many changes were occurring in the company. The chairman continued to appoint white associates in leadership positions. I continued to research the company and read in the amended complaint filed on April 22, 1999, that a black male associate with a high paying position in the company stated that he'd had a conversation with the chairman. In that conversation, the chairman stated that it would be at least twenty years before he saw a black man hired in an essential decision-making position in The Coca-Cola Company.

I remember how angry this brother seemed as I read the information he shared. Despite denials by the chairman and the spokespersons for the company, their actions aligned with the statement not their denial. Now, two years later, the chairman of the company reorganized and surrounded himself with six white males reporting directly to him while at the same time demoting the once highest-ranking black in The Coca-Cola Company.

A few weeks later another company bulletin appeared announcing the leadership of several other key positions in the company. I searched the bulletin carefully only to find there was not one black among those placed in these essential positions. One could conclude that the chairman was certainly putting his plan and beliefs into action. I often wondered what the decision-makers of The Coca-Cola Company were thinking.

Did any board member at any time think to ask the race of any of those who were being promoted? Did it matter to anyone? Or, were they simply handling business the way the company has always handled it?

Once again, the weeks and days passed with little news of the lawsuit in the media. Many associates would ask me if the case had been settled. I did not mind responding to their questions. I knew that most blacks were deeply concerned with the case for one reason or another. Most were genuinely concerned, but not all had the greater good in mind.

For instance, I disliked when an associate would come to me and ask, "When do we get paid." The person asking this foolish question probably had done nothing to support the struggle. These people were probably the ones who just sat back as they have always done and simply waited on a handout.

This lawsuit was clearly not about money, but righteousness. We four original plaintiffs did not set out on the journey to try and become rich while others who were in the same position continued to suffer. While a few freeloaders wanted our cause to be a meal ticket for them, we were in it for righteous reasons and justice. I disliked answering these few but I remained focused on our goal.

It was so wonderful to have associates ask how I was doing, especially because it became harder each day to work in such a racist environment. It seemed like the more I came to work, the crazier the stares and comments became. It seemed that the problems of the company were growing.

Because of my role in the lawsuit, I had first-hand knowledge of the many tactics the attorneys representing The Coca-Cola Company were using. I often smiled inside when the attorneys for Coke would pass me in the corridors with angry looking faces. I knew that no matter how they tried to hide the truth, the company's database would soon be released and the world would get an opportunity to see statistics that would confirm that The Coca-Cola Company had indeed discriminated against blacks.

It was a chilly Tuesday morning when the plaintiffs gathered to discuss the depositions. As I sat at the conference room table and looked around at each of the ladies, I became filled with a sense of joy.

I knew what each of them had gone through to get to this point. Each of

them like myself, probably thought of giving up somewhere along the

line, but when we thought of what we'd been through and what we

knew others were going through, we persevered.

The room was filled with warmth and well wishes. Our attorneys

were present. They appeared to be savoring the moment and I could tell

that each of them felt privileged to be in the midst of the four

courageous plaintiffs. For hours we just sat and talked about how and

why we have come this far. The sister who had been working with me

for the longest time shared some of the experiences we'd had in

meetings and in preparing for certain conference calls and so forth.

As one would talk, the others would listen with a great deal of

respect for the voice that had the floor. Each of the women voluntarily

shared some intimate thoughts about what they had been through and

how difficult it had been. One sister said that if nothing else happens in

this we have already done enough. She was tired, as we all were. I

knew she was ready for the ordeal to be over. As she finished sharing her concerns about the case and the depositions, I knew that I needed to say something.

I quickly and assertively dismissed the notion that we had done enough. I made it known that the reason that blacks were given more positions in the company was because of the lawsuit and for no other reason. I maintained that this was simply the reactionary response when white directors and managers looked at their groups after finding out what the lawsuit stated and they realized there was not equality. They were simply and consciously trying to cover up the discrimination in their groups.

By no means I stressed, should we mistake these actions as being a long-term strategic effort to correct the racist environment of The Coca-Cola Company. Instead, this reactionary mode was how many in leadership positions responded when they realized news of what they had grown accustomed to doing to blacks in the company had reached the public and would soon reach the courts. I suggested we should approach the depositions and the rest of whatever was to come with the attitude that nothing positive yet has happened and we must keep on keeping on.

Surely, I stated, that it would be helpful to know that the black community supports us, but this was not the case. I asked the plaintiffs and attorneys to consider whether the dollars The Coca-Cola Company donates to the black community causes have an effect on whether black organizations will or will not speak negatively about the company in regards to the lawsuit? Of course it does. I charged them that we must continue walking by faith and not by sight. Like soldiers in the army of the Lord, we all agreed and began planning to move forward.

A deposition was one of the most important parts of being a class representative. It was also the most stressful. There were meetings to prepare for. Other meetings were more informal and allowed questions or concerns to be shared and responded to by our attorneys.

As the case progressed, I developed an understanding of the importance of having thorough, professional and ethical legal representation. Each of the attorneys specialized in a particular area of law and was willing to share their knowledge with us. I remained cautious for I knew that at any given time, The Coca-Cola Company had enough money to buy each one of them if they were for sale. I was thankful to have attorneys that were dedicated to this case.

We began preparing for the depositions several weeks in advance. As time grew close, I became more concerned about the three ladies given the task of conquering the beverage giant with me. I was not concerned with whether or not they would be successful in completing the depositions; I was more concerned with the type of demoralizing tactics the attorneys representing the company would use.

I tried to think of ways to relieve them from the misery and aggravation that the deposition would surely thrust upon them. The day before the first deposition, we met with our attorneys to connect and answer any last minute questions. I listened to the sisters' concerns and on several occasions I smiled. My desire to relieve them of the unnecessary pain they would soon have to endure grew stronger.

I saw no reason why the ladies needed to go through the days of questioning by the defendant's attorneys. I on the other hand, welcomed the challenge and opportunity to speak. I had a mother, wife and sister, and was protective of women to the point where I was willing to sacrifice myself to ease their burden, for they had already done so much for the betterment of conditions for blacks in the company. But despite my protective instincts, we all had our turn.

196

The schedules were set. Lady Two was the first to be deposed. I thought this was excellent for the group. She was very strong, intelligent, and committed to completing what we started. I knew she would do extremely well and that the attorneys for Coke would not be able to rattle her or use their unkind tactics to break her spirit. She was indeed an asset. My feelings were echoed by the other plaintiffs and we all offered Lady Two our encouragement. At the end of the meeting we hugged and carried on as if we were family. I thought to myself, after all we have been through, if we are not blood relatives, surely we have connected in spirit.

Two days passed and Lady Two's deposition was over. She did great as we had expected. Coke's attorneys did what we expected them to do, and of course we responded appropriately. But what the attorneys of Coke did not expect was for Joe Beasley, Regional Director of Rainbow Push Coalition, to be present for the deposition. His presence caused the attorneys for Coke to panic.

The attorneys were furious that he would have the audacity to show up for the deposition. They argued then huddled among themselves wondering what he was doing in the room. It was obvious that Coke's attorneys did not have any idea of what to do, so they threw him out of the room.

Why would a company behave in such a manner if they had absolutely nothing to hide? The chairman and spokesmen for the company consistently denied that the company discriminates against blacks. *Was this the truth? Why would they insist that a man who has very close ties to Jesse Jackson be removed from the room?*

It was a very ugly scene. The uncertainty of Coke's attorneys became apparent. They were not expecting, nor were they prepared to respond to the situation. Nevertheless, they allowed Mr. Beasley to make a statement on record. In the midst of being in shock and ill-prepared for his presence, Mr. Beasley was given the opportunity to directly address the forum and indirectly address the judge.

Lady One was next. Her deposition was done by one of Coke's female attorneys. Our attorneys felt that Coke would try and use this attorney to intimidate her because if one did not personally know Lady One, one would think that she was very fragile. Make no mistake however. Lady One worked in the company each day, and fragile she was not.

The plaintiffs called and caught up with each other for encouragement. One day Lady One called me and shared a note that was left by one of her white male managers telling her of a task that had to be completed immediately. Because of the degrading language and tone in which the manager wrote the note, she went to him and told him that she would not complete the task because she found the note to be harassment. She believed his offensive note was a direct reaction to her participation in the lawsuit.

The manager who left the derogatory note went directly to his boss and tried to get her disciplined. When the manager told her of the discussion with this man, she demanded that if they were going to have more meetings about this incident, she insisted on being present. She was not weak. She was a support person to more than five white managers and had quickly gained their respect as the black woman that was not willing to take or accept unprofessional behavior.

Following the deposition, she described it as mentally draining but it did not defeat her. The attorneys for Coke spent a great deal of time arguing against restrictions that the Judge had already put in place.

199

Coke pressed her for the names of each black that the plaintiffs spoke of in the lawsuit; however, the judge ruled against that. Lady One went on expressing how demeaning and inappropriate many of the questions were and how difficult it was to remember things from her past dating back twenty or more years.

Regardless of how demeaning the questions were she remained focused and even used reverse psychology on the attorneys. She later described how easy it was to anger the attorneys for Coke with the truth. Rarely should there be yelling or arguing from any attorney in depositions, but these attorneys were angry.

She will always have the memories and scars from this time, as each of us will. We all paid a price for stepping forward and speaking out against the company. As a group we believed these scars could not be avoided as black men and women whom refused to accept racism as a part of society.

The third person to be deposed was Lady Three. I knew she would have the most difficult time. But, I also knew she had the resolve to deliver a believable testimony. She prepared with phone calls with the attorneys. Just a small sliver of the thousands of hours spent on the telephone for the past number of years.

I had come to know Lady Three well. I also knew her claim was more delicate because it affected some very personal aspects of her life. I knew Coke would take each and every opportunity to try and discredit her with these elements.

A few of us had personal things in our life that we felt Coke had no business making a part of this case. However, because of the seriousness of the claim and the amount of evidence the attorneys had already compiled and were continuing to gather, we knew that nothing would be beneath Coke's attorneys. The time they had used to stall gave us more time to prepare for the case.

While I was more concerned about Lady Three than any other plaintiff, I knew that once she focused and realized what the company's intentions were she would be fine. During her depositions there were times when she had to take a moment and gather herself because of the pain she had experienced when recalling the racist experiences. Afterwards, she too described the entire situation as mentally exhausting.

201

Each of the ladies that came forward was strong. They were unique and uniquely strong; I fed off their strength. They were also women of faith with a love for Jesus Christ and I too shared that common bond with them. Jesus was the glue that kept us together when we were tired, afraid and even unsure. We had come far by faith.

As you might expect, Coke's attorneys all wanted to find out how they came to be in touch with me. Coke's attorneys had different styles of interviewing, but at one point or another they all would focus on how this particular woman came to meet Greg Clark. While the attorneys for the company attempted to tear us down individually, Jesus was right there to hold us up. Even when our own attorneys were unsure of exactly how a particular situation would turn out; for the most part, we knew. Our strength came from the Lord.

On Monday, December 6, 1999, the chairman of The Coca-Cola Company sent an e-mail to all associates informing them that he decided to resign from his position, effective April 2000. This was "hot" news, but his statement surprised few.

Initially, I felt sad for him. I spoke with many associates about his actions. Both blacks and whites agreed he was not the right person to lead the company. Many associates felt that I was to blame for the chairman's resignation. I was not pleased with these statements.

I knew the lawsuit that was filed had merit and that the company would probably try and use him as a scapegoat to get the lawsuit out of the public eye. By removing the chairman, the company probably thought it could cleanse its name. There was speculation that the big wheels on the board of directors asked the chairman to step down from the position; but this was only hearsay.

Fortune magazine's article titled "What really happened at Coke?" cited many reasons that the chairman was forced out. The writers stated that Doug Ivester was a demon for information, but he couldn't see what was coming at the showdown in Chicago. They wanted to first of all clear up any mystery about why Doug Ivester, at age 52 and after only a little more than two years on the job, suddenly resigned as chairman and CEO of Coca-Cola. He was pushed...hard. Sure, he was beleaguered by a string of setbacks in his short, unhappy tenure.

But aides who worked with him every day, and who were as shocked as anyone when the dogged executive threw in the towel, reported that everything was business as usual on the first day of

December, 1999 when Ivester flew from Atlanta to Chicago for a routine meeting with McDonald's restaurant executives.

Upon his return everything seemed to have changed. What had not come to light until now is that while Ivester was in Chicago, he attended another very private meeting called by Coke's two most powerful directors, Warren Buffett and Herbert Allen. During this meeting, the two directors informed Ivester they'd lost confidence in his leadership.

For most of the year Buffett had remained in the wings, while Allen had numerous conversations with Ivester about his cramped management style. This time it was different, according to well-placed sources close to the situation. Together, Buffet and Allen, the board's two 800-pound gorillas, told Ivester that they had reached an irreversible conclusion: He was no longer the man who should be running Coke. It was time for a change.

Apparently, the meeting was non-confrontational, even sympathetic, and it ended without a conclusion as to the next step. Conceivably, Ivester could have decided to fight. But it's also conceivable that Buffett and Allen could have decided to force the issue, perhaps as early as the next board meeting scheduled two weeks later. Their influence as directors is immense considering that Buffett's Berkshire Hathaway (of which he owns 31%) controls about 200 million shares, or 8.1%, while Allen owns or controls about nine million shares.

Whatever they were thinking when they left the meeting, Ivester returned to Atlanta and called an emergency board meeting on that Sunday at which he quit. His announcement stunned executives, directors, employees, and Wall Street, as well as the man who was named to replace him, Doug Daft. Daft was a 56-year-old Australian whose experience had stemmed mostly from running Coke's businesses in Asia.

It was hard to believe that a man who once said, "I know how all the levers work, and I could generate so much cash I could make everybody's head spin," had come to such a quick, stark end as a corporate leader. Or, that a man almost obsessed with doing things in an orderly and rational way would leave behind such a mess, the article stated.

Some might ponder as to how a man that seemingly had everything in the world could be so cold. Not only was Doug Ivester cold to Americans, but foreigners as well. The troubles in Belgium began the decline; an ill-considered comment Ivester made about developing vending machines that could automatically raise prices in hot weather further angered bottling executives, who are the ones actually in the vending-machine business. Finally, significantly raising the price bottlers had to pay Coke for concentrate seemed an unconscionable affront and decreased their stock value even more.

"We're big boys with big businesses," says one high-ranking bottling executive. "But the perception on the street was that Ivester was running the Coca-Cola Company at our expense. Some had the view that he was raping the bottlers." But Ivester continued trying to do it alone. At one point, Don Keough sent him a six-page letter with constructive suggestions on how he could improve his situation.

What did Ivester do? He sent Keough a one-line response thanking him for his input. Ivester was never one to show weakness. "I just don't know what it's like to feel a lot of stress," he told *Fortune* last summer in the heat of the Belgian crisis.

Ivester seemed to have adopted an almost breezy attitude since turning in his resignation. He told Coke executives that he was not embarrassed and was essentially well off. He was right; he did make a lot of money. As of last February 1999, he owned 5.3 million shares of Coke (including 2.5 million shares he could acquire by exercising options), which at mid-December's 1999 price of about $60 a share, would be worth $318 million.

In 1998, Ivester's salary was $1.25 million with a bonus of $1.5 million, which according to the proxy, reflected the company's performance and "the committee's confidence in Mr. Ivester's leadership in difficult times."

What happened? How could a brilliant CEO as Roberto Goizueta have dialed such a wrong number? Simple. Goizueta was planning on living a long life, stepping back into the role of chairman, and letting Ivester run the company with his discreet guidance. That probably would have worked, for Ivester was indeed a brilliant Number 2. But what played out was different.

Some say we should have seen this coming. In October of 1994, Ivester, the then newly named president and COO; took center stage at a big industry trade show and delivered a speech that was unforgettable for its surliness. It was called "Be Different or Be Damned," and it was some debut. Ivester seemed to be trying to differentiate himself from the larger-than-life Goizueta. He described himself as a wolf, highly independent, nomadic, and territorial. "I want your customers," he told the stunned audience. "I want your space on the shelves. I want every single bit of beverage growth potential that exists out there." Make no mistake; he told them that he was their competitor. He would not pretend to be their statesman. He would be different or be damned. In the end, it turned out he was both.

Ivester was criticized for many things, particularly his handling of the racial discrimination lawsuit. Many might ask who in their right mind would demote the highest-ranking African American in the company in the midst of such a publicized lawsuit. Nobody seemed to have a good answer for that question.

Ponder the situation for a moment. It had already been established that Ivester was arrogant and felt good about stirring things up. He obviously enjoyed being in the limelight regardless of whether the limelight was caused by positive or negative news for the company. As chairman of one of the largest companies in the world, one might have presumed he'd be one of the most respected leaders. This was not so.

This man grew up in New Holland, GA. The black population at the time he was growing up was likely near an all-time low. His expectation of blacks being employed probably did not stretch far but rather considered jobs in fields such as cooks, maintenance, housecleaning, farmers and landscaping or lawn services. I believe his upbringing likely affected his judgment as a powerful man in those days.

I imagine that like anyone, a person who rises to the top of an organization and great wealth, still also remembers his adolescent experiences, beliefs and thoughts. I think that a solid foundation plays an essential role in how one interacts with, depicts and coincides with others. The race of people a man often saw doing meaningless or even degrading jobs is not to be discarded however. These people deserve respect as human beings and a chance to grow and rise to more fulfilling and rewarding occupations.

Does a COO of a company magically forget his or her childhood experiences? I say not. Maybe, if Doug Ivester had forgotten some of that history and thinking about blacks, Carl Ware would not have been stripped of his dignity as he was. Mr. Ware even towed the company line that there were no "glass ceilings" at The Coca-Cola Company and that the company does not discriminate. In the end, if anyone experienced racism and had knowledge of it in the company, surely Mr. Ware did.

On May 30, 1999, the *Atlanta Journal Constitution* featured Mr. Ware and listed many of his accomplishments that helped propel him to his position. Approximately six weeks after the lawsuit went public Carl was quoted in the paper stating, "I, myself, am a good example, a proof that "glass ceilings" do not exist at The Coca-Cola Company." When I first read that article I was sick.

Often times, we create a false belief of how some people may think of us and begin behaving in this perceived perception we've created in our minds because we want to belong and be respected. This is a very dangerous game to play. To create a false image of your being with the intentions of impressing someone suggests that one be ashamed of what God has created you to be. Such a game reveals you are not man or woman enough to play the hand you have been dealt.

Why Mr. Ware felt compelled to go public with his statements, only he knows. I am curious as to how he felt when Ivester later told him the news that he would not be reporting directly to him anymore. *Did he still feel that he was a proof that "glass ceilings" do not exist at The Coca-Cola Company? Or, did he feel that anyone believed him when he made that statement?* Surely he knew nobody believed him anymore. I am curious if he thought that Ivester ever considered him as an equal human being. *If so, and he was rightly valued, then why did he demote him in the middle of a highly publicized racial discrimination lawsuit?*

It is not hard to see that the chairman's actions were a direct depiction of what the four plaintiffs were alleging in the lawsuit about the culture of the company. As much as Mr. Ware probably did not want to leave the company, this reshuffling led to the announcement of his retirement. Mr. Ware stated that he wanted to spend more time with his family. That is a noble and honorable desire and a blessing if one is able to do so. But why was his retirement announced suddenly, when it was slated to occur a year later, at the end of 2000?

Did Mr. Ware intend to resign? Was he encouraged to retire instead due to the sensitive surroundings in the company? Surely the public would better receive a retirement than his resignation, which would be a direct slap to the face of the company he had so adamantly defended.

Most of the newspapers and magazines wrote articles suggesting that Ivester must be crazy to make such a move in the middle of a racial discrimination lawsuit. I did not think he was crazy at all. It was typical of his cocky mode of operation. He was going to set up the power in the manner that best suited him.

It is my belief that Mr. Ware's resignation during such a trying time for the company was the worst thing that could have happened to the company's culture. *Should he have used his alleged power of position and circumstances to challenge the restructure? Or was his power so limited, as was that of other blacks in the company? Why didn't Mr. Ware speak up?* Perhaps he was ashamed of his now famous, bold statement that he was "proof that The Coca-Cola Company does not discriminate against African Americans."

My mother told me as a boy that if a person told a lie, they would have to tell lie after lie to cover up that initial lie they told. Sometimes the first lie told is so damaging that it not only hurts the person who told it but also demolishes his or her credibility down the road if he or she wanted to come clean. Few people would believe a person who appeared to lie for no apparent reason, but in reality many people lie out of fear – fear of the truth and what might surface once it is known. A lie often starts because of fear of losing face. In time, the fear may transform into fear of losing a comfortable or luxurious lifestyle that the string of lies has bought for them.

I often pondered upon whether this arrogant man ever came to the realization that his heart was not right to lead the company. I am not suggesting that his heart was any different from any other chairman, but I wondered how he reconciled his heart to his position. I am a firm believer that different strokes may very well yield the same folks. One man's leadership did not cause all these troubles from 1998 to 2003. He was simply one link in the chain.

Each of the past leaders of the company had a responsibility to blacks and the world to make sure that the numbers of the company depicted an environment of equality. It appeared that nobody in the

upper levels at this time cared enough to do anything about the

appalling numbers brought forward in the complaint filed in April

1999. I recall once being on one of the executive floors where I

overheard the conversation of two white male executives. One

gentleman stated that he was embarrassed by the numbers of blacks that

were in management positions in the company, and if anyone found out

this truth it would be terrible, for there was no way the company could

explain the numbers. They knew the truth and chose silence. I remained

focused and chose not to be silent.

Chapter 9

My Turn: Sixteen Hours of Depositions

December 1999 was a busy month. Normally I would be looking forward to spending time with my loved ones, but this year there were a few things standing in the way. December 8th and 9th were the days set aside for my deposition.

I was not sure what to expect and it did not matter much to me. I knew Jesus was the source of my strength and He would be there by my side whatever might come. The Coca-Cola Company sent the very best it had to offer legally to perform my deposition. Two of the company's heavyweight attorneys were present along with a Court Reporter. It was not going to be a short ordeal.

My attorneys all entered the room before me, and it was as if I was the 'number one contender' being led into the ring for a heavyweight championship fight. The tension in the room was thick. The attorneys all shook hands and greeted each other as they began to take their places around the table.

Coke's attorneys greeted me as if they were pleased to see me. For months I had seen these people at headquarters and never did any of them even speak to me. I was well aware of the tricks they wanted to play before, during, and after my deposition. I took my seat and ignored their obvious attempt to get me to lower my shield. Just as I was not impressed when they ignored me while in the company, I was not impressed with them this day either.

I was informed of the process and procedures for the deposition. The Court Reporter asks me to raise my right hand and swear to tell the truth. This was not as easy as it sounded because as the attorneys for Coke soon learned, I did not swear. I was raised to believe the only oath one takes is before the Lord, not man. I was not willing to compromise my religious beliefs. Furthermore, I was not going to raise one hand while the other is placed on a bible and use the word 'swear' to make some glamorized crooks think that I would tell the truth because I swore that I would. I am a man who tells the truth regardless of the audience.

Shortly after a conversation between the attorneys, I was affirmed and the process was under way. The first few minutes of the deposition were uncomfortable because I was not familiar with the setting of the forum. The attorney questioning me had spent hundreds of hours and many months going over the documents and preparing. In contrast, I had little time to prepare because I worked two jobs to make a living. Working ninety-five hours a week with no days off could have gotten the best of me, but instead I treated work as therapy and necessary.

Keeping busy helped to minimize the stress and frustration of the lawsuit as it dragged on. So, while I lacked formal preparation, I was ready to share my testimony. It started out fine until about fifteen minutes into the deposition when one of the company's attorneys appeared to be speaking down to me.

I speak respectfully to others and expected the same courtesy. This was the turning point of the deposition. I remember being asked if I thought that my evaluations were done fairly in the company. What a silly question. Bearing in mind that the complaint that was filed spoke clearly of our position on the evaluation process, this question was completely unnecessary.

It was not the wording of the question that got my attention, but the arrogance in which the question was delivered. When the question was asked, I saw the same white, disrespectful, arrogant male faces I'd become familiar with for the past four years. They had no desire to listen to me until now, so what would make today any different?

Therein lay my resolve. I was reminded of why I was in the room and from that point on, I was no longer uncomfortable. I sat tall, looked the attorneys in their eyes and spoke with honesty and sincerity, as I relayed the facts as I saw them through the eyes of an educated black man who was not afraid.

While at times I tried, I could never really escape the fact that I filed a major lawsuit against one of the largest companies in the world. I felt the weight of every past and present black that has worked in Coke on my shoulders. I also felt the prayers of those who had taken their pain to Jesus and were awaiting an answer. I remember the commitment I'd made a few years ago and realized that this deposition was another sacrifice to be made for that commitment to unearthing the truth.

Sixteen hours divided into two days was more than enough time for the company to ask questions about the racist culture which they represented. The days were long and tiresome. As the other plaintiffs told me, it was an absolutely mentally exhausting task. I would not wish this type of mental abuse on my worst enemy.

At times I grew sick of the meaningless questions the company's attorneys were asking. I knew it was a part of the process, and what they were trained to do. My wife tried to help me before each day by giving me a card that she thought would be helpful. I thank God for her. She helped me to see strength in myself that I did not know existed. I gained strength because one line of the card said that she found strength in many things that I did.

I never imagined that she was paying me so much attention. I was simply doing what I thought was necessary to take care of the household. It was very encouraging to know she knew I was prepared and I would do well. Imagine standing on a solid rock with shepherds in front of you, angels above you, goodness and mercy behind you, your rod and staff on your sides, and the Holy Spirit inside of you. How could I fail? I thank God for the angel that He has given me to share my life with. My wife has been my backbone through it all. She often reminded me that God did not bring us this far, to leave us. So, she lovingly reminded me that I continue to be the man that she knew. Leaving home each morning, I knew that I had all the ammunition I needed to go to battle.

After my deposition, several days had passed quietly. Lady One and I praised each other as we passed in the hallways. I knew I had one supporter in the company who was willing to protect me without limitations, and I would do the same for her. Our relationship grew strong through it all. I was grateful for her presence.

When Coke earlier had gone public in denouncing the allegations, the stronger the possibility appeared that the allegations were in fact, real. Now in the relative silence, most white associates were probably thinking in the silence, that Coke found a way to dismiss the charges very quietly, but that had not happened.

On December 17, 1999, I read that the Martin Luther King Jr. Center would be giving The Coca-Cola Company its "Salute to Greatness" Award in January 2000. According to the King Center, "Salute to Greatness" awards are presented in recognition of outstanding efforts and contributions for the community. The recipients are recognized for "notable contributions toward improving the quality of life for all, for giving valuable partnerships with the corporate community, and making outstanding contributions to the universal quest for social justice and worldwide peace in the tradition of Dr. Martin Luther King, Jr."

I also learned that Jesse Hill, past chairman of the Atlanta Life Insurance Company, would chair the awards dinner along with Ambassador Andrew Young, Chairman of Good Works International. The article also stated the 2000 King Holiday Observance would mark the 71st birthday of Dr. Martin Luther King Jr., the 32nd annual King Center program and the 15th national holiday in his honor celebrated around the world.

I knew where the pressure for these accolades stemmed from. Coke had funneled money into the community intentionally. I saw this event as just another opportunity for the company to try and buy its way into the public eye. My concern was with those who made the decision from the King Center to give such an award to The Coca-Cola Company. *How could anyone choose a company that was in the middle of a highly publicized racial discrimination lawsuit?*

I firmly believe that if Dr. King were living, he would have nothing to do with such foolishness. I refused to believe the family most looked upon by blacks, as the leading family for civil rights and equality for all

221

mankind, compromised the very purpose for which one of the greatest men ever to live gave his life.

In all fairness, one must ask for what reason could the King Center possibly have for honoring The Coca-Cola Company at this particular time? Is it possible that one of the two most public blacks in the company had a personal relationship with the family and was simply asking for a favor? I would like to think that the King Center had not yet heard about the racial discrimination lawsuit filed against the company, but with all the publicity that was unlikely.

I did not allow myself to become unfocused by the actions of the so-called leaders of my race. During my research period, I learned that many of those who are given leadership positions in the black community are not always interested in our people. Certainly there are election processes for these leaders in which speeches are given that are filled with everything one might want to hear. But as soon as true challenges come along and one has to stand against a rich powerful company, they often change colors.

Be careful who you elect as political and community leaders. These elect become decision-makers in services that affect our families. As much as I dislike the thought of selling out, it is reality. There is evidence of black leaders worldwide who have sold their souls for material gifts. It is far better to place your trust and faith in a man who shall not ever fail; his name is Jesus and I dare you to try Him.

While I fought in The Coca Cola Company to be treated as an equal, my home state of South Carolina was in a battle of its own. The black citizens of South Carolina were fighting a war to have the rebel flag removed from the state's Capitol, and ultimately from existence. Many religious and civil rights leaders that spoke out publicly; all stated that the flag was an embarrassment and it had to come down. I was proud to see that many blacks were coming together to voice their opinions and participate in a process that dealt with such an important issue. I was filled with joy because the people of my home state were not bowing down to the racist acts of a few.

Nevertheless, I was deeply saddened so many of our leaders were afraid to turn up and speak against Coke. It appeared that some were willing to speak out against racism, but not when it is fueled by a large, powerful and rich organization. The flying of a flag over a state where a group of people perceive the flag to be a sign of racism, is no less discriminatory than denying a person an equal opportunity to provide for their family in a corporation.

I remember hearing that the King Center had joined to do whatever was necessary to make sure the confederate flag, which flew over the state, would soon come down. I wondered why we did not get the same consideration. This puzzled me, until one day while on my way to lunch I met the most public black woman at The Coca-Cola Company. She was walking holding hands with the wife of one of the most famous civil rights leaders of all time.

There was an entourage of people surrounding and walking beside the two. I then knew why the King family had not taken a stand against the company and the allegations we plaintiffs had brought forth. It was obvious that there was a personal relationship between this woman and the most public black female at The Coca-Cola Company. The black Coke employee looked at me and gave me a little smile unlike any she ever had in the past. I knew then the battle to erase racial discrimination in this company was just a high price game in which many would suffer and few would benefit.

I had been on my way to lunch, but I'd suddenly lost my appetite. I did not want to read too much into what I just saw, but I knew it was a very peculiar scene. That visual gave me more understanding of why there was not a public announcement about the racial discrimination lawsuit against The Coca-Cola Company. After all Coke had been an annual contributor to the King Center for over thirty years.

I then tried to analyze the situation even further. I thought if I had a friend that was working for a company in a position that was respected by many blacks and most certainly very visible to the public eye, I would simply ask that friend 'what in the world was going on in The Coca-Cola Company?' This probably would have been a safe way of getting the inside track of such a serious issue. *Was the information the Center was receiving about the lawsuit distorted?*

The company was preparing internally to deal with some of the changes that resulted from the firing of Doug Ivester. Shortly after the announcement by Mr. Ivester, the Board decided that Doug Daft would be a wise choice to lead the company in the direction where it must go to gain the respect of its consumers around the world.

As I mentioned earlier, Daft's experience was largely in the Asian markets. He had been with the company for 30 years and was very welcomed by the associates. He appeared to be a relational leader and seemed to have friends within the organization. Based on the articles I read, he seemed to be just what the company needed to get back on track. When asked what employees could expect from his management style, Daft responded: "I learned over the years to delegate, and once you delegate, don't manage it and lead it."

He also believed that the company needed to continue to evolve our business, learn of and take advantage of new opportunities. These messages were a breath of fresh air considering the leadership style of the former chairman. Ivester made the mistake of trying to lead the company by himself. I did not believe that the newly appointed chairman would make the same mistake.

It was a busy December and people were preparing for the holiday season of 1999. A happy and joyous mood was evident in the company. I imagined everyone was looking forward to spending quality time with their families and loved ones. I too enjoyed the Christmas holiday season, when families around the world gather to honor the birth of Lord and Savior, Jesus Christ.

Not everyone was counting down the days to holiday rest, however. Our attorneys had been working day and night for the past few months on a surprise that would surely give the decision-makers of the company something to think about over the holidays. In December of 1999, the *Atlanta Journal Constitution* ran an article that the attorneys for the four blacks who had filed a racial discrimination lawsuit against The Coca-Cola Company were now seeking to add four more plaintiffs to the lawsuit. The growing number of plaintiffs certainly gave the company something to think about!

On January 10, 2000, The Coca-Cola Company surprised the world by announcing that the company would be cutting 6000 jobs and 2500 of those would come from the headquarters in Atlanta, GA. Despite the company's arrogance, it was not immune from economic realities such as cutbacks that were needed to maximize shareholder earnings. The company had been weathering trying times, but the associates never imagined such large cutbacks. Newspapers around the world rushed to conclusions about why they thought the company was downsizing.

Many reasons were cited including the decline in foreign markets, and the recent scare in Belgium. Others chose to assign some of the blame to Doug Ivester's "bulldog" style of leadership.

It was the first Wednesday of the new millennium when I remember getting dressed early to head to "The Plantation". I saw a news report that Carl Ware, The Coca-Cola Company's top African American, had decided not to resign from the company and was given a promotion to senior vice president's level. I could hardly believe what I was hearing.

I wondered how much more could a black man stand for, or should I say fall for. I wondered if the company realized how unstable it appeared. *Or did it even matter to the decision-makers that the world at this point must have been viewing the company as one big soap opera? How could a company that for the past 116 years claimed to hold dearly its mission and core of operations now seem so changeable and inconsistent?*

When I arrived at work, I expected to see an in-house memorandum posted on all the bulletin boards that Mr. Ware had reconsidered his position and had decided to remain with the company. This was the normal means of communications to associates about executive promotions within. These memos usually included a photo and a brief biography of the person being promoted. To my surprise, this time there was no memorandum or photo posted of Ware. *I thought to myself, how could this be?*

Thirty minutes ago his picture was posted all over the television, but inside the company he was invisible. Maybe news of his promotion was not visible because The Coca-Cola Company views his leadership was just that, "invisible." Once again, even in this newly appointed position by the chairman and president of The Coca-Cola Company, Ware was given a post that was not top notch. It was not a position that dealt directly with generating revenue. It was obvious that The Coca-Cola Company wanted to sway its badly damaged reputation in the public's eye but didn't want to promote Ware to one of its most critical senior vice president positions. The company simply wanted to impact the media and public in a manner it considered positive.

On January 19, 2000, I learned that Jack Stahl would be the president of the company. Many speculated that Mr. Stahl would be the likely choice to assist Mr. Ivester in running the multi-billion dollar company. Mr. Daft did not waste any time in deciding who would help him make the decisions that would determine the fate of so many

shareholders. Again, the newspapers and magazines wrote stories about

the new appointment and how the company might help restore its name

by sharing some of the responsibilities of leading the company.

As many of the articles spoke of the newly appointed leaders, they

also shared the many serious problems facing these men. As much as

the city of Atlanta wanted to forget about the racial discrimination

lawsuit, authors around the world took the allegations seriously and

saw the lawsuit as an issue that needed to be resolved quickly.

After many weeks of anticipation, the dreaded February 15, 2000

finally presented itself. It was sad to know that many people who'd

dedicated a large part of their life to The Coca-Cola Company would

find out on this day that their services were no longer needed. As much

as I wanted to find a way to mend the many broken hearts and spirits, I

knew I was powerless.

I thought of the many children who would be affected by the laying

off of their parents. My hope and my prayers went out to the parents

whose lives were about to be turned upside down. I prayed protection for the innocent hearts of their children, and that the parents who had a personal relationship with God would find a resting place in His arms.

In an unstable economy, it was unlikely that many of these associates would find quick employment elsewhere. I prayed for them to find new work and also that the leaders of the company would fall to their knees and confess Jesus Christ as Lord. Maybe then they'd see the real impact of their sweeping decisions.

At approximately 8:00 a.m., Lisa Calhoun, a God-fearing sister who attended New Birth Missionary Baptist Church, took the initiative to lead associates in a brief, but very inspiring prayer service. Hundreds of associates gathered to render a word of prayer in harmony concerning the news they'd soon hear. My heart was filled with joy. The company had been faced with one of the worst periods in its history, and its people were finding a way to connect and face the uncertainty by taking their fears and burdens to Jesus.

Later that day, I was approached by both of my shift supervisors on post and told that the manager of security needed to see me. I asked what was up and neither admitted knowing what the meeting was

231

about. Having heard the "I'm just the messenger" drone more than once, I knew better than to believe their proclaimed innocence.

When I arrived at his office, Keith Marks, the manager, acknowledged my presence and asked me to please sit down. I thought to myself this was certainly a switch from the last time I was in here. I also began thinking of the power of prayer.

He began the meeting by shifting the blame for the decision I was about to hear from himself to the Operations department. He began by stating that he was told that because of some of the comments that have been directed toward me, Operations thought it would be best if they removed me from having so much contact with the associates of the company.

I responded by stating, "I did not ask for any protection nor am I going to hide from anyone." He then stated, "This will only be for ten business days or until things calm down on the campus."

I thought this was a joke. The very same people who have made my life a living hell now want to embrace me with their protection. I knew the real reason was that upper management was simply trying to cover its tracks. I was not the core of their concerns. Keith then stated that he was concerned about an alarm that sounded in the console earlier that morning. He asked, "What were you doing around room 2029 in the USA building?"

I knew exactly what his concern was, but I acted as if I was not aware of what he feared most. I told him that a police officer and I were simply responding to the request from the console. He nodded his head as if he wanted me to think that it was fine that I had knowledge of 'the room.' I then stated that we could not find a room numbered 2029. Keith did not respond. He knew full well that the room was not numbered, and really was only concerned with the knowledge I had of this room and the shredders that dwelt within it.

Several months ago one of the security officers told me that he stumbled across this room and entered it because the door was open. The officer stated that the room was filled with documents and paperwork pertaining to the lawsuit. He went on to say that he saw newspaper articles about the lawsuit all over the room. He also added that there were machines that he thought the company initially stated to the judge, were not being used in preparing for the lawsuit – shredders that is.

I did not let Keith know that I knew of the room, nor did I want to arouse any suspicions he may have had. My only concern was to play ignorant and wait on those that were working on the case for the company to make another mistake so I could then respond appropriately.

An old man told me once that most whites do not think blacks are intelligent. He advised me to use this to my advantage. He also said that it would not be wise for a black man to become discouraged when he is not treated as an equal. He then advised me to take a moment and think carefully about what it is you are truly seeking and use the game to get what you desire.

I now had first-hand knowledge of what that old man shared with me. The leadership of The Coca-Cola Company made the mistake of focusing on my job title instead of the man who wore the uniform. This, I promised myself, would prove to be fatal to the company. I left Keith's office that day convinced that Keith believed I was not at all concerned with the room, and that was exactly the way I wanted him to think.

The next day I was posted on the 20th floor of the USA building. Again, I was reminded of just how committed some white associates were to hiding the racism in the company. There I sat at the desk in front of the elevators that divide the floor, when Dela Harrison, the human resource representative for the security department, got off the elevator. As our eyes met and I greeted her with a hello, she acted as if she'd seen a ghost. Normally, one of the receptionists would be sitting at the desk rather than a security guard. So, I imagined that I was last face she expected or desired to see.

It became even more amusing when she asked if I knew where room 2029 was located. Before I could respond she seemed to suddenly remember for she stated, "I think it's on this side." Here was another white person treating me as if I was ignorant. Again, I remained quiet and acted as if I believed she really did not know where the room was. I wondered what the big secret about the room was.

Earlier in the case the judge asked Coke about the shredders that were seen in the room that came to be known as the "War Room." A few days later it was learned that not only were there talks of shredders in the room, our attorneys received documents that pretty much

235

confirmed the shredders to be present. *The racial discrimination case was common knowledge so why all the secrecy about the room if it was only set up to work on the case?*

It would be no surprise for the team working on the lawsuit to need a place to congregate and prepare. *That being said, why were there so many people trying to keep this room invisible? Moving this workroom to the executive floor may have kept it out of view of many associates but why?* There was nothing wrong with the purpose or premise of the room unless activity in the room was inappropriate or unethical.

Somehow things always seem to work themselves out. Keith, the manager of security, called a meeting for all supervisors to attend. I felt at this point that my presence on the floor of the "Invisible Room" made several people uncomfortable, and I would probably not be scheduled to that floor again until the lawsuit was over or the room was once again moved. I was pretty sure this meeting was to remind supervisors of the locations I was not to be posted.

Starting the next day, I was placed on posts that were designed to keep me out of the building. This was not a coincidence, but I was wise enough to do my job and do nothing to draw any added attention to myself. I knew management wanted a reason to show me just how angry they were, so giving them a reason to discipline me would be fuel to their smoldering fire. So, I did my job and laid low.

I was saddened when I received a telephone call from Lady One informing me she'd just finished meeting with her manager and learned that her position was being phased out. I listened as she described how she was told. My heart grew heavy for I felt I was losing a dear friend. I realized I'd no longer have the luxury of seeing her, encouraging one another or sharing with one another the things we were forced to endure as we stood our ground. I knew Christ might have simply decided it was time to move her on to bigger and better things, or smaller and better things.

Whatever the case, I knew that she was ready to move on. I was happy that she had found peace in the decision made by the company that thrives on chaos.

Chapter 10

The Company Offers Severance Package...But With A Twist

On February 23, 2000, the *Atlanta Journal Constitution, Wall Street Journal and New York Times* wrote articles of how a black fifteen-year associate and assistant pastor was terminated after he met with Jack Stahl, President of The Coca-Cola Company. He spoke of the concerns that many blacks had about signing a severance package that would force them to give up their legal claims to all or any damages recovered by the plaintiffs in a racial discrimination lawsuit. The *Atlanta Journal Constitution* stated that the plaintiffs' attorneys reported in a legal motion that Larry Jones, a company associate, told Jack Stahl about organizing a meeting at his church a day before he was laid off. The company responded that the layoff had "absolutely nothing" to do with the meeting.

The article went on to say that Jones, a human resources manager who had worked for Coke since 1985, called the meeting at St. Philip A.M.E. Church in Decatur to deal with employee "apprehension and confusion" over a key issue involving the suit as well as planned job cuts, the plaintiffs' attorneys alleged. In order to qualify for enhanced severance benefits, laid-off black employees would have to sign a release form relinquishing their rights to share any monetary reward that could be recovered if the discrimination case became a class-action suit. On February 12, Jones and 150 other African American employees, as well as the four plaintiffs' counsel, met at St. Philip to discuss the issue of the release form. Jones, an associate pastor at the church, said he'd organized the meeting after scores of African Americans had approached him for advice.

On the same day as the meeting with Stahl, Jones claims that a human resources director told him that he had nothing to worry about when additional job cuts were announced on February 15. However, it appeared that an overnight change of heart regarding Mr. Jones' employment occurred. He was terminated, and it appeared to be as retaliation for the meetings he'd had with potential class members and the objection to the releases he raised with Mr. Stahl as alleged by the plaintiffs' attorneys. I was not at all surprised with the way the company handled this situation. Senior white decision-makers in the company were arrogant. I was not surprised that another black had lost

239

his job, but I was infuriated with the dogmatic and devious way the young brother found out about his termination.

This was just another example of the foolishness blacks were forced to endure in the company on a daily basis. We must remember, there was never a war without casualties. I had the opportunity to meet with brother Jones. While I had my personal opinions about why it was being arranged, I kept them to myself. I knew that a meeting with this man would first and foremost acknowledge Jesus Christ before concerns were spoken. The children of God were crying out and the company was not paying attention. He was one of the first people to confront me when the lawsuit surfaced, and he applauded the effort we took bringing change to the racist environment of the company. I reminded him of the article that identified him as standing up for people treated poorly that had run in the newspaper, and that Coke didn't like noisy employees. Surely that article's public claim and his dismissal were not coincidental.

One day Jones and I discussed concerns about the manner in which he was terminated and the reasons why he was terminated. He spoke of how angry Jack Stahl, a man he knew for almost fifteen years, became when he had presented facts to him. Jones had asked Stahl when they met if what they discussed could be kept confidential – just between the two of them. Confidentiality agreed, Jones began expressing some of the concerns of the blacks in the company. Stahl repeatedly became angry as the two men talked. Although Stahl went out of his way in public to acknowledge and speak to many blacks in the company, there was anger underneath the surface. Personally, I was never impressed by this obvious "barrier breaker approach", for I knew that the president of the company or any division head had access to the numbers of blacks in the company and blacks in key positions, and probably felt that since this lawsuit did not affect their own job security, why worry. Jones then continued to speak of the sour way in which the meeting ended. He stated that he knew from his experience of dealing with The Coca-Cola Company that something was about to happen to him, but never in a million years did he imagine he would be terminated.

When Jones was terminated, a white female manager called him in her office. She greeted him and then said, "You went to see Jack, didn't you?" Being the man he was, he firmly stated, "Yes, I did." The female manager then began to cry and told him he was being let go from the company. Being the God-fearing man, Jones' first was concerned about the manager's tears and sought to calm her down. I too was concerned for the manager. Her color did not matter, I felt sorry for her and for the fact that her superiors forced her to render an unjust dismissal to an undeserving black man. Her tears proved that she knew what "right" was and she was being played as a pawn by the company.

How many more decisions had been made like this one? I doubt this was an isolated instance. I think this was an established and accepted practice of many of the leaders of the company. Without challenge, it would continue; to the harm of both the dismissed employees and the conflicted messengers.

Jones' dismissal sparked talk and helped many blacks see just how the company felt about blacks who were competent and capable employees. While many employees and consumers had fallen in love with the company, they had struggled to believe talk of wrongdoing. Some now were starting to see. It amazed me that people could be so loyal and in love with something that cannot possibly love in return. Chaos or abuse was common outcomes of such one-sided relationships.

This I thought provided an excellent example of how the company's leaders valued its black employees.

The Company wanted its black employees to give up their right to receive compensation they were owed, because it was alleged it treated its black employees unfairly. Coke also decided that it would be fair to its black employees to demand if they were to accept a severance package as a result of the lay-offs; every black would be required to sign documentation forfeiting any funds they would be eligible to receive from the lawsuit if a settlement was reached. There it was; a good example of how the leaders of the company viewed its black employees. One had nothing to do with the other. *Why link them together?*

Most of the blacks in the company heard about the meeting that was scheduled at St. Philips A.M.E. church on Saturday, March 4th, 2000. This meeting was no longer a secret. In an exclusive interview where Jones, the terminated human resources manager, shared his feelings about how the company treated blacks and how he felt about the company, the time and place of the meeting were given. Because of where I had been stationed, I had not been in contact with very many

243

blacks in the company, so I wasn't sure how many people might turn out for the meeting.

I wondered what purpose shuffling my station really served the company. Keeping my face less visible to blacks in the company would not cause the lawsuit to lose its momentum. The battle went on and was already won. I wondered how low the company was prepared to let the stock drop before it came clean to the world. The lawsuit was not the only reason the stock value plunged in the market; however, it was most certainly one of the most talked about issues that the company needed to deal with.

March 4, 2000 turned out to be a good day. I did not know what to expect from those who were coming to the church. The culture of the company had certainly dampened or stolen the spirits of many. I didn't know what to expect except the certainty that Jesus would be there. As I got dressed to go, I reflected on just how good God had been to me. He gave me the strength to step out on faith and make such a bold proclamation of discrimination. He gave me strength to face the giant – Coca-Cola.

Greeted with warm smiles and hugs, I was glad to arrive at the church. Attorneys and paralegals as well as citizens were there to take part. The meeting was a place to give voice and plan the strategy of how we were going to tell the world we were sick of the racist environment at The Coca-Cola Company. The meeting organizer, Jones, was one of the first people I met. He hurried to complete last minute details when we connected. I firmly shook his hand and looked into his eyes hoping to let him know that I understood the fear he was feeling about speaking out. I knew he did the right thing in instigating the meeting. I knew what it was like to launch one of the many battles of this war. It could at times feel like you're fighting alone as one steps out in front.

So, I assured him he was not alone. Even if the 500 blacks in the church fled, I would surely stand beside him. He was set in his mind. He said he was ready to do whatever was necessary to bring change to the racist culture of The Coca-Cola Company.

This day proved to be one of the most exciting and appreciative days of the struggle. For the first time in almost three years, I had the opportunity to see the numbers of blacks willing to stand up and tell the company they were tired of its racist practices and were demanding change. The meeting started with a prayer and God being glorified. Jones then told the story about his February 14, 2000 meeting with Jack Stahl. He was still very angry and hurt, but used humor to tell the story in an impacting way. Brothers and sisters who had felt similar pains in the organization resonated with his story. He shared how angry Jack became when he tried to get him to realize that the waiver was unfair. He said it was then that he realized and expected some type of retaliation; although, he never expected to lose his job because he was told by both his manager and a human resources manager that his job would not be affected.

As he addressed the crowd that had waited so patiently, he struggled to hold off the tears. Sharing his story was painful and not something he looked forward to doing; rather it was something he knew he had to do. I respected him for standing his ground and not turning and running like so many others had. I knew the true test of character was not when you were popular and had a large following, but rather when you had to stand alone, face-to-face with the devil and call him a liar. Jones had taken his solitary stand.

The press conference was fabulous. I was proud to stand out front facing the crowd and witness the many blacks who came to stand and be heard. People were tired of being treated as less than human and they were ready to say so publicly. Local television stations were ready to share the news with their viewers. The organizer spoke very eloquently as he shared the injustices he was forced to face as a black employee of The Coca-Cola Company. His voice was loud and bold, demanding attention. He revealed the pain and frustrations that many blacks had endured as employees of the company, and he announced that no longer would we allow ourselves to be second-class employees in the company.

My heart was filled with joy as I listened to his speech. I was proud of him and knew he'd sleep a lot better after having cleared some of the concerns of blacks in the company. Whether he knew it or not, he was speaking for thousands of people who may have never had the opportunity to speak for themselves. As the press conference was ending and the crowd was getting smaller, I chatted with many brothers and sisters currently working in the company who had felt for one reason or another they could not approach me. Today, they shared with me their experiences at Coca-Cola. I guess this was their way of saying that they too felt the pain that racism renders. I was pleased to finally have an opportunity to say to each of them that I understood and shared their pain.

Many of the attorneys representing the class were there. I remember standing next to one of them and heard him say; when lead counsel made a move that no one predicted, the spirit probably moved him. We all chuckled and realized just how powerful the gathering had turned out to be. A few of the attorneys spoke; each resounded with sincerity. I sensed that the group knew that these were some of the good guys. One of the attorneys presented an animated illustration from the *Wizard of Oz* as he spoke of our common goal. .

His story resounded with the audience. Perhaps they felt they were on their own journey to see the wizard, of sorts. The applause rolled and the audience was on its feet. The speaker lit up when he saw he'd connected so well with the crowd.

I could hardly wait to see just how the media would depict this scene of electricity to the public. On the 11:00 p.m. news, I had opportunity to see a few seconds of the press conference flash across the television. That was it?! It was barely a sound byte. All of the pain and frustrations that the tens of thousands of blacks shared from years of working for the company, and the media didn't even give it a full minute of coverage.

It was as if the TV producers were on Coke's side. After all, threat of a boycott would harm the company and might impact media spend. What was presented was so sliced and diced, and replayed lines that had already become so familiar in the press for the past year. This was not a coincidence. The stations didn't want new news of solidarity to reach the public.

Did the decision-makers of The Coca-Cola Company set out to take care of their own? Was it unrealistic to believe that the news stations had people working behind the scenes to prevent such a large and important client from being portrayed negatively? At the time, I did not want to believe that the company again poured money into an area to minimize its possible losses by distorting information, but I could think of nothing else.

I was at the church and heard every word that was spoken. I witnessed hundreds of blacks all coming together to say that enough was enough. Hundreds of us covered the steps of St. Phillips Church and held empty coke cans above our heads as we shouted, "No more. We will take no more." It wasn't long before bumper stickers were printed with the same slogan to show the company that we were serious.

As the case dragged on, the more incriminating evidence that surfaced against the company. What started out as a personal battle against an arrogant and racist manager who kept me from making a fair living to provide a better life for my family was now a much bigger battle. The voice of hundreds of blacks had been stirred. They were moved from silent frustration to a roar.

The Monday after the meeting, headquarters was buzzing. Black associates hugged and encouraged one another. I had not expected this at all but I certainly welcomed it. The recent layoffs had affected thousands of associates. The mood in the company had been damp and dark for weeks, but not on this day.

Recently, senior management had changed the dress code to business casual and this had lifted spirits a bit, but that little freedom was nothing compared to the joy and jubilation I saw in black associates after this meeting. I thanked the Lord for the turning tide. My soul cried out for the glimmer of hope and for the Lord's salvation.

What if the leaders of the company would stop for a moment and take their minds off the plaintiffs? Would they then have recognized this as the handiwork of God?

The gathering on that weekend brought nearly 500 blacks into the house of the Lord and they cried out to Him. They leaned on Jesus to see them through. The meeting, the spirit, the location were not coincidental. God was letting us know that in order to move mountains one must first seek Him. I read in the Word that God said, "Wherever two or more gather in my name, there I will also be." No doubt, He was there!

The Spirit moved in that room and even as I write this today, I feel him. No matter what trial you face my friend; God has something prepared for you. Hold onto His unchanging hand, come what may.

On the Tuesday following the press conference; new Chairman, Doug Daft, released a statement to all the associates of the company. Daft said he wanted to assure every associate that the company was working to resolve the lawsuit as expediently and equitably as possible.

251

I thought this was the company's way of trying to discourage other black associates from becoming active in the lawsuit. I think the company realized that 500 angry associates were more than enough to damage the company's already tarnished image for a very long time.

Senior management could no longer sit on the sidelines and watch legal wrangling demolish business plans. While I applauded the message, I suspected that management's heart remained unchanged. Racism had not just suddenly died a quick and mysterious death. I knew that whites in management didn't really believe blacks were equal and should be treated as such in all levels of The Coca-Cola Company.

I am not saying or insinuating that all whites in the company are racists or act with racist behavior. Rather, I am saying that the ingrained policies, practices and beliefs that allowed things to get as out of balance as they had, could not change overnight or easily. There were some beautiful white associates who went out of their way to let me know they respected me and had given me their blessings for doing what I felt was right. But those people were not indicative of the overall corporate culture at that point in time, and certainly not of the upper echelon of management.

I had long awaited the weekend of March 10, 2000. The original group of plaintiffs had grown to include four others. Eight black plaintiffs refused to continue and accept racial abuse at The Coca-Cola Company. March 11th was the first time all eight lead plaintiffs would come together with our attorneys. I could feel the momentum growing.

This was the first time I'd met the two plaintiffs from The Minute Maid Division in Houston, TX. I looked at our growing group in that conference room and my eyes grew full and my heart heavy. I was reminded of the first time I met with the other associates back in 1997 and first heard their pain and stories. I was sad because some of the familiar faces from back in 1997 were no longer here journeying with us.

Most of the day was spent with the attorneys sharing the strategies that we would take to the table regarding a settlement. Many times when I caught the eyes of the attorneys in the room, they seemed amazed at what they were experiencing. I was thrilled to be a part of the team and it seemed the attorneys had great respect for us. I felt we had a good team.

During our breaks that day, the lead plaintiffs huddled together. It was as if we had known each other for many years. Our common pain and desire for justice bonded us quickly. I even bought a camera to capture some of these connected and historical moments that day. There was much love in the air. The attorneys smiled, embraced the plaintiffs and embraced each other. More than a common cause, it was as though we had become family. Not once did I doubt the power and ability of the group that had assembled.

I believed in my heart that this group was selected a long time ago and that the Captain had already prepared each of us to go through the storm. All we needed to remember was that no matter how hard the wind might blow, or how long it might rain, we just had to hold firm to His unchanging hand and everything would be fine.

Through the battles, I never once stopped believing in or leaning on the Lord. Many tears had fallen from my weary eyes and my body began to show signs of pain and a lack of rest. When asked, "Brother Clark whose side are you leaning on," my response was always the same. I answered, "I am leaning on the Lord's side." I believed we were blessed with one of the most courageous and intelligent legal teams ever assembled, but it was Jesus that I depended upon. I will never forget the power of the Lord.

There was one nagging thought though. Although the hours of discussion that day were so positive and joyful, one comment made by one of the attorneys stuck with me. The attorney shared that someone had informed him that Rev. Watts was raked over the coals for announcing that he would ask at the NAACP Convention for a selective buying campaign against The Coca-Cola Company's products in coming weeks. This infuriated several of the lead plaintiffs. I was not angry; instead I looked around the room and tried to read others' feelings. I had faith that God would work that situation out, so I knew there was no need for anger.

Long ago in this journey, I learned I could only depend on one person for my help and strength, and his name was Jesus. I imagined along the journey there would be people who appeared to be for the cause and genuinely with the group. I also knew that many groups that called themselves a Civil Rights Organization would embrace The

255

Coca-Cola Company. The company has been funding these groups for many years, so when an issue such as this one presents itself, the organizations feel its loyalty would be best placed with those that have financially supported them for years. Before this experience and from the outside looking in, I might have once thought that the effect of corporate funds on the action or inaction of Civil Rights Organizations was limited. But, I had seen enough to know different.

In the fall of 1997, I sat with Rev. Watts and Mr. GS in homes of current and former black employees and listened as they told stories of how the company had discriminated against them. I imagined the so-called Civil Rights leaders, sitting pretty with their hush money, never thought of the pain these people were enduring. Not only had the company figured out it could disrespect black employees, it also figured out the price at which it could buy these so-called Civil Rights leaders. The company thought it was in the clear it seemed.

The company knew that no matter how guilty the company looked and was portrayed in the media, it could pay, and these Civil Rights Organizations would remain quiet. Instead of inciting indignation and speaking up for blacks, the organizations nursed their purses.

What about the songs blacks have sung for generations like "We Shall Overcome"? What exactly was the price of silence?

When I wondered why so few organizations seemed to not have a price tag, I understood why Rev. Watts kept pushing so hard for justice. While so many could be bought, Rev. Watts stood as an example of what was "right." He led even when others didn't always follow. I had become a member of the NAACP because of the leadership I saw in Rev. Watts. I know there were others like me who saw the Truth, and knew we had to search for youthful members who would stand for Truth as well so that they could become a proud part of Civil Rights Organizations.

Sadly, the system many corporations seem to have in place resembles the old "house nigger" mentality. Believing that we have overcome, many blacks have become complacent in our thoughts and daily activities. But all it takes is one look around to realize that we, as blacks, have not made it yet. All we have to do is look around and see that our face is one of the few in this environment that shines with dark skin.

Corporation icons realize that if they place a few blacks in what appears to be key positions, they can sway the public to believe their lies should racial issues surface. This was vividly displayed in the placement of The Coca-Cola Company's top and most public black associates. The white leaders of the company probably thought these token black executives would be quick to cover up the company's racist wrongdoings should they surface. I prayed that one day each of those who had taken advantage of the sweat, pain and frustration of the many blacks who had labored at The Coca-Cola Company would ask God for forgiveness and the strength to face their fears. I did and He has not failed me yet.

Time continued to pass and courtroom tactics were in play. The war continued and I started to feel the pains physically. When I began this journey, I knew that my stress level would rise as the case proceeded, but never did I ever imagine so much pain.

I would retreat to the Run & Shoot Gym to work out and relieve stress. One day, I planned a three mile run on the treadmill and when I looked down, I had gone five miles in the time it normally took me to cover three. I played a few pick-up games of basketball only to find that I could not focus on the game. I felt like I was moving in slow motion. This time of night, the competition on Court #4 was usually at its best, but today the guys asked if I was sick. I answered, "No!" But, I knew I wasn't simply having a bad day. I was not well.

That night when I arrived home, my wife too asked about my health. I answered as honestly as I knew how, but it appeared the more I answered the more she asked. I could not see what she saw, but I knew she was asking because she saw that something was wrong.

For some time I had not been sleeping well. I was working long hours as well as trying to keep my house in order and get ahead. I reached the point however where I could not pretend that I was just lacking a little sleep. My body was breaking down under the stress. I lacked an appetite and wasn't eating well. I called and made an appointment to see my physician.

When I went to see him, I shared the story of my stress and months of not eating or sleeping well. He was a professional and I knew I could trust him. I told him about my place of employment and the situation. He seemed to know instantly what I was speaking of. He examined me and found I was extremely tight. My muscles were knotted and I was in severe pain. Simply turning my neck left or right was painful. I'd also experienced sharp chest pains on and off for months. What I had been ignoring I could not ignore any longer. The doctor said he's rarely seen someone so tight and locked up.

He gave me a referral to see another doctor to help me deal with the nucleus of the pain. I didn't want to tell my wife that my next appointment would be with a psychologist. I always thought that only people who could not manage their lives and those that wanted a "way out" saw psychologists.

I took the doctor's advice and made an appointment. I realized within the first few minutes of meeting with the psychologist that my initial impressions of his profession were totally unfounded. One of the most relaxing things about the first visit was the fact that he was drinking a Pepsi when I arrived in his office. I thought for a moment that maybe this was one of the games he'd learned in medical school. After a few minutes of small talk, I realized it was not a game at all. He was a solid professional and I found my time with him to be fruitful.

During our visit I shared how I secretly held meetings with many blacks trying to bring about change in a company that was

260

discriminatory. As was standard for me, I did not trust him completely right away. I shared information only in a general sense. I could tell by his reactions that some of what I shared shocked him. The more I talked, he listened. The more I talked, the angrier I became.

For so long I was trying to hold it all together but if I were "all together" I wouldn't have been in his office seeking help. By the end of the first session, I was pleased that I had followed through with the appointment. Dr. Allen Carter suggested that I take some time off from the company while under his care. So I did.

March 20, 2000, the *Atlanta Journal Constitution* wrote that "Coke Critics Plan Justice Ride." The article claimed that Larry Jones along with other current and former employees had planned a bus ride from Atlanta to go to the Shareholders Meeting in Wilmington, DE. The article quoted Larry as saying that one of the purposes of the bus ride was to raise the public awareness about life inside The Coca-Cola Company for black employees.

The article went on to say that the unusual civil rights actions against the world's largest soft drink company came at a time when Coca-Cola was trying to improve its image among employees and shareholders in the face of a racial discrimination suit, and financial

troubles that had contributed to major company reorganization and the

layoff of hundreds of employees. Before reaching Wilmington for the

April 19th annual meeting, Jones said the convoy of three buses would

stop for rallies in Greensboro, NC, Richmond, VA and Washington,

DC. The article also stated there would be seats for about two dozen

members of the media. In addition to a rally on the steps of the US

Capitol, Larry said the riders would be meeting with members of

Congress to discuss the case.

The next few weeks was a continuance of articles and reports that

black employees were meeting at St. Phillip A.M.E. Church in Decatur

to try to force the company to a speedy settlement. One of my greatest

concerns was the fact that it appeared that blacks were responding

emotionally and had not carefully thought through all that they were

embarking upon.

By this time my body was at the point where it could shut down at

any moment. Chest pains and splitting headaches were plaguing my

already sleepless nights. Despite the pain, I didn't want the case to be

settled hastily before the truth reached the world in the manner it should. I wanted the leaders of the company to have to own up to the wrongdoings. I didn't think we'd come this far to settle quickly before the truth was fully known. Unlike some civil rights leaders, we couldn't be bought when former and current Coke employees paid such a high price.

What good would it have done if we fought for eleven rounds only to be told that we must now take a dive in the 12th round because the promoters of the fight were losing millions of dollars?

I knew that we could not rush to a settlement to please and silence those that were losing money and were angry. I too was a shareholder. I too was losing money, but "what does it profit a man to gain the entire world and die and lose his soul?" Absolutely nothing. From my conversation with the other lead plaintiffs, I could tell some wanted the case to soon be over, but felt that if we turned or bowed down to the racist practices of the company, nothing would have been gained from our many months of fighting.

Several days after "The Bus Ride for Justice" became public knowledge, the company began shuffling a few blacks into some key positions. Because of layoffs and voluntary retirement packages, one of the highest positions in the human resource department became available – the position of vice president.

Thus, on March 23, 2000, The *Associated Press* wrote an article titled "Coke Names Human Resources Director". The article went on to say that the company named a 46 year-old black woman as head of human resources as the nation's biggest soft drink company continues to grapple with fallout from massive job cuts and a racial discrimination lawsuit. It added that Coretha Rushing had worked in Coca-Cola for four years and had nineteen years of experience in human resource management. It stated that in her new position, Ms. Rushing would be responsible for overseeing recruitment, staffing, compensation, benefits and employee training and development. The article also stated that the suit filed by eight current and former employees seeks class-action status for 2000 of the company's black salaried employees in the United States.

The second appointment announced to Coke employees and the world was the appointment of Juan D. Johnson to the position of Vice President and Director of Diversity Strategies. He was to report directly to the new chairman. The writer then acknowledged, "Juan has been a vice president of the company since 1993 and has worked in senior

positions in Human Resources, Corporate Communications, Marketing

and Finance. In addition, Juan had been an important figure in the

Diversity Advisory Council since its formation last July. In the new

position, he would be responsible for developing and executing

company strategies for building, maintaining and leveraging diversity

throughout our business."

Chapter 11

The Enemy Within

On March 23, 2000, an article appeared in the *New York Times* that surely sent shock waves through every Coke shareholder. It opened by stating that black employees had held empty Coke cans outside an Atlanta church to protest Coca-Cola's treatment of blacks and that Larry Jones, Coke's terminated human resource manager, was quoted stating, "We have an interesting story to tell at the shareholder meeting. The company has done such a good job at telling the world what a good company it is, but on the inside it absolutely does not practice what it preaches." The article went on to acknowledge that Mr. Jones said he had not been given a time to speak at the shareholder meeting.

Clearly, the racial discrimination lawsuit filed by a group of Coke employees nearly a year prior was no longer just one of many side issues at the company. Stock analysts reported that the lawsuit was harming the company's image with investors. Coke was trying to make itself attractive again after turning in one of its worst business performances in its history the previous year. The article stated that Coke's stock price closed on March 22, 2000 at $47.625, about 23%

266

lower than the opening price on December 6, 1999, when Doug Ivester announced plans to step down as chairman and chief executive.

As for my physical condition, I had not been on company grounds for nearly two weeks based on my doctor's advice. The daily stress level and hatred I had been shouldering had taken its toll on my body. My attempts to offset stress with exercise could not counteract the effects of the mental and physical stress I was under. While I took some time to rest, there were associates who kept me informed about what was going on at "The Plantation".

On March 29th, I was informed of a conference call that Rev. Jesse Jackson was to participate in. It was to be a call with the lead plaintiffs, our attorneys and Rev. Jackson. I was excited at the prospect of such a prominent man taking an interest in our cause. I looked forward to the upcoming call which was to include him. After all, for over a year I had been wondering why civil rights organizations were so gun shy of speaking out on our behalf and not willing to ask Coke for some worthy explanation.

A few days later, when the time arrived for the conference call, I dialed in with great hope for the power of help from Rev. Jackson.

When I called in through the familiar maze to the conference connection, I heard a few of the other lead plaintiffs already on the line making small talk. Soon all the attorneys and lead plaintiffs had connected and it was time to get started. The lead counsel shared some of the recent events and reported that things were pretty much moving in the direction that we expected. He then asked us to hold while he tried to connect with Rev. Jesse Jackson.

Seconds later the connection was made and we heard the Reverend's familiar voice. I was thrilled to have such an opportunity to be a part of this fight, to fight to bring change to the culture of Coke and to corporate America as a whole, and also thrilled that I might be soldiering alongside Rev. Jackson. The Reverend stated how proud he was of each of us and told us that he felt that each of us should consider ourselves pioneers for justice and change. He applauded our efforts in such a way that I could tell he was a man who had indeed traveled long roads and fought many battles for the cause of equality for all people.

His words that evening will forever be a part of my life, and words that I too will share with my children. He was interested in our backgrounds and experiences, so we each took a few moments to share a little about our experiences at the company. As we shared, he made comments like "My God" and "Lord, Lord." I think he was shocked by some of the things that he was hearing. I had imagined that the token blacks scattered in the higher levels at The Coca Cola Company lived a life of wealth and privilege contrasted with those of us common employees who had stories to tell Rev. Jackson on this day.

I knew Rev. Jackson had probably been told a very different story before this day when he heard our stories. That's what corporations do when they are caught with their hand in the cookie jar; they spin a story to suit themselves. Rev. Jackson sounded genuinely concerned and after hearing our testimonies, he began asking questions of our attorneys.

His expertise and experience were obvious. He asked our attorneys some point blank questions that we'd never even thought to ask. His first question to the lead counsel Cyrus Mehri was, "What is the amount of money the attorneys were taking off the top?" My mouth was open and I know the other plaintiffs were in the same posture. You could hear a pin drop across those phone lines.

The conversation continued with a little small talk from the attorneys. I suddenly realized, as did others, that the question was never answered. The Reverend's keen ear noticed that too. So, he asked again, "Cyrus, what is the amount of money the attorneys are taking off the top?" Cyrus, realizing that he could no longer ignore the question answered, "twenty-five percent." His reply puzzled me and for a brief moment the line again went silent. Cyrus's answer – 25% - puzzled me because I didn't recall ever reading that number in my contract.

The conversation continued and a breakfast meeting with the plaintiffs was scheduled for the next morning with Rev. Jackson. The Reverend again thanked us for our time and said he looked forward to seeing us in the morning. He seemed to be concerned with our cause and more than willing to help us bring change to "The Plantation".

With Rev. Jackson off the line, I told the group still on the call that I thought he was sincere and that I welcomed his presence. Everyone on the line appeared to be on the same page. For the first time, I actually thought that both the plaintiffs and the attorneys all felt there could be closure to this long, exhausting ordeal very soon. Cyrus then asked all plaintiffs to hang up the telephones and all the attorneys to stay on the line.

One by one I heard the lines click as the plaintiffs said goodnight and hung up. Before I could say goodbye, the thought of the exchange between Rev. Jackson and attorney Cyrus flashed through my mind. A deep sense of doubt crept into my psyche. Like walking down a deserted street and peering back over your shoulder because you thought someone was following you; my senses were peaked. An inner voice said to me, "Gregory, do not hang up the telephone." Before I could make a decision internally to answer that message, the attorneys began talking.

The legal counsel did not realize I was still listening and one of the female attorneys said, "Hey guys, can you believe how quickly Jesse won Greg over?" The attorneys replied with words like, "Yeah, that was great" and "Wow! That was interesting". One of the attorneys stated that he did not think it was a good idea for the plaintiffs to meet with the Reverend without the attorneys being present. I sat silent and dumbfounded.

Each of the attorneys agreed that it was definitely not a good idea for us to be alone with Rev. Jackson. Cyrus then asked, "Well, who wants to call Greg and inform him that we have decided that the attorneys should be at their meeting?" J spoke up to say, "I'll give Greg a call and let him know what we have decided."

I was processing. Every attorney on the line agreed that it was not a good idea for the plaintiffs to meet with the Reverend alone. They knew Rev. Jackson was a man of power but none of them ever suggested a prayer meeting with the Reverend. As I sat and thought about what I had just heard, J told Cyrus that one of the female lead plaintiffs kept asking about individual claims.

Before J could finish talking, Cyrus said, "Hey guys, listen, I've got it all worked out. First, I'll call each of them [the plaintiffs] individually and tell them that their individual case is only worth $20,000 each. I'll then ask Judge Story to hold $2.5 million from the settlement to be divided equally among them. They won't be pleased, but what can they do, the case will be over."

J then said, "You guys know Greg won't be pleased with that amount." Another attorney commented that he cared little about what

Greg's concerns might be. S then said, "That will leave us with around, around…" he paused as if he was computing the numbers as he was speaking, "That will leave us around $87 million dollars." And another attorney confirmed, "Yes, which sounds about right," and the other attorneys on the line agreed.

I could not believe what I was hearing. While I wanted to shout, I said nothing. I wanted these snakes to continue thinking they had pulled the wool over the eyes of some fools. They were chuckling and having a grand old conversation. The attorneys spoke as if each of their comments were not new news. It was as if they'd had this conversation before or many just like it.

I almost lost my mind. These bastards! One attorney, Jamey, who we initially wanted to be a part of the case in order to watch Cyrus and the other attorneys, was on the line agreeing with all of them. He wasn't looking out for our best interest.

During the conversation, J then asked Cyrus, "What are you going to do about Larry Jones." The question was asked as if they were trying to calculate how much money it would take to make him go away. Cyrus responded, "I don't know, I don't know. We will just have to see how things work out." After Cyrus spoke, he then reemphasized to each of them what needed to be done to make the meeting with the Reverend go like clockwork.

I sat and listened to the greed in their voices as they carried on about the amount of money they would receive. Their voices were familiar yet strange. My anger was familiar too. It was as though they were acting on a stage when speaking to us, their clients; but now they spoke what was really in their hearts and on their minds. When speaking to one another, their true motives were revealed.

As the call drew to a close, I waited for the very last click before I hung up. I was livid. I could not believe these dogs had a hidden agenda and had been playing us for fools. I acted on my anger and impulse. I dialed Jamey. He answered right away and when he said hello, I shouted at the man calling him everything but a child of God.

Initially, he was silent. A few minutes into my tongue lashing he asked, "Well Greg, just what did you hear?" I shouted, "You bastard, I heard every word." He repeated, "Well, then tell me what you thought you heard." I slammed the telephone down so hard it broke.

I'd never been so angry in my life. My next calls were to each of the lead plaintiffs. In the past when we wanted to talk with everyone, we'd call one another on three-way lines until everyone was on a single call. We did this again and when everyone was on the line, I told them verbatim what I had just overheard. The phone lines sounded like they went dead. Nobody said a word. Shocked silence was all that resounded.

Stunned, disappointed, disillusioned and frustrated, we sat quietly listening for someone to find the words that might ease the pain. While we hung on the line with each other, call-waiting beeps started interrupting on each person's phone. Before anyone could swap over to the incoming call, I told them that I knew it was those bastard lawyers calling.

One plaintiff agreed to switch over to see what they wanted, then return to the call. Once we were all on the line again, that plaintiff shared that Cyrus wanted to have another conference call. All plaintiffs received phone calls.

I protested and told the group not to listen to their bullshit. I suggested that we wait and talk the next morning to decide what direction we were going to take. For me, it was crystal clear. *If those low down dirty dogs had not done or said anything they shouldn't have, why was there such a desire for another conference call?* Cyrus was a master at manipulating people and he did exactly what I expected. While the attorneys called all the plaintiffs, he himself telephoned the weakest and most emotional female of the group.

Cyrus knew this woman was in a crisis. He knew that she had been out of the company for an extended period of time and was pressed for money. He knew that if he stressed that a breakup of the group could prolong any type of settlement, she would look to him for answers. He knew she needed him in more ways than one, and she more than likely could possibly persuade a few of the other plaintiffs to also ignore the overheard conversation.

As a group, we agreed that the other plaintiffs would listen to what they had to say in another conference call and when the designated plaintiff gave the signal, we would all hang up. This second conference call began with a female attorney telling a few flat jokes trying to break the silence as we waited for everyone to join. The silence on the telephone revealed our lack of trust. While I wanted to hear nothing the

276

attorneys would have to say, I agreed to participate because the others wanted me on the call.

So we sat on the line waiting for Cyrus to join us. Seconds later, he answered, "Hello guys, I guess we need to clarify the conversation that was supposed to be between the attorneys that Greg allegedly overheard." He tried to be as smooth and as careful as he could. But, he didn't know what I had heard.

He didn't know if I heard all or just parts of the conversation, so he stumbled across a few rehearsed words only to find himself sounding like a broken record. After the designated person felt he'd heard enough, he gave the signal, and one by one the plaintiffs began hanging up without saying goodbye. I listened to the attorney voices as they realized what we were doing. They shouted, "Wait! No! Don't hang up!"

We had all agreed to think overnight of what our next move needed to be. What next? This would surely be our most important topic of discussion in the morning. I realized that the attorneys knew exactly who the weak plaintiffs were, and who would be easiest to convince that the conversation I overheard did not happen.

The Practice, Wall Street Journal

Ever wonder what lawyers talk about when their clients aren't listening?

Ask Gregory Clark. On March 29, Mr. Clark, a security guard with Coca-Cola, participated in a conference call among eight would-be plaintiffs, their five lawyers and the Reverend Jesse Jackson. But when the Reverend Jackson and the other plaintiffs hung up, Mr. Clark stayed on the line. The lawyers speaking to one another did not know the line was still live.

Mr. Clark's account of that conversation, which reads like a made-for-TV script, is laid out in delicious detail by R. Robin McDonald in the July 18 *Fulton County Daily Report*, which you can read at www.overlawyered.com. Mr. Clark says his suspicions were aroused when the Reverend Jackson asked about the lawyers' cut, and attorney, Cyrus Mehri of the Washington, DC-based Mehri, Malkin & Ross, responded 25%. That surprised Mr. Clark, because he said his contract had a clause putting the amount at 33%. The lawyers, he says, also discussed a settlement in the neighborhood of $250 million.

Of this amount, the lawyers would get $87 million, while the eight plaintiffs would split only $2.5 million, while the rest would be divided among 2,000 current and former Coca-Cola employees. The arithmetic sums up the logic of the class-action vehicle: while a plaintiff may stand to get more from a successful individual suit or settlement, lawyers clearly have an interest in applying their percentage to the much bigger "take" from a class action.

The *Fulton County Daily Report* puts it as follows: "'Hey, I've got it all worked out,' Clark recalls Mehri saying. He would first tell the lead plaintiffs that their individual claims were worth no more than $20,000 each. Later, he would ask U.S. District Judge Robert W. Story to set aside $2.5 million for them as class representatives, Clark recalls, "Mehri acknowledged that the lead plaintiffs won't be pleased with that, but what can they do? The case will be over."

Mr. Mehri denied Mr. Clark's account, but was quoted as saying he couldn't go into detail because of attorney-client privileges. What he did do, in the uproar that followed, was drop Mr. Clark and two others as plaintiffs. The ex-plaintiffs then hired their own lawyer, Mr. Willie Gary, who filed a separate $1.5 billion suit the same day Coca-Cola announced a previously secret settlement with the original attorneys.

In the latest wrinkle, Judge Story last week put some restrictions on Mr. Gary's ability to make deals with other Coca-Cola employees. But the story is far from over. Ultimately, the final resolution will await claims and counter-claims not only between the lawyers and Coca-Cola, but also among competing groups of lawyers.

Anyone still think tort reform too dry for the public to understand?

I received a telephone call from one of the attorneys that worked in a local firm, JB. He was not on the previous conference call. He sounded very humble and appeared to be sincere when he apologized for what I had overheard. As far as I know, JB was the only one of the attorneys that had an open relationship with Christ. He did not try to tell me what to do, nor did he ask what I was going to do, and for this I respected him. Instead of trying to fix things, he stated that his only reason for calling was to see if I was alright and to apologize for what I overheard. To this day I don't believe the other attorneys knew he called me. I thanked him for calling.

That night, I could not sleep. I knew when the sun rose again the attorneys would have reached several of the plaintiffs. I prayed and prayed. I cried and cried. I got out of bed and called on Jesus like I never called on him before. My body was racked with pain, stress, confusion, uncertainty, and I was just tired.

I still knew that I had to fight and do the things I felt were right in my heart. I was representing people who, for one reason or another, could not fight for themselves. I felt that they depended on me to do the right thing, come what may. That night I had to know Jesus. I prayed and cried but the more I called out to Jesus, the heavier the burden felt.

My mother told me when I was younger that I must be prepared to pray until a breakthrough came. So, on bended knee and with a heavy heart, I continued to pray. "Jesus! Jesus! Oh Jesus!" I cried. I told the Lord, "If I've never needed you before in life, I sure need you now." I knew that whatever decision I made, many would be angry. I knew some would treat me like a dog, but all I wanted was to do what Jesus wanted me to do.

Knowing enough to not be a fool, and think I was rich or powerful enough to fight this group of attorneys, I needed direction. Suddenly, I remembered how the saints would run and jump and shout in church. I also remembered my mother testifying that Jesus was all I ever needed. He was a doctor on the operating table she said. Jesus, she said, is a mother to the motherless on Mother's Day, a father to the fatherless on Father's Day and a lawyer in the courtroom. He was her Alpha and her Omega, her beginning, her middle and her end. Jesus was everything and everywhere. To me he was those things as well, and my decision was made to stand for righteousness.

The next morning three of the attorneys met me as I arrived in the lobby of the hotel where the Rev. Jackson was staying. Two of them were each partner of their prospective law firms. They stood at a distance appearing to be sizing me up to try and determine my mood. One of them walked toward me very cautiously. He had not been on the conference call the night before but I knew he was aware of the plan. "Good morning," he greeted me. I replied, "Good morning." I looked at him and added, "Although you were not on the call last night, I have nothing to say."

As I was speaking, the other approached and tried to speak to me. Angrily, I told him to get out of my face. He complied. Next, Joe Beasley, Southern Regional Director at Rainbow Coalition, then entered the lobby and we greeted each other. Soon after, three other plaintiffs walked into the lobby and two of them embraced to console each other. The third however, went directly to the attorneys and spent her time listening to them, not engaging with us.

At 6:00 a.m. it was time to go up to Rev. Jackson's room. I had decided that once the correct opportunity presented itself, I would share the conversation I overheard with the Reverend to see what he thought. When we arrived at the room, Mr. Beasley knocked on the door and the Reverend answered and invited all of us in.

After some initial small talk, I asked the Reverend did he object to talking to the plaintiffs without the attorneys being present in the room. The Reverend responded, "Certainly not, and I am sure that they would not object to that request." The attorneys then leapt to their feet and tried to act like that was the best idea they had heard in a long time. They were grinning as if trying to dump a great big snow job on the Reverend.

Once the attorneys were on the other side of the door, I asked the Reverend and Mr. Beasley to follow me to the bedroom where I shared with them the conversation that I had overheard. I also told Rev. Jackson that the twenty-five percent quoted by Cyrus did not appear in my contract. The Reverend remained quiet as I spoke. He then asked, "What was the percentage in your contract?" I responded, "thirty-three percent." The both of them stared at each other as if they had been down that road before. This was apparently a high percentage of a very high dollar case, far above the norm in such suits. The Reverend then thanked me for having the courage to tell him the truth.

Upon returning to the room where the other plaintiffs were sitting, we discussed some changes we felt needed to be made within the company. The attorneys were still outside the room as we spoke freely to the Reverend. He was very attentive and took notes to share with the leaders at the company who he'd soon meet for breakfast.

Before long it was time for that meeting. He encouraged us to stay together and continue to be strong. As I was leaving, the Reverend and I continued to discuss what he thought needed to be done to make "The Plantation" into a workplace all could be proud. I welcomed his input and I appreciated his concern. I was pleased he was going to meet with representatives from the company.

A few days later Cyrus called a meeting with all the plaintiffs and attorneys. He was trying to carry on as if nothing changed. By this time, I knew he had persuaded at least four of the eight plaintiffs to believe that I misunderstood the conversation I had overheard. I believed that the attorneys wanted to talk to each of the plaintiffs and to sway their perspective on the overheard conversation. Yet in the days that passed, not one of those attorneys called me. I knew they were concocting a secret plan. I had a few days to collect my thoughts and had reached the decision that it no longer mattered what they might throw my way, I was going to stand for righteousness.

Realizing we could no longer trust the all-white group of attorneys, Rev. Jackson dialed Mr. Willie Gary from his cell phone to arrange for us to meet with him later that day. The four of us agreed that if we no longer trusted our current group of all-white attorneys, something must be done to secure a fair settlement.

The four of us arrived for a meeting that Cyrus had rushed to call. To his surprise however, we did not arrive alone. Mr. Gary and one of his attorneys went with us. When we walked into the room, the faces of the all-white group of attorneys turned red. At first, I think they thought these gentlemen represented one of the civil rights organizations in town.

Cyrus was the first attorney to walk up to me, hand extended as if we were old friends sitting down to get to the business of the day. I thought he was a snake. Instead of shaking his hand, I looked in his eyes and introduced Mr. Gary and his associate to him. I then added, "You have proven yourself not to be trusted. These are two black attorneys we feel need to be brought into the case to ensure a fair settlement." Cyrus' stupid grin vanished. His cheeks grew red and he looked a bit faint. Another attorney suggested we take this matter to another area of the office.

My group followed them down the hall to another room with a long meeting table. More symbolic than it seemed at the time, the white attorneys were on one side and we were on the other. When the door closed, all hell broke loose. I looked at each of them and began reciting verbatim the conversation I overheard. Nobody said a word. They sat back in their chairs looking like children caught breaking the rules. My

285

voice rose to a yell and my posture was that of a warrior. Nobody moved.

Cyrus then looked in my direction and tried to suggest that perhaps I had misinterpreted the conversation. I told him I was only fluent in one language, and that was English. The meeting carried on and it got ugly; a bit like a legal sparring match. One of the white attorneys said he could not see where there was a communication problem, and as far as he was concerned there were no problems. The way in which he spoke was as if he were disrespecting Mr. Gary and the other attorney. Mr. Gary stood up.

As he stood facing this attorney, he pointed his finger in his face and shouted that surely he did see what the problem was and if he couldn't, then indeed it was he who had the problem. Mr. Gary then turned to Cyrus and shouted, "The contracts the plaintiffs signed were slave contracts." Mr. Gary continued to say that if he had made any of his clients in Florida sign a contract like this one Cyrus had used, there was a strong possibility that he'd be disbarred. Cyrus dropped his head. Body language can say so much.

Cyrus then lifted his head and replied that he was not the person who had written the contracts. Mr. Gary erupted again, looked him directly in his eye and asked him, *"Do you think blacks and the civil rights organizations give a damn if you wrote this sick shit or not?"* Cyrus repeated himself, "I did not write them." Mr. Gary and his associate both looked at Cyrus and the other attorneys like they knew they were dirty lawyers.

That was what I had come to view them as. Mr. Gary and his associate however were quickly earning my respect. While Mr. Gary entered the room humbly with the intention of helping to get the best settlement for everyone, he clearly was not about to let this man or anyone else disrespect him. Another attorney then suggested that maybe everyone else should leave the room and let the attorneys talk. We left the room.

As we stood outside the conference room, the weakest and most emotional plaintiff got off the elevator and greeted the receptionist. The attorneys were called out of the conference room to meet with her. They were sure to turn their backs to us and speak in whispers. The attorneys finished and returned to the meeting. When they did, I went over to address that plaintiff. She immediately told me that I better not try and poison her mind against Cyrus and the other attorneys. Clearly she was a fool and I had no tolerance for her ignorance. I left her alone.

Hours later, the attorneys surfaced and invited us back into the room. One of the attorneys stated that he thought it would be a good time to call the other plaintiffs who were out-of-state to see if they agreed with bringing Mr. Gary and his partner aboard. A conference call was set up to include the out-of-state plaintiffs while we were there. Once we had congregated and gathered the others on the phone, Cyrus gave his recollection of the events that had occurred that day. I spoke up to say that I could not sit back and be bamboozled any longer by Cyrus. This wasn't a game, I explained, it was our lives we were dealing with.

For almost one year we had been asking for a copy of expense reports to ascertain some idea of the amount of money the attorneys were spending on the case. I told them that all of us had talked amongst ourselves about how unfair we felt we were being treated and I had enough of that. I went on to say that before launching the suit, I had secretly researched the company for years and established the "Right to

Sue" letter that set the whole deal in motion. I'd established that the case had merit and could potentially encompass over 2000 African American employees. I had not entered into this process blindly.

Most of the people in the first set of plaintiffs had journeyed with me in secret meetings before we had hired the law firm. It was my intent to let the lawyers know that they weren't the glue that held this group together. It was our cause.

We were fighting for more than ourselves. Those not present depended on me to fight for justice. And, after hearing that conversation, I would be remiss not to ensure we added some attorneys to the team who were looking out for our best interests – preferably a black attorney with strong trial experience. We needed someone who had a reputation for helping people from all walks of life.

The plaintiffs who joined by conference call were angry that I did not consult with them prior to bringing Mr. Gary and his associate to the forefront. I did not care what they thought. Each of the four had been out of the company for an extended period of time; three of them out of state. They were leaning more and more towards a quick settlement and were not so connected to the cause and people in the company anymore. My loyalty still remained to the people still currently working for The Coca-Cola Company and the fight against racism for them. By the end of the call, the other plaintiffs agreed to bring Mr. Gary and his associate aboard. Cyrus was furious. His face was red. He barked at me like a spoiled child, "Greg, you are the reason for all this."

By the end of the day, everyone left the office believing there was an agreement. Mr. Gary, his firm, and each lead plaintiff felt comfortable moving forward with the settlement process. The attorneys had started to plan how to present the new attorney to the media. Despite the consensus from this meeting, I didn't trust Cyrus. I knew that he would not take easily to having the famous Mr. Gary take the spotlight away from him, yet he was not in a position to battle with Mr. Gary either. I expected Cyrus to prey heavily on the weaker plaintiffs and salvage whatever relationship he could with them.

The original eight plaintiffs in the case sent a letter to Cyrus to say that they had concerns. The letter stated, "We believe we now have a major credibility gap. This gap has created a sincere lack of trust; and emotional outpour and a wakeup call for us as plaintiffs. We now believe it is imperative that we take charge of this case as if it were our business." We asked to be treated like shareholders in a business. We wanted to be taken seriously. Further, we asked about expenses and said, "We want to understand the following: expenses to date, and if this amount is unknown at this time, we would like to know when this information will be available; a formal communication process on either a daily or an as appropriate basis. And, a clear indication of next steps, a specific calendar of events, all meetings, press contacts and telephone logs." We asked for a detailed discussion concerning individual awards within 7 business days. Having outlined our lack of trust, this letter let Cyrus know that we were not pawns in his game. We wanted information, details and accountability.

The next morning I received a call from one of Mr. Gary's attorneys who informed me "the deal had gone bad." The other attorneys had switched everything around, and would not now allow Mr. Gary to be part of the case to represent the class. Just as I had suspected, those snakes were never going to allow a famous black attorney to steal the spotlight. Immediately, I called the Bondurant, Mixson & Elmore, LLP, firm, one of the firms we'd been working with until now. The receptionist told me that none of the attorneys were available to talk to me. Next I called Cyrus' firm, Mehri, Malkin & Ross, and the result was the same. I called each of the firms many times that day only to be placed on hold over and over again. I knew their plan was to ignore the plaintiffs who refused to trust them.

After realizing what the all-white group of attorneys was doing, I called Mr. Gary and shared with him what happened. He responded, "Don't worry; we will work things out together." I believed Mr. Gary and his associates were honest men. Finally, we were working with attorneys who prayed before every meal and openly confessed their success was nothing less than a blessing from God. I researched this man whom everyone seemed to love and found fascinating things about him. He appeared to be a personal friend to every media outlet in the country. I thanked God for the two, and their firm.

The next day I received a Federal Express package. In it was a letter written to the courts stating that because of monetary issues we allegedly raised, they felt the courts would not accept us as lead plaintiffs. What liars! We never talked about money during any of the meetings. The spineless cowards!

I was curious if anyone thought it strange for three lead plaintiffs to be removed by their attorneys a few days before settlement talks started. These greedy attorneys were determined to let nothing stop them from getting their millions. After all, Cyrus did tell his associates, "Hey guys I've got it all worked out." He had a story concocted to explain the reduction in plaintiffs.

What kind of attorney would concoct such a lie and present it to the courts? I was curious as to how many times this had been done. *Was this truly how the rich got richer and those that are fighting to be treated equally are robbed? Was this not an excellent example of how the greed of money causes officers (lawyers) of the courts to lie and falsify documents for personal gain?*

Cyrus's group of attorneys assumed that Ms. Williams, because of her quiet demeanor, would stay with them, but she did not. Wanda continued to work at "The Plantation" so she saw those she was fighting for every day. I will always respect her for the stance she took against the attorneys. I believe she followed her heart when she decided to leave the attorneys. She told me that she believed the Mehri group of attorneys had one of the female plaintiffs call her in attempt to get her to remain with them. She said her decision was not a difficult one; however, it did cause her pain. "All Greg wanted was to bring Mr. Willie Gary aboard to make sure everyone was protected," she tried to explain to her instead. She will always be a soldier in my eyes.

The Mehri group knew that it would look bad if they went public with the split. Instead of bringing one of the most powerful black trial attorneys aboard, a telephone call was then made to a law firm in Alabama. They added at least one black attorney from that firm who'd appear at the next press conference, and where it was announced that he was joining the case. The Mehri group of attorneys thought they had it all worked out.

While someone once said that if you want to hide something from a black person, put it in a book; I am the book. I would document this nonsense. It was time to denounce such an ignorant myth. I would be sure that those attorneys didn't think they'd won. I committed to telling the story.

Many articles were written that shared various views as to how or why a split of this magnitude could come at such a late stage in the case. I knew the time would come when the group of attorneys would be exposed for greed. For now, I knew to be patient.

The next few weeks were spent getting familiar with The Gary Firm and trying to get our documents together that the firm would need to prove our individual cases. I must admit, I did wonder what the Mehri group of attorneys told the other lead plaintiffs when they asked why we were kicked out as lead plaintiffs. This was not an easy question to answer. They probably told them that we asked to be released so the Gary Firm could represent us. If this was told to the lead plaintiffs however, it was nothing more than a blatant lie.

It was the second week of August 2000, and I was approaching the fifth month of medical leave from the company when I received a certified letter from the manager of security. I was not at all surprised with the contact because in my research of the company, I learned that when a person was approaching the end of their short-term disability, the company would gladly send them a letter stating its position. The letter was confusing; it read that the department had done an analysis, which concluded that because of the business needs of the security department; my position could no longer be held. However, once I was released from either short-term or long-term disability, I would have 45 days of unpaid leave to find a position within the company. The letter also stated that the company would do everything that it could to place me in a similar position.

My position was gone. I had 45 days to find another position in the company. And, I'd be helped in this pursuit? I knew this letter was nothing but a bunch of hogwash. However, to prove that the company was still playing games with me personally and cared nothing about my well-being, I again needed documents, and I found them. I knew of several other security officers that had been ill and forced to take short-term disability, and they probably still had the letter they received from the manager of the security department.

I located some letters sent to other security officers that were also on leave at one time or another. Just as I suspected, my letter was written differently than any of the others. It was obvious that the manager and those involved were trying to send me a message that was not as clear in the other letters I located. The message to me was that my job was no longer there. It appeared that rather than the standard letter to inform the associate of the department's policies and position, the manager of security and a white female, who served as the human resource representative, along with one of the attorneys from the legal department, wrote my letter to make it appear that I no longer had a job. Additionally, they tried to cover all the bases so they even faxed a letter to Mr. Gary's office.

I received a call from Mr. Gary's office and told them that I was aware of what was going on, and if I needed their assistance with this matter I would call. The same people whose games made me need five-months of disability leave were now playing with my life and career. I knew the only way to make the company stop playing these senseless games with me and with other blacks was to expose them publicly.

This was one way The Coca-Cola Company manipulated people into doing what they wanted. I must admit that it is not always the leaders at the top of the organization making all the bad decisions. Often times there were middle level managers who thought they could make whatever decisions they preferred without being held accountable; managers who tried to eliminate people rather than deal with real issues.

In The Coca-Cola Company, there were thousands of people and many levels and channels used for processing decisions. It was not unrealistic to believe that some of the executives at much higher levels in the company had little daily contact with middle level managers. Hatred and racist acts committed by some managers, which led to the disgrace, embarrassment and possibly destruction of a successful organization.

After some months of much diminished stress, it started again. I knew what my manager wanted to do. He wanted to keep me from returning to the company. I stayed focused and tried to ignore the arrogance I knew would soon be their downfall.

Chapter 12

Dramatic Changes: Who's Side Are They On?

In the end, I was back at work, in my previous position. At least in this small instance, pointing out the injustice led to the "right" outcome in a timely manner. Perhaps this was a small sign of what might happen on a larger scale by our group speaking up with regards to racism.

In September of 2000, my wife and I became two of the happiest people in the world. We waited, planned and prayed until we felt it was the right time to begin our family. Both in our early thirties, we'd talked about one day being parents and were thrilled about the idea of raising a child. We found out that my wife was pregnant and I was so happy. I could barely comprehend the thought of us finally becoming parents.

For days my feet didn't even touch the ground. At night we'd sit and talk. We'd discuss the names we thought would be excellent. Many things needed to be done before the little one would arrive. Being close to both sets of parents, we decided to share our news with our parents first. We planned to take the first weekend of October to travel to South Carolina to share the wonderful news with them.

They were all very happy and ready to welcome our first child. My grandmother and my Uncle William were among the first to congratulate us. They wished us well and cracked jokes - all the things that a family does at such times.

Suddenly, my life had a new meaning. I was still playing the hand that I was dealt, but I realized that now some of the struggles became more important while others did not matter as much. Oh! How I prayed and thanked God for blessing us! I thought of the school my child would attend. I thought of the neighborhood that would be safest for my child. I thought of bringing my child to Sunday school, Bible study and prayer service. I wanted to do all of the things that my parents and my wife's parents did when raising us. I believed in my heart that we were ready.

On October 9, 2000, I took my wife to her second visit to the doctor's office. I was a proud soon-to-be-father. My joy showed in my walk, my talk and my eyes. My wife often commented about how my eyes would light up when I spoke of our child. The initial part of the exam was done and all seemed well. Next we would get to see the baby on an ultrasound. It seemed to take longer than expected.

My senses told me that something was going on, but I could not quite put a finger on it. My wife asked the midwife if everything was going well, but her response confirmed that sadly, something was wrong. She answered my wife very briefly and quickly exited the room. We waited for about fifteen minutes before she returned and told us that the doctor would see us now. This confirmed for me that something was wrong.

The doctor introduced himself to me. The sad look on his face was accompanied by the worst news. The baby was dead. Several weeks ago all was well but now there was no heartbeat. My legs went numb. I could see his face and his lips moving, but I could not hear anything that he was saying. My eyes had already begun to fill with tears, but I had to catch myself and remember my wife.

As much pain as I felt, I knew she felt that much and more. As a boy my father once told me that once I became a man, one of my responsibilities would be to put my feelings last and think of my family first in all things. Never did I imagine that I would be confronted with such pain and having to ignore it. I had to put her pain first. It did not matter what it took or how bad it hurt; all I wanted to do was comfort her.

I blamed myself. I could not help to think maybe it was my fault the baby died. She was supportive of me in my struggle. Surely the stress had taken its toll on her body. She did what she felt was right in her heart by choosing to support me on this hard road and for that my heart will always belong to her. She had to surrender one of the dearest prizes a wife could surrender, and she took on that grief and loss for me.

I was angry. I had sacrificed much in this battle and now I was more focused than ever. Night after night I held my wife as she cried, trying to ease her pain. There was absolutely nothing I could do to help her so I prayed. I asked God to take away her pain as I sat holding her as she cried herself to sleep.

For me, a burst of energy came into my life and over my body. By any means necessary, I wanted to impose the injustices that contributed to her stress. While my wife never once blamed me or said much, deep down inside I knew this struggle and the time and energy it consumed in our lives caused us to lose our child.

I rededicated myself to exposing the company and others like it to the public. I was only one person and I knew that what I could do was limited, but as long as I focused on God I continued to learn that He has no limitations. Besides, I'd been many places and seen many things, but I had never seen the righteous forsaken.

I walked the hallways as usual but something was different. When the associates refused to speak to or acknowledge me, I spoke. I wanted them to know that I was still in the company and was not afraid to play the game they created.

Several months passed and the company began announcing plans to bring about a more diverse workplace. I thought one of the most ridiculous things implemented was a Mentoring Program. While I actually agree with mentoring programs, in principle, unless all wanted an equal playing field and a healthy culture it would not work.

At this time in history and sports, Tiger Woods was on top of his game. The Williams sisters were tearing up the tennis court. Such successful black sports heroes were a better indication of what a level playing field looked like. Hard work, not unearned privilege was required to soar both in sports and with diversity at work. The culture of unearned merit and privilege at The Coca-Cola Company had to go for true change to occur. If the company, like these athletes was ever going to be "the best" at its game, it had to earn it, work for it, and win it.

I knew this program and others like it were established to gain positive press. Instead of just launching these programs, the company alerted the press. It wanted every bit of credit it could get to help counteract the negative press from the lawsuit. Ivester's early comments denying the merit if the lawsuit were long gone. Now, it was time for positive press attack. The problem was that the programs being reported on were not so carefully plotted out as the publicity campaigns.

When I reviewed the diversity plan, I believed it to be window dressing. *Would anyone address issues like what should happen when a black person goes to interview for a position and a less qualified white person has already been given the position before interviewing was complete?*

What would be done when a manager rates a black subordinate with a lower than deserved performance review because the manager feels threatened by someone with more credentials than he or she has?

What would be done when a manager showed a history of not promoting blacks or giving fair reviews and continued to prefer hiring other whites who were likeminded in dislike of minorities?

There were countless issues that the company's diversity plan would not address. An upper echelon of management that only included a few token black "yes men" and "yes women" was not the place to work from to set up a truly fair and effective diversity plan.

For a company to get rid of its racist culture, a new culture must be born. People must set personal feelings and beliefs aside and build from the ground up. Opinions and feelings are just like shoes; we all wear them but we can also take them off.

The companies that will be leaders and pioneers of the 21st century will be those that realize that attitudes that are focused on anything other than the organization's success are best left at the door. Instead of babysitting people's feelings and fears, a successful company has to choose to do what's right for its people, consumers and shareholders. In this day and age of a multi-cultural community, racially biased opinions and fears have no place in a successful company. Filter out the fools and work with a modern, global, colorless, talent-focused mindset instead.

And I must add that it seems to rarely be a person already at the top who's seeking more in the realm of justice. Usually, it is a little person that everyone has ignored and looked over that has the courage, time and faith to fight to bring change to a culture that perpetuates racial injustices.

Some have asked, "What will a man die for?" Others have asked, "For what will a man live?" I am curious if the answer to one is the same as it is to the other.

Chapter 13

Family Matters

As I was fighting for equality at The Coca-Cola Company, I faced personal challenges too. The loss of a baby and other family stresses were difficult. Sometimes I wonder if we are given many challenges at once so we must soldier on not having time for self-pity. God promises never to give us more than we can bear, but sometimes more seems just unfathomable.

One more family matter was added to my plate. My oldest brother had experimented with drugs in high school and he eventually became addicted to Crack. This demon stole many years of my brother's life and it was about to take more. Missing for four months, I could not find him anywhere. I searched the jails, the drug programs and everywhere I thought he might be.

I spoke to people who had overcome drug addiction and were in process of turning their lives around. My father contacted friends in the FBI and various law enforcement agencies to try and track my brother down. We followed each lead or snippet of information we received.

307

My parents were consumed with trying to find and help him. They blamed themselves for his illness and had poured out tens of thousands of dollars to try and get him help. Nothing seemed to help. Over the years he had visited some of the finest rehabilitation centers in the country only to be clean for a few weeks or months and then return to the streets and crack houses.

This time he had been in a program and was reported to be doing well. He then was kicked out for some reason and had virtually disappeared. He was back on the streets. He had a car which was a dangerous equation. And I had to face this reality every day as well as the other struggles on my plate.

There was a time when I would become angry with my brother for the burden he placed on my parents. He'd been missing for over four months. I did what I could to help search and alleviate my father's burden. He felt he was somehow to blame for my brother's struggle but I knew better. My sister and younger brother called all the time in hope of a breakthrough.

My missing brother's family needed him. His daughter, my niece, called me one day. She told me of a little girl in school who accused her of thinking she "was all that" because she had long hair. This sweet girl said to me in the gentlest voice, "Uncle Greg I told her that I don't think that I am all that, I think Jesus Christ was all that." She needed her father and asked me often where he was. I told her that he was away working.

I didn't want to lie to her and neither did our family, but we knew we needed to protect her gentle spirit. And I knew we needed to find him. I could not understand how a man-made drug could be so strong that it could make a father turn his back and forget about a child as precious as my niece. Nevertheless, she would never go without. I prayed for her.

I prayed for my brother wherever he was. I called jails and then even morgues in search of him. At times it seemed like I was carrying a thousand pounds of iron on my shoulders, but I focused on Jesus and spent time consoling my parents amid our search.

Back at work, in the last quarter of 2000, The Coca-Cola Company was in the midst of implementing many changes to its culture. Seminars were held in the auditoriums so each associate had an opportunity to hear of the changes the company apparently was making to create a more diverse culture. I attended one such meeting. And just as I suspected, the mentoring program was focused on putting blacks in contact with people that could possibly help them become more comfortable with the culture as it was. The company had done a wonderful job of selecting a few black employees to participate in a video to share why they thought the Mentoring Program would be successful. The Coca-Cola Company even went as far as interviewing blacks from other corporate companies just to let the viewers know similar programs worked. Interestingly, the black vice president who spearheaded this program and introduced the program was one of the very people that I had reached out to for help.

Apparently, years ago, The Coca-Cola Company would sponsor meetings at some of the most elegant hotels in town. They were meetings designed to afford blacks an opportunity to meet and mingle with other blacks in the company as well as blacks in senior management. This practice had not been present since I was hired in the company but was reinstated in 2000-2001.

I attended one of these meetings in Buckhead. About twenty minutes into the meeting, I felt sick to my stomach. The room was filled with people that were all black in color; at least that's how it appeared. The affair was held after hours so most were dressed in professional business attire. I looked for familiar faces as I wandered through the room and overheard snippets of conversations as I looked around.

Those conversations spoke for themselves even in just these small sound bytes. Most were about what title each person held in The Coca-Cola Company and how long had they been there. Eventually, I saw people that I knew from "The Plantation" including one or two who had invited me to attend. But nobody wanted to speak with me now that I was there.

I was dressed as sharp as any of the other black males there, and I was very comfortable speaking with anyone. Yet the people I knew at the event acted as if they were a bit uncomfortable or just did not want to be seen with me when I approached them. Naively, I did not understand why there was so much peculiar behavior in the room.

So I stood off to the side and observed my people. Everyone in the room appeared to be on a stage performing as if they were competing for a part in a Broadway show. No one appeared to be real. As much as everyone appeared to be having a good time, I sensed that most of the group could not wait until the evening grew old and they could find the right moment to leave.

Even the black senior executives there to represent the company appeared to be putting on a show. These meetings were designed to allow blacks to meet other blacks and ultimately share their views of The Coca-Cola Company and how they might become successful in the company. That's what the purpose was said to be on paper at least. But in reality, people were faking it. I couldn't help but ponder for a moment.

If we are pretending like this and putting on a show for each other in a private establishment away from "The Plantation", what in God's name would we be doing on "The Plantation" surrounded by white folks?

I soon realized the meeting was probably a fact-finding mission for the company to find out which blacks in the company had problems with the system and were willing to voice their opinions in that particular forum. Although the senior blacks in the company were presumed to be sponsoring the meeting, they had nothing to gain personally. The company was already affording them a very comfortable life. After an hour or so, I decided I'd skip this sort of event in the future. While it appeared that most of these blacks were willing to become puppets to please and be accepted by whites and other blacks in positions of power at "The Plantation" so they might become successful there, I was not.

The company spent a lot of time on programs to give the cause of equality lip service. Coca-Cola stock had been suffering for almost two years and it was now beginning to show more stability. There is an old saying that when people are desperate they will try anything at least once. I believed that once a company has treated a person or a race of people wrongly, in order for the company to be successful again, it has to find a way to repent or apologize to the very people it had taken advantage of. But The Coca-Cola Company didn't ascribe to my theory.

The company appeared to believe it just needed to appeal to the public, not with an admission of guilt, but by appearing to implement programs designed to improve conditions of those who complained. At a time when all else seemed to be failing or not showing profit fast enough, the leaders of the company felt they should place their faith in someone or something other than Almighty God. Instead of admitting that they had made some mistakes concerning black employees, they hid behind talk and programs that touted equality and fairness in theory even if not in practicality within the company.

The company even grasped at some crazy straws like looking into feng shui. Feng shui is Mandarin Chinese for 'wind' and 'water'. An article was sent to all associates explaining this theory and how it could benefit the company through the idea that buildings and landscapes are conduits for certain kinds of energy. Adherents believe that the shape of a building and its rooms can channel energy.

It was not an original idea. *Time* magazine had written articles on the growing influence feng shui had on corporate America. Real estate developers and corporations like Universal Studios, Merrill Lynch and Coty Beauty Products had all hired the same "consultant" to help them improve their energy flow. Some of the leaders even sent e-mails to associates sharing their perspectives on feng shui. The Coca-Cola Company apparently believed that if it frosted some of its doors, placed a gold disk in the Central Receiving Building, moved the flag poles and water fountain in front of the building, and replaced artwork around the building, its profits would rise.

Upon reading the memos sent to all Atlanta-based associates, I realized that the company was simply trying to find another way to undo, and turn back all of its wrongdoing. I knew that the feng shui belief was very real in countries like China and Hong Kong. The tradition was inherited and in most cases was a way of life for them. The Coca-Cola Company was not at all concerned with any tradition or belief that people held dear to their hearts. I believed that the only reason the leaders of the company wanted to adopt such an idea was because the company had at least two terrible years of business, and they were searching for anything that might change the fate of the company. Think about it.

The Coca-Cola Company has always positioned itself far above its competitors. *So, why would the leaders now be concerned with beliefs or tactics of companies like Hewlett-Packard, Citigroup, British Airways and HSBC? Could The Coca-Cola Company have been thinking that what was good for the goose was good for the gander?*

315

I laughed as I realized the sad state of being the company was obviously in. I failed to believe that the leaders wanted to do anything other than raise the stocks and gain back some of the momentum that was lost from all the lies and behind-closed-door meetings that constituted this mess. If they only knew that it was not me, nor feng shui principles trying to get their attention. The Word plainly states, "Thou shall have no other God before Me." Worshiping idols such as money creates greed and it shames and angers the God that has brought us thus far. *Why couldn't they see it?* What was on the minds of the leaders of the company that kept them grasping at straws instead of realizing that their misfortune was due to a dire situation that needed real attention?

As time passed, I learned more about why the hatred for me was so great at work. Many of the associates, both black and white viewed Coke as a God, and as far as they were concerned nothing else mattered. If anyone got in the way or attempted to make their god look bad, they were in opposition. A truly successful company puts people before profits, but at The Coca-Cola Company, the god of the company – its bottom line – reigned supreme. To Coke it was imperative that staff trust its leadership and any sign of lessened employee loyalty was interpreted as lessened productivity.

I believe in my heart that The Coca-Cola Company has discriminated against blacks since its foundation was poured. It was there before the walls even went up. And, if it takes the destruction of those very walls to get the attention of the leaders and the world, then so it will be.

On a lonely Sunday, the Rev. Larry Jones and a few other ministers from around the city decided to come together and acknowledge those brothers and sisters that had taken a stance against racial discrimination. At 5:00 p.m. that evening at Big Bethel Church A.M.E. on Auburn Street in Atlanta, there was a worship service where employees from The Coca-Cola Company, Georgia Power/Southern Company, Lockheed and the Waffle House were present to praise the Lord for what he had done and for what he was getting ready to do. I attended the service because I wanted to hear what others were experiencing at other large corporations in the city. I was speechless when I heard that there were similar claims in these powerful companies.

I met people who were forced to work around nooses while the managers made fun of them if they complained. Others had been in companies for 20-25 years and never once received a promotion. These people were discouraged.

How could it be that all this was happening in a city that was "too busy to hate," without a single civil rights organization taking a stance against any one of the companies? I knew a long time ago that most of the civil rights organizations had a price for which they'd sell their silence. But never did I imagine that all of them would be silenced like this. *How could these organizations consider themselves to be activists when they did nothing? How could people back these organizations when they shied away from standing up to wrongs in such large corporations?*

If there was ever a time to give college students and others with sharp minds and able bodies a reason to fight, it was now. It would not be hard to mobilize support, unless an organization didn't want to. I firmly believed that the leaders of many of the civil rights groups were on the payrolls of most of the large and powerful corporations in one way or another.

Could this be true? I dare you to think about it. Although some of the leaders of these organizations marched alongside Dr. Martin Luther King Jr., faced prison, and knew those who lost their lives fighting for equality; their motives seemed to have changed and resolve weakened.

Was it possible that so many of these leaders had lost the passion of achieving equality for blacks? Had the comfort of their popularity and notoriety made them complacent? Did they sell their souls or was it simply easier to write media-pleasing speeches and tell people what they wanted to hear but never really challenge the corporate bullies?

It seemed to me that while they said the "right" things in a room full of hurting, down-trodden blacks, they also said the "right" things to the corporations. I believe the latter was where their true colors showed. It seemed that the deal to be silent always won and somehow the black civil rights leaders and company both came out smelling like roses as they covered each other's backs.

After having the privilege of meeting with some of the civil rights leaders of this country, I knew that the fire that I always read about and visualized based on snippets I saw on TV had been snuffed out for many of them. *Did they just get tired after fighting for equality for so long?* I got tired too working day after day in a company where I was hated for the public stance I took. I understood the weariness but couldn't imagine turning my back on a just cause.

In the beginning, just a handful of people reached the conclusion that The Coca-Cola Company had to be held responsible for its actions. Two years down the road, some people who chose to ignore problems rather than speak up to fight the system, were suddenly wondering about when they'd get *their* money. Some laughed and joked as if the racial discrimination that we suffered was funny.

Eventually, I decided to challenge each person that came to me wanting to know how much money they were going to receive. I would let them say their piece then I would ask them, 'why do you care?' My question was met with peculiar stares and some simply just walked away. Over seventy-five percent of blacks on "The Plantation" sat back and allowed the company and the team of all-white attorneys determine their fate. Just a few were willing to speak up about what they had observed.

In November 2000, the company was doing its best to appear as if it had changed. Meeting after meeting and program after program were touted to be fostering diversity and fixing things. One night as I watched the evening news, the reporter said Coke had given 8600 employees equity raises.

The news station reported that The Coca-Cola Company recently benchmarked its current salaries against similar companies and discovered that its salaries were much lower than what the market demanded. The station also stated that the company had also implemented a diversity plan after eight black, current and former employees filed a racial discrimination lawsuit against the soft drink icon.

My supervisor called me at home that same evening to tell me I would be receiving a second raise. Like the television news, he said it was because of a benchmark with other companies in the market place.

Coke still claimed to be second to none, yet here it was looking to others to be sure it was compensating its employees adequately. The high dollar earners at the upper levels were more concerned with their own gains than with fair pay it seemed to me, it was trying to realign salary levels. Embarrassing enough to face a racial discrimination suit and now they had to admit publicly that they underpaid staff.

It brought me pleasure to see the leaders of the company squabble and squirm as they tried to hide years of discrimination at the company. I was curious if any of the executives really thought they could buy their way out of the mess or pay a legal team to find just the right shaped loophole.

They would walk up to me and call me by my first name, as if we had been buddies for a lifetime. They appeared to be flaunting their assumed power in my face. I studied the whites in the company for several years and I had a pretty good understanding of how and why they did things. I knew whether they were truly happy or whether they were simply trying to depict an image of happiness. I knew when they were angry and wanted to hide it. I also knew when they realized that this lawsuit had tarnished their presumed uncharitable image of over 100 years. With their hello, I could tell if they really wished they were saying goodbye. Those comfortable in the system disliked me for exposing a system that suited them just fine while causing pain for so many others.

The Coca-Cola Company's 'Good Ole Boy System' allowed executives to live very lavish, comfortable lifestyles partially because they had the right color skin and knew someone who could place them in a job where few questions would be asked. I wondered if some whites thought I believed myself to be better than other blacks because I was educated and therefore also assumed I was owed something.

In reality, I did not expect a free ride at all. My experiences at the University of South Carolina and Mercer University helped me prepare for the future. I was prepared to work hard and prove myself. I quickly learned however that others might not give me that courtesy. Whether in South Carolina or Georgia, many whites have a general perception of blacks and how they should deal with them rather than believing everyone deserves a fair shot.

My department was going through change after change. When a position would come open in my department, the application process seemed to suddenly change. It took months after interviewing to fill openings. Several black officers applied for a team leader position only to be told they did not have the necessary supervisory experience or they lacked in some other manner. Then, the position was filled with a white male who had neither the education nor experience required for the role. In another case, a white female was hired from outside the company with a totally unrelated Bachelor's degree and supervisory

experience in warehousing, not security. Apparently, little had changed.

Despite token raises and efforts to appear better on the surface,

change was not deep. We were still being played. In a December 23,

2000 article in the *Atlanta Journal Constitution,* Judge Story

encouraged class members to settle. He discouraged people from

pursuing individual suits saying that "An individual suit could take

three to five additional years to resolve, including appeals. Most

individual employment discrimination suits are unsuccessful." It would

be years before I fully understood why this was the case.

Managers still thought they could do whatever they wanted to do,

how and when they wanted without being questioned. When I spoke to

a few of the officers who were passed over for these roles, I found they

had both experience and education that were a better fit than those who

were hired. The officers shared with me their frustrations both about

the hiring manager and evaluation system, but as the initial shock of the

racist evaluation process wore off, they simply joked about it.

It seemed the manager realized he screwed up badly because after

he hired the last two people, he acted as if the other candidates already working in the department didn't even exist. They were frustrated at being passed up for the role and also with being ignored. I watched it like an experiment to see how they'd respond to the injustice they were recently rendered.

I did not initiate conversations, I let them approach me. I knew talk was cheap however. Of the potential candidates, four of whom were black, only one was not afraid to speak out about this biased system. I was not surprised with this revelation. After being in the company for almost 5 years, I knew most people were comfortable just having a job and getting by. I was not.

Work went on amid frustrations. The company took a lot of pride in securing and protecting its assets as well as the people viewed to be essential to the daily operations. The executives and their families were in many cases given access to the Special Operations Unit of security to report anything of a peculiar nature or anything of concern around their homes. One morning I heard that an executive's wife called the night before and she was extremely angry. The officer telling me the story said she was complaining because the power went out and she wanted someone to come check on her family. The wife grew angry and said if she was the wife of a white executive she'd have no problem getting someone to come out. She threatened that when her husband returned to the country she would tell him of the lack of response and then someone would have to answer to him. Her anger and demeanor floored the officer.

I soon connected the dots and realized that the women he spoke of was the wife of a high ranking black in The Coca-Cola Company. The officer then waited to see how I would respond. I showed no emotion. I was not at all happy about the news. I was actually angry and shared her frustration and pain. I imagined all she wanted to do was be treated as an equal and with respect, or treated as if she was the wife of an executive of The Coca-Cola Company and not the wife of a black man who happened to be an executive of The Coca-Cola Company. I never met the women that called with her concerns, but I was very familiar with the pain and anger she felt.

Then I thought back to this woman's husband. I distinctly remember an article in the *Atlanta Journal Constitution* where he said he did not know any of the plaintiffs, but he was certain they were wrong in their assessments of the company. I felt neither pain nor sorrow for him. I imagined that it was awful living in a world where success depended on how well one could hide the true reality of problems within a company.

One of the most precious gifts God gives man is a wife. It was sad to witness this man's wife being treated unfairly and hear that she was upset. *What if her husband had confessed that the company did discriminate against blacks and actually had enough faith to depend and lean on God in doing so? Could he have been the change agent we all had been hoping for if only he'd been brave enough to trust God and speak the truth?*

After the lawsuit was filed, I remember speaking to a woman who received a promotion. She made no excuses for why she felt she received the promotion. After being in a contract position for at least seven years, this black woman was quickly given a permanent position and promoted once the lawsuit hit. Although the new role meant she had to relocate, she didn't mind because it also included a company car. As she and I spoke, a well-dressed black man came along and greeted her with a hug. She introduced us and as he was leaving she stated that

327

the man who just left had prayer with a high-ranking black in his office here at Coke.

When she saw my look of surprise, she said, "Yes, he told me how bad things got at times and they actually had prayer." I was shocked! But, I believed her. She was an upright, bright woman. She was a graduate of one of the historically black colleges in the Atlanta University Center. She explained to me that initially that gentleman brought her to the company to be mentored, but it didn't take long for her to realize what was really going on in the company.

Someone helped these men who had broken through the race barrier to succeed. They came from the same roots as the rest of us. *How could they forget where they came from?*

Furthermore, it still astounded me how most civil rights organizations listened to these token blacks in companies who were paid to tow the company line. There was one black male that worked in The Coca-Cola Company who had a very active role in the black community. When there were meetings or events linked to any of the civil rights organizations, he would be there. "Was he like all the others?" I wondered.

I'd met this person back in 1999 and he proved to be extremely helpful to me. After each meeting he would attend with various civil rights organizations concerning The Coca-Cola Company and the lawsuit, I would get first-hand information on what happened in the meetings. After attending a meeting with the NAACP and several other so-called civil rights organizations he said, "It appears that all of these Negroes are going to do nothing but sit back and accept the money that the company has been giving them." He knew that wasn't the information I preferred hearing.

He spoke of the sad state our civil rights leaders were obviously in. He agreed with me that it was a crying shame. Throughout this struggle I knew that the company was doing a snow job on the organizations that at one time stood for hope for blacks. The organizations could be bought for a price these days.

I was not for sale, however. I am so thankful to my mother for raising me in the church, where I learned at a very young age that man would fail you, but Jesus always prevails. These were comforting words to remember when it was apparent that many men failed to stand for what was clearly right – a cause that many had risked their lives for over the years.

It was already the middle of November 2000, yet there was no word from the company or the attorneys that were representing the people. At work, people would approach me to ask if I had news. I would suggest, "Why don't you call the attorneys that are representing the class or any one of the four lead plaintiffs that represent you?" The typical response to my suggestion was, "They are not representing us, they are only looking out for themselves," or something of the sort.

Not one to be shy, I also told them that if they stood up to the company and the attorneys representing them, and demanded information then maybe they'd get it instead of sniffing around for rumors. I asked a few if they thought the silence meant the attorneys were fighting for them or in cahoots with Coke instead. The people always replied they imagined the lawyers were "in bed" with the company, not fighting the good fight.

My heart grew sad when I thought of the blacks in this country that would rather sit back and wait on a system that has never worked on their behalf to render a righteous judgment. *Where did all the fear come from? And for those who called themselves children of God, how could they rationalize their fear?*

While many blacks in the company were afraid to face their fears, I knew that if God is for you, then foolish is the man [or company] that stands against you. At the same time I wondered in the midst of one of the largest, public racial discrimination lawsuits, with scandal after scandal being uncovered, who would help me lift Jesus?

One day, a sister approached me with a smile that gleamed as bright as a full moon on a summer evening. She introduced herself and told me how proud she was of me. Her focused demeanor caught my attention. I could tell that she was speaking freely from her heart. I ignored our surroundings for a few moments to give her the respect her eyes asked for.

She told me how much her family prayed for me and for the cause for which God had obviously placed in my life. She spoke very softly, but her words rang loud in my heart. I needed a word of encouragement and there she was. When she finished speaking, she gently reached over and placed an envelope in my hand, looked straight into my eyes and said, "Thank you, for all that you have done."

Curious about what was in the envelope, I opened it. I read the card and my heavy heart ached. Her words showed she clearly depicted someone that understood my pain and was willing to let me know just how much they appreciated the suffering and the sacrifice I endured. The card read, *"Hi Greg, I am too long and far too late in writing this note to you. I should have written you two years ago. I want to thank you for being such a strong, Godly vessel of hope for the hundreds of blacks at Coke who were and are too afraid, for whatever reasons to come forward. It is sad that so many of them are trapped by fear. You are a shining example of what God wants us to be, not fearing men and systems, but God. Thank you for standing. Thank you for your stamina. I pray without ceasing for you and your family. Thank you for listening to the Lord."*

Just when I needed a reason to smile, God sent an angel to lift my burdens. I will forever be a witness that Jesus never fails. He may not be there when you want him, but he will be there right on time. I found so much peace in remembering the testimony of others who've been through struggles that seem larger than life, only to find out in the end that there is no struggle larger than Christ. I decided when I knew of nothing else to do, I would call on the name of Jesus, for He was my

rock in this weary land and shelter in the time of a storm.

Chapter 14

A Settlement in Principle

On November 16th, 2000, a press conference was held at the Sheraton Hotel in downtown Atlanta. In the conference, the attorneys would release some details about the settlement. The news about the release was broadcast in the media and while I did not know exactly what to expect, I knew that the attorneys did not get anything close to what the case was worth.

I distinctly remember all eight plaintiffs being together for the very first time in Atlanta and Cyrus opening the meeting by stating that the case was worth about $20 million dollars, but [we] must find a way to get the company to think outside of the box. I knew then he had no inkling of the pain that racial discrimination causes. Even then it seemed such a low number to place on the lives of more than 2000 blacks. Although the attorneys were known for settling prior class-action lawsuits, I doubted they really understood the pain of the plaintiffs. They did not know how it felt to be black so I thought it would be hard for them to fervently represent us according to their hearts and the law.

334

I waited until I was absolutely sure that the numbers I heard represented the truth. After speaking with Mr. Gary and his attorneys, I learned that the case settled for $192.5 million dollars and only $58.7 million dollars in compensatory damages. I wondered where would the other $133.8 million dollars that was not represented in the cash figure go.

I soon learned that $79 million dollars went toward a number of programs that the company agreed to establish as a way of trying to create a more diverse environment. The agreement also awarded $23.7 million dollars in back pay, but there was a catch to receiving this money. Coke could award any amount of money it wanted to the black associates, but if the associates disagreed with the amount of money they were receiving, each associate would then be forced to hire an individual attorney. Basically, in separate lawsuits each associate would have to prove that he or she were worthy of his or her back pay.

The cash part of the settlement also included a $10 million dollar promotional achievement award fund that would be distributed over a decade at Coke's discretion as bonuses to black employees who were promoted and who succeeded in their new jobs. This was one of the most sickening parts of the agreement. This fund would be awarded to blacks who received jobs that blacks did not normally get. If they received an evaluation rating where they at least met the requirements of the position and were in the position for at least a year, they would then be issued some of this $10 million dollar fund. Coke even went as far as saying that if the money at the end of the 10-year period was not all gone; the remaining amount would then be given to some local black colleges.

What were the attorneys thinking when they made such a deal? How does giving money to the black colleges help the blacks that have been discriminated against? Yes, the students and the colleges deserve as much help as possible, but giving money to colleges and rectifying racial discrimination issues were two separate things. Surely colleges needed funding. Surely they should not be waiting for ten-year-old road kill from a lawsuit against the race they seek to educate. Why wait to see if blacks excel for ten years – why not deal with both issues in a timely and effective manner.

I was not at all shocked with the outcome of the settlement. After learning what the attorneys who represented the class were truly like, I did not expect much from them. It seemed to me that on the journey to fame, fortune and notoriety, integrity was a victim. Even officers of the courts seemed to prefer ego boosts to following the letter of the law. While shades of grey are certainly open for interpretation, Jesus will be the ultimate judge.

When I considered the $20.6 million the handful of attorneys would be receiving, I couldn't help but compare it to that which would be spread among 2000 blacks. It was nearly ¼ of what the 2000 workers would be compensated with in terms of $58.7 million in compensatory awards and $23.7 million in back pay.

I wondered if these dollar amounts were really what would be paid out. While reportedly one of the largest settlements of its kind in history, I wondered if it would be what we'd hoped for – change. I doubted this money and the stipulations for its distribution would really bring about the change that the other plaintiffs and I were aiming for. After all, a historically large settlement was not our goal – change was.

While I hoped change would come and that the world would see it, I wondered if the snow jobs would continue instead. Money was no fix if the cover up carried on. We did not expect or like the fact that the lawyers were announcing that an agreement in principle had been reached. We wanted a real, valid, tangible settlement that would constitute real change, not just words meant to appease those who'd been hurt. We didn't want a settlement in principle and a settlement agreed upon to the public without discussing it with us first. Settlement in principle meant that hopefully nobody in the class would dig in and scrutinize the difference in money for programs verses real change and compensation.

For the plaintiffs, the settlement was not just about dollars. There was nothing in writing to protect the jobs of the blacks that were currently working in the company. The others and myself certainly didn't want a gag order that would keep vital information from reaching the people who might benefit from the lawsuit.

I firmly felt the settlement reached by the attorneys benefited the attorneys more than the lead plaintiffs, and certainly more than the perspective class members. Before filing the lawsuit, I researched all phases of a class action lawsuit. Through that research I realized what amount the attorneys would probably have taken from the overall settlement. I believe that a successful lawsuit should be one where all parties are pleased with the cash awards as well as the programs designed to bring true change in the company. In this case the numbers looked good on paper but were misleading to both the public and the people the lawsuit represented. It did not come close to getting what the case was worth for the class members.

The night the settlement was announced I received calls from many major newspapers and magazines asking for my comment on the settlement. Never one to treat anything about the case lightly, I answered them honestly. I told each of them I thought the attorneys did not fight for the people and that each of us should be concerned with the message that The Coca-Cola Company had just sent to the world.

Doug Ivester was given a package to leave the company as large as or even larger than the cash amount the case settled for. *Is The Coca-Cola Company suggesting that it cared more about one privileged man than all 2000 blacks represented by the suit?* Actions speak louder than words. The organization had a golden opportunity to shine, but in fact, company stock raised little after this even.

On November 17th, 2000, the leaders of The Coca-Cola Company called a meeting to inform associates about the details of the lawsuit.

This meeting was via teleconference from headquarters in Atlanta and included employees across the country. Initially I did not plan to attend, but curiosity got the better of me and I attended to hear how the leaders would share the news.

It was just a few minutes past the time the meeting was set to begin when I arrived. I was told the room was full and was directed to the overflow room. I heard this gentleman clearly and realized he was only doing his job, but my feet kept walking. I reached the auditorium door and a sister there told me, "Yes we are full, but you can come in." We shared a smile as she opened the door and I entered the meeting.

The auditorium was one of the prettiest rooms on the campus. Being a Kappa Alpha Psi man, red was one of my favorite colors. The auditorium's carpet was red like an elegant theater. The meeting had not yet started and so I walked down the steps to find a seat. The tension in the room was so thick you could have cut it with a knife. Pure silence. That familiar angry tension showed across the faces of most whites. Conversely, the blacks smiled and waved as I passed each row.

Clearly some were angry that I was present. I was not afraid. I had long ago learned to ignore the angry looks and find peace instead of discomfort in their shadow. Today more than ever I was focused on the positive, not the hatred.

I found a seat by a sister I had spoken to about the meeting that morning. She waved and smiled with pleasure that I had decided to come. The meeting started shortly after I sat down. Company Chairman, Mr. Daft, President Jack Stahl along with Carl Ware, the highest ranking black in the company, hosted the meeting. They took turns discussing parts of the lawsuit. Hearing their voices, I knew the company felt that it had come out on top.

Of course they felt like victors. The Coca-Cola Company escaped without paying one cent for punitive damages. The leaders were very careful with their words and appeared to be genuine with the deliveries of their message. I, on the other hand, knew a lot more about the lawsuit and was able to identify where the leaders were shying away from key details.

The employees were very attentive and asked excellent questions during the Q&A session. Many of the blacks wanted to know what was

341

next. One sister asked the question, *"If the lawsuit did not make the company step back and take a look at how it treats blacks, then when was the company ever going to correct its discriminatory practices?"* Many whites expressed their disapproval of the lawsuit by asking questions like, *"Why were all of the blacks getting paid?"* Some of them even showed their legal ignorance with many of their comments. I remember one white associate stating that because of the lawsuit, her manager was afraid to discipline black associates who were not meeting the standards of their job. Personally, I felt that her comments reflected a bit of bad judgment. If any manager, free from color, does not know how to discipline any employee that was not up to par in his or her job, then maybe that manager does not need to be managing.

It was interesting to watch how the leaders of the company made eye contact when a difficult question was raised from the audience. I was disturbed when the president of the company suggested that he would leave it up to each individual to share in their communities how Coke got itself into this situation. I was not at all pleased with that statement. I knew better than anyone why and how the company got in this mess. I decided to speak.

I was not sure what I was going to say, nor was I afraid. I remembered my mother telling me there was never a time when Jesus would leave me or not show up. I prayed when I rose to address the employees of The Coca-Cola Company. God would decrease my physical presence and increase His Holy Spirit instead.

When I rose I could hear the crowd gasp collectively as I stood for a few minutes before I was recognized to speak. I remember leaning over to take the microphone, not sure exactly what I was going to say. So, I decided to speak from my heart. I shared how I grew up drinking Coke products in a small town in South Carolina. I told how excited I was to be offered a job at the very company that was so prevalent in my childhood. I shared that although I had a Master's degree, I was not ashamed to enter the company at its lowest level, for I knew I had prepared myself and it would only be a matter of time before I would be given an opportunity to show what I was capable of doing. In reality I told them how the weeks, months and then years passed, and I continued to be given countless reasons that just did not make sense as to why I was not being promoted. I then told the forum that I got so tired of my manager playing with my life, I got angry. I decided that if one manager wanted to ignore me, then I would dedicate my time to get the attention of the entire company and the world. I told them that I spoke with everyone in my chain of command trying to get a feel for what I needed to do to better provide for my family however, it seemed the more people I spoke with, the more I heard that I wasn't the right "fit." Everywhere I turned I kept hearing I was not the right "fit."

I shared that here I was with a Master's degree and the only use the company had for me was as a security officer. I commented on disrespectful moments like managers conducting phone conversations in the middle of a discussion with me. I ended by challenging each officer that the next time an associate walks into their office, to try not to focus on the uniform that he or she might wear, or the salary range they probably are in, but rather focus on the character of the individual that stands or sits before you and base your decision on that.

I sat down and the room exploded with applause. I was shocked and afraid because suddenly I realized that I did not understand why the entire auditorium was on its feet applauding. The room erupted and yells and cheers carried on. While I was in the room, for whatever reason it seemed like I was not in my body. I could hear something coming out of my mouth, but I could not remember what I'd said. I remember all the sisters that were sitting around me crying and applauding as they stood. My face was wet from the tears of faces pressed against mine with hugs and kisses of appreciation.

I still was not clear about why all these people were standing, applauding and crying. I know I never physically left the room, but I did leave my body. After all the applauding, Mr. Daft stood and said, "Greg, I don't make shallow promises. I think I can learn a lot from you and certainly you can learn a lot from me, so I will mentor you." I raised my hand to acknowledge that I had heard him and the room again exploded with applause. It was an experience I know I will never forget.

I waited a few minutes then left the room. As I walked up the stairs, many of the whites who peered at me with hatred when I entered were now red-cheeked and teary eyed. Jesus showed up in the midst of a Coca-Cola Company meeting. He came unannounced when no one was expecting Him. He spoke through the lowly bottom-rung security guard. He used the least expected person to get the attention of one of the richest, most powerful and influential companies in the world. God used me.

While I was no one in the eyes of the leaders, I was someone when I stood on post each day to make sure that company security policies were being followed. In the twinkling of an eye, I became the most powerful person in the company all because I feared God and trusted Him enough to deal with man. Oh! How I thanked and praised Him for showing up when He did. I didn't mind being used.

I wanted people of all colors, shapes and sizes to realize that a title of a position does not make you anyone special. God sees and believes that we are all special. Over the last few years of my life, I saw how Christ humbled me to a point where I could be used to get a message to a powerful company. I struggled to understand why I was going through such unfair situations until this meeting. I continued to give His name all the praise and the glory. I no longer saw my trials and tribulations as negative, but rather as vehicles to strengthen my faith. I now had a clear understanding of why God places obstacles in front of his sons and daughters.

As I exited the auditorium, my heart was full. Nevertheless, I was not prepared for what happened next. As I pushed open the second door, which leads back into the main building, there stood a group of employees waiting to embrace me. All races alike; first Indian, then Black then White hugged me with tear-filled eyes and told me of their own personal pains and how they had identified with my words.

Nobody cared about color – we were all the same. It was one of the most moving experiences I had ever been a part of. Their eyes were windows to the struggles, frustrations and disappointments they experienced. I was delighted to know there were witnesses unafraid to share that they too had struggled with the pains of inequality.

In a strange way, I felt the chairman of the company, Mr. Daft, also shared the pain of the people. Perhaps that was why he had offered to mentor me. It was a gesture I did not expect, but again it warranted a standing ovation from the crowd.

As I stood post later that day, I was overwhelmed with the number of employees that stopped to share their personal experience with the 'Good Ole Boy System'. Instead of the looks of hatred I had grown accustomed to; people approached me and introduced themselves.

Suddenly it appeared that no one cared that I was black. People responded with their hearts. No longer did associates care who saw them speaking to me. This was a change from past experiences when my "friends" would be watching over their shoulders to see who might be noticing that they were talking to me. Instead of discomfort, people now were at ease with me. I openly welcomed the presence of each employee that wanted to share or just stop and say hello.

Days after Mr. Daft made the offer to mentor me; I began receiving calls from the media. Most were interested in knowing if Mr. Daft had contacted me since that time. It was the holiday season of 2000 and I imagined he was very busy. I knew the company was working on closing some big deals before year-end. I hoped he took me seriously because I telephoned his office several times trying to set up an appointment.

After meeting with Mr. Gary in reference to the mentoring process, it was decided that it was not a good idea for me to meet with the chairman and other vice presidents alone. Although I personally welcomed the challenge, Mr. Gary believed it was just a trick trying to win me over so blacks would accept the settlement offer without resistance.

I sent an e-mail to Mr. Daft sharing that because of the many legal parameters; I would like my attorneys to be present when I met with him and his group. He immediately responded and stated that because of the lawsuit neither he nor his staff could meet with any of the attorneys who had been involved with the lawsuit. This was no surprise. Yet, I was puzzled as to how he thought it was acceptable for him to mentor the person that started the lawsuit and ignore my legal team.

It seemed the company was going to try and find a way to make it appear it was I that refused to be mentored, rather than he or the company being the inflexible. I guess that was why the chairman and the corporate attorneys felt it was safe to forward this e-mail to me:

> Greg,
> I want to reiterate my commitment to development opportunities for all Coca-Cola associates and to let you know that my offer to mentor you remains in place. I appreciate your desire to discuss your case with me and I know that you understand that the litigation prevents that. But I am disappointed that you decided not to go forward with lunch to discuss career development. I was looking forward to starting

the mentoring process with you. Mentoring is one of several important tools that will help us realize our organization's potential through maximizing the capabilities of our people and I believe it will be of great value to the Company. Greg, if you change your mind and would like to discuss career development, the offer stands open to you. Simply call my office and we will arrange a meeting. In addition, I want to extend my best wishes to you and your family for a very happy holiday season.
Regards.

Doug Daft.

This email confirmed his offer was nothing more than a hoax designed to try to win over the associates at the meeting. Although I never had a desire to discuss my case with him, I felt I was blessed with one of the greatest trial attorneys if that particular desire did arise. The language of the e-mail was that same old typical corporate garbage used when white folks want a black person to think they have their best interest at heart. I responded with the following e-mail:

December 12, 2000

To: Mr. Daft, Chairman
From: Gregory A. Clark
Re: Response to Memo

Thank you again for responding and also for understanding my position with the litigations. I, too, continue to look forward to the time when we can begin our mentoring process free from discussing any parts of my case or the lawsuit. I apologize for the disappointment you felt by the postponing of our initial luncheon. I never intended to cause you any discomfort. I have been a committed and dedicated associate to this company for several years and through it all, it is safe to say that the disappointment you felt about one meeting being cancelled, I've felt too many times. I often pray that God keeps you humble and gives you the strength and the vision to lead the company to heights that Wall Street has never imagined. There are many legal issues that have prolonged our first meeting. Please make no mistakes that I have or I am taking your offer lightly. I take my career as well as career development extremely serious. It was the very questions about my career and career development that will later in the correct forum prove to be the nucleus of the lawsuit. While litigations are hindering us from meeting, I am continuing to aggressively search for a career opportunity within the company. Over the past few years I have had the opportunity to speak with thousands of past and present black and white Coca-Cola employees. It is a mutual belief that the leader for the future must be one that will place people before profit, not profit before people. I agree there is a lot that we can learn from each other, but somewhere, somehow along the line to achieving an environment in which all associates can be proud of, free from color, some feelings must be hurt, sir. I wish you a very Merry Christmas and a peaceful and Happy New Year. God bless you and your family. Take Care!

Chapter 15

Sprinkling Water on a Corporate Fire

Over the years of fighting for equality, I met many journalists; some good and some not-so-good ones. I imagine objectivity is hard even in such a job since we are only human after all. Perhaps objectivity wanes when reporters allow themselves to become personally involved with a story. It seemed to me a particular reporter for the *Atlanta Journal Constitution* now wrote reports strongly favoring one side and presenting jaded information. In my opinion, they did not present the truth to the public and potential class members. However, as a God-fearing man I knew the tricks being played could not withstand the wrath of Christ. Regardless, how unequal some situations may appear to be, one must always remember that Jesus is the equalizer.

Despite biased reporters, there were odd occasions when I met a journalist who did his or her research. Robin McDonald, a staff reporter for Atlanta-based *Daily Report* had been covering the case for some time. She was one of the few reporters I spoke to over the years who possessed the desire to bring the truth to light regardless of how deep or hard she had to work to find it. Her questioning was different than that of the other reporters who called.

One day when we spoke, she said she found it interesting that Mr. Daft would have made any offers to the man who instigated the lawsuit. I think she was even more curious as to how he expected to mentor me with a powerful attorney like Mr. Willie Gary in my realm of counsel. When she heard of the mentoring offer, she made calls to The Coca-Cola Company to try to pinpoint when Mr. Daft would begin this mentoring process.

I presume it was media calls to the chairman's office that stirred the pot. Eventually, I received calls from the offices of the chairman and executives designed to determine how best to approach me. Meanwhile Robin continued to publish reports that clearly depicted fairness and were directly related to the behavior within the company. Even the *Atlanta Journal Constitution* appeared to have less favorable slant and fewer articles running. It almost seemed that their bubble had been deflated and they realized they could no longer get by with just publishing information that would only benefit The Coca-Cola

Company. The primary reporter assigned to cover the case went oddly silent.

I thanked God for Robin and her tenacity, commitment to her career, and the respect that she openly shared for others in providing truth and clarity to a situation that was intentionally designed to confuse and frustrate the public. Each time The Coca-Cola Company released information to the public, she would dig just a little deeper and uncover essential information – and often missing – information. Usually it was information that the public and class members needed to know.

As the days passed, associates continued to stop and greet me at my post. They'd linger and chat for a few moments to share how they felt during the meeting in which I spoke. Many of the stories were similar to those I'd encountered while researching the issues at Coke.

What amazed me was not so much the stories these people shared, but the fact they were the same people who had been passing me in the hallways for years and said nothing. I had assumed they were all doing wonderfully and did not have issues with the system because that was the impression they gave. Little did I know how many of the people wearing "I'm ok" masks were actually also shackled by the chains of discrimination in The Coca-Cola Company. I discovered many of these people were silent for so long because they felt they had more to lose than gain because the inequalities and unfairness were so prevalent in the company.

I didn't just hear from blacks. While the unfair treatment to blacks may be more blatant, there were many whites and people of other races who were also not pleased with the way in which the company operated in the arenas exposed by the lawsuit. I listened carefully to the stories they told. I was careful also with regard to who I trusted because I knew caution was imperative in the war for equality in which I was fighting.

On January 18, 2001, one day after more than 2000 settlement packages were said to have been mailed to the class members, I was eating lunch in the USA building-dining hall. An associate approached me to tell me about a report that was recently generated. The report generated just a day after the settlement packets were mailed allegedly showed pay adjustments made for many white females in the company.

355

I later looked on the intranet and externally but could find no information about this increase. But, I was not surprised.

In corporate America, the white male is 'large and in charge.' I had little doubt that females, white or otherwise, were underpaid when compared to white males in the company. I heard enough venting to believe that was the case at The Coca-Cola Company as well as in many other companies across the nation. I knew that the company's research was not limited to pay disparities by race, but in relation to gender also.

A rumor had surfaced after the lawsuit went public that white females in the company intended to file a lawsuit as soon as the lawsuit was settled. As far-fetched as that rumor sounded, I learned many years ago there was often some shred of truth contained in most rumors. And in this case, I knew some of the white females who were secretly plotting against the company. While many people in the company guessed that any leaks probably came from blacks in leadership positions, I knew that was not usually the case.

It had been weeks since I addressed the company at the November meeting and people still wanted me to know they appreciated all I shared. People of all races approached me. One comment made by a white male will never leave me. He was well dressed and looked me straight in the eye. He said he had been waiting for weeks since the meeting for an opportunity to speak to me alone. He wanted me to know what I had said had changed his life forever. He spoke his piece, smiled, and then shook my hand and turned and walked away.

I wish I could remember all the details of what I had said that day in that meeting, but I soon found peace in knowing that although I could not remember, God touched many people's lives that day. God turned up. Even the company's most prominent attorneys now appeared to have a newfound respect for me. If they had only given me an opportunity to share with them before, they would have known just how pure my heart was.

After receiving the settlement packages, blacks in the company became very upset. I received many negative comments about the "agreement." No one understood why the attorneys, who were being paid to represent the people, would agree to such a small amount and release such a confusing document. It had been a long struggle for many blacks, and time after time they were asked to sit back and trust the company and the plaintiff's attorneys to do right by them.

Now reality hits. After waiting so patiently, the agreement in the end did more to protect the defendant (The Coca-Cola Company) than it did to help the class members. There was no disputing that fact. It is my belief that the attorneys partnered with Coke to get the dollar amount they themselves desired, and then abandoned the interests of the class.

Apparently, I was not the only one who reached this conclusion. The people knew what the attorneys did and were not afraid to voice their opinions. One of the most disturbing things about the settlement was the amount of empty intellect the company and the attorneys actually gave the people. There were countless senseless clauses placed in the agreement that had nothing to do with racial discrimination. *Why were they there? Was it carelessness? Was it an attempt to bamboozle and confuse people?* Whatever the reason, I believe the attorneys only wanted to get their money from this case in order to easily finance future cases that were placed in their hands as a result of this one.

I prayed that God would give the victims of this crime a clear understanding of what had transpired, as well as the courage to make a statement to The Coca-Cola Company and the attorneys, who I believed betrayed them and tried to hide behind the very law they were sworn to uphold. Instead of obeying or upholding the law, I believe they intentionally misled common people, who in most cases could not represent themselves. The attorneys also needed to be reminded that God's children are precious to Him and are not to be taken advantage of.

In January 2001, the lawsuit had not been settled, although the majority of the class members had received their notices. I had a funny feeling that the case was far from over and that further company problems were getting ready to surface. I started noticing peculiar behavior exhibited by many leaders I saw in the building. By this time, I was not a stranger to the ways of corporate America, nor was I naïve to the games of its bureaucracy.

It was almost as if many of them knew that the company was trying to pull wool over the eyes of the people. It often seemed like people were just wondering how much I knew. I always smiled and greeted each of the leaders professionally. Many I did not know personally called me by my first name and made an effort to be familiar with my face. Sadly, there were still some whites in the company who did not accept blacks or other minorities. Their lack of acceptance had nothing to do with the educational level or lifestyle of blacks, but rather with instilled racial biases that no discrimination lawsuit, judge or chairman was going to change. And so, I watched the behavior of the various people and walks of life that passed me each day on my post.

Listening to the complaints of folks day in and day out, I could not help but think back to April 2000 when the Mehri Group of attorneys announced it would be in the best interest of the class if Plaintiff X, Plaintiff Y and I were removed as lead plaintiffs. Partial truths published in the newspapers, rumors, animosity and pure lies were just some of the things that made it hard at times to return day after day to work. In truth, all we wanted to do was protect our interests as well as the interests of the people.

It took almost eight months to finally have the very thing I accused the attorneys of doing in April 2000 to play out like a well-written movie script. Now, countless blacks and some whites in the company suggested that the attorneys did just what I had said they were doing. They realized they were lining their pockets and not representing the plaintiffs or class well.

The $192.5 million dollar settlement was just a bunch of inflated numbers, and a lot of hot air coming from the Mehri Group of attorneys and The Coca-Cola Company. Even the attorneys knew that the settlement was not going to be looked upon as good legal work. It was obvious the attorneys wanted to secure as much money as they could for themselves and while making it appear as if The Coca-Cola Company was committed to diversity and blacks. So, they released an inflated number to the public. Of the $192.5 million, less than half went directly to the class. The attorneys did this before and knew how to maximize their earnings while inflating the settlement numbers and burying much of it into "program" funds within the company.

Meetings were again held at churches with a focus on prayer and then discussion of the issues blacks continued to face. I was not fooled by the initial response of my people. While many seemed eager to attend at first, I knew that the meeting would include only a few. Sadly, many of us find courage for a moment to speak and often say what we think another person wants to hear, but far fewer are courageous

enough in the long run to walk the walk and not just talk the talk.

Walking the walk means taking real action and ignoring one's fear.

Walking the walk takes sacrifice and is usually a long journey because

real change is a slow process.

History has shown that when blacks fight for justice and equality

the initial fervor is strong. But when things get rough over time, many

abandon the fight or simply run out of time, energy and resources to

continue. The same was true at The Coca-Cola Company. The long-

suffering soldiers were far fewer than the initial idealists who said they

wanted to join the cause.

For months nothing appeared in the media about the lawsuit. Most

blacks in The Coca-Cola Company grew impatient. Those silent all this

time now began to ask me questions. They did not seem to care about

the toll the struggle had taken on the lives of those that started the

lawsuit and continued to fight. Lady One lost more than any of the

eight plaintiffs, and she was still holding on for justice.

I will always have a great deal of respect for her. She could have

turned her back on the people she was fighting for. She could have believed the attorneys' lies when they said I had misinterpreted the conversation. She could have decided to stay with the Mehri Group. After all, she was laid off from the company during a downsizing period and spent more than two years jumping jobs to try and make ends meet. Glory Hallelujah! She did not complain. She accepted her losses, and they were huge, and even found ways to capitalize on them. As a single parent with a daughter in college, she depended on God to see her through this war whatever the cost. In the beginning, it was just the two of us holding on to each other as we dealt with racism in The Coca-Cola Company.

I could not understand how the four plaintiffs that chose to stay with the Mehri Group of attorneys could stand in front of the media and act as if they were truly in the trenches during any part of the lawsuit. Three of them lived out of state and the other was on leave for an extended period of time. Cyrus tried to make it appear as if his four remaining plaintiffs were the only ones involved in the lawsuit. I wished one of the reporters had asked Cyrus or one of those plaintiffs how the lawsuit started.

They chose to count their chickens before they hatched. The day of the settlement announcement, newspapers ran stories and photos of the four plaintiffs who "so proudly represented the class." Those stories were the first glimpse that many class members had of those plaintiffs. On the other hand, Lady One and I were never afraid to show our faces and own the fight. You cannot fight a war without the enemy knowing who you are especially when you claimed to walk by faith and not fear man. Long ago we had decided we would not hide in this battle.

In early March 2001, I was told that my manager, Keith Marks, wanted to see me. Someone came to relieve me of my post and I made my way to his office. When I arrived in his office, the security representative from human resources was sitting in the room. I knew Keith was up to something. I sat down and listened.

Keith told me that it had come to his attention that I was overheard by an associate who passed by me while I was standing post. He said I was discussing money and a lawsuit with another associate and did not look at him passing by nor ask for his badge. Keith said the associate claimed to have intentionally walked by again with his ID badge deliberately hidden in his pocket in order to get a response from me.

At this point, the human resource representative chimed and stated she met with this associate and asked him was he playing some type of game with me, to which he responded, "Yes." She said she informed him that his behavior was inappropriate.

I sat and listened quietly as these two, who obviously disliked me, tried to trump a disciplinary charge to place in my file. I saw through their intentions and simply asked why I was in the office. They both sat dumbfounded and seemed to try to back out of the situation at that point.

Before I left the room, I stated again, I was still confused as to why I was asked to meet with them. Realizing their little plan had backfired; neither said anything else. I left the office knowing that these two devils were up to no good. I also knew I had better document the entire situation on paper. I did just that.

March 9, 2001

To: Keith Marks/Security Manager
Subject: Meeting on 3/07/01

On Wednesday, March 7th, 2001, a Console Operator told me that you requested a meeting with me. Once I arrived in your office, present was the Human Resource Representative for the

Security Department. You began the meeting by stating approximately two weeks ago an associate informed you that he passed a post in which he assumed the officer was Greg Clark and he overheard [me] saying something about $8000 and a lawsuit.

The City of Atlanta in the past year has had several of its major corporations confronted with class-action lawsuits. There are several that have not yet gone public, local or national of which I have personal knowledge. You also stated this person said I did not ask him for his I.D badge. You continued by stating this same associate later came back to you and said again he passed my post and only this time he intentionally placed his I.D. badge in his pocket or out of my assumed vision to test me.

You then alleged because of this complaint I was obviously not being attentive to my duties and I had extended visitors while standing post. I immediately corrected you and asked as a practical matter I think it would be best if these accusations were treated as nothing more than accusations. The HR representative then agreed and voluntarily shared she spoke with the associate and asked him did he intentionally place his badge out of plain view in an attempt to get a response or play some type of game. He in return stated, "Yes, I did." She then stated she immediately informed him that his behavior was inappropriate.

These are provided as just a few examples of the harassment and retaliation, which have created a hostile environment since my filing of the lawsuit.

I am well aware of the position I've chosen to take against the company. I understand many are angry and wish I would go away. I cannot and wish not to change the minds of those who are not yet convinced The Coca-Cola Company is guilty of racial discrimination. However, I have a right to work in my choice of workplaces, free from a hostile environment, harassment and retaliation.

Because of the actions of the white associate who admitted he intentionally hid his badge in hopes of getting some type of reaction from me, I feel his actions constitute harassment and have helped create a hostile work environment for me.

In the past I have stressed concerns of unfair treatment to you, only to witness two days later, you and the very white male I complained about embracing and laughing as you both approached my post. Two years ago, I met with a member of the corporate security team and a Human Resources representative only after one of my fellow officers reported some comments they perceived as threats to you in regards to my safety.

At that time the gentleman from corporate security asked me to report any action I deemed unusual from any associate to management. However, because of my focus and desire to right the wrong the company has rendered, I chose to remain silent about much of the treatment I received here at headquarters from the white associates.

I am now bringing this matter to your attention as a complaint and as an example of harassment I have experienced while working here at the company after the filing of the lawsuit. I would like to be informed as to how this matter is concluded. I am appealing once again internally to you as a manager and representative of The Coca-Cola Company. Thank you for bringing this concern to my attention.

This memorandum precisely was to inform Keith I was not going to play these senseless games. Nor was I going to allow any associate, white or black, to dictate my behavior. I entered the company as a gentleman and by all means I was going to continue to conduct myself accordingly. I spoke with another member of the human resources department after sending this memorandum to my manager but it appeared that call was a mere formality. Once again, the company was simply trying to cover itself should this ever be brought up as harassment.

In early 2001, a new position became available in the security department. The job was for an Operations Manager at job grade 10. Starting pay would be approximately $40,000 more than I was currently earning. After all these years, I still wanted a chance to use my skills and prove myself. So, I wrote to Keith requesting a meeting with him to discuss the position. I realized that I was definitely the last person he would want to meet with; nevertheless, I requested to see him. I wrote:

March 26, 2001

To: Keith Marks
Subject: Operations Manager Position

I have received your e-mail in reference to the Operations Manager's position and I am confused and concerned about several items listed on the posting. I am requesting a meeting with you as the hiring manager at your convenience, to discuss my concerns.
Thank You!

He replied and wrote:

March 26, 2001

To: Greg Clark
Subject: Re: HQs Security Department Operations Manager Posting

Greg thanks for taking the time to review the POP posting and contacting me.
However, I anticipate a very busy week and therefore I would like you to e-mail me your questions and/or concerns regarding the new position and the POP posting.

Once I've had a chance to review your questions and/or concerns then I'll coordinate both of our schedules to set up a time, in the near future, that is mutually convenient for us to meet. Also, by knowing and understanding your questions and/or concerns prior to the meeting, it will make for a more productive meeting to address those questions and/or concerns.

Thanks,
Keith

My reply was:

March 28, 2001

To: Keith Marks
Subject: Re: HQs Security Department Operations Manager Posting

I would like to sit and talk with you, the hiring manager for a position that currently is under your direction and supervision in our department. Yes, I have questions; however, my follow up questions and responses will stem from your comments during our meeting. As much as I would like to prepare a list of questions, it will be useless in reference to bringing clarity to my concerns.

Thanks!

He wrote back and stated:

March 28, 2001

To: Greg Clark
Subject: Operations Manager Posting

Greg, your request for a meeting is not a problem and I fully understand that you may have some follow-up questions and/or responses generated by our discussion. However, I would still like you to e-mail or forward to me your initial questions and/or concerns so that we can have a starting point for the meeting, which will make for a more productive meeting. I do not agree that having your questions prior to the meeting "will be useless..."

Thanks,
Keith

Although little things had changed within the company, it was still window dressing for the public's benefit not real, substantial, incremental change. In March 2001, the company announced the appointment of an Advisory Council to oversee the company as it fulfilled its obligations under the settlement agreement. Wow! All this process and oversight and yet the leaders continued to say they had done nothing wrong.

I studied this board and found that it contained people who would do an excellent job if given a chance. The board consisted of black, white, Hispanic, and Native American men and women. I am curious why The Coca-Cola Board of directors or leadership for that matter, did not reflect the same diversity. Again, I contest this was just a maneuver to make the company look like it had changed.

If the company felt so strongly about diversity, certainly its Board should represent that. Over the years, I learned that most executive boards having one black man or woman and one white or Hispanic female probably were not reflective of companies with good diversity in its ranks. Instead they likely had a host of discrimination charges hidden deep within the core of the company.

Why not have a board of all women, some white and some black? Or what about a board that only had one or two white men? I wonder.

There were many quiet battles still being fought within the company. Some blacks were still catching hell from white managers who were not willing to accept the fact the company had been exposed. One sister had been fighting an individual battle within her group for years. She was not willing to allow whites or blacks, who were obviously not qualified, to evaluate her poorly.

Could it possibly be that after a particular person has been identified as a problem by management, the human resources representative then begins to work with that manager to try to find ways to terminate that employee? Or was the tactic to simply place the employee under severe stress and mental abuse so he or she would leave the company permanently or on short-term disability?

This very sister, who addressed the forum at two of the last three shareholder meetings, had become so frustrated that she appealed to the top leadership of the company.

As the date for the Fairness Hearing on May 29, 2001 approached, more associates were voicing their opinions about the settlement and what they thought was fair. Many of the whites in The Coca-Cola Company did not have a problem with the eight plaintiffs who came forward with the lawsuit, but were strongly against 2000 blacks getting $3700 a year for compensatory damages. They also didn't like the idea of an undisclosed amount of money for back pay for doing nothing more than being born black.

I understood their paradigm. For more than two years, I had the opportunity to watch the behavior of blacks in the company. When the lawsuit went public, many didn't believe anyone could beat the company. I understood what it was like to be the focus of scrutiny. When I was focused on, I focused on Jesus. It was God not me who made things happen so the world would finally hear these matters. It was going to take more than shuffling top leaders and creating new programs. Token programs would not be mistaken for real change.

After reading what the attorneys and the mediator had concluded as a settlement package, I knew the Fairness Hearing would be a circus. Only twenty-three of approximately 2000 blacks opted out of the lawsuit. I arrived in the courtroom that morning a few minutes after the session was scheduled to start. The entire room was filled. Some of these black faces I had not seen in several years, and others I saw daily on "The Plantation", but they never bothered to speak to me. One side of the room was 98% black, the other attorney and decision-makers side was 98% white.

Standing in the Federal Courtroom on Mitchell Street in Atlanta, I gazed at the beautiful paintings on the walls, assuming they were current and former judges for they covered the room from one corner to the next. Only one of those paintings hanging was of a black person. After seeing how the attorneys originally hired to fight for justice for the people had obviously partnered with Coke, I had a pretty good idea of what the Judge's decision would be. I knew some of the very people he would hear from today had lied and intentionally distorted and kept many facts about the case from him.

Before taking my seat, I mingled. I was pleased so many took the time to come out although I knew the majority of them were just there to make sure their money was on the way. As the day began, the first person to speak was Cyrus Mehri. As I expected, he began telling lies. One of the first lies was that the lawsuit was started by one of his female lead plaintiffs who wanted change for herself and her people in the company. The truth was that this plaintiff was out of the company on disability leave before the lawsuit was filed, and only worked a few days before she decided her environment was too stressful for her to work. So in reality, she had no contact with the people he said she wanted to help.

Once upon a time, this lie would have upset me but I'd traveled a long, dark, rough, lonely road and I was not about to let trickery and deceit spoil the day. I knew how the fight had started. So, I sat and smiled to myself as the day passed. I thought about the time nearly four years ago when three now-terminated blacks and I sat in our very first meeting wondering what could be done to improve the conditions for blacks at The Coca-Cola Company. At this meeting, it was the right to sue letter that I had researched and received in October of 1998, which sparked everyone's interest in the case.

As I listened to the opposing sides share their points of view, it became more apparent a partnership definitely formed between attorneys on both sides. Even more sickening was the fact the mediator, the plaintiff's attorneys and the attorneys representing the company acted as if they had an early breakfast together and could not wait until the judge let everyone know he approved the settlement so they could all celebrate privately together. I was not the only one who noticed the unusually close connection between the sides. It was so obvious that many of the blacks in attendance asked me if I felt like the entire day was just for show and all minds were decided a long time ago. While I was pleased that the charade did not fool people, the class members'

hands were tied. They could do nothing.

It was August 2, 2001 when I imagined Keith felt it was time for

him to drop his bomb. The e-mail was sent late in the evening after my

shift ended and it read as follows:

ATTN: HQs Security Associates

I am pleased to announce that Mr. Chandler Beacon will be
joining the Company as the HQs Security Operations Manager
effective Monday, August 6th, reporting to me.
Chandler 's fifteen years of professional security operations and
management experience includes various positions of increasing
responsibilities, including positions as a U.S. Air Force Security
Forces Shift Commander, Operations Officer, Staff Officer and
Squadron Commander.

He has attended and instructed numerous specialized security
and law enforcement courses during his military career.
Chandler holds an M.S. degree in International Relations from
Troy State University, a B.A. degree in Criminology from St.
Leo College and a B.A. in Political Science from the University
of South Florida. Most recently, Chandler was enrolled in Law
School at the Oklahoma City School of Law.

In Chandler's new operational management position, he will
manage the day-to-day operations and activities of the HQs
Security Department. Additionally, Chandler will assist as we
continue our transition to the Service Source, specifically as we
review and refine current processes, implement new processes
and continually update and improve our service offerings to our
clients.

Please join me in welcoming Chandler to the Company, the Service Source and our HQs Security team.

Keith

I was interested in knowing if Keith really thought this announcement was a surprise to anyone. Several months before the position was posted this man was seen with Keith many times on "The Plantation". He was black. It was also learned that the two had been stationed on the same Air Force base at one time.

Knowing Keith as I did, I had no doubt he personally recruited Chandler for the position. Keith went out of his way to recruit a black male with my educational background. Never in the past had a hiring memo included the display of the new manager's educational credentials for the entire security team to see. It was obvious Keith and the men he reported to were determined and would even risk losing their jobs just so long as Gregory A. Clark did not get the opportunity to prove himself in a management position.

This was not a surprise to me, nor was I upset. I was well aware of how Coke did business. What I found more interesting was the fact there was no system in place to check or confirm policies were being adhered to. These racist white men had been in the system long enough to know they could do whatever they wanted. They knew that neither they nor the company would be penalized. They were wrong. It only took the racist acts by one of them to expose an entire company. And still they tried to play games within The Coca-Cola Company.

A few days passed when I first heard that some of the checks had been received by a few blacks in the company. Suddenly it was socially acceptable to publicly discuss the money they would receive from the lawsuit. The whispers were loud and filled with joy. I was very pleased to see my brothers and sisters smiling and enjoying life, although I knew the money the case settled for was not close to what they deserved.

Their acceptance of less than what was fair and happiness at having received anything was an example of institutionalized racism. I saw the many different ways the company discriminated against blacks, but what was even more disheartening was the disrespect and discrimination most blacks were willing to endure. While many of them knew this was simply hush money, they took it gladly and didn't seem to care that real change was not likely to come.

An officer I knew for years quickly signed his disclaimer letter and was eager to receive his check. Another associate had contractors start work on her house and then was disturbed when her check didn't arrive quickly enough for the contractor's timetable. Most blacks were counting their chickens and making plans to spend the money that was coming. Many of these people were unwilling to speak up about discriminatory experiences, but now were happy to receive their payout – not because they spoke up but because of the color of their skin. They seemed to find it harder and harder to look at me or speak to me these days.

I really wanted to ask them how they felt about benefiting without fighting. Although the payout was less than deserved, it was more money than some ever received in a lump sum. I also wondered how the blacks who worked in positions such as the internal EEOC and diversity in the workplace group felt knowing they did everything in their power to discourage me from feeling I had been racially discriminated against. What were their feelings now that it all had played out and they too would be receiving thousands?

I'd often see the woman that tried so desperately to get me to believe I was just an angry black man whose situation was just an isolated case. I knew the other plaintiffs did not opt out of the lawsuit, and this made me more curious as to what they were truly thinking. Part of me wanted to suggest they were the biggest hypocrites this side of the equator. However, once I studied their profiles, I knew their positions in The Coca-Cola Company were not roles they could be proud of. They were contained in roles they'd convinced themselves were necessary to find a lifestyle of success and happiness. They were not so strong for the fight as I had thought. They were held hostage in a way; hostage to lying and deceit to keep jobs that would never let them sour to their full potential.

It seemed that whether these associates made eye contact with me now depended on the white associates in their company as we passed in the halls. I wished I could have an opportunity to tell them that while they were trying to stop me from correcting a wrong, they forgot about the almighty man himself, Jesus. By this time any logical thinking person must have known I could not have been responsible for all the terrible things the company was experiencing. God has a way of getting one's attention and keeping it. After more than two years of fighting The Coca-Cola Company, I did not believe the leaders realized who was in control. I imagined they tried to label different situations that could have caused them so much pain and financial hardship. Did any of them think of divine intervention?

Days passed and more checks were received, and the smiles of the brothers and sisters in the company grew even larger. I was not fooled with their assumed looks of praise and contentment. After fighting for years and being the "scapegoat" for many associates who were not satisfied with many of my comments in public, I prayed they would not be fooled by the "hush money" the company paid.

As time went by, the checks continued to arrive. Many whites began to harbor feelings of hatred and resentment regarding the fact all blacks could be and were being paid as part of the class action suit. Only a few, however, stood to voice their concerns. I could see flashes of hatred across some of those faces still as they passed me in the halls. Years of those looks had not intimidated me and they didn't bother me now. If only they knew I wasn't paying attention to them as they glared at me. I was concerned with staying focused on God as I did my job. I thought after almost three years of being in The Coca-Cola Company

after the lawsuit went public that surely many of them would have

realized that I, a mere man, was not trying to get the company's

attention, God was.

Throughout this struggle I have learned that generally people

believe what they want to believe, and most likely that which is easiest

to comprehend and causes the least amount of involvement or effort is

normally what is chosen. After several years of embarrassing numbers

in profit performance by the company and a racial discrimination

lawsuit alerting the world to misdeeds behind the walls of the giant, the

same old games continued to be played.

Associates continued to approach me daily to stress concerns

nothing had changed in the company. Many of them felt the diversity

training programs were designed to do everything except deal with the

real issues that got the company involved in the lawsuit in the first

place. The first associates to attend the diversity training programs were

the managers in The Coca-Cola Company. After spending 2-3 days in

the class, several black managers stated it was a waste of time. They

shared many whites were angry they were being forced to attend the classes. They also shared that after attending the classes; the white managers now knew how to legally continue in their same old ways. I knew what they meant for I had first-hand experience with post-lawsuit behavior that was just as it has always been.

Chapter 16

The Collapse of an American Icon

September 11, 2001 began a normal day for me. At 10:15 a.m., I was on a break and decided to go to the Assembly Room where officers meet in the mornings for briefings and to eat. I arrived at approximately 10:20 a.m. and saw several officers staring quietly at the television. The room was never this quiet. I looked at the television and saw a building burning. In the blink of an eye, I saw a plane appear out of nowhere and vanish inside of the building beside the one that was already burning.

I was astonished and devastated, for I did not know what to think or feel. I thought for a moment we were all watching a movie someone brought in. This horror could not be real. I was sadly mistaken. The national news channel reported America had never experienced a terror attack. The news station showed the plane crashing into the World Trade Center over and over again. Each time I saw the scene the more unreal it appeared.

Next an anchorman reported there had been some sort of crash at the Pentagon in Washington, DC. Soon cameras there showed a plane crashed into the side of the historic and important building. I was

384

afraid, but I did not know what to fear. I grew angry, but I did not know where to direct that anger. More than anything, I was yet in a stubborn state of denial.

How could this be? Who or what could hate America so much they would kill innocent Americans to get attention? Where did all this hatred come from? Who would claim the responsibility for such a horrific disaster?

Time slowly passed. I observed the behavior of the officers in the room. For the first time in many years, I ignored my personal pain and all that I'd experienced at The Coca-Cola Company. I've lost loved ones and friends that were dear to me in life, so I had a thorough understanding of what the families and friends would soon experience.

I began to concentrate, meditate and pray for every person with missing loved ones. I knew it was not possible for anyone to quickly have an accurate count of Americans that were missing. I could think of nothing other than the children that kissed their parents goodbye earlier that morning, never imagining that kiss would be their last. I am certain many wives and husbands did the same that morning; never realizing it would be their last goodbye. I also couldn't forget about the parents that may have spoken to a son or daughter the prior evening not realizing it would be the last conversation they'd share with that child.

The tragic news spread around the globe. As I continued working, watching and listening, there was not a group of people whom I passed who were not talking about the incident. The associates of the company were obviously shaken and afraid, for they did not know what to expect next. The chairman of The Coca-Cola Company, Doug Daft, responded very quickly and appropriately, I thought. It seemed like only minutes after the news was reported that an e-mail to all the associates was sent, stating that because of the horrific and tragic events that had occurred, the company would be closing immediately.

It only took moments for the entire company to be evacuated. There were several different entrances to the complex, all heavily manned with security. I was stationed with five other officers and an Atlanta police officer at Marietta Street. As the associates hurried out of the building, many with broken hearts, they were crying and in shock as they told us to be very careful. I felt some of these people who had made my life a living hell at the company were very sincere in their concern and well wishes that day.

By the time I arrived home, the Federal Airline Association (FAA) had stopped every flight in this country. It was obvious whoever perpetrated this terrible crime had crippled the movement of every American in the United States and abroad. I sat for hours watching the events that occurred that day over and over again. I listened to specialists share thoughts on who might be responsible for such a tragedy. To my surprise, they agreed only a few people in the world could be capable of committing such a senseless act. Osama Bin Laden was the name declared by every military and terrorist specialist's mouth. I knew little about Bin Laden; nevertheless, he quickly got my attention and of every American too.

My heart grew sad as I watched and listened to those who were given the task of reporting this disaster to the country. I could tell as they shared pictures of Americans who decided to jump from floors near the top of the World Trade Center, they were struggling to hold back tears. Pictures of Americans running while covered with thick white dust and debris, panicking, stumbling and trampling over each other were posted on every news channel. It was a nightmare. *Who would have thought that the actions of a few would forever change the*

lives of 270 million Americans?

There was a silent, unwelcome gloom across the country. Every

conversation began or ended with talk of September 11th, 2001.

President Bush did a remarkable job of taking control of the situation

and assuring Americans the perpetrators of these tragedies would be

caught. I listened to his speeches addressing different audiences and

Congress, and was proud of the way he spoke. He did not waste time

trying to find words that would make him sound like a professor. He

was not at all concerned if he offended the friends of those who had

prior knowledge of the events. However, he was extremely careful to

make absolutely sure the Muslim people knew that neither he nor the

country in any way blamed the Muslim religion or its followers for the

tragic events.

President Bush made it perfectly clear he felt the religion was one

of peace, and those guilty of this crime would be hunted down and

brought to justice. I believed he had in his corner a strong military mind

in the man of General Colin Powell.

Having a support system as strong as our military, I was confident those responsible would be found. For many days I did little else aside from think of the sad state of our country. Everywhere I looked and everything I heard all suggested the need for prayer. I cannot remember listening to a single anchorperson that did not begin or end their broadcast with the familiar saying of "God Bless America."

It appeared that America, a country of people with many different origins and nationalities had become one. For just a few days in the United States of America, the color of a person did not matter. The pain of September 11, 2001 was so great that it forced Americans to look beyond the obvious physical appearances of people and search for any kind of comfort to ease the pain. I wondered how long this would last.

How long would there be decisions made in corporate America where the color of a candidate's skin was not a part of the selection process? How long would little girls and boys who had never played together be allowed to swing on swings and play as children, instead of as black, brown or white little girls and boys? How long would the leaders of the country ask its people to pray for America? How many more times would CNN ask Bishop T. D. Jakes to pray for America on

national television?

It seemed like yesterday the same anchor people reported that the leaders of our country had decided it was no longer acceptable to have prayer in schools. As a young child I remember watching a few Americans hold rallies and lobby to have prayer taken out of the school systems. I was a young boy then and remember vividly how angry I was when the leaders of the country decided it was inappropriate for children to pray in school. Back then; I wondered where all the Christians were when this unacceptable act was passed. I wondered now what they thought as the whole nation prayed in desperation.

In the blink of an eye, thousands of lives were lost and hundreds of millions changed forever. *How would America respond to such a tragedy? What might our children tell their children? Was it possible that the creator was trying to get the world's attention?* One thing I knew for sure was that we could not afford a repeat of this tragedy.

Months passed and the country was still trying to recover. I knew in my heart the road to recovery would be endless. The pain and the memories were too exhausting. Nevertheless, President Bush continued pleading with Americans not to allow the terrorists to rain upon their freedom. He was precise and persistent in telling the country the only way the terrorists would win was if we allowed them to change our lives and how we lived each day.

All the fear and anger that I initially felt, I channeled in prayer. As much pain as the events of September 11th brought, I believed that if the entire country began to call on the name of Jesus, astronomical healing would take place. Although the terror of September 11th caused great pain, it was imperative for those who lived by the word of God to remember Romans 8:28 – ALL things work together for good, for those that love God and are called to his purpose. In a time of suffering and horrendous pain, I found comfort in His Word.

It was amazing how this one event forced people of all colors to unite. A few days after that terrible day, I remember working in the USA Lobby and seeing dozens of black, white, yellow, red and brown associates holding hands in the courtyard praying in a big circle. When they finished, many of them upon coming inside walked up to me to shake my hand and say "God Bless You." I looked peculiarly at each of them. Most of them saw me each day at work and never once thought enough of me to open their mouths to say, "Hello." Wow! The sweet Holy Spirit was working on the hearts of many associates in the company amid the tragedies.

More than fourteen months passed with little being said about the plaintiffs that opted out of the class action. Some former executives of the company were brought out of retirement and given positions to try and regain some sort of stability in the company. Men who should have been enjoying their senior years found themselves once again in the rat race trying to get profits to acceptable levels for Coke shareholders.

I wondered why the company remained in such terrible shape after years and years of success, the death of a great chairman as well as the resignation of another not so great chairman. The company busily marketed its products, particularly in black communities, and carried on with business as if there was never a discrimination lawsuit filed and settled. I felt despite the continued denial by most company leaders, daily racist business practices were more prevalent than ever.

I continued to hear stories of how blacks were being evaluated unfairly, being placed on Performance Improvement Plans, and given a false sense of hope when open positions were posted internally in the company, only to be disappointed. It had been more than three years since the lawsuit went public and the people in the company were doing the exact things that tarnished the company's name. I was not at all surprised with what I heard or what I saw because I knew the deal stunk, and the settlement was a joke. The continued blanket denial of all allegations could have possibly paved the way for white managers, who were angry at blacks working in their groups who'd received checks, to humiliate them and make their life at work unbearable.

I remember one of the black females who while being deposed shared the only time she had seen any discrimination in The Coca-Cola Company was when a white manager was fired for calling a black associate a nigger. The attorney, in questioning her, asked whether that was the abuse a black person must suffer before the company acknowledged or admitted there was discrimination. She stated after almost 20 years of being in the company in her position in the EEOC department, this was the only time any investigation, to her knowledge, found racial discrimination. The world must know this medieval paradigm was prevalent in The Coca-Cola Company.

I was not at all surprised by the lack of attention the core plaintiffs were receiving in the media. We had become accustomed to receiving coverage from just a few loyal, sympathetic news reporters. The company continued to do damage control in the media by introducing new products, hiring celebrity talent, and supporting community causes that appealed to ethnic consumers. My only concern was to quietly prepare for the next step and continue to pray without ceasing for the families of those that had enough faith in God to step out from the 2000 class members to be heard.

I believed the leaders of the company probably felt that since the class action part of the lawsuit was settled there was now little to be concerned about. Their arrogance was too great for them to believe seventeen blacks who refused to accept their pitiful offer could possibly hurt them. They had no idea what was forthcoming.

Many years before the lawsuit, I planned for a fight that I expected to linger for years. My desire was never to accept pennies from the company or allow them to silence me so it could continue to hide racial discrimination in the workplace. After being in the company for six years with a good relationship with many black employees, I had first-hand knowledge of the practices that occurred before the lawsuit was filed as well as thereafter. I imagined The Coca-Cola Company thought the fight ended once it received the signed disclaimers from the blacks that accepted the settlement packages. They were wrong.

As time passed, the very people who accepted the packages were soon literally catching hell. Part of the company's plan, which was not disclosed until later, was to carry out layoffs across the board. Known throughout corporate circles as 'downsizing', many of the class action participants found themselves pawns in the company's hidden master plan.

The class action group of over 2,000 employees, who when compared to the originators of the lawsuit, had done very little to receive $3700 per year of employment as compensatory damages, plus back pay. Meanwhile, the company publicly denied that it had done anything wrong, and had settled the lawsuit for the "historic" amount of $192.5 million. Now with layoffs it was more apparent than ever the attorneys representing the class did not truly have the interest of the class at heart.

It remained a mystery, even a secret, as to how the settlement amount would be dispersed. The attorneys allowed The Coca-Cola Company to structure an agreement that paid the plaintiffs a combined total sum of approximately $80 million to be distributed among 2,000 current and former black employees. As a side note, again this amount was smaller than the retirement package given to Doug Ivester, the outgoing chairman of Coca-Cola. Meanwhile, the attorneys benefited to the tune of $20.6 million dollars plus $1 million for expenses!

This historical amount of money -- $192.5 million dollars-- became a public relations platform for The Coca-Cola Company. It allowed the company to announce the payment of a huge debt to society, repair its image with few promises, and move on. From the press conferences to news articles and magazine stories, their plan was revealed to the world. The plan included keeping $10 million to fund a ten-year program designed to give bonuses to black employees who were promoted and then succeeded in positions where there were traditionally few minorities. I thought this was all one big circus.

Approximately $100 million of the settlement money was just numbers on paper, set aside for the aforementioned program as well as various types of training and leadership development programs. I could not believe anyone could be so naïve to believe such foolishness. For years the company never even admitted to one act of racial discrimination despite numerous claims filed with the Equal Employment Opportunity Commission (EEOC). Black as well as white upper level employees of the company flat out denied any racial discrimination had ever occurred in The Coca-Cola Company. Yet, all of a sudden after such a difficult mediation process, the company agreed to pay the largest amount of money ever in the history of any racial discrimination case.

Why would the company pay one dime if it had done absolutely nothing wrong as it alleged? I often thought that The Coca-Cola Company took its consumers to be fools. *Was I the only person in America that saw this was nothing more than trickery?* I contest that every person that took part in composing the settlement agreement knew it was ridiculous. I believe the most difficult aspect of the lawsuit, for the settling parties, was not the content of the agreement, but deciding how in the world they would come up with an explanation that would hide what a terrible agreement it was! Despite the games, I was not fearful; for I believed in my heart that Jesus was still in the business of working miracles. I knew it would only be a short time before something else would happen to expose the company.

Each year the company holds its annual stockholders meeting in Wilmington, DE. However, after September 11, 2001, the company decided to have the next shareholders meeting at Madison Square Garden instead. The Coca-Cola Company has made billions of dollars by presenting itself as a place where all are treated equally, so this change of location made sense. After many years of studying its culture, I knew it was just another way of trying to depict an image. Because the tragedy of September 11th claimed the lives of people from all races, the company saw a golden opportunity to market itself in the eyes of the world as being seen as present in a city trying to recover.

I received another e-mail from Keith Marks stating he was available for me to discuss why I was not selected for an interview for the operations manager position. I thought this was interesting. As usual, my experience and education more than qualified me for the position, but over the years I learned at the company, education and experience were useful only to whites or blacks who were liked by the hiring

manager.

Keith Marks wrote:

> Greg,
>
> I wanted to follow back up with you regarding your non-selection for an interview for the HQs Security Operations Manager position. Although you previously indicated that you would pursue this "outside of the department," I am still very open to providing you meaningful feedback on the selection process and the decisions I reached as they apply to you, and would welcome the opportunity to share that information. Please let me know if you would like to meet and I will determine a time convenient to both of our schedules.
>
> Keith

Now all of a sudden he wanted to meet with me to share why I did

not get an interview. Little did he know my concern was not with an

interview, but with the job. I have never measured my success by the

number of interviews I received. Once again, Keith was trying to

appear to have my best interest at heart but really he was documenting

and covering his tracks, which were already far too traceable.

Chapter 17

A March for Justice

For months I had planned to take a bus of protesters to New York City. I wanted to show the people of New York that The Coca-Cola Company still discriminates against blacks and nothing has changed since the snow job called a settlement was completed. There were many things to be done.

First, I needed to secure transportation and lodging for the soldiers who wanted to join the trip. Some soldiers used funds from their lawsuit earnings to help fund the trip. And, at the very last minute, I shared my plans with those who'd opted out of the lawsuit. Most of them had not been deposed, and thus I wanted to make sure their knowledge of the journey was limited.

After my sixteen-hour deposition, I knew the games lawyers played in their interview tactics. I felt the lawyers were guilty too – guilty of prolonging the case so they could rack up a larger and larger legal bill. I found myself still operating cautiously when I wasn't sure of the impact of sharing information with those who might in turn share it with the attorneys. The attorneys for Coke had their backs against the wall.

April was a busy month and many things demanded my time but none more than the cause I fought for at Coke. For several years I met and shared my experiences at Coke with blacks working in various companies throughout the city. I learned in the process there were many companies in Atlanta that discriminated against blacks. I also learned most blacks in the South have developed an enormous tolerance level for racism.

As I met with various groups of blacks from some of the largest companies in the city, I heard some of the same stories I uncovered when I first started researching The Coca-Cola Company. It seemed for the most part, many whites seem to have a particular lifestyle and acceptability level of achievements in mind for blacks. The conversations I heard seemed so universal. Other Atlanta companies were squirming at the thought of facing racial discrimination charges. Lockheed Martin, Southern Company, Georgia Power, Waffle House and Cracker Barrel were some of the companies where a few blacks decided to stand and speak out against racist practices.

I spoke at many places sharing my testimony. Some sociology departments were interested in hearing how a security officer was capable of bringing a successful lawsuit against such a powerful

organization. These professors wanted to share with their students that

racism does still exist in America. I traveled sharing my experiences

with thousands of young minds that would soon be the leaders of our

country.

In April 2002, I spoke at Central Michigan University in Mount

Pleasant. I was amazed at how well the students responded and how

pure their minds and hearts appeared to be. Most of the students and

faculty were shocked to hear of my experiences.

Before I traveled to speak, I prepared thoroughly. I am a firm

believer that failure to prepare is the same as preparing to fail. During

the Q & A sessions, many of the students boldly stated how

disappointed they were with The Coca-Cola Company. Some even

stated they would boycott Coke products for the rest of their young

lives. I was very open as I shared with them that The Coca-Cola

Company is very powerful and has countless ways to manipulate the

minds of consumers. I told them it was imperative for them to continue

educating themselves to bring change to racist organizations that

cripple our country. I cautioned them to make decisions based on truth and credentials, not color. I also urged both faculty and students to realize that racism and racists exist, and not to become or be a part of either.

The groups welcomed me warmly and their gifts were appreciated. The host professors were extremely excited for the students. I was extremely thankful and appreciative for another opportunity to share what truly happened behind the walls of "The Plantation" with young impressionable minds that could make a difference. I prepared for this speaking engagement as I prepared for the trip to New York.

I arrived in New York City on April 16th from Michigan and was exhausted. The bus riders arrived earlier that evening and were all out having a good time. I could not wait to finally lie down. The next morning we met downstairs in the lobby and discussed strategy for the march. Spirits were high as the soldiers prepared to begin the march for justice.

We decided to march two blocks and gather in front of Madison Square Garden. The streets were jammed with people. As I walked slightly in front of the group, I was one of the first to witness the shock in the eyes of the New Yorkers when they read our signs. As busy as they were trying to get to work, many of them stopped to ask what was going on. I was pleased with the attention we received and looked forward to what was coming.

When we arrived in front of Madison Square Garden and 7th Avenue, we were shocked. There were so many organizations there picketing; there was little public area for us to march. We were met by a city police officer. He stood at least 6'6" and appeared to be about 300 pounds. I was shocked at how professionally he dealt with the large number of picketing blacks. After we introduced ourselves and he learned that we did not have a permit to picket, he called his Sergeant.

Within five minutes, his boss arrived and I was introduced as the leader of the group and the voice of the protesters. The Sergeant, very professionally explained his position as well as the law, and informed us that he would gladly clear an area for us to march. I was again pleased with the amount of respect and professionalism we were shown in New York, by the Police Department.

Before we began marching, we gathered to pray. It had been a tiring journey but we had a message to share. As we prayed, many New Yorkers stopped and prayed with us and for us. My heart was touched by the amount of love we were shown by strangers. I couldn't help but wonder why we had to travel so far to be heard.

I did not think The Coca-Cola Company respected its black employees as much as it valued the black community's dollars. I however welcomed the black community and New York community's prayers. What a great place and platform from which to tell our story.

Shareholder's meetings were a place where the company tried to depict an image of diversity and solidarity. It was the perfect way for us to get the leader's attention. Coca-Cola had spent millions of dollars trying to convince the citizens of New York it was indeed a company every nationality would want to be a part of. The meeting started with about fifty people of all colors, sizes and shapes singing 'What a Wonderful World We Live In' because Coke's products are marketed as bringing people closer together.

The show was long, predictable and boring. One of the things I adored about the people of New York was their openness to express themselves. As we sat and watched The Coca-Cola Company bring celebrity after celebrity on stage sharing why they felt the company was so wonderful, many of the shareholders verbally acknowledged they thought the show was ridiculous. For two hours we listened to song

after song. I'd been in the company for six years then, and I could

scarcely recognize the company they were speaking of. In my opinion,

The Coca-Cola Company did nothing but hide its negative aspects from

the public and pay money to silence its critics.

As the show went on, the crowd became more restless. I wondered

what the producers of this showcase were thinking. It was an obvious

attempt to hide the true reality of The Coca-Cola Company. *Profits*

were down so why was so much money spent on one show? The

company had recorded a loss. I realized the company was willing to

spend any amount to influence its consumers.

Finally, it came time for the shareholders to ask questions of

Chairman, Doug Daft. I had just returned from a press conference

outside with approximately 200 supporters when I heard his voice. The

voice that was coming from microphone #1 captivated the entire

auditorium. You could have heard a pin drop. When I approached the

microphone, one of the bus riders that rode for more than thirteen hours

to speak her peace was in tears as she shared an e -mail that she'd

received from her white male manager. I looked at the stage where the chairman and the other vice presidents of the company were sitting with clear looks of embarrassment about their faces.

After such a long high-priced extravaganza to launch the meeting, I knew it would only take one brave soldier to stand to snap the meeting back into reality. I was proud of the sister who spoke. Two years before she traveled to Wilmington, DE, and addressed the shareholders at the annual meeting. At that meeting she shared that before she allowed herself to continue to be treated as a slave, she would rather lose her life and go home to be with Jesus. Her sincerity again captivated the audience in April of 2000, and her very presence in New York was nothing less than courageous.

It was discouraging to say the least that after a historical settlement of $192.5 million, one of the black females who was an essential part of the "Justice Ride" was still fighting racial discrimination in The Coca-Cola Company. I firmly believed the very arrogance that allowed the white leaders of the company to behave the way they did would be their downfall.

As the sister appeared to be weakening, I approached and embraced her. With the large spotlight on the both of us, I leaned over into the

407

microphone and said, "Mr. Daft." The chairman looked up as if he had

seen a ghost and immediately told the sound crew to "go to microphone

number 2, go to microphone number 2." His voice had lost its usual

calm and was now stricken with a ring of panic.

Most members of the company at the meeting recognized me, and

probably felt Mr. Daft did the correct thing by not letting me speak.

After all, the last time I addressed a concern in front of an audience,

Jesus showed up! He showed up, showed out and spoke to the hearts of

those who could empathize with the pain racial discrimination, or any

discrimination renders. In that meeting, the standing ovation the crowd

gave was in response to the Holy Spirit, not Greg. The last thing the

chairman wanted on this day was a similar response with this crowd.

Six microphones were strategically placed around the auditorium.

There were at least fifty people waiting to address the forum or simply

ask a question of the chairman. After asking the people of New York

and the shareholders to sit patiently through an almost two hour

Broadway musical, the chairman decided to terminate the meeting after

hearing from approximately six people. The roar from those who had

stood patiently awaiting their opportunity to speak suggested they were not pleased with his decision to end so abruptly. Once the gentleman at microphone #6 was finished speaking, Mr. Daft knew I was anxiously, yet patiently awaiting my opportunity to address the leaders of the company, as well as the shareholders.

After he announced the meeting had ended, I watched as he and the other leaders of the company found other ways to try to make it appear the meeting was scheduled to end at that specific time. I was not worried at all. I continued to pray for those that were making decisions to depict an image of diversity in a company that continued to treat employees as unwanted guests.

I spoke with many reporters there on the streets of Manhattan, who appeared to have a passion for their jobs, but none like Ben White, who wrote for the *Washington Post*. He looked me straight in my eyes and asked questions that some whites may have been uncomfortable asking if they were racist. I appreciated his desire to share with the readers of this great paper, information that the *Atlanta Journal Constitution* and other papers that operated in the backyards of The Coca-Cola Company did not share with their readers. Ben wrote an article titled "Black Coca-Cola Workers Still Angry."

NEW YORK, April 17, 2001 -- Protesters lined Seventh Avenue

outside Madison Square Garden today to press criticisms of Coca-

Cola Co., which was holding its annual shareholders meeting

inside.

     With labor and environmental activists were dozens of black Coca-Cola employees who said conditions have not improved at the Atlanta-based company since it agreed in November 2000 to pay $192.5 million to settle a class-action race-discrimination lawsuit and promised to change the way it manages, promotes and treats minority employees. Greg Clark, one of 17 employees pressing individual discrimination suits against Coca-Cola, led the African American protesters, many of whom said African Americans remain underrepresented in top management at the company, are paid less than white employees and fired more often. Clark accused the company of engaging in a public relations offensive to convey a new, more racially sensitive image while failing to back it up with concrete changes.

     "Coca-Cola has done a wonderful job of fooling the public into believing that the racial discrimination lawsuit is over," Clark said. "It's not over. And I'm not interested in settling. The only way to expose the racism at Coca-Cola is to have our day in court."

     Clark flipped through a glossy brochure given to shareholders at the meeting and pointed to a photo and description of a black female employee who, Clark said, is suing the company for discrimination. "They feature her, they market her," he said, shaking his head.

     Coca-Cola spokeswoman Sonya Soutus did not comment on the photo but said the company remains "committed to a diverse workplace." She pointed to the work of a diversity committee mandated by the 2000 agreement and headed by former labor secretary Alexis Herman. "We are

working diligently to implement the agreement. And from our perspective we are certainly making progress."
Soutus did not offer figures to show progress, calling the effort "an ongoing process." Protesters handed out material claiming that 16 percent of the Coke workforce is black, but that blacks have just 1.5 percent of top-level jobs.

When I returned to the company the next day, one of the sisters that worked in the media relations department thought I needed to know just how angry the whites in that department were at our protest and media attention. I thanked her for sharing with me. Although the company was trying to hide the many evil things it had done over the years, it appeared every other week there was something negative about the company in the papers. I guess the old saying that, "What is done in the dark, shall soon be seen in the light," was becoming a reality for Coke.

On Tuesday, May 21, 2002, the Associated Press wrote:

Dallas Workers Accuse Coke of Reselling Soda to Minorities.

Dallas - - Several North Texas employees of Coca-Cola Co. have accused the soft drink maker of repackaging nearly out-of-date soda cans and bottles and then reselling them at stores in minority neighborhoods. One worker who made deliveries to stores in predominately white and black Dallas neighborhoods said the practice was widespread and well known when he started working as a Coca-Cola merchandiser in

1993. Coca-Cola officials denied the allegations, which they said were not brought to their attention internally.

Llewellyn Hamilton, 49, said so-called "near dated" items were shipped from white neighborhood stores and sold at a discount in predominately black and Hispanic stores. "They'd lower the price and ship them to the black and Hispanic stores," Hamilton told the Associated Press on Sunday. "It was common knowledge that we'd recycle it to that neighborhood."

For example, he said about-to-expire 2-liters of Coke that sold for $1.19 was marked down to about 69 cents. "I thought it was strange," he said. "They (customers) knew it was something they had to drink right away."

Rick Gillis, division vice president and general manager for Coca-Cola Bottling Company of North Texas, located in Dallas, said after a newspaper reporter brought the allegations to their attention about two weeks ago they did an internal investigation and spoke with everyone involved in the supply chain. "We believe without a doubt that these allegations are totally without merit," Gillis said.

But Hamilton said company officials knew of the repackaging and did nothing to stop it. "You'd get those "don't ask any questions, "He said

Kenneth Newsome, a dairy manager at a Sack-N-Save in Oak Cliff, said Coke merchandisers took near-dated soda off the store shelves and repackaged it in the store's back room. The old soda also was put into the store's vending machines, said Newsome, who has worked at the store for 16 years and first noticed the repackaging about five years ago. "When it got close to the date on the box, it would just sit there (in the back room) with the chips and damaged goods," said Newsome. "They would bring extra boxes and repack them with tape."

Hamilton now works a new route, delivering drinks to five grocery stores in Garland and Mesquite, both suburbs of Dallas. There, the policy on about-to-expire soft drinks is much different, he said. "If it gets within a month of going out of date, we ship it out," he said. The aging soda is then returned to the bottler, he said. "It is racist. There are some things you just live with. We're giving it to them for dirt cheap, but still, you wouldn't do that out here, "he said.

Dave Lydia, President of the Dallas branch of the NAACP, said they are still investigating the allegations. "To this date we have not come up with a final on this," Lydia said. "We need some hard fast evidence before we make that claim." Meanwhile, Hamilton and others have filed an unrelated lawsuit against Coke. Attorney Brett Myers represents 10 plaintiffs in a lawsuit that claims that Coca-Cola Bottlers of North Texas had discriminatory promotion practices at its three facilities in Dallas and Fort Worth.

He said the case, which is pending class-action status in federal court in Dallas, includes numerous examples in which white workers with little experience were given promotions while black workers with years of employment were passed over. "Six months or a year later, these white employees are supervising these 20 year veterans," Myers said.

Myers said while the case is unrelated to the claims of date manipulation, it shows the mindset of the company. "It certainly indicates the prevailing attitude that they think they can get away with certain practices within the black neighborhood that they don't even try with whites," he said.

In regards to the discrimination lawsuit, a lawyer representing Coca-Cola, Kevin Wiggins, said, "We do not believe the allegations are sustainable as they've been pled by the plaintiff. We've taken steps to ask the court to dismiss them."

In 2000, Atlanta-based Coca-Cola settled a racial discrimination suit for $192.5 million.

It was obvious that the company had done wrong to many people that the settling of the class action did little to stop its pain. It was senseless to think over the past years the setbacks the company had experienced were simply because of a down economy. A wise man

413

once said, "Every dog will have its day." After years and years of intentionally harming blacks, Coke's "day" was here.

After the settlement, it was not a secret the company wanted to make sure its customers felt it changed the way it treated blacks and that it treated everyone equally. By continuing to work in the company, I knew it wanted to make the world think that the only change that had happened was to strengthen not weaken the racist 'Good Ole Boy System'.

Chapter 18

The Greatest Father of All

As I looked back over the years, I realized the fight for equality took a tremendous toll on my life and taught me many lessons. But nothing could have prepared me for the telephone call I received on Thursday, September 5, 2002. I was working overtime and posted in the Central Reception Building. I was chatting with another officer when I answered the call. I could hear nothing on the line but I was able to identify the number was from South Carolina. I sat puzzled for a few seconds and wondered who would be calling me from an unfamiliar telephone number in South Carolina. When the telephone rang again, it was one of my father's most trusted friends.

Charlie's voice sounded very nervous, and there was a lot of noise in the background that sounded like people were yelling, shouting and crying. Charlie then said, "Greg! Bo Doug just shot Boley!" My heart stopped beating, as I struggled to breathe. I couldn't hear anything around me and time seemed to stand still.

Finally, I responded by shouting, "Charlie, what did you say?" Charlie again said, "Bo! Doug just shot Boley." Boley was my father's

415

nickname. Doug was my youngest brother. I ran from my post as fast as I could to inform a supervisor what had happened. He shouted to me, "Go, just go."

I ran as fast as I could to my car, hardly able to breathe and my heart practically beating out of my chest. Buckets of sweat poured off my face, my mind went completely blank, and my body was numb. I drove as fast as my car and Atlanta traffic would allow. When traffic stopped I was in a motionless state of shock.

Calling back home to see if I could get any information as to how my father was doing, my neighbor, Charlie's father, answered their telephone. I told him that I was on my way to South Carolina, but I needed to know where my father had been shot. He said, "Greg, son, I really don't know, but I think it was in the face."

The tears flowed down my face. I could not remember or focus on anything else for chills suddenly came about my body. My hands grew cold and my legs began shaking uncontrollably as if they were running, but my body was not moving. I decided to call my best friend, George Goodwin (Duke), to tell him to hurry to my house to see what was going on, but there was no answer. My thirty-minute drive home seemed to take hours.

As I pulled into my garage, my cell phone rang again. I was afraid, but anxious to answer it. This time when I answered, the voice was one I was extremely familiar with; it was my best friend George. He was calling from my house in Holly Hill, South Carolina, but I had just called his house in Santee and there was no answer.

Why in the world would he be calling me from my home in South Carolina? I shouted, "What's going on?" For a few seconds there was not a sound on either telephone. Then he said, "We lost him." I started shouting at the top of my voice, "No! No! No! No! No! No!"

I felt faint, cold, afraid, lost, puzzled, powerless, confused, angry and helpless. I took off running and crying in my neighborhood. I ran as fast as I could, until a neighbor stopped me and asked what was wrong. The pain that I felt momentarily paralyzed me. I could not talk, just scream, shout and cry. I did not know what to feel, but I knew I had never felt the pain that I was feeling.

When I arrived home my neighbor met me and I was slumped across his shoulder when wife pulled into the garage. We made eye contact, and I imagined she was wondering why I was in the state she saw me in. She opened the car door and before she could ask, I shouted, "Chef is dead, Chef is dead, my daddy is dead." She struggled but lost the battle with her tears as she ran towards me and embraced me. She helped Tim bring me in our home and I collapsed on the floor. My heart was crushed, my precious father was gone.

By this time all the neighbors gathered in my driveway hoping for the best, but at the same time realizing something was drastically wrong. There was no pain or void any larger than what I felt; until I thought of my mother and sister that were there at the house where Chef was killed. The shouting, yelling and screaming in the background was that of my mother and my sister. My brother lived in Atlanta and had already called me to say he was on his way home to South Carolina. My life, the pain, the shock, and the uncertainty were too much for me to handle. I actually thought I was going to lose my mind.

As we threw some things together to rush home to be with our family, my life had little meaning and direction. There were so many questions, and for the first time I started feeling hatred for my brother who shot and killed my precious father. I knew it was not Godly to hate, but for me to say that I did not hate him during this time would have been a lie.

He took the life of the most precious and adorable father in the world. When I thought of the many lessons he taught me, I cried. When I thought of the many Western movies we'd stay up late to watch, I cried. When I thought of the times we spent just being around each other, I cried. As I am writing and sharing the type of relationship we had, I'm crying. Oh! How I miss him.

I didn't see how my heart would ever be the same. Nothing mattered anymore. During that time I cared about few things in life. For the first time in my life, I knew firsthand what a broken heart truly felt like.

I drove for more than four hours numb, shocked, powerless, weak, angry, and stunned in a total state of denial. *How could it be that my youngest brother would take the life of the one man that loved him unconditionally?* I had many questions to ask and so much pain. I found myself at the weakest point in my life. As I drove, I thought of the pain my mother and sister were experiencing. Normally, when one of them would call for something, I always found a way to work out whatever they needed. But for the very first time, I could do nothing to undo that which was done.

I arrived home after midnight to the home I grew up in. The mood, the calmness in the air, the quiet and the stillness of the wind said something was wrong. My mother and older brother were waiting for my wife and me to arrive. They met us outside. I could not enter the house where my father and my family shared so much love. My mother came outside and we just held each other. I had many questions, but I did not know where to start; nor did I want to cause my mother any more discomfort. I did not ask, but the look in my eyes probably told her I needed to hear what happened.

She started by saying there was some sort of disagreement between my father and my brother, and as she watched, one thing led to another and before she knew it, my brother ran to the garage and within seconds returned shouting, "I've got something for you, I've got something for you." The gun was pointed up towards the upper part of my father's body and Doug kept shooting she said. After shooting my father, he threw the gun in some high grass nearby and ran towards the town of Holly Hill.

I listened quietly, stunned in disbelief that my youngest brother took the life of my precious father. As she told me what she had witnessed, my mother had a very peaceful demeanor about her. She; being saved, sanctified and Holy -host-filled; had a peace beyond all understanding. I stood and watched how calmly and easily she spoke of how a child who she gave birth to shot and killed the man she married more than forty years before. My heart was broken, and my body was more tired than it had ever been. Still, I did not enter the house.

That night was the longest night of my life. I lie in bed awake all night waiting for the sun to rise. Regardless of the pain I felt, my father always told me to ignore it and be strong for my family. I could see his bright eyes, hear his stern voice and feel his presence as I remembered his words. I knew that the days to come would take every ounce of strength, and I had to find a way to push forward. My family needed me and depended on me for leadership; I was not going to let them down. I made up my mind to ignore my pain and to put my anger aside for my family, but it was not easy.

421

The morning came and I rose knowing there were many things that needed to be done to prepare for my father's funeral. I remember sitting in the house with family members and friends surrounding us, but yet feeling alone. I was still in a state of shock. I could not believe that Chef was dead. He was so full of energy and so looking forward to his final year at the Augusta National Golf Club where he'd worked for twenty-nine years as head Chef.

I was so proud of him and wanted to always let him know that he made me the man that I am, but I never got an opportunity to tell him those words. Instead, I tried to live my life and apply the many principles he taught me. It was surreal preparing to bury my father. Certainly, I knew that just as a man was born, one day he would die; but facing it was hard. I was so shocked because Chef, after working more than fifty years in the hotel restaurant business, was finally preparing to live a peaceful life full of lots of rest and many rounds of golf.

Eutawville Community Funeral Home owned by the Pickney's of Cross, South Carolina, handled the services and prepared Chef to be viewed. We believed there should be a wake where other family members and some of the many friends of our father would have an

opportunity to gather and share what Chef meant to them. Ordinarily, I

would not have agreed with a wake, but my father was a legend, and to

deny others the privilege to tell their stories of how Chef touched their

lives we thought, would be robbery.

The wake was held Sunday, September 8, 2002. Three limousines

arrived at my mother's house to take the family to the wake. I stood

away from my family and watched them as they gathered and began

entering each of the cars. I knew Chef was dead, but I could not believe

it. My heart was torn, and was filled with a sorrow and a void unlike

anything I had ever felt. I didn't know what to expect, but I knew I had

to be strong for my family, and most of all for my mother. We rode the

quarter mile to where my father worshipped at Greater Target African

Methodist Episcopal Church in Holly Hill, SC. As we rode, I thought

of the Father's Days when I would come home and we'd ride in the

golf cart to the church, no matter how hot it was. Chef insisted on

riding his golf cart to service on Father's Day and every other Sunday

we went to church together.

When we arrived at the church, there were more than a thousand people waiting patiently for the family to come. As I write to share this experience with you, my tears flow freely. The congregation stood with sorrow as we entered the church. I walked down and sat on the left side of the church, in the front row. There, my precious father lay in a blue casket dressed in his navy blue suit. When I got closer to the casket and saw him, I almost fainted. My legs grew weak; my thoughts were empty and my body, ice cold. Yet, somehow I kept it together. I stood trying to be strong for my family.

As we sat and the choir began the service, I could no longer hold it. It seemed like thousands of pounds dropped on my heart and I burst into tears. I wanted to cry out and I did; I felt like screaming, so I screamed. I could no longer fight the pain. I wanted to be strong for my family, but the loss of my precious father and seeing him breathless lying there in church did it. I broke down like I never had before. The pain was so strong, I felt like my heart had first been stolen and then crushed. I remember friends and family surrounding me and holding me and wiping away my tears; yet I felt like I was alone. My body was cold, my heart was crushed, and nothing they did comforted me. I was in an unfamiliar territory of pain that I hope never to experience again.

As I sat on the front row venting, I thought of many of the wonderful times Chef and I shared. For several moments, I forgot where I was. My family who surrounded me also tried to be strong but we all failed. We tried to be strong for each other but we failed. The deep, unfamiliar pain would not allow much strength to be shown.

As the service continued, many of my father's friends stood proudly and shared from their good times with Chef. The chairman of the Augusta National Golf Club at that time was Hootie Johnson, a man Chef loved and greatly respected. He was one of the first to tell what my father meant to him and the Augusta National. Chef's golf partners told humorous stories of the times they shared on various courses. As they spoke, many of them had to be consoled and embraced. Some even had to stop and wait for the tears to cease before they could carry on.

One of my father's dearest friends was "Charlie" of Holly Hill, SC. Although my father knew his name, he insisted on calling Mr. Johnson "Charlie." For as long as I could remember, these two were as close as brothers. He tried to share what Chef meant to his life, but he too lost that battle to pain and tears. I never felt so helpless in all my life.

Normally, when there was a problem in the family, I always found a way to make things better for everyone. My mother would call when something was on her mind and she wanted my insight. Chef and I talked about everything from family issues to politics and life's challenges. The conversations we shared will always be cherished, but none of those talks had prepared me for his death.

After the wake, family and friends gathered at our home hoping to bring comfort. I knew it was essential I try to regroup and be there for my mother, my sister and my brother. I prayed that God would give me strength to be the man my father would want me to be at his funeral. When I heard his voice, I grew stronger. When I thought of all the wonderful times we shared together, I became happy. I knew he would want me to be strong for the family, and that was exactly what I was going to do. There were no weaknesses about Chef. The very sight of him made me feel like I was strong enough to conquer all.

Again, I couldn't sleep that night even though I knew the next day would be the most painful of my life. I remember Chef saying one way a man could test his strength was with his ability to ignore his pain to comfort others. I lay awake that night thinking of the pain my family was feeling. As I lay there, all of a sudden I felt a warm sensation come over my body and remove my tiredness. I did not understand it, nor did I give it much thought, I simply concentrated on thanking God for all that He had done and all that He was going to do.

I found thinking of the goodness of Jesus Christ comforting, soothing and relaxing. I prayed because I knew of no other who could wipe my tears away. I prayed, because I needed Jesus to see me through. I prayed because God sent His only begotten son, so that we might have a chance to live and live life more abundantly. I prayed, because I knew of a solid rock on which I could stand when all other ground was sinking sand. I prayed, because he said, "I will never leave you or forsake you." I prayed, because I needed supernatural strength to see me through. I prayed, because I can remember my mother telling me as a little boy, "When all else seems to have failed, try Jesus." I prayed. He has never left me nor forsaken me. I prayed, because He is the sweetest thing I know. I prayed.

Secrets, Lies, and Betrayals

Monday, September 10, 2002 came quickly. That day marks the burial of the greatest man I have ever known. I did not know how I would continue without him. Preparing the last-minute details before my father was laid to rest was my final gift to him. My gift to my family would continue however. I was determined not to let my family down. I did not know how, but I knew my father would expect nothing less of me.

The family all gathered in the front yard for prayer before going to the church. As the car approached the church, I could see hundreds of people outside waiting, for the church was filled to its capacity. They waited for the family to arrive and be seated. As we waited to go in, I prayed for strength to help my family get through the day.

My emotions were running high and many thoughts crossed my mind as we waited. There was still so much anger inside of me. We were forced to bury our father because one son chose not to listen to him as a child. I thought of how senseless my father's death was. The car was so quiet. You could hear the tick of a wristwatch and the swallow of the person in the seat beside you.

We all tried to be strong, but I knew it would be a difficult day. I felt so alone. My father and I talked about everything, like men. He would look me directly in my eyes, and I would return the same courtesy. As hours passed he always shared many of his personal experiences with hope that I would learn something that would help me along my way.

Who would I turn to for advice now? Who would guide me along my way? Damn! Damn! Damn! So many thoughts at that present time did not matter. *So why were they running rampant in my mind? Was this a normal response of dealing with death?* At that time I really did not care. My only concern was taking care of my family.

The time came, and the funeral directors opened the door for my mother and I to exit. My eyes grew heavy, but I was determined to be the anchor my family needed. My pain on this day I decided would mean nothing; I was determined to ignore it. The doors of the church opened with my mother hanging on to me, as she was drooped over my shoulder we very slowly walked down the aisle of the church. My father, again in his baby blue casket in front the alter. The service was a beautiful service. My mother asked the women in the family to wear white and the men to wear dark suits. The songs were some of the favorites of Chef's. I was proud of all the wonderful things that were said about my father.

It came time in the service for me to rise and share some of the good times we'd had as a family. I remember sharing about the week after I graduated from the University of South Carolina. Chef and I were in the backyard fiddling around when all of a sudden, Chef looked at me and paused as he always did before speaking, and asked me, "Greg are you ever going to have enough sense for me to talk to you like a man?" I thought the question was a no-brainer. Before I could answer, he would say, "That's ok I already know the answer; that was a waste of my time." Then I'd always laugh and smile as he walked away. I'd watch him to see if he was going to turn around and allow me an opportunity to answer; but he never did.

My mother was pleased with Chef's going home service. I knew I'd forever miss Chef asking me if I had sense enough for him to talk to me like a man. But a man I was, and now I was the man my mother needed to be strong for her and the rest of the family.

There were many issues that needed my attention concerning

Chef's death, and the next few months were spent taking care of the

family's business. I was not mentally or physically prepared to return to

Coke but eventually, I did.

Chapter 19

Will It Ever End?

Shortly after I returned to work in 2003, another supervisor position became available. The position was posted several months before; however, for whatever reason, it was never filled. I decided to apply for the position, regardless of management's behavior toward me.

After applying for the position, several weeks passed before any news was posted from the staffing department. Many officers felt the position would probably go to the acting staff member who held it for several months. After all, the department set a precedent of showing that education and experience were good only if management chose to recognize those attributes. I thought no differently than the security officers of the department. I knew the people who worked in management already decided who would be the next supervisor. A few years ago, applying for a position knowing I would not be considered would have bothered me. Not anymore. I learned the heart that plagued the leaders of my management team could not be cured even with prescribed medicine.

It was a Friday morning when I was asked by one of the officers who also applied for the position if I had received my interview time. I responded, "I have not checked my e-mails, but I will let you know shortly." An hour passed before I could check my e-mails, although I found no surprises when I did. My email said I was denied an interview because more qualified candidates were found, same old story, but with a twist.

In the past, although I only received one interview in 7 years, and had been overlooked for more than 30 positions, it was business as usual. Previously, they found ways of sharing news with me without putting it in writing. I could not believe that I actually received an e-mail from the staffing department stating I was denied an interview because more qualified candidates were found. I knew the only way the company could find more qualified candidates was if it accepted resumes from outside of the company.

I shared this information with many of the security officers. They were stunned I didn't get an interview, especially after the lawsuit. Some asked, "What reason did they give you this time?" When I shared the reason, most of them just shook their heads in amazement. One of the oldest officers told me, "You should feel good for exposing racism in The Coca-Cola Company. Since its existence, Coke discriminated against blacks; and it was just time for someone who was not afraid to beat them at their own game."

The interview process began on a Friday, the same day I was told I would not be getting an interview. I was fortunate to be working in the CRB where visitors and guests would enter the company. As I was working that day I saw each of the officers who were granted interviews. Three of the five candidates had only high school diplomas, and the other two were twenty year army veterans who had recently completed their Bachelor's degrees.

As the candidates entered one after the other, I became more convinced this was nothing more than retaliation. My Bachelor of Science degree in Criminal Justice and Master's degree in Management was not a secret to many in the company, and certainly not to the management of security. It became evident the reason given for not being allowed to interview was a lie. It was neither a truthful nor intelligent response.

After I learned who was being interviewed, I decided to write my management team and the chairman of the company, Doug Daft, as well as the company's number one legal man. I wrote a memo simply asking if any one of them could give me an intelligent response that might explain the "no interview" decision made by my management team. Their response was predictable. They sang the song the security management team sung.

It was Wednesday, April 23, 2003, when I first visited the Federal Equal Employment Opportunity Commission. It was my first time ever visiting the office, and I was very disappointed with the manner in which the investigator spoke to me. When I thought of the rude tone in her voice when she questioned me, I was puzzled. I can still remember how disheartening it was to share situations that I felt were demoralizing and embarrassing.

After sitting for only a few seconds, a middle-aged black gentleman approached me and introduced himself as a supervisor. He then asked if he could speak with me for a moment. I responded, "Certainly." I then followed him to the rear of the building into one of the offices used for interviewing. He then asked me to tell him a little about my case. I

435

began by telling him that almost five years ago I received a right to sue

letter and that I was the original plaintiff in the racial discrimination

lawsuit brought against The Coca-Cola Company. I continued and

shared that although the class settled; I had not, and that I was suing the

company individually. I shared I had continued to apply for promotions

and was continually being denied because of the role I played in the

lawsuit. I then stated I spoke with my attorneys, and I was there to file a

complaint against the company. He then very rudely interrupted me and

said, "Just because Coke did not give you a job does not mean they

have retaliated against you."

I tried to share with him the paperwork I brought, which I felt

clearly provided evidence of retaliation by the company, but he did not

want to hear it. His voice became louder and louder until he was

shouting. He said, "If Coke wanted to retaliate against you, all they

needed to do was fire you." I was shocked, not expecting this type of

behavior from any employee and certainly not a supervisor.

I grew tired of his ignorance very quickly. I then told him that Mr.

Willie Gary was my attorney and it was he that suggested I file this

complaint. The supervisor then said that he was going to kick it back and that the complaint was not going anywhere. I told him I did not need his legal advice; I had an attorney and was very pleased with his team. By this time both of us were shouting. I realized that the intelligence level of this brother was limited to say the least, so instead of continuing to shout and argue, I picked up my cell phone and called the Gary firm. As I dialed the number, this gentleman was still telling me if my attorneys did not fax their desire into the office, he was going to kick out my complaint.

I spoke with one of the partners, and it was at that time that the gentleman walked away stating, "Go have a seat, I will get somebody to talk with you." I wondered if he would have felt so strongly about my complaint if it were not against Coke. His behavior was truly unacceptable. I was not concerned with his personal thoughts of my case. *Why was this person clowning about a situation where his knowledge was truly limited? Was this the normal way a supervisor responded to each employee that exercised their right to file a complaint?*

I returned to the waiting room and waited for about ten minutes before I was again called to the rear. I was called back by a black female, who obviously had been briefed by the supervisor. As I shared

my situation, her body language told me she was no more interested in

my complaint than the other man. After I shared some of my situation,

she then asked me to return to the front while she typed up my

complaint. A few minutes later I was called back to sign and receive a

copy of my complaint. In that few minutes, the attitude of this woman

had apparently made a 360 degree turn. She was somewhat pleasant

and smiling. Obviously, she took a few moments to read my

documentation, and she therefore understood why I was there. I

thanked God for giving me strength to endure this unexpected battle.

When I returned to the company the next day, a black female that I

did not see for several months, approached me. We greeted each other

with a smile and shared a little small talk. She spoke of a situation that

caused a lot of stress in her life. She explained that in October 2002, a

white male approached her while she was working in her area and was

on the telephone. She stated that this man looked her in her eyes and

shouted, "I am sick of your black mother-fucking ass, and you getting

every fucking thing you want." As she spoke of this incident, her voice

trembled badly. She then shared that her white female manager was standing nearby and told the gentleman to "stop it; do not use that kind of language." He then stated, "I am sick of her black ass getting everything she wants." This incident had been witnessed by at least fifteen employees. Because she felt threatened, she ran out of the building crying.

She was so hurt and shocked that she went directly to the doctor. Her physician immediately insisted that she be removed from the company for an unspecified period of time. Once she arrived home and tried to rest, she concluded that she must report the incident to the Human Resources department. The next day she telephoned and reported the incident to her human resource representative. She was told that an investigation would be done, and she would get back in touch with her.

It was several weeks later before she heard anything from the HR department. After interviewing over fifteen witnesses, during which each of them gave identical accounts of the incident, she was floored by what she was told next. The human resource representative stated, "The Coca-Cola Company does not terminate employees for verbal abuse." As she told me this, she burst into tears. I too cried for I felt her pain.

After all the lying and misrepresentation that The Coca-Cola Company had done in the media, and after the settlement of the racial discrimination lawsuit; nothing had changed. If you believe that it has changed, please explain how anyone could still be an employee of an organization after using such offensive language towards another co-worker.

Chapter 20

What Is It About Power, Anyway?

Trouble for the famous soft drink giant seemed like it would never end. I wondered what it was about power that caused corporate executives to make such unethical and fool hearty decisions. The same decision makers, who were fresh out of the fire, public embarrassment and the media circus regarding the racial discrimination case involving more than 2000 employees, found themselves yet again embroiled in another debacle that was sure to make stock prices plummet to their lowest point ever. It seemed the sun had forgotten to shine on the company, and the once untarnished and most recognized trademark would continue to suffer loss.

Thursday, July 17, 2003 was the date of my fourth deposition. The first sixteen-hour marathon should have been enough. The next two were also long and largely a waste of time. I didn't expect this one to be any different. I was sick of the attorneys for the company and the other law firms trying to find some sort of technicality to have the case thrown out of court. I believed that any objective thinking judge would look at the case and conclude there was more than enough evidence to take the case to trial. However, I never forgot that I was in Georgia.

I wondered why there were so few, if any, racial discrimination cases heard in federal court on Coke. I found the number of cases that actually made it to trial appalling. I was not at all naïve about the many connections and power the company and the law firms representing the company wielded. They were infinite.

I was prepared for the upcoming deposition and focused not only on that, but the events that would occur afterward. I was well aware of what I was facing. My attorney and I waited in the law firm's reception area as Coke's attorneys and Keith Marks came out to begin the day. Each of them approached me with a greeting and handshake. My response was simply, "Good Morning; however, there is no need for handshakes." Not one of these people cared anything about me. So, I simply refused to play that game.

I believed depositions were designed to frustrate and humiliate the plaintiff or the deposed. I knew it was just another formality I had to endure to get to where I wanted to be. The arrogance of the attorneys kept me grounded. Much like I expected, it was the same old garbage I heard years before. Throughout the humiliating experience, I remained focused and only thought of the people that would somehow be vindicated when the story was told. Many of the questions asked had absolutely nothing to do with my case, and this I expected.

The attorney tried to put on a face of stone, but he was transparent. His hatred for me was as obvious as was the tension in the room. He tried to appear tough. It was not a time to be tough, but rather smart. The attorneys spent the day trying to focus on issues that would stop me from telling my story. The Constitution of the United States of America provided me with the opportunity to tell my story to the world. The attorney for Coke and those that were hired to fight us, all took the position that I was all about the money. If they had only known that my blessings came from Jesus not from man, favor ain't fair.

People discriminated against for years, for one reason or another, had not taken a stand. But Pray! Prayer changes things. Please remember the fight that you choose not to initiate today, is the very same fight that your precious loved ones will face tomorrow. I sat in the deposition knowing just where my motivation came from and just who was on my side.

I joined Coke with the hopes of doing wonderful things for a company I thought welcomed all races of people. I realized when the Mehri Group of attorneys kicked me out as a class representative, the prospect of winning an individual racial discrimination lawsuit against an icon like Coke in the state of Georgia would be all but impossible, for obvious reasons. But, my new attorneys and my determination to secure justice led me on.

I secured good counsel, and I never forgot what my father told me: learn all you can learn, for you never know when it will be essential to use. I have accepted the fact I will never be free from the pain of my experience at The Coca-Cola Company. I am not suggesting a boycott of Coke products. However, Coke products are not welcome in my home. My family and friends have taken a stand against such a culture. *Will you?*

I only ask that you think twice about what products you purchase in a restaurant or grocery store. *Is it intelligent to support any organization that treats any race of people the way Coke treats blacks?*

Again, please do not be misled by what might appear to be generous financial contributions to any organizations, communities, countries, scholarship foundations, churches or families. These contributions in many cases are simply tricks, and are a part of the game to appear to be something the company is not. Be very suspicious when one, two or even a group of blacks emerge from the organization shouting that Coke is a wonderful place to work and claiming they have never seen any racial discrimination. These people have probably accepted a token position in the company and are comfortable knowing they have sold their souls.

It was September 10, 2003, when I received a telephone call from Mr. Gary. He asked if I was busy and I responded, "Never too busy for you." He continued and told me that he just received a fax from Coke stating I was terminated for presenting an inaccurate resume. I paused for a moment, and then shared that I expected the company to come up with something, but wow! Coke had hired me more than seven years ago.

After over seven years of committed employment, my background was how the company chose to attack me. My attorney shared that he

445

believed Coke terminated me because of a part-time job I held in 1993 which I had not listed details of in my resume. I told him that was more than ten years ago, and I had only worked that job for twelve weeks so the details seemed irrelevant. Furthermore, I'd had many jobs over the years to make ends meet and not all of those were listed on my resume.

I am certain if a background check of this sort was to be done on each associate in the company, or on the attorneys at Coke for that matter, there would be few people left to work. He chuckled, but I later learned that his assessment was accurate. After our conversation he faxed a copy of the letter to me.

The fight against Coke over the years opened my eyes. I had a new awareness. I often saw the desperate measures the company would go to for damage control. Consequently, I did not allow myself to become alarmed when I lost my job. I saw my termination as just another attempt to try to rekindle a fire that was fading. I realized for more than four years I was a thorn in the sides of the leaders who tried to forget about the negative impact the lawsuit had on the company's rich history. The last thing they wanted to do was continue looking in my face each day when they came to work.

I realized many of the associates chose to hide their hatred for me while others did the very opposite, and showed it each time an opportunity presented itself. But through it all, the attorneys and the leaders of the company discovered I was not going to leave the company on my own. So, when they thought it was safe to get rid of the one black man that dared to stand on the Word of God, and proclaim that all of God's children are special and must be treated accordingly, they did.

Little did they know that terminating my job at Coke was the beginning of a new path to continue walking by faith and not by sight. After all, the Bible speaks of the number seven as a number signifying completion; and at the time I was terminated, I was in my seventh year. I realized that I was being moved from Coke because my assignment there was completed. Awesome God is He!

After dinner that evening, I read the termination letter and carefully thought over my last months in the company. I, in reflection realized I saw and felt in my spirit that a change was coming. I found it interesting a black female initially hired to replace the white male that was ultimately responsible for the company being sued, was the person who signed my termination letter.

As people of color we must always be cautious and aware of the games that are so prevalent and easy to become a part of in corporate America. At first, I often spoke to this sister when she was hired to manage the very department where the largest racial discrimination lawsuit in this country's history originated. I knew when I spoke to her someone had probably told her a little about me. I remembered how uncomfortable she appeared when we spoke. If she only knew that her focus should have been on the white males that hired her to do their dirty work, and not the black man that provided an opportunity for her to be employed. Nevertheless, I understood that she was only doing what she was hired to do.

One advantage I had by staying in the company so long and facing those that committed the discriminatory acts, was that it afforded the opportunity to see how the company tried to change behind closed doors. I learned one of the most common ways the white leaders in the company tried to counter many of the allegations was by simply hiring more blacks. It appeared the company strategically decided it would place certain blacks in positions that were previously filled by whites. It also appeared the gender of choice for the company was most certainly female.

It never ceased to amaze me the lengths a company would stoop to when trying to hide its racist and discriminatory culture. Little did they know that an apology would have gotten things headed in the right direction. After all, black folks are seemingly one of the most forgiving races on earth. But instead, they continued to place bandages on wounds that needed surgery.

Even today, the company is still squandering about trying to present some type of positive image that will produce great revenues for its shareholders. If they only knew that the answer to their problems was not in boring commercials and stale advertising gimmicks. If only they knew the answer wasn't in training programs that mostly whites attended only because it was mandatory, not because they felt a need for change. I believe there is no training class in existence that can teach a person how to remove the hatred that one might have in their heart toward another. I knew of a "doctor" that made house calls as well as visits to corporate America. Only He could cure those hearts, and so I wondered if any of the executives, vice presidents or leaders of the company had a personal relationship with Him.

It was Spring 2003, and still there was not a ruling on my case. I was not worried for I knew a ruling would soon come from the courts. Mr. Daft, the second chief executive officer since the filing of the lawsuit had now announced his retirement. It was interesting to me that Mr. Daft had been given credit for coming into his position and quickly settling the class action suit. Although Mr. Daft had been given credit for settling a portion of the lawsuit, the fact still remained that the person who started the entire racial discrimination lawsuit had not settled and the courts had not ruled on my case.

The timing of the announcement ensured me that a settlement on my case would be rendered before Mr. Daft's retirement. Over the years, I learned how large the world was and at the very same time, how small and closely knit the people who inhabit it were. I also learned that the powers that be, the real decision makers in our country, traveled in a very small social circle. The chance of me crossing paths with a judge who would rule in my favor was small. However, the chance for one of the senior executives of the company or senior partners of one of the law firms whom Coke hired to cross the judge's

path was highly likely.

I was well aware of how crucial decisions might be made, and I was

even more convinced that the ruling would be in favor of the company.

The company and its attorneys had painted a picture that the lawsuit

was over. There had been absolutely no talk of the lawsuit for a

substantial amount of time in the media. This was just what the

company desired. If the judge ruled that there was enough evidence in

my case to go to trial, then all of the hundreds of millions of dollars that

the company spent trying to remove the lawsuit out of the public's eye

would have been wasted, again. As I continued to pray, I prepared

myself for the judge's decision and looked to the throne of grace for my

strength.

Over the years of fighting for equality, I learned many priceless

lessons. I saw how attorneys and companies would manipulate

reporters to read the way they desired. I saw decisions made from the

bench that supported the rich and powerful and shunned common,

everyday hardworking Americans. I quickly learned this was simply

how the game was played.

I knew a decision would be made soon, and it would not be in my favor. I thoroughly understood the decision made would be the right "fit" for the company. I studied the company and its leaders for many years and could almost predict their actions. This was one of the most important variables needed to launch such a powerful lawsuit against the icon.

My life was blessed and so full of love from family and friends. Each day brought examples of love from someone who thought enough of me to show they cared. I always welcomed the telephone calls and friendly cards. I continuously thanked God for all that He had done and all that He was going to do. I believed oftentimes that which we want is not necessarily what God has planned for us.

There have been many times I wondered why God chose me to fight the battle against this giant. No one answer came to mind when I thought of this incredible struggle. I knew that my chance of winning an individual lawsuit in Georgia, against Coca-Cola was zero; it was not the way things were done in the south. Nevertheless, I never stopped praying for strength to tell the truth to the world. I believed every individual who were aware of the class action lawsuit and how the company relentlessly tried to keep its documents out of the public

eye would know it was guilty. On the other hand, proving racial

discrimination in an individual case was virtually impossible in the

eleventh circuit district court, for one reason or another.

One only needed to study the precedent the courts established to

understand how many of the judges felt about racial discrimination

cases. I studied some of the history of this district, and if one did not

know better, one might assume some of the judges were racist and

believed that discrimination like blacks had its place in America. I

struggled with this concept along the way.

On Friday, May 28, 2004, I received a telephone call from a

reporter. He stated his name and that he worked for the *Atlanta Journal*

Constitution. He had written some of the stories on the lawsuit, which

made me somewhat familiar with him. I answered the telephone,

"Hello," and the voice on the other end said, "Hey Greg, I just heard

that the judge dismissed your case, and I guess you know that means

that it's over, there will not be a trial. *What are you going to do now?*"

In the end, I simply told him, "I'm fine with whatever the judge has

decided." That was what was printed in the May 29th article entitled,

453

"Coke wins one bias case, worker opted not to settle." What a surreal and succinct way to summarize such a long battle. The article also mentioned this book but none of the details contained within it.

I was somewhat startled when I received this call. After all, it was not one of my attorneys calling, but a reporter who worked for the *Atlanta Journal Constitution*. The information didn't startle me, for the decision of the judge was certainly not a surprise, but the enthusiasm and the excitement in his voice was. I listened very carefully to make sure that I was hearing what I heard. I was right; it sounded like this reporter was leaping and rejoicing over this decision.

He continued by sharing he was writing a story as we were speaking, and he wanted to get a quote from me. I paused a moment. *Why was there such a rush to get the story out?* I had informed him that my attorneys and I had not spoken, so I asked, 'what was the need for such a quick release on his story'? I knew exactly how this story would read and who was behind it.

I became curious as to how and where this reporter, who was supposed to be professional and neutral, received his information. *Who could have peddled this information to the media so quickly? Who would benefit most from sharing this information with the public?* It had been approximately 2 years and there was nothing of our cases in the media, *why now?* I asked, "How and where did you get your information?" He never answered. Instead he continued asking me questions. I didn't bother to answer any of them; I had a pretty good idea of how that article would read and wanted no part of it. Maybe years ago, when I was green in the lawsuit and to the ways of corporate America, this would have concerned me; however, experience has once again proven to be the best teacher. I thanked God for direction and for peace of mind.

The following day the article was printed in the newspaper and just as I'd anticipated; it was written to make The Coca-Cola Company appear innocent. Yes, the judge ruled there was not enough evidence to go to trial. Wow! If they only knew how predictable they were. If only the leaders of the company and the attorneys who fought to keep the lawsuit out of the public's eye knew my true desire. The sad part of it all is that our precious children are the ones who will suffer because of our greed. *How as a people do we continue telling them we love them, when we have embraced the very things that will later cause them so much pain? My brothers and my sisters, black, brown, red and white, we must stand for righteousness. What does it profit a man to gain the entire world, only to die and lose his soul?* Throughout this journey, I have been many places, I've seen many things, but I have never seen the righteous forsaken, nor his seed begging bread. When all else seems to have failed, please continue to stand. And never forget, the fight is not yours, it's the Lord's.

Later that evening I received calls from some of my friends who'd heard the news on the television. They heard the judge ruled there was not enough evidence in Greg Clark's individual case to go to trial. Each of them spoke freely as to what they thought of the judicial system. Many of them could not believe after years had passed and with almost everyone believing the lawsuit was in the past, Coke would want to remind the public of such an embarrassing period in its history. I more than anyone, understood their anger as well as their frustrations. Nevertheless, I reminded them that I too knew of a judge. Just as we yearn for water when we thirst and for food when we are hungry, so must we yearn for a greater understanding of the Word of God.

Chapter 21

The Blinders Come Off

The years from 2003 to 2009 were essentially new chapters for me. I was occupied with taking care of family business for my mother who was now on her own. I worked at building my own, independent security services company. The building of my own enterprise had new meaning after my experiences at The Coca Cola Company. I was driven to offer quality service to my clients and quality leadership and management to my staff.

My new life was in full swing when my phone rang. It was in October 2007. I had just returned to my car after working out at Metro Fitness, formerly known as The Run & Shoot Gym. My cell phone showed a stream of missed calls when it rang again. I answered and the voice of a professional woman said, "Mr. Clark I am calling from Mr. Gary's office, he wants to speak with you."

I paused for a moment. It had been years since I'd heard from Mr. Gary. I waited on the line until he answered. Next I heard Mr. Gary's voice say, "Hey buddy how are you doing", I responded, "well, and you?" He replied that he was just trying to keep things rolling.

457

Why after several years of silence was Mr. Gary calling me?

After a few minutes of small talk he let the cat out of the bag. He

stated two young ladies, former clients of his, were spreading a lot of

lies about him and some of his closest friends. I listened carefully. I

was very familiar with these ladies; they were strong-willed sisters.

They were two of the seventeen who had opted out of the class-action

lawsuit against Coke in order for Mr. Gary to represent them

individually.

Mr. Gary asked if it was ok if he placed me on speakerphone, I said

certainly. Once on speakerphone, the other attorneys present in the

room introduced themselves. I was familiar with most of their voices

and names.

Mr. Gary then got down to business. He stated that these two ladies

put up a website about he and some of his friends and colleagues and

he needed me to give them a call and try to get them to take the website

down. He was very upset and his voice depicted that of a man that was

nervous and frightened. This startled me.

Although several years passed since I last spoke with Mr. Gary, I

could not remember hearing him sound so shaky. I asked him what was

458

on the website. He replied, "A whole bunch of lies. These damn girls are talking about that I took $40,000,000 from Coke and sold you guys out. Greg, you know we are all black and we are just trying to make a living."

I thought to myself, *"Yes, we are all black, but you my brother are living on a totally different level than we are."* The conversation continued with a few of the lawyers stating what legal grounds they might pursue to take down the website. I listened as they went back and forth with their ideas. I was amazed at what I was hearing. It seemed like a lot of focus for one little website. The conversation ended with Mr. Gary giving me his new cell number and me assuring him that I would give the two ladies a call to see if I could help. One of the attorneys gave me the number on which to reach the two ladies.

Driving home that night I thought about this most unusual call. Years had passed and I heard nothing from the attorneys who had represented me in a highly public case against a corporate giant. I was just a former client to them. They were the experts in their legal rights and avenues. Yet, Mr. Gary saw it necessary to call me for help. I was curious about what was really going on.

The next day, I called the number given to me and left a message letting the ladies know that I wished to speak with them. A few hours had passed and they indeed returned my call. We exchanged a bit of small talk and then I shared with them the purpose of my call. I asked if they would consider taking down the website about Mr. Gary. To my surprise, these two sisters went off! They started yelling and cursing. I was shocked.

This was not the demeanor of the sisters who'd stood with me during the lawsuit against The Coca-Cola Company. I gave them time to vent and then I simply suggested maybe that day was not the best time to call and I hung up the telephone. I was puzzled; I could not believe how angry they were.

I took a few moments and sat quietly, asking myself why in the world they were so angry. I then called Mr. Gary on his cell phone and shared with him how the first call went. We chatted for a while and just before ending the call he told me to keep trying. I decided to let a few days pass before I would reach out to the ladies again. That proved to be a wise decision.

I had mixed feelings about calling the ladies again, but I did. Once again, I left a message and they returned my call together. This time they seemed to be more willing to listen to what I was saying. I told them Mr. Gary asked me to give them a call because he did not like the website and he wanted it down immediately. They laughed! They began saying things like, "so what, he'll get over it," and "don't worry, tell him his day is coming." Then they focused their attention on me.

One of the sisters asked, "Greg, don't you understand what they did?" I grew silent. She went on to say, "Greg they stole from us." I replied, "They did what?" The other sister stated, "We know Mr. Gary paid you, you were his partner." I responded, "Paid me for what?" She then went off again but this time her anger was directed at me. She shouted that I knew what he was up to and I had allowed him to use me to steal money from the 16 others he represented.

I did not know what to say, so I said nothing. It was obvious these sisters believed beyond a shadow of a doubt Mr. Gary and his team of lawyers stole from them, and because it appeared there was a special relationship between us; they assumed I assisted in this horrific crime. They were adamant. They were also wrong about me.

461

I spent years fighting for the cause at Coke. I had spent hours and hours trying to do what was right. By this time I had spent years rebuilding my life. But, financially I had gained nothing. Not a single penny. I received nothing from The Coca-Cola Company except my termination letter. I received nothing from the large settlement. I certainly had received nothing from these slick lawyers. Cyrus Mehri nor Willie Gary. Wow! And it was my case.

I waited as they took turns sharing information they gathered over the past few years. They stated there were taped telephone conversations and videotapes of depositions, which proved Mr. Gary and his cartel were guilty of operating unethically, and that they had established a pattern of stealing from their clients. Arriving like heroes to save the day, the attorneys would promise their clients justice and retribution but most often those clients would walk away with very little or nothing. Yet somehow the law firms seemed to thrive and survive just fine.

I was floored but willing to listen to all they shared. Our conversation lasted for well over an hour. Before hanging up they said they knew my family and I had been through a difficult time to say the least; nevertheless, they urged me to take some time and think about how things had happened in our case. I assured them I would.

I called Mr. Gary the next day and told him they had no desire to take down the site and the ladies said they had evidence he secretly took money from The Coca-Cola Company. Much to my surprise Mr. Gary started shouting this time. He screamed, "What fucking evidence, they ain't got shit! What I am going to do is shut the mother-fuckers down. They don't know whom they are fucking with. They ain't got shit on me." Mr. Gary then asked if I could get their addresses for he was going to have them arrested.

I was shocked to hear Mr. Gary speak about women in this manner, and was stunned to hear him lose his temper. *Why did he get so angry?* If the ladies truly had done him harm, he would have no problem having his day in court. Because of the way he spoke about these ladies, I became curious as to what was on the website, ***www.employeesforchrist.com.***

He went on and on in his fury, "Greg they have even implicated a dead man, Johnnie Cochran, in this shit." I listened as he raved about putting those "bitches" in jail. *Again, why was he so angry?* This

463

brother had the power, connections and money to bring about strong legal actions against these sisters if he so desired. *Why was there a need to degrade them with all the name-calling?* They had only done what they felt was right. They were only protecting themselves. If they were wrong then surely this intelligent man had legal recourse.

I called the ladies back a few days later and shared with them that Mr. Gary said he was going to have them arrested and shut them down. To my surprise, this news gave them the biggest laugh. Here we had a rich and powerful attorney, out of character shouting ugly profanity towards two women who had lost everything trying to right the wrong they believed was committed against them. They remained constant in their claim that Mr. Gary took millions from The Coca –Cola Company and sold us out. They went further and gave me their address so Mr. Gary would know where to find them when he filed charges to have them arrested.

Previously, I would call Mr. Gary to update him on the conversations I had with the ladies, and he would call me to see if there was any progress being made to get the website down. This time, Mr. Gary called me first and asked if I had heard anything else from the ladies. I responded that last time I spoke with them they told me to tell you to please send someone to arrest them. The telephone went silent.

Mr. Gary then stated," Well Greg, I am not losing any business. I am as busy now as I have ever been. No one is paying them or that website any attention. Keep trying and keep me posted." Interesting! It was as if Mr. Gary apparently changed his mind about having the two ladies arrested. Suddenly arresting them was not on his agenda. He was not going to file any charges against these ladies in court.

This was puzzling; or was it? A few weeks ago, he reached out to me after years of silence. When my business with him wasn't even done yet he didn't bother to call me. He'd never even called to tell me that my case was dismissed, yet here he was comfortable enough to call and ask for my help. Something about this situation stunk and I was determined to find out what it was.

I spent the night recalling the events that recently happened concerning Mr. Gary and looked through the ladies' website. To my surprise, at first glance, the site appeared to be obvious slander. There were pictures of Mr. Gary and several very influential prominent black men who held very high positions in various organizations. There were headlines that read, "Gary threatens Hillary's Presidency" and "Gary accused of Sexual Assault." These were just a few, but the others were just as damaging.

I now knew why Mr. Gary was so anxious to get this website down. I could not believe the amount of information on the site. The website was an embarrassment to Mr. Gary, his firm, family, business partners, friends, lawyers and most certainly to his wife. *Why would he not go through the courts to have the website taken down?*

I decided to consult with a dear friend of my late father. He's a retired FBI agent. I sought his input to see how I might proceed with my concerns and gave him the website address. He visited the website and called me back. He agreed that it was obvious slander, unless that is, it was all true. He too was concerned that Willie Gary did not immediately go to the courts to file the necessary paperwork to have the website taken down.

After talking for a while we concluded there was definitely more to this situation than Mr. Gary was telling. My friend stated he would check out a few things and get back with me. A few days passed before

I would hear from him again. This time when we spoke he sounded

certain that Willie, as he referred to Mr. Gary, was hiding something.

He alluded to the case of Kubik, et. al. v. Gary, et. al. This was a

case where more than forty female former clients of Mr. Gary's

accused him of taking $51.5 million dollars from the company that the

clients were suing. Instead of protecting his clients, it claimed that Mr.

Gary made a secret deal with the company and returned to his clients to

tell them they had no case against the company. Yes, Mr. Gary met

with the attorneys that represented Ford Motor Company and the

Visteon Corporation and a deal was allegedly made. The deal,

according to the complaint that was filed, was worth $51.5 million

dollars. Apparently, Mr. Gary would be given $51.5 million dollars if

he would get his clients to drop their claims against Ford.

What actually happened in that case? Mr. Gary informed his clients

they did not have a case against Ford or the Visteon Corporation. Even

more disgusting was learning that this deal was allegedly made prior to

Mr. Gary having a retainer agreement with any of the ladies filing the

suit. If true, this was not a coincidence. This was an intentional act of

fraud. The complaint that was filed against Mr. Gary and several other lawyers in his firm was simply appalling. (See full complaint in

Appendix C.)

After reading this complaint it became crystal clear to me that those women were sold out by Mr. Gary. It also became crystal clear that the same thing had happened in our cases too. I believe Mr. Gary, along with others from his firm, entered into a secret deal with The Coca-Cola Company in return for having the plaintiffs withdraw their cases.

This too was what the sisters who posted that website had also concluded. One of the website authors, a woman who'd lost her job at Coke, was led to dig deeper, had a hunger for justice. She went on to law school and her study of these cases helped bring the dirty truth to light. In my opinion, her conclusions were right on the money. Furthermore, I think the Holy Spirit, not a desire for vengeance, led this God-fearing woman down this track. She was simply led to uncover the truth.

The truth uncovered was a pattern that was not new. It had been seen before. Cyrus Mehri and his cast of attorneys settled with the majority of the class. However, the 17 plaintiffs Mr. Gary represented were still enough to scare The Coca-Cola Company, and so the company was looking for resolution. Willie Gary made his reputation on bringing large companies to their knees and hitting them hard and deep in their pockets. Sadly, rarely would his clients benefit from his hard hitting tactics it seemed. When we were together during the case and even at press conferences, Mr. Gary would say although there has been a settlement with the class, "The final resolution must come through Willie Gary, The Giant Killer."

I remember having a meeting with Mr. Gary and several of the lawyers from his firm in his hotel room. Mr. Gary was to be featured on 60 Minutes that evening I learned after I arrived. We sat and watched as the television show highlighted his fame and fortune, and praised Mr. Gary for showing such an interest in our children who represent our future. They did a wonderful job of making him seem like he was larger than life. They portrayed him as truly caring about his family, friends and most certainly his clients. I watched as the theme from "Rocky" played and Mr. Gary jumped up from his seat and started shadow boxing as if he felt he was the heavyweight champion of the world.

469

But what happened next gave me great insight into just how powerful and connected Mr. Gary was. His cell phone rang. He answered, "Hello," and then replied after a pause that he was just a country boy trying to make a living. This I'd learned was his way of appearing to be humble and modest. He then looked at me and said," It's the President." I thought to myself, "The president of what?"

As he continued to converse, I learned it was the President of the United States on the telephone talking to Mr. Gary as if they were old buddies. Then Mr. Gary spoke as though he was repeating the President's words by asking "What did you say Mr. President? You have a way for us to make a lot of money?" I was floored; Mr. Gary then lowered his voice and walked to another area of the room while continuing to talk.

I sat in stunned silence when one of the attorneys then joked about how well dressed I was and commented on my gators. My street sense told me I was not supposed to hear that part of the conversation, but I did. I thought to myself that if the President of the United States called Mr. Gary on his cell phone, then Mr. Gary was indeed a very powerful man.

Coke knew the racial breakdown statistics on the company were an embarrassment, especially for a company claiming to be the forerunner in diversity. Willie knew all he needed to do was publicly appear to be pushing for a trial and he'd create pressure. This would be enough to scare Coke and let his clients think he was fighting hard for them. Yet in private, he would say he had 17 opportunities to break their bank. Unlike the Kubik case where there was not a related class action suit, just 42 brave women fighting for their rights; this case had more leverage. Mr. Gary apparently thought this time it would be easier to walk away with tens of millions of dollars from The Coca-Cola Company.

I imagine he thought this one would be a cakewalk. After all, The Coca-Cola Company had already established the amount of money each class member would receive. It would be easier for Willie and his lawyers to encourage the 17 of us to accept the money we would have received if we'd not opted out of the class action, rather than presenting our case in court with the possibility of not receiving any monetary gain. The funds were already waiting to be distributed, and surely they thought we'd settle for that versus nothing.

471

It is my belief that Mr. Gary approached The Coca-Cola Company and stated he would make 16 of the 17 cases go away for the small price of say "millions" of dollars. My case was well on its way to summary judgment, so he could not stop it; but rather than worrying about that, he simply decided to not properly represent me. Instead he just let it sit there until the judge decided to rule on it; however long that might have taken. Once a secret deal in principle was agreed upon, he left my case to grow stale and focused his attorneys on the other clients and getting them to withdraw their claims or accept a nominal settlement.

I too received a call at one time. An attorney called me and asked if I would consider accepting less than $24,000 for the settlement of my case. While Mr. Gary told me time and time again that my case was worth millions and had even documented this claim in correspondence to me, now it was suddenly worth little. He also knew it was unlikely I would accept pennies to be silenced for life, yet he suggested that Coke was offering me much less than this amount. In reality, I wasn't his, the other 16 were. He knew I was willing to walk away with nothing if that's what it took for justice to be served.

472

He did get to the others. I remember also when several of the 16 plaintiffs called and said something went wrong. They spoke of telephone calls each of them received from lawyers of Mr. Gary's firm urging them to take the settlement. Several of them stated it was somewhat appalling how the attorneys spoke to them. They shared in their own ways the stories of how they believed Mr. Gary had sold us out. All of a sudden, the cases against Coke which Mr. Gary and his lawyers had been all over the media ranting and raving about, were suddenly nonsense in their eyes.

When we signed our retention contracts, Mr. Gary told us our cases were strong and they were going to fight for us to the bitter end. That was an empty promise. After more than three years, our cases were now apparently too weak to proceed. This was the same thing Mr. Gary had done to the women in the Michigan case. He and lawyers from his firm told those clients they did not have a case against Ford Motor Company or Visteon Corporation and that they therefore needed to drop the charges.

Our spiel was a little different. The Coca-Cola Company had already allotted each class member a particular amount of money. So,

473

instead of convincing us to walk away empty-handed, he just had to get

the 16 plaintiffs to accept the money they would have received as a

class member, and it would "be a win" for each of the parties involved.

In the Kubik v. Willie Gary Civil Action No. 03-73350 case, Mr.

Gary and several lawyers of his firm were accused of legal malpractice,

conversion, breach of fiduciary duty, contract in contravention of

public policy and fraud. I found it easy to believe after carefully

pooling all the facts together that Willie Gary, Tricia Hoffler, Robert

Parenti, Sekou Gary, and Gary, Williams, Parento, Finney, Lewis,

McManus, Watson & Sperando, P.C., were accused of committing a

crime.

After reviewing that information, I realized our cases were no more

than a joke to Willie Gary and his firm. He has created a well-

organized system of defrauding his clients out of millions and the

companies paying him are as guilty as he. It was clear they never

intended on helping us. All the meetings, conference calls and

correspondence from the firm were just a joke and a part of the scheme

that led down a road where a man who seemingly had everything stooped as low as a snake. He was led by his personal greed, not his desire for justice for his clients.

I lost all respect for Mr. Gary and the lawyers from his firm. I have even less respect for the companies that go to these lengths to hide discrimination, mistreatment and wrong doing with regards to its workers, who in many cases were nothing less than loyal, committed employees.

Mr. Gary, the self-proclaimed "Giant Killer," did not choose to have his day in court to defend his firm against the charges these women had made. *Why not?* He is after all a trial lawyer. If he were innocent, I don't believe it would have been hard for him to defend himself against accusations of legal malpractice, conversion, breach of fiduciary duty, contact in contravention of public policy and fraud. Surely if he were innocent he'd want to clear their names.

Being accused of criminal acts, punishable by imprisonment, should have angered Mr. Gary and his team. It should have made these attorneys furious to the point that if nothing else, they were going to have their day in court to clear their reputations. But it did not. *What is exactly is their reputation?*

Instead of fighting to defend himself, Mr. Gary hired a firm out of Michigan, and they did not battle in front of a jury to clear their names of such serious charges. Rather, they settled the case quietly as if they were wealthy guilty criminals, and sealed all documents so the world could not see their dirt.

Wow! How do lawyers, agree to take $51.5 million dollars from the company that their clients hired them to fight? How do they then return to those very clients and tell them they do not have a case and advise them to drop all charges without ever mentioning the $51.5 million dollars their firm would receive if all the cases simply went away? The thought of this sort of corruption is beneath any decent thinking human. To those who have taken an oath to uphold our precious Constitution of the United States of America, it should have been even more appalling. These were dirty lawyers.

This man prayed before every meal. At the time, I thought he was sincere but maybe this was just a ploy to win over clients. I have since seen him on the religion television channel confessing how good God has been to him. In my opinion, Willie Gary and these attorneys should be incarcerated for an extended period of time and never allowed to practice law again. In reviewing the facts, it seems obvious they were guilty and wanted to settle quickly and then bury this case deep in the archives of the judicial system.

I was convinced that Mr. Gary committed the same crime in our cases as he had in the Michigan case. I decided to get as many of the seventeen former clients of his together to see what they thought of my suspicions. That's what I did. Several phone calls later, a group of us agreed to meet in Buckhead, Atlanta.

When the group began to arrive we caught up with a little small talk. It was great seeing everyone after several years passed. I counted nine and realized almost everyone was there. I began the meeting with a short prayer and quickly moved on to say why we were meeting.

I shared the communication Mr. Gary originally initiated with me after several years of silence. I then told the group why Mr. Gary had called me and what he wanted me to do. I then told of the attitudes I encountered with the two ladies he wanted me to call. I asked if any of them felt Mr. Gary made a deal with The Coca-Cola Company and was paid millions to get each of them to accept the money they would have received as a class member.

Every one of them looked at me with certainty and said they knew

that was what he did. One of the sisters shared how she refused to take

the settlement amount even after the attorneys from the Gary Firm

badgered her to do so. She worked at Coke for almost twenty years at

the time the class settled, and she shared how the attorney called her

trying to make the amount of money she would receive seem like a

treasure on which she could retire and live happily ever after. Many

others shared how they tried to contact Mr. Gary and lawyers from the

firm when they had questions, but rarely were able to speak with

someone and even when they did, their questions were not answered.

After giving everyone an opportunity to speak, I simply stated Mr.

Gary played each us for fools, but me as largest of all. As clients we

trusted him to represent our struggles in corporate America. I went on

and shared we felt comfortable with him because being a black man he

was not ignorant to our pain. He certainly knew all the right things to

say, to get us to trust him.

One of the sisters, an original plaintiff, reminded me of how Mr.

Gary spoke to her when she was unsure about leaving the class and

allowing him to represent her. She said, "Greg, remember when I asked

Mr. Gary how did we know that he would not mistreat us like the first group of attorneys and he responded to me, 'just pray about it.'" She continued saying she believed he had it all planned from the beginning.

I told them when we met with Jesse Jackson Sr. and he introduced me to Mr. Gary over the telephone, I believe they were already working together. Mr. Gary was waiting on that call, I'm sure. I also explained why Jesse Jackson Sr.'s presence was significant. He was also present in the Michigan case. *Another sister muttered softly, if you cannot trust a preacher, a man who said he was a friend and walked beside Martin Luther King Jr. and your lawyer, then whom do we trust?*

I affirmed I was going to do all I could to bring light to this terrible crime. I knew he was rich and powerful with connections throughout the country. But, I believed if we pushed the right buttons, anyone having knowledge of the settlement would not commit perjury to protect Mr. Gary, certainly not the attorneys from Coke.

I then shared with the group a document where one of the attorneys who now serves as a judge in the state of Florida, wrote Coke voluntarily withdrawing the claims of one of the 17 the Gary firm represented, and went even further stating the client was consulted

479

about her withdrawal. It was not until this sister realized that Mr. Gary

cut a secret deal with Coke and requested a copy of each

correspondence in her file did she find this document of withdrawal

buried in one of her boxes. The letter stated that HR files for the

plaintiff's Caucasian higher-paid counterparts indicated that their

higher pay level was due to longevity and performance reviews;

therefore the plaintiff was withdrawing her discrimination claim. The

former plaintiff does not recall voluntarily withdrawing her claims nor

did she approve this move at the time it was made. In fact, she

maintains that she was unaware of it. Had she not requested those files,

she would not have uncovered the deceit.

Add to this discovery the fact that the young lady I am referring to

is one of the very ladies Mr. Gary asked me to call and plead with her

to take down the website. He knew she had uncovered dirt and had

hoped I might help him to resolve the problem. Little did he know I'd

not resolve his problem but further uncover it. Little did I know just

how big the problem and corruption was.

Collectively, we could not understand how an attorney could lie and

surrender a client's claims without her knowledge and not be held responsible for it. This was obvious deception. I can only imagine how

this sister felt when she stumbled upon this piece of documentation. For

years she thought Mr. Gary was fighting for her. She now had proof he

was not, but on the contrary made a deal and sold her out. *What kind of*

games were Mr. Gary and his lawyers playing with our lives? This was

dangerous.

The group decided to write and request each of our files but to do

so collectively. Each of us was curious to see what was actually

contained in our files. But we also knew that Mr. Gary did not intend

for that document ever to be seen by anyone outside of his firm,

especially not the client that he stated had knowledge of wrong doings.

The group was aware of Mr. Gary's slickness and expected many

excuses when requesting our documents. We believed Mr. Gary cut a

deal with The Coca-Cola Company and this would be one of our first

steps to proving it. Having fought the two sisters who established the

website for several years, we knew Mr. Gary most definitely had

cleaned the files lest there be another slip up or document request like

the last one.

A letter was written to Mr. Gary requesting the complete files for the nine signatures appearing on the document. I did not sign the document. I wanted my file but I knew Mr. Gary, especially because there were things to hide, would call me to see if I had any knowledge of the letter requesting documentation. I was the common link to the nine.

The letter to Mr. Gary was simple and straightforward. It said: "We are writing to request a copy of our individual files to be sent to the addresses below. We have signed our names beside each address giving the firm permission to send the files. We would like to receive these files within ten business days. Please be advised there will be others requesting copies of their files. We thank you in advance." That letter was signed by nine of Mr. Gary's former clients in this case and once it was mailed, we waited.

We knew he'd not be in a hurry to answer and in expected fashion; Mr. Gary's first response arrived with some delay and without adequate response. His letter indicated that there was a problem with the money order we sent and said it was enclosed to be returned to us, but it was not in the envelope.

Mr. Gary's letter said, "In response to your letter, enclosed is your money order. You will note that the Money Order was not signed by the purchaser nor was it correctly made payable to us, and, therefore, would not be negotiable. Further, your letter does not indicate if all copies should be sent to the address on the envelope or if they should be sent to individual addresses. Please clarify. As we previously advised, if any pleadings are urgently required, the federal courthouse in Atlanta would still have access to all pleadings that were filed in your case including copies of what transcripts were filed."

Just as I anticipated, both Ms. Hoffler and Ms. Diaz lawyers that worked for Mr. Gary called me a week after the letter was mailed. Ms. Hoffler started with a bit of small talk as she tried to get a feel for my mood. Ms. Diaz was also very polite. Then Ms. Hoffler informed me they received a letter from what appeared to be some of their former clients from the Coke case.

Ms. Diaz asked me if I knew why they would be requesting copies of their files. I said, "No." Ms. Hoffler then asked, "Greg, isn't this the group that worked on the technical side of the company? I responded, "I am not sure." I then asked what the letter said.

483

Ms. Diaz left the call for a few minutes then returned and read the entire letter to me. After reading the letter, the ladies began to talk among themselves as if I was no longer on the call. Ms. Hoffler stated the files were several years old and after the tornado destroyed their building, she was not sure if they even had those files any longer. She then asked Ms. Diaz what the going rate for copying documents was.

Ms. Diaz replied, "I think it is between $1.00 to $2.00 per page." Ms. Hoffler then stated a letter would be drafted explaining the damage that occurred to the building and how some of the files may have been destroyed. Then, she stated the cost per page would be mentioned in the letter and the full payment would be required before any files would be released.

It was amazing to hear how freely these women spoke. Ms. Hoffler even asked me if I knew the statute of limitation on the case and I said I did not. Interesting. *Why would one of Mr. Gary's brightest attorneys ask me if I had knowledge of the statute of limitations?* After a few more minutes, the call ended but not before Ms. Hoffler and Ms. Diaz spelled out exactly how they were going to respond to the letter requesting the files.

Each of these ladies had knowledge of the fraud committed in our cases. I wondered how they would feel when they realized I was the author of the letter just read back to me. After the conversation with the two ladies, I knew Mr. Gary had not told them of our earlier conversation where I requested to meet with him, and he suggested that we meet in Stuart, Florida. That suggestion made over a year ago was never followed up on. He did not give me a meeting place nor did he return my phone calls. I guess he assumed he had gotten rid of me.

The first response we received from Mr. Gary and his firm regarding the letter was exactly what we expected it to be – a stall tactic. His second response to us did include the money order but once again, it did not address the issue of the records and files we were requesting. We decided to make it absolutely clear what we thought. We sent the following letter to Mr. Gary making it clear that while his firm was messing around with the details of a small money order, our real interest was in receiving the information we'd requested.

The group of former plaintiffs decided to enclose a copy of the voluntary dismissal letter the one lady had received so Mr. Gary would know exactly what was being asked for. Again, as we expected there

485

was never a response addressing our concerns. It was obvious that something was wrong. *If there was nothing to hide why not give an affidavit?* We were the same clients for whom Mr. Gary chartered a private plane to fly all 17 plaintiffs to Florida to meet at his office, take a tour of his home, and later return to Georgia that evening. A meaningless trip, I once thought. Not unless the trip provided Mr. Gary the necessary time to close the deal with The Coca Cola Company in lieu of fallout among his clients.

What if Mr. Gary had already given an affidavit stating that he or no one from his firm received any money from representing the seventeen of us? What if Mr. Gary and other lawyers in his firm perjured themselves? The two sisters responsible for creating the website had already received affidavits from Mr. Gary, and other lawyers from his firm. Among many things, it stated neither they nor any attorney working out of the firm did wrongdoing in representing them.

They proclaimed they were nothing less than professional in their handling of all complaints. Wow! This was meaningless to me knowing these attorneys probably used some of the same language in their denial in the Michigan case. Nevertheless, each of the affidavits stated the same thing, "Contrary to Plaintiffs' allegations, there was never an agreement whereby Defendants attorneys, their law firm, or MBC would receive $40 Million dollars, or any other sum of money, as part of a settlement package in exchange for Plaintiffs' permanently dropping their claims against The Coca-Cola Company, and Defendants attorneys agreeing never to pursue litigation against The Coca-Cola Company again in the future."

In researching Mr. Gary and this crime, I became more familiar with how attorneys respond to questions. I found it interesting Mr. Gary nor any other attorney from his firm were willing to give the ten of us affidavits as they did the two young ladies whom created the website.

We have to ask in a different manner, I thought. As a group, we specifically asked Mr. Gary to give us an affidavit "as to whether or not he, his firm, or anyone else working on his behalf or on behalf of his firm, received any monies or consideration of any nature whatsoever from the defendant, The Coca-Cola Company, in settlement of any and or all cases filed on behalf of The Coca Cola Company clients, and if your answer is in the positive, please provide the exact dollar amount

received and/or the type of consideration received if not monetary." No

affidavit was given.

However, Mr. Gary's response to the bar association specifically

stated, "there was never an agreement whereby attorneys, their law

firm, or MBC would receive $40 million dollars, or any other sum of

money, as part of a settlement package in exchange for plaintiffs'

permanently dropping their claims against The Coca-Cola Company,

and Defendants attorneys agreeing never to pursue litigation against

The Coca-Cola Company again in the future."

I found it interesting that Mr. Gary, Ms. Hoffler and Ms. Diaz all

stated in their affidavits there was never an agreement whereby

Defendants attorneys, their law firm, or MBC, which is a cable

television network Mr. Gary once owned a part of, would receive $40

million dollars, or any sum of money, as part of a settlement package in

exchange for Plaintiffs' permanently dropping their claims. This only

means the monies were paid through another entity with the

understanding it would later be routed to Mr. Gary. Just like it was

done in the dreadful Michigan case.

I knew he could not give the sworn statement, for if he did and stated he did not take any money or consideration, he would have committed perjury; a crime for which he may have been disbarred. I imagined after consulting with his team of lawyers, they simply decided to ignore our request. Rather than defending themselves, they chose to make us prove they took millions of dollars from The Coca-Cola Company. Here is a first step in that process. *Is it so difficult to believe?*

Mr. Gary and the attorneys in his firm were not under any court ruling stipulating they must surrender an affidavit to us, but if they were innocent, they would have gladly complied with former clients. Put yourself in their shoes. *If you were innocent would you have given a sworn affidavit saying you had not stolen from your clients? Would there be anything to hide, provided you were innocent?*

Once again, former clients are accusing Mr. Gary's firm of stealing from them. Once again, it appears that the "Giant Killer" has taken the cowardly way out.

It doesn't end here however. One of the former plaintiffs – the woman who went on to law school and helped establish the website that Mr. Gary was upset over – took things a step further. She filed

motions with the courts documenting where judges recused themselves

until the Coke discrimination lawsuit filings would eventually land

with Judges Story and Scofield. She also filed a motion seeking to have

both of these judges disqualified based on prejudice.

Think back to that December 23rd, 2000, article in the Atlanta

Journal Constitution. Judge Story was discouraging class members

from pursuing individual cases. My co-plaintiff, the woman who went

on to law school, has since dug up documents showing just how many

racial discrimination cases originally given to other judges somehow all

were assigned to Judge Story instead. *Someone may ask did he know*

more about the underhanded way these cases were suddenly invalid, or

was he the reason that they virtually never reached a fair courtroom in

Georgia? You be the judge based on Judge Story's words in that

article:

> "The class members, current and former African American
> employees of Coca-Cola, will then have about two months to
> decide among three options. They can accept the settlements for
> compensatory damages, back pay and other damages, which are
> expected to total about $40,000 apiece on average.
> Class members who think they have strong evidence that they
> were discriminated against in a past promotion decision can
> accept a partial settlement for compensatory damages, typically

expected to total $28,000, while taking their promotion case to a U.S. magistrate judge. The third option is to "opt out" of the settlement and pursue a case on their own.

Story, however, strongly urged members of the class-action lawsuit to weigh the risks of a separate lawsuit against the "very substantial and significant monetary benefits of this major proposed settlement.

"An individual suit could take three to five additional years to resolve, including appeals. Most individual employment discrimination suits are unsuccessful," Story stated.

He noted that Coca-Cola said no individual race discrimination cases against the company in the past 10 years have resulted in either a judgment against the company or settlements with awards higher than the class-action suit's average settlement.

"The judge is correct that most individual cases are unsuccessful. We understand that 80 percent of the cases in the Atlanta area are thrown out on summary judgment," said plaintiffs' attorney Cyrus Mehri.

He called Story's preliminary approval "an important step on the road to justice at The Coca-Cola Co." Now more than 10 years have passed and not 1 Title V11 racial discrimination case has been awarded in this court.

One of the sisters and co-author of the website featuring Mr. Gary, decided after attending law school she would research the entire racial discrimination case or cases as well as the judges, lawyers and court system. What she uncovered is astonishing. What she uncovered may be considered criminal. What she alleged and confirmed with documentation could possibly be one of the largest scandals of our time. She filed two documents; the first being a response to her summary judgment which referenced the cases in which judges recused

themselves until the Coke cases landed within the chambers of Judges

Story-Scofield. The second was the motion to disqualify both Story &

Scofield based on prejudice. I received a copy of each of the

documents, filed under Civil Action 1:01-CV-2866 (RWS), they blew

my mind. Please see **Appendix A & B** in the rear of the book.

Discrimination in the corporate icon, The Coca-Cola Company was

a given. Fraud and corruption among the lawyers; we all have heard

stories. *Fraud among the judges; was it possible? Corruption and*

manipulation in the judicial system; alleged or in fact true. You be the

judge.

After the filing of these documents with the courts; attorneys from

The Coca-Cola Company and King & Spalding were soon on the

telephone asking to meet with her she shared. *Why? She was claiming*

injustice and fraud in the judicial system, so why was that a matter of

concern to the company she had formerly tried to sue for racial

discrimination? Why did those attorneys have any interest in the claims

she made against judges in the Northern District? She was not

attacking The Coca-Cola Company in her court filings or on her

492

website. Why did Elizabeth Finn-Johnson, Coke's attorney and Michael Johnston from King & Spalding become interested in or worried about her actions? Is it possible that this type of behavior ran rampant in the Northern District? *Is it possible that other cases brought before the court by the King & Spalding Firm were ruled on the same way?* After all, the company did a wonderful job proclaiming to the world that through its historic settlement all was done fairly, and from then on the company was committed to treating all of its employees equally. It did set aside approximately one hundred million dollars for programs, such as sensitivity training for employees. *But, what if nothing was done fairly? Is it possible that the racial discriminatory attitudes of many of the leaders of the company could now be found in federal court amongst judges?* I want to believe there are honest fair judges in the northern district, but something about this stunk.

She agreed to meet with Coke's attorneys as requested. According to her account, there was one male, Michael Johnston and one female attorney, Elizabeth Finn-Johnson whom sat with her in a room. She then stated Michael Johnston who is believed to be one of King & Spalding finest attorneys sat with a notepad and looked her directly in

493

her eyes then asked her what she wanted. These weren't lightweights.

In the room were the big players of the legal department at The Coca-

Cola Company and King & Spalding. I saw them many times during

this war. Her reply was, "Nothing." She recanted that the female lawyer

nearly fell out of her chair when she gave her answer. This sister fought

so long and hard with us, and not for the purpose of being awarded a

nest egg of hush money. She simply wanted justice. She simply sought

for the truth to be told. And, here it is in the pages of this book.

Why did the attorneys ask her what she wanted? Her claims were of

judicial fraud and injustice against the judges involved in her case, my

case and all those before Judge Story and Magistrate Scofield. Could

they have been asking to keep hidden an inappropriate relationship the

company had with federal judges? Wow, if not, then why?

They weren't disputing the claims she made. She wasn't asked to

give proof of the claims; instead she was asked what she personally

wanted. *Why would these powerful, intelligent attorneys be willing to*

risk it all, to pay to keep this information from going any further?

Could Coke's attorneys have realized that if her research reached the

public and prompted an investigation that proved her allegations were accurate, the company would again be involved in another

embarrassing position it could not explain to its shareholders or

consumers? Did they realize that her findings may prompt an

investigation among all of the federal judges in the northern district?

Who would investigate federal judges, or for that matter the entire

eleventh district?

Why were all the discrimination cases shuffled off to Judge Story &

Magistrate Scofield? Why would nobody else take them? Or who

encouraged them not to take them? Is this one isolated case of

seventeen, or is it a common practice? Is this hidden racism or simple

blatant abuse of judicial power? Why?

I remember so well years ago, when it was time for the class

members to make a decision to accept or reject the settlement package.

It was at that time that I stumbled across the article where Judge Story

described how difficult it would be to win an individual racial

discrimination case in Georgia's northern district. I am thankful that

now I have a thorough understanding of why it is so difficult. *Again, I*

ask the question who would investigate federal judges? These were not small allegations that she made against the judges, but all Coke's attorneys wanted to know was what she wanted to go away.

Many years have passed and a prominent leader who was a pastor died in Atlanta, and I knew Rev. Jesse Jackson Sr. would certainly make an appearance, because that's what he does. I decided to go to the memorial service and speak with him. I arrived at the service two hours before it started to get a seat. Time passed quickly as the service began and just as I thought towards the end Rev. Jackson made his appearance. He was given time to speak to share some of his memories of his friend that had gone on to be with the Lord. I sat patiently yet anxiously waiting the opportunity to once again speak with him and it came. I positioned myself outside of the door that he entered and waited but he exited through another door. I swiftly made my way around to the front of the building and walked directly to him. I told him that I was the lead plaintiff in the racial discrimination lawsuit against The Coca Cola Company and that I was concerned that the attorney he introduced me to Willie E. Gary stole tens of millions of dollars from his clients and I was one of them. I went on and shared that after not having heard from Mr. Gary for several years, I received a telephone call from a reporter telling me that my case had been

dismissed. I called the law firm countless times and could not get

anyone to respond to me. I felt at that point that something was wrong

but I couldn't put my finger on it. I then told him that Mr. Gary called

me back but it was several years later. He was not calling to provide

clarity to my case but to ask for my help. I shared Mr. Gary asked me

to call two of the other clients he represented along with me, to see if I

could get them to take down a website that depicted him and several

prominent business men and leaders as organized criminals. I told him

that he was one of the people mentioned as being a part of this criminal

activity. He looked stunned but I knew how close he and Mr. Gary

were and that he probably had knowledge of the website. It was at that

time when Rev. Jackson told me that he was running late for a flight

and that he would call me once he settled himself on the flight. I waited

an hour and yes my cell phone rang, but to my surprise it was not Rev.

Jackson Sr. but one of the gentlemen (Bishop Tavis Grant) whom I did

not know nor had the pleasure of meeting but was travelling with Rev.

Jackson. This I found strange. A short time ago we stood as men face to

face and I shared my concerns about an attorney that you introduced to me in the presence of Joe Beasley, Regional Director of PUSH, during

the time of the Coke racial discrimination lawsuit and now it appears

that Rev. Jackson wants to act like less than two hours ago we did not

have a conversation and he did not tell me that he was going to call me

once he was off.

The conversation with Bishop Grant appeared to be for

informational purposes only. As this gentlemen asked questioned that

he had no knowledge of it was obvious that he was being told what to

ask. I listened as he tried maneuvering his way to finding out just how

much evidence and exactly what I knew. Weeks passed before I

forwarded this letter to Rev. Jackson Sr.

Rev. Jesse Jackson Sr.
930 East 50th Street
Chicago, IL 60615

Rev. Jackson,

I was first introduced to you during the Coca-Cola class action
lawsuit on a conference call where the percentage of money the
attorneys believed they would have received was intentionally
misstated to you by lead counsel Cyrus Mehri. The next morning, I
met you and Joe Beasley along with a few of the other lead plaintiffs at
the hotel where you were staying in downtown Atlanta, GA. During
this meeting, I asked you if I could speak with you alone, without any
of the attorneys present. You responded, "Certainly" and turned to the

attorneys that were there from the Bondurant, Mixon and Elmore law firm and said, "Surely the attorneys would not mind if you spoke with me alone."

On August 5, 2011, I met you at a memorial service for the late Pastor W. Howard Creecy Jr. at Olivet Baptist Church in Fayetteville, GA. While walking beside you to your vehicle, I shared with you that Willie Gary, the attorney that you without the help of any others introduced me to during the Coca-Cola class action lawsuit, stole money from me. I told you that I could prove that Mr. Gary had the company forward tens of millions of dollars to an organization that was not directly linked or could easily be traced to his law firm. I also shared that one day after realizing I had missed numerous calls from Mr. Gary, we spoke. Mr. Gary asked me to give two of his former clients, Sharron Mangum and Marietta Goodman, whom I knew and were also represented by him, a call and ask them to take down a website that depicted you, his firm and several others as criminals that designed an elaborate scam to heist hundreds of millions of dollars from companies that were facing class action lawsuits. I shared that Mr. Gary and I spoke for several weeks concerning the ladies taking down their website. In one of our conversations Mr. Gary stated that he might be willing to give them a few pennies, a couple hundred thousand. But, he could not do that because what the women would do at that point was go to the media and say, "Look what Willie Gary gave us trying to make us go away." I told you that I called Mr. Gary and simply told him I needed to meet with him immediately. Mr. Gary started stuttering and appeared to be at a loss for words and said he would call me back. In less than five minutes Mr. Gary called back and asked if it was ok if he could bring Gloria and I could get my wife and we could sit down and have dinner. I stated "Yes," and I would await his call. To date, I have not heard from him.

Before exiting in your vehicle you stated that you would contact me and look into what I shared with you. You then told one of the gentlemen that travelled with you to give me a card and to take my number. As you requested, I texted Bishop Tavis Grant, the name that appeared on the card, with several of my concerns. Someone responded they would check into things and get back with me via text messaging. A few days later, I received a call from someone who said his name was Bishop Grant asking what exactly did I know. He stated that if he were going to try and get to the bottom of things he needed to know all that I knew. He then went on and asked me a series of questions. The questions were centered on finding out how much information I could prove that I made reference to the day I saw you, and of the text messages I later forwarded. I shared very little with him. I found it interesting Rev. Jackson that you personally called my cell phone several times during the lawsuit before there was a settlement. On one occasion while riding in a car with Mr. Gary, my telephone rang and you asked to speak with him. I am puzzled as to why you are now appearing to be hiding your hand or trying to take a backseat to the issues at hand when in fact, I would never have known Mr. Gary if it were not for you.

Approximately one week later, I received a call from the same gentleman whom stated his name was Bishop Grant, only this conversation was different. I answered my telephone, he immediately asked me to wait for a moment while I was placed on hold. Before being placed on hold I heard several voices in the background. It appeared he was only being used to try and find out once again how much I knew. He asked me a number of questions, but this time I told him in so many words I was sick and tired of the games that Mr. Gary played and was currently playing with my life. He asked me if I had gotten a lawyer yet. He asked if I had thought of an amount of money to settle. He wanted to know what documents I had in my possession to prove that Mr. Gary took money from The Coca Cola Company. I once remember sitting at a round table as questions and strategies were laid out to go forward against The Coca Cola Company, where Mr. Gary dictated and controlled the conversation. There were always lawyers from his firm present. I imagine the call that I received was no different. Bishop Grant made it clear that he "had no dog in the fight." The conversation ended with Bishop Grant telling me that he would be in touch with me in a few days. Weeks, now months have passed and my initial concern has never been addressed by you, sir. Why did Willie Gary steal money from me? He did not have a case against The Coca Cola Company. I would not have been a victim of this horrific crime if you had not introduced us. Rev. Jackson, because of your actions and the way that you have not responded, I now have reasonable knowledge to believe that a crime or crimes have been committed by Mr. Willie E. Gary in his representation of my case against The Coca Cola Company.

Since then, I've researched and learned of several cases where clients have accused Mr. Gary of stealing. It appears that a well-organized scheme has been perpetrated on corporations to include, but not limited to The Coca Cola Company, Ford Motor Company, and Microsoft. It appears Rev. Jackson that although the cases differ, they are alike as well. These cases received national publicity. The companies make public blanket statements acknowledging they do not and will not tolerate discrimination of any kind. Meetings were held between the lawyers, some secret, some not. Threats were made by Mr. Gary that suggests he has enough information to shut the company down. The companies realized that it would be best if it settled behind closed doors to save its image. The companies, along with Mr. Gary agree they will not admit to any wrong doing. In an effort to begin rebuilding the company's reputation, some sort of unified public display of both sides of lawyers is seen depicting togetherness and solidarity. Meanwhile, the lawyers have agreed to the terms of the Gary Firm and also have agreed to have the settlement paid to other organizations, but never directly to the Gary Firm. If there was an amount paid to Mr. Gary's firm, it would not be the full amount for which the case settled. Obviously, if the money that Mr. Gary has rerouted through other entities and there is not a direct link to him, I'm curious if there are any taxes being paid after Mr. Gary has received these funds. In other words sir, this appears to be racketeering.

60 Minutes once featured Mr. Gary. At the time it was airing, I was in a hotel in downtown Atlanta, GA with Lorenzo Williams, C.K. Hoffler and Mr. Gary. After the show, Mr. Gary jumped up and started shadow boxing. I imagined he felt good for the show depicted him as an attorney that grew from rags to riches, and one that loved fighting for those that for various reasons could not fight for themselves. After a few jokes were told, Mr. Gary's cell phone rang. Mr. Gary answered

the phone and said "Hello Mr. President, how are you sir?" Mr. Gary looked at me and made a hand motion pointing to the telephone and said, "It's the President." It was the President of the United States, President Bill Clinton, calling him on his cell phone. A bit of small talk took place before Mr. Gary said, "I am just a country boy trying to make a living." He later asked, "What did you say Mr. President? You said you have a lot of money for us to make?" Lorenzo and Mr. Gary made eye contact but no words were spoken, and that was when Mr. Gary quietly but swiftly walked into the other room. In my research, I learned that President Bill Clinton appointed Judge Richard Story. Ironically, all seventeen of the cases somehow mysteriously landed in Judge Richard Story's courtroom. I wonder if a federal investigation was done who would be damaged the most, Rev. Jesse Jackson Sr., The Coca Cola Company, King& Spalding, or the Gary Firm.

In July of 2005, Mr. Gary settled a case where the very clients whom hired him to fight Ford Motor Company and Visteon Corporation on behalf of discrimination claims, ended up suing him for contract in contravention of public policy, breach of fiduciary duty, legal malpractice, conversion and fraud. In this case (Civil Action No. 03-CV-73350) in the Eastern District of Michigan Southern Division. The law firm of Rundell and Nolan P.C. hired Mr. Gary's firm to serve as co-counsel for the plaintiffs. After being retained by Rundell and Nolan P.C., Mr. Gary implemented a scheme designed to compel Ford Motor Company and Visteon Corporation to resolve the pending lawsuits on terms extremely advantageous to Mr. Gary and the other attorneys. A few months later, and without the knowledge and consent of any of the plaintiffs that hired him, Mr. Gary entered into a secret agreement whereby he would receive $51.5 million as part of a settlement package in exchange for the plaintiffs dropping their claims. Rev. Jackson, this may have been pleasing to the plaintiffs, but Mr. Gary never told them of this agreement. But what he did do was go back to the plaintiffs and told them their claims were without merit and they would never prevail against the companies. Mr. Gary insisted the plaintiffs permanently dismiss their claims against the companies without receiving any compensation. Upon receiving intentionally false and erroneous advice, and the non-disclosure of the sums Mr. Gary and the other lawyers received, the plaintiffs signed various documents that purported to permanently dismiss and release their claims against the Ford Motor Company. After this, Mr. Gary received the $51.5 million from Ford Motor Company and the plaintiffs never knew. Certainly Rev. Jackson, you must agree, being a trial lawyer (the Giant Killer), if Mr. Gary were innocent of these charges, he would have gladly gone to trial to clear his name. But no! Mr. Gary settled the case and petitioned the court to have all files sealed, trying to hide all depositions and other related material from the public.

Mr. Gary entered into a similar agreement with The Coca Cola Company, but this one was a little different. He certainly learned from the Ford Motor Company case. All he had to do was get as many of the seventeen clients to accept the money they would have received as a result of being a class member. Once again, several of the attorneys from the Gary Firm called their clients and told them they did not believe their case would be won in court and many of them accepted the money. Mr. Gary received tens of millions of dollars for doing so, just like he did in the Ford Motor Company case. The plaintiffs that did not accept the money were poorly represented in court and their cases did not survive summary judgment.

I grew curious after not hearing anything from the Gary Firm for several years. I received a telephone call from an Atlanta Journal Constitution reporter informing me that my case was dismissed. I was the original plaintiff. I researched and organized groups that led to the class action lawsuit. If not for my efforts, there would not have been a lawsuit. The company settled the class action lawsuit for $192 million, and Mr. Gary wants me to believe that he walked away with nothing. I must admit, some time passed before the wool was pulled off of my eyes. After the death of my father, my attention was on taking care of my mother, sister, and even the brother that shot and killed my precious father. Please Rev. Jackson sir, make no mistake, I SEE CLEARLY NOW. I am aware of the scandal and your part in it. I want the money that Mr. Gary and his team of lawyers stole from me. Please, allow me to make it crystal clear. I am not trying to exploit or extort anything from Mr. Gary or anyone else for that matter. I want the money that Mr. Gary and his team of lawyers stole from me. It amazes me that I have to fight the attorneys that I originally hired to help me and others fight a racist culture. I fail to believe that Michael W. Johnston, or William A. Clineburg, Jr., of King & Spalding will perjure themselves to keep Mr. Gary out of prison. Likewise, will Elizabeth Finn-Johnson or Robert Boas of The Coca Cola Company, nor Jeffrey E. Tompkins. of Thomas, Kennedy, Sampson & Patterson, or any attorney from Paul, Hastings, and Janofsky & Walker law firm. This was a terrible crime that has been committed and it appears that no one's hands are clean.

If the need arises where I must obtain a legal team, we will first depose Jay Schwartz of Jay Schwartz Law Firm of Farmington Hills, Michigan, and Lawrence C. Falzon of Wigod, Falzon, McNeely & Unwin, P.C. of Southfield, Michigan. They will be able to testify and provide proof of the sworn statements of Mr. Gary's along with a host of lawyers. Regardless of the clever disclaimer contracts I'm certain they signed before receiving any money as a result of the settling in the Michigan case. As officers of the court, they will testify to Mr. Gary's behavior when asked did he commit this scheme on any other companies. Likewise, to his answer when asked what were the names of the other companies. Furthermore, they will testify to the number of stalling tactics that were used to keep Mr. Gary from answering these questions. They will be asked to physically demonstrate Mr. Gary's posture before these questions were asked, while they were awaiting an answer and after he gave his so-called answers. I also think it would be imperative to depose each attorney that would or should have knowledge of settlement talks. Each of the attorneys from Ford Motor Company and Visteon Corporation will be vital to exposing this crime. In addition to all this I have been blessed with a ram in the bush.

I once heard Mr. Gary remark that in picking a jury, he was not concerned with all twelve jury members wanting him to win. He just needed one that refused to let Willie lose. I am curious if and when a lawsuit is filed, it will most certainly receive national attention when one considers the level of ruthlessness and greed that has been uncovered. How difficult will it then be to find that one?

I realize the significance of what I have uncovered and I have not mentioned my smoking guns. It appears that maybe lawyers were not the only officers of the court that have committed unthinkable acts or have knowledge of them. I also remember Mr. Gary used the term "smoking gun" during one of the press conferences as he shared how he has become so successful, if that's what you want to call stealing from clients. In doing so, I have forwarded a copy to a family friend that is well insulated within the Federal Bureau of Investigation, a seasoned veteran that can't be bought. If there is any harm done to me, he will go forward and provide this letter as well as the other documentation to the proper authorities.

Respectfully,

Gregory A. Clark

Months passed without hearing anything from Rev. Jackson or Mr. Gary his partner in crime. Nevertheless, I continued to research. I reviewed many of my documents and compared my case to others I knew were similar. I continued to pray daily, for I knew the day would come when all that was done in the dark would soon be brought to light. I often reflected back to the beginning where I sought for a promotion that would have increased my salary by $20,000. Lawyers and people like Rev. Jackson who call himself a political leader have been exposed. I continued calling the offices of Rev. Jackson just to keep him reminded that I was not going away. A telephone call I made in the fall of 2013, sparked a telephone call from Mr. Gary.

My cell phone rang and I recognized the number as being from the

Gary Firm. I answered, "Hello" and Mr. Gary said, "Hey Greg, this is

Willie Gary. What's going on buddy? I have been out of the country for

the past 3 weeks and I'm just getting an opportunity to call you back."

He immediately began talking about how much money he'd lost

because of the website the ladies authored. As he continued ranting I

sat quietly and listened. Each time we spoke he continued to boast

about the amount of money he lost and was losing because of the site,

yet, he never took the authors of the site to court to have it removed. He

was a man that had hundreds of millions of dollars and the ladies had

nothing, what was his fear? Obvious slander if not true, prison if it was.

After realizing that I was not responding to him, Mr. Gary stopped

talking long enough to ask me, "Greg what's going on?" I told him that

I did my own investigation and I could prove that he stole money from

me. Once again he lost it. He began raising his voice and cursing. At

this point I was so sick of Willie and his bullshit, I too raised my voice

and gave him a few choice words. The louder he got, the louder I got. It

was clear that he had an audience and was trying to impress them. He

kept shouting, repeating, "I thought you said you did not believe the girls, that's what you told me". He said this several times before I

replied, "I never said that, you believed that because you always

assumed you had me in your pocket, but I received no money". He

replied, "Greg why are we talking about some fucking shit that

happened 8 years ago?" I replied, "Because that's when I realized you

stole from me". He yelled, "Greg, this shit is crazy, why are we still

talking about this shit?" The conversation never calmed, it became a

screaming match between lawyer and former client. I found this

extremely interesting. I remember years ago when Willie called me

seeking my help of getting the young ladies to remove the website.

Time has passed and I'm now telling him that I have proof that he stole

tens of millions of dollars, and he is screaming and yelling at me as he

once did concerning the ladies. He was definitely a showman, he put on

a great show for his audiences. We shouted back and forth for almost

20 minutes before his arrogance led him to say, "Well Greg then do

what you gotta do." I responded with a few more choice words and told

him he did not have to worry about that, I was going to do all that I

could to make sure he and his accomplices went to prison. The

telephones went dead. I was furious and so was he. I had a right to be, he did not. Mr. Gary realized that I was no longer the fool that he played me to be for years. He knew that I would not stop until I was satisfied. Although he tried to talk tough, I knew he was worried and afraid, for the crime that he committed not only would send him to prison but all the other lawyers involved. I continued my research.

While my initial fight was with Mr. Gary and Rev. Jackson, The Coca Cola Company was far from innocent. The Coca Cola Company paid to hide its dirt. This entire case reeked of the most unpleasant scent one could imagine. Coke did not have a reason to forward any amount of money to anyone on behalf of Willie E. Gary, for he had no case against them. The fact the company agreed to send money to another law firm with the understanding that it was on behalf of Willie Gary, and his role in representing former employees who sued the company, was criminal. The Coca Cola Company paid Mr. Gary to make the cases go away. Nothing is more apparent and clear of this when the federal documents of my case are viewed. They told the story. Mr. Gary and the lawyers that represented me were seasoned trial lawyers. What they did was appalling. Please see **Appendix D**.

This document is designed primarily to be used as a flow chart to capture the different filings of briefs and motions and rulings of the judge. It can also be used to surmise what a judge will allow and what he or she will not. While these documents are public record rarely do attorneys expect them to be reviewed. The reviewing of my docket further confirmed that Mr. Gary and The Coca-Cola Company had partnered. I was alarmed at the number of highlighted documents which represented they were filed under seal, which simply meant the only way they could be viewed was if the judge approved to have them unsealed. The more I researched the more I uncovered.

What was alarming about my case was the number of documents that were sealed. Twenty four (24) documents which were primarily depositions all highlighted were sealed so no one could see them. What was the big secret? The Coca-Cola Company claimed for years publicly that it was innocent. So what could have possibly been said by current employees whom many worked with me while being deposed that needed to be hidden from the public? The Coca-Cola Company and Willie Gary knew that once the documents were sealed it would take a court approved order by a judge to have them unsealed. Not one time did Mr. Gary or any lawyer from his law firm inform me that any documents were being sealed. What was the big secret? Why so much privacy? My case was about racial discrimination. There were not any trade secrets or formulas to making Coke products they were being asked about. None of the employees that were deposed were ever asked to give any personal information about themselves, such as, social security numbers, credit card numbers etc., so why was it necessary to seal the numerous amount of documents in a discrimination case. Again, why would Mr. Gary agree? Obviously, an awesome partnership was made.

The release agreement that I was encouraged to sign by my attorneys sealed the deal for The Coca-Cola Company. The company made sure that it admitted to no wrongdoing as well as made certain that I would never work there again. Little did they know employment at Coke was the last thing on my mind. I shared my release agreement with more than 30 attorneys, and to my astonishment each of them stated that the only time they would have asked a client to sign such an agreement was when they knew they got everything they could for the client. Several of them stated that the manner in which Willie Gary

510

represented you gives lawyers a bad name. They further stated they are sworn to make certain in each case they are fighting, that their clients are made whole. As my Jewish attorney friend stated, it was clear in your case the only person that was made whole was Willie Gary. Please see **Appendix E**.

The blatant disrespect in which Mr. Gary spoke to me, fueled me every day. He spoke with such arrogance and as if he was untouchable. I chuckled each time I thought of how he ended our last conversation, "Well Greg, then do what you gotta do." Some time ago, I contacted a dear friend of my family and most certainly someone who had great respect for my father. He was a retired Federal Bureau of Investigation Agent (FBI) and he was essential in helping me. Knowing that attorneys are most comfortable in the courtroom and working within the judicial system, I researched Weldon Latham. He was the attorney that The Coca-Cola Company hired to handle the financing of the lawsuit. I became curious if Coke's attorneys new that Willie and Weldon were the best of friends. However, he was no longer with Holland & Knight. I pondered if he was asked to leave the firm because the partners gained knowledge of his involvement in the criminal activity. Nevertheless, he was then working for Jackson & Lewis PC, in

Virginia. Many may describe the entire ordeal as "Gangster." I

personally thought the attorneys and all that were involved were

nothing more than cowards. I could not stop asking myself, if the

website was truly slander, why didn't Mr. Gary take the authors to

court to have it taken down. Instead, he like his partner Rev. Jesse

Jackson Sr. kept hiding their hands and banking on the fact they were

rich and famous and no one would believe it anyway. I imagined he

hoped that most people would view the site as just a couple of

disgruntled clients that lost their cases and would not go away. They

probably would say the same about me. My answer is simple. I would

let every reader allow the "Holy Spirit" and the God that lives within

them to guide their hearts to a decision.

Knowing the deck was stacked against me trying to have a day in

courtroom with these giants, where very shady things have happened

was meaningless at this stage. My research brought about the name

Weldon Latham. I called telephoned him at Jackson & Lewis in

Virginia. The telephone rang twice before the administrative assistant

for Mr. Latham answered. I asked to speak to Mr. Latham. She asked if he was expecting my call or knew why I would be calling. I answered,

"No", then "Yes." She then stated he was definitely in the building but

at that time was not in his office. I then asked if I could have his

voicemail, she said certainly and connected me. I told Mr. Latham my

name and that I was the original plaintiff in the racial discrimination

lawsuit years ago in which he was a part of the handling of funds. I told

him that I had reason to believe that he and Mr. Gary stole money from

me and other clients. This money came from The Coca-Cola Company

and was wired to Holland & Knight. I repeated my name and gave my

telephone number requesting that he give me a call.

On Thursday, December 19, 2013, at approximately 3:30 p.m., one

day later, I received a call from a number within the Jackson & Lewis

firm. I answered, "Hello", and a male's voice asked if I was Greg Clark

and if I was the gentleman that called Mr. Weldon Latham yesterday. I

replied, "I am and yes I did." He then stated that his name was John

Bryson and that he was a partner of the firm. He asked if I was

represented by counsel, and further stated because as an attorney he

could not speak with me. I informed him at that time that I was not. He

went on and shared that Mr. Latham has been out of town all week and

513

that he was checking his voicemail and returning his calls. This I found

to be interesting. Wow! A partner of a law firm that has over a

thousand lawyers and are known throughout the country has time to

check the voicemail of another attorney. I found it even more

interesting when I called just one day earlier, Mr. Latham's

administrative assistant stated he was in the building but was not in his

office. Mr. Bryson's casualness in addressing me was not a surprise,

over the years I'd gotten accustomed to it. It normally occurs when the

person whom is speaking thinks they have the upper hand.

Nevertheless, he continued and stated that he would ask two things of

me. As I searched for a pen, I replied," and they are." He asked if I

would put my concerns in writing and forward them to the firm. "And

the second?" I asked. He stated "Well I guess that's the only one". Just

before hanging up, Mr. Bryson, a partner of Jackson & Lewis said that

my information was inaccurate. I responded, "I assure you that it is not,

thank you and happy holidays". Why would a partner of a major law

firm seek to give me his opinion of a case that happened years ago, at a

firm where he was not employed and could not possibly have enough

information to make an intelligent decision? Obviously, Mr. Latham was indeed in the office and shared his side of the events that occurred.

I wondered if they knew of my "smoking gun" would the conversation

have been the same. I have someone that can verify that, YES, The

Coca Cola Company sent tens of millions to Holland & Knight law

firm in Washington, D.C. on behalf of Willie E. Gary, and the money

was received by Weldon Latham. My focus is on protecting her from

these spineless, embarrassing, cowards who call themselves attorneys.

On Thursday, January 8, 2014, at approximately 4:10 p.m., I

received a call from (202) 506-0183. I answered, "Hello," and the voice

on the other end said, "This is Weldon Latham, did you call me?" I

responded, "Yes, I certainly did". Mr. Latham said, "I don't know you,

who are you." I responded, "I imagine you would not know me." I then

told him my name was Greg Clark and I was the lead plaintiff in the

racial discrimination lawsuit against Coca-Cola in which he and Willie

E. Gary stole tens of millions from clients, and I was one of them. He

immediately responded, "First of all your facts are not accurate. Let me

explain to you that The Coca-Cola Company hired me". I chuckled then

laughed and told him that I was well aware of that and his statement

meant nothing to me. I went on to explain I called him yesterday to get

515

the current address of his place of employment, but I found it on the

firm's website. I also shared that I have done an intensive amount of

research and that I would be going public with my findings. Mr.

Latham began shouting, "If you print anything about me I will sue you

for defamation and slander." My voice raised as well, I quickly told

him to shut up. I told him that he was a coward and a pitiful excuse for

a man, not to mention a lawyer. I reminded him that he needed not to

use the excuse that The Coca-Cola Company hired him and not Willie

Gary. As I continued to shout at the spineless coward, I told him the

words he just used were the words his partner in crime Willie Gary said

years ago when he called me and asked me to call the ladies who

authored the website to try and get them to take it down. He even went

as far as to say that he would throw them some pennies, a hundred

thousand a piece, but he then caught himself and said well he couldn't

do that because all they would do was run to the media. I went on to

remind him that not only was his name on that website but a picture of

him as well. I then shouted, "Why haven't either one of you well

established, well connected, rich attorneys filed one motion in court to

have the ladies prosecuted? Why have you not sued them for

defamation of character and slander as you are threatening me?" I promised him that once the federal officers and prosecutors arrested he and Willie, that's when they would realize they could not continuously screw clients and hide behind the name of major law firms. I then told him there was not a rock for him to hide and neither was there a valley deep enough for him to run trying to escape, I was not going away. The conversation lasted for almost 6 minutes before Mr. Latham decided to hang up the telephone. I found it interesting that Mr. Latham would return a call where there was not a voicemail left. It was obvious when he called that I was on speaker phone and there were others in the room. This was the exact scenario of the telephone call I received a few days prior from someone who introduced himself as John Bryson, a partner of Jackson & Lewis. I got the impression that Mr. Bryson as well as Weldon Latham were trying to see just how much I knew and would share about the crime Mr. Latham and Willie Gary and a host of others have committed. I find it interesting that the brilliant Hillary Clinton in her quest to become the first female President chose Willie E. Gary and Weldon Latham as Chairman and Co- Chairman for her campaign. I'm curious how the 42 women in Eastern Michigan where

Willie Gary took $51.5 million dollars to sell them out and the millions

of respectful women that have helped build our country would vote

having the knowledge of what has been shared in this book.

It is my prayer that someone that has read this book will feel

compelled to place it in the proper authorities' hands to begin an

investigation that will right the wrong the attorneys have done as well

as the eleventh circuit if any wrong has been uncovered within it. I also

pray the federal government will look at all the evidence and the .

peculiar ways of all involved, and initiate one of the largest federal

investigations to uncover all the crimes that have been committed, and

put each of the attorneys who have disgraced their oath to achieve

personal gratification in prison. If I were a federal investigator or

federal prosecutor I would begin my investigation by deposing the

following attorneys. Each of them have information that may be vital to

exposing these criminals. However it is essential to have all the files in

the Michigan case unsealed to pave the way to incarcerating Willie E.

Gary and his co-conspirators.

Willie E. Gary, Maryann Diaz, F. Shields McManus
Gary, Williams, Parenti, Finney, Lewis, McManus
Watson, & Sperando, P.L.

221 Osceola Street
Stuart, FL 34994
(772) 283-8260

Weldon Latham
Jackson & Lewis
10701 Parkridge Blvd., Suite 300
Reston, VA 20191
(202) 506-0183

Elizabeth Finn-Johnson
Larry D. Thompson
The Coca Cola Company
Once Coca Cola Plaza
Atlanta, GA 30313
(404) 676-3736

Michael W. Johnston, Samuel M. Matchett
King & Spalding
191 Peachtree Street
Atlanta, GA 30303
(404) 572-4600

Jeffrey E. Tompkins, Thomas G. Sampson
Thomas, Kennedy, Sampson & Patterson
3355 Main Street
Atlanta, GA 30337
(404) 688-4503

Jay A. Schwartz
Schwartz Law Firm, P.C.
Suite A, 37887 W. 12 Mile Road
Farmington Hills, MI 48331
(248) 553-9400

Lawrence C. Falzon
Wigod, Falzon & Dicicco, P.C.

Secrets, Lies, and Betrayals

29500 Telegraph Road, Suite 210
Southfield, MI 48034
(248) 356-3300

Paul Kiernan
Holland & Knight
800 17th St. N. W.
Washington, D.C. 20006
(202) 955-3000

Jesse Jackson Sr.
930 East 50th Street
Chicago, IL 60615
(773) 256-2709

This lawsuit started because one manager refused to allow me an equal opportunity to advance in my career but look at what has been uncovered. When the lawsuit was filed, not one supervisor in the security department had a bachelor's degree. Now, years later, all of them have their degrees, earned along the way to hide skeletons in the company's closets. *What other steps has or will the company take to keep its skeletons hidden?*

Far too many people have been hurt, and too much pain hidden behind the walls of the company. Far too much corruption has gone on for silence to prevail – both in relation to corporate, legal and judicial injustices. And so I have spoken.

What started out as a story of racial discrimination has turned into something greater. The naïve and angry young man I once was is not the man I am today. I have hope and faith that others can, like me, step beyond what is uncomfortable and hard for a higher purpose.

I have come to realize that we all are prejudiced. It may be human nature to prefer people who are "like" us whether it is according to race, religion, size, shape or some other measure. The question is not about counting the number of minorities in a particular company, the question is about the state of the human heart in our society.

I pray the story I have shared will bless you and encourage you. I pray you will be encouraged to look into your own heart to assess the biases that you hold. I pray that you will be inspired to speak up instead of stand silent in the face of injustice. I pray that you will come to know the incredible source of hope and strength that can be found leaning on Jesus Christ no matter what trials you might face.

Fighting for equality falls flat. Celebrating talent and diversity does not. Uncover your own personal biases and learn to live beyond them. Learn to love people as the Lord commands – love your neighbor as yourself. Let's face it, few people love anyone more than self.

My story is not an attempt to flatten The Coca-Cola Company. It is just the stage for my story. It could have taken place in any company, organization, religious organization, government, school system or foundation; and it does.

The bitter taste that this season of my life left in my mouth is a common reaction to hurt. I find now, over a decade later that the taste is not so bitter even though the level of corruption is far worse than I ever imagined. I realize that I am simply a vessel being used to tell a story that I hope resounds with your heart and encourages you to be proactive rather than bitter about the challenges in your life too. Don't suffer silently, speak up and you will find as I did that you are not alone.

Speak up and respond to injustice by calling others to be respectful and sensitive to those in their charge. Honor the sacrifices others, like your parents and grandparents have made, so that you can reach for your goals. Fight for justice, fairness, truth and righteousness for all human beings wherever they may work, live and play.

Unless and until we appear as a blind people that cannot see color and other biases, are united and demand that we be treated fairly as individuals and employees, will there be change. There will be no

justice. There will be no peace.

This has been my testimony. God Bless!

Appendix A

FACTS

1. September 21, 2001 the Gary Firm filed a joint complaint, Civil Action File No. 1:01-CV-2525 [DOC. 1], for Plaintiff and three other individuals, Jacqueline Everson, Wanda Starks and Tinlyn Graham. On this exact date, CASE was REFERRED to Magistrate Judge Joel M. Feldman (Herein Judge Feldman).
2. October 15, 2001 an ORDER [DOC. 3] issued by Judge Willis B. Hunt, Jr. recusing himself and the case was reassigned to Judge Richard W. Story.
3. October 17, 2001 CASE REFERRED to Magistrate Judge E. Clayton Scofield.

   a. Likewise in the highly profiled discrimination class action lawsuit, Abdalla et. al., vs. Coca-Cola, Civil Action File No. 1:98-CV-3679, did Magistrate Judge John R. Strother, Jr. issue an ORDER January 11, 1999 [DOC. 3] to recuse himself and Magistrate Judge John E. Dougherty issue an ORDER January 15, 1999 [DOC. 4] to recuse himself as well. Finally, on March 10, 1999 the case was REFERRED to Magistrate E. Clayton Scofield.

   b. Likewise in Tangela Gaines vs. Coca-Cola, Civil Action File No. 1:02-CV-2046 did Magistrate Judge Linda T. Walker issue an ORDER December 4, 2002 [DOC. 8] recusing herself and CASE REFERRED to Magistrate Judge E. Clayton Scofield.

   c. Likewise in Darryl Wallace vs. Coca-Cola, Civil Action File No. 1:03-CV-2590 did Magistrate Judge Janet F. King issue an ORDER October 30, 2003 [DOC. 11] GRANTING Defendant Coca-Cola's "motion for reassignment and transfer of case to District Judge Richard Story" and CASE REFERRED to Magistrate Judge E. Clayton Scofield.

   d. Likewise in Darryl Wallace and Sharron Mangum vs. Coca-Cola, Civil Action File No. 1:03-CV-2739 was removed from Superior Court of Fulton

524

County (03-CV-73797) and on September 12, 2003 CASE REFERRED to Magistrate Judge E. Clayton Scofield.

e. Likewise in Marietta Goodman, Sharron Mangum et. al., vs. Gary, et. al. Civil Action File No. 1:03-CV-3387 did District Court Judge Richard W. Story take assignment of this case through a CONSENT ORDER December 8, 2003 [DOC. 2].

    i. This action under the Racketeering Influenced and Corrupt Organizations Act ("RICO"), 18 U.S.C. § 1961, et seq, arose from an illegal scheme that was created, owned, operated, managed and controlled by Willie Gary (Herein Gary) and their co-conspirators the Coca-Cola Company, wherein, twelve of the seventeen Coca-Cola individuals represented by Gary, were fraudulently induced into settling their claims with the Defendant, Coca-Cola.

    ii. Additionally, three of the four remaining individuals allege that Gary and his co-conspirators acted in a manner to commit: racketeering OCGA § 16-14-3(8 & 9); theft in violation of OCGA § 16-8-1 et seq.; securities fraud in violation of OCGA § 10-5-24; mail fraud in violation of 18 U.S.C. § 1341; obstruction of justice in violation of 18 U.S.C. § 1512; influencing witnesses in violation of OCGA § 16-10-93; tampering with evidence in violation of 16-10-94; and extortion in violation of 18 U.S.C. § 1951.

        a. See also Laosebikan vs. Coca-Cola, Civil Action File No. 1:01-CV-3040, Goodman vs. Coca-Cola, Civil Action File No. 1:01-CV-1774 and Everson vs. Coca-Cola 1:01-CV-2525.

Secrets, Lies, and Betrayals

4. October 25, 2001 Judge Story entered an ORDER
SEVERING the claims of Plaintiff and three other
individuals, Jacqueline Everson, Wanda Starks and
Tinlyn Graham and DIRECTING the clerk to assign new
and separate civil case numbers [DOC. 4].
   a. Likewise in joint Civil Action File No. 1:01-
   CV-1336 against the Defendant, Coca-Cola, did
   Judge Story issue an ORDER SERVERING the claims
   of plaintiff's Motisola Abdallah, Ajibola
   Laosebikan, and Gregory Clark November 13, 2001
   [DOC. 23].and DIRECTING the clerk to assign new
   and separate civil case numbers.

   b. Likewise in joint Civil Action File No. 1:00-
   CV-1774 (Originally filed in Superior Court of
   Fulton County, 00-CV-6139.) against the
   Defendant, Coca-Cola did Judge Story during a
   TELE-CONFERENCE October 12, 2001 [DOC. 66]
   "raised concerns regarding case assignment" and
   on October 22, 2001 [DOC. 68] issue an ORDER
   SERVERING the claims of plaintiff's Marietta
   Goodman, Kathy Fain, Dana Allen and Angela
   Graham and DIRECTING the clerk to assign new
   and separate civil case numbers.

   c. Likewise in joint Civil Action File No. 1:01-
   CV-2105 against the Defendant, Coca-Cola, did
   Judge Story issue an ORDER SERVERING the claims
   of plaintiff's Diletha Waldon, Nicole Suddeth,
   Lesmer Morton Orr, Velma Thomas, Bonnita
   Thomas, and V. Freeston Warner October 25, 2001
   [DOC. 13].and DIRECTING the clerk to assign new
   and separate civil case numbers

5. Each of the aforementioned cases, whether joint or
successive individual complaints, as enumerated in
paragraphs 3 and 4 above have been DISMISSED WITH
PREJUDICE with the exception of Laosebikan vs. Coca-
Cola, Civil File No. 1:01-CV-3040, Wallace vs. Coca-
Cola, Civil File No. 1:03-CV-2590, Goodman and
Mangum et. al. vs. Gary, et. al, Civil Action File
No. 1:03-CV-3387 (in which Coca-Cola stands accused
of collusion with the Gary Firm arising from the
joint cases and their successive individual cases as
enumerated in paragraphs 3 and 4 above), and the

526

above styled action. A total of seventeen (17)
cases against the Defendant, Coca-Cola, in which
fraud has been alleged, have come before this Court
between 2001 and 2003 and were referred to
Magistrate Judge E. Clayton Scofield and District
Court Judge Richard W. Story, and consequently
dismissed in favor of the Defendant, Coca-Cola.

LAW PURSUANT TO 28 U.S.C. §§144, 455

6. Plaintiff charges Judge Scofield and Judge Story
   with personal biases and prejudices against
   Plaintiff for various reasons, including, but not
   limited to, denying, depriving, and overlooking
   Plaintiff's Due Process Rights; violating the
   Constitutional Rights of Plaintiff to have
   Plaintiff's motions heard and ruled upon in a timely
   manner, which denies Plaintiff meaningful access to
   the courts; manipulating hearings to deprive, and to
   deny, Plaintiff a meaningful hearing on the merits
   of Plaintiff's cause; issuing orders, which did not
   provide Plaintiff with any meaningful time to
   respond to the exhibits of the Defendant; violating
   Plaintiff's duty to comply with the Supreme Law of
   the Land; and violating Plaintiff's duty to apply
   the Law even if the judge does not agree with the
   Law.

7. This personal prejudice and bias evidenced by Judge
   Scofield and Judge Story is an extension of the
   prejudice and bias of the Georgia Federal District
   Courts and the Eleventh Circuit Court of Appeals
   towards non-represented litigants, as evidenced by
   case law from the time of Haines v. Kerner, 404 U.S.
   520, 92 S.Ct. 594 (1972), to present.

8. Judge Scofield and Judge Story violated their Oath
   to be a Judge, when they did not uphold the U.S.
   Constitution in this matter. Judge Scofield and
   Judge Story's actions in denying, depriving, and
   overlooking the Plaintiff's legal and constitutional
   rights were prejudicial against the Plaintiff
   pursuant to 28 U.S.C. §453. Judge Scofield and
   Judge Story did not faithfully and impartially

discharge and perform all the mandated duties
incumbent upon them.

9. Judge Scofield and Judge Story intentionally and
effectively denied the Plaintiff's constitutional
right to effectively "petition...for a redress of
grievances".
U.S. Constitution, Amendment I. The
Plaintiff has filed Motions with this court,
which this court has refused to hear and rule
on at a meaningful time. The failure of
these judges to promptly hear, in a
meaningful manner and at a meaningful time,
the Motions of the Plaintiff does not satisfy
the constitutional right to a redress of the
Plaintiff's grievances. The failure of this
court to hear at a meaningful time and in a
meaningful manner the Motions of the
Plaintiff deprives the Plaintiff of her legal
and constitutional rights; it is prejudicial
and biased against the Plaintiff. Some of
the Petitions-Motions include, but are not
limited to, "Plaintiff's Motion to File
Amended Complaint", Plaintiff's Motion to
Compel Defendants in Discovery Requests",
Plaintiff's Response to Defendant's Motion to
Dismiss" and "Plaintiff's Motion for a
Proposed Settlement of Sanctions".

10. Judge Scofield and Judge Story effectively denied
Plaintiff of her rights of equal protection under
the law under Article VI of the U.S. Constitution.
Judge Scofield and Judge Story have been prejudicial
and biased against Plaintiff, by refusing to rule
pursuant to the Supreme Law of the Land. Judge
Scofield and Judge Story have deprived Plaintiff of
the equal protection of the law, by not applying the
Supreme Law of the Land to the Plaintiff's position.

11. The United States Supreme Court stated, "Chief
Justice Marshall had long before observed in Ross v.
Himely, 4 Cranch 241, 269, 2 L.ed. 608, 617, that,
upon principle, the operation of every judgment must
depend on the power of the court to render that
judgment. In Williamson v. Berry, 8 How. 495, 540,
12 L.ed. 1170, 1189, it was said to be well settled

that the jurisdiction of any court exercising
authority over a subject 'may be inquired into in
every other court when the proceedings in the former
are relied upon and brought before the latter by a
party claiming the benefit of such proceedings,' and
the rule prevails whether 'the decree or judgment
has been given, in a court of admiralty, chancery,
ecclesiastical court, or court of common law, or
whether the point ruled has arisen under the laws of
nations, the practice in chancery, or the municipal
laws of states.'" Old Wayne Mut. L. Assoc. v.
McDonough, 204 U.S. 8, 27 S.Ct. 236 (1907). By not
complying with the law, Judge Scofield and Judge
Story have prejudiced this Plaintiff.

12. While this court has limited discretion, it must
rule pursuant to law at all times. The Seventh
Circuit, Chief Justice Marshall state:
"Courts are the mere instruments of the law,
and can will nothing. When they are said to
exercise a discretion, it is a mere legal
discretion, a discretion to be exercised in
discerning the course prescribed by law, and,
when that is discerned, it is the duty of the
court to follow it. Judicial power is never
exercised for the purpose of giving effect to
the will of the judge; always for the purpose
of giving effect to the will of the
legislature; or, in other words, to the will
of the law." ' Littleton v. Berbling, 468
F.2d 389, 412 (7th Cir. 1972), citing Osborn
v. Bank of the United States, 9 Wheat (22
U.S.) 738, 866, 6 L.Ed 204 (1824); U.S. v.
Simpson, 927 F.2d 1088 (9th Cir. 1990).

While a judge may have discretion to make a ruling
which may be erroneous, he has a duty to rule on all
valid issues, especially those issues which deprive
a party of his/her constitutional rights, presented
before the court. Littleton, supra." Failure to
rule on the issues presented to this court denies,
deprives, and overlooks this Plaintiff's
constitutional rights. Judge Scofield and Judge
Story have repeatedly acted in a manner prejudicial
and biased against Plaintiff.

13. Judge Scofield and Judge Story have manipulated the judicial process to deny, deprive, and to overlook the rights of Plaintiff. Judge Scofield and Judge Story have selected only those motions that they want to hear, mostly those of the Defendants. Judge Scofield and Judge Story have intentionally selected only those specific demands of the Plaintiff's motions that they desire to hear and to grant, while intentionally ignoring, not considering, and not ruling on the other specific demands of the Plaintiff's motions that they do not desire to grant. Such manipulation of the judicial process is prejudicial and biased against the Plaintiff.

14. Judge Scofield and Judge Story must not be an advocate for either side; yet they have acted as an advocate for the Defendants.

15. Judge Scofield and Judge Story must give advice to a non-represented litigant, otherwise he has deprived and denied the non-represented litigant of his/her legal and constitutional rights. Judge Scofield and Judge Story must inform the non-represented Plaintiff at every stage of the proceedings of the Plaintiff's rights, whether Federal, State, or Local, in a timely manner and in a manner that the Plaintiff can understand. If the court fails to observe this free and natural person's rights in every respect, if the court denies, deprives, or overlooks any legal or Constitutional right of the Plaintiff, the court invalidates the judicial process. The failure of Judge Scofield and Judge Story to advise the non-represented litigant of all of her rights, as above, further evidences the prejudice and bias of the judge against this Plaintiff.

16. Judge Scofield and Judge Story must comply with the Federal Code of Judicial Conduct. Judge Scofield and Judge Story must comply with, among others, Canon 3. They do not have discretion to pick and choose which Canon or Canons they will, or will not comply with. Littleton, supra.

17. By Judge Scofield and Judge Story's failure to comply with the mandatory requirement of reporting

the misconduct of an attorney, U.S. v. Anderson, 798
F.2d 919 (7th Cir. 1986), Judge Scofield and Judge
Story have acted prejudicially and biased against
the Plaintiff.

18. The hearings scheduled and manipulated by Judge
Scofield June 14, 2004 and September 1, 2004 is
another "sham" hearing. If the purported non-
party's have no valid claims against the Plaintiff's
subpoenas for depositions and discovery, then the
purported non-parties have no standing to bring a
motion to be heard before this court, specifically
if they do not appear. The validity of the
purported claims against the Plaintiff, must be
first heard in a meaningful manner.

19. Plaintiff states that it is unquestionable that a
reasonable person would consider that Judge Scofield
and Judge Story' actions were prejudicial and biased
against the Plaintiff.

20. Though this court has set extensions of time and set
dates for hearings, this court has not ruled in any
substantive matters, and Plaintiff is entitled to
disqualification of judge, pursuant to 28 U.S.C.
§144.

21. Under Article VI, clause 3, of the U.S.
Constitution, every judge or government attorney
takes an oath to support the U.S. Constitution.
Whenever any judge or government attorney violates
the Constitution in the course of performing his/her
duties, then that judge or government attorney is
acting without lawful authority, has defrauded not
only the Defendant or the Plaintiff involved, but
has also defrauded the government. The judge or the
government attorney is paid to support the U.S.
Constitution. By not supporting the Constitution,
the judge or the government attorney is collecting
monies for work not performed.

A judge is not the court. People v. Zajic, 88 Ill.App.3d

477, 410 N.E.2d 626 (1980). A judge is a state judicial

officer, paid by the State to act impartially and

Secrets, Lies, and Betrayals

lawfully. A judge is also an officer of the court, as well as are all attorneys.

Appendix B

Secrets, Lies, and Betrayals

IN THE UNITED STATES DISTRICT COURT
**FOR THE NORTHERN DISTRICT OF
GEORGIA
ATLANTA DIVISION**

SHARRON MANGUM   }
                           }
                           }
    Plaintiff,   }   CIVIL ACTION

                           }   FILE NO. 1:01-CV-2866
    Vs .
                                    (RWS)
THE COCA-COLA

COMPANY   }
                           }
                           }
    Defendant.   }

PLAINTIFFS MOTION TO DISQUALIFY MAGISTRATE JUDGE E.
CLAYTON SCOFIELD AND DISTRICT COURT JUDGE RICHARD W.
STORY PURSUANT TO 28 U.S.C. §§144, 455 AND MOTION FOR
DEFAULT SUMMARY JUDGMENT BASED ON COLLUSION

NOW COMES the Plaintiff, Sharron Mangum and hereby moves

this court to issue an order disqualifying Magistrate Judge E. Clayton

Scofield III (Herein "Judge Scofield) and the District Court Judge

Richard W. Story (Herein "Judge Story") from this matter, pursuant to

28 U.S.C. §§144, 455, and any other applicable statutes and/or rules, due

to their personal biases and prejudices against Plaintiff.

I.   INTRODUCTION

March 19, 2001 Plaintiff entered into a contractual agreement

with Gary, Williams, Parenti, Finney, Lewis, McManus & Sperando(Herein "Gary Firm")

for legal representation of her claims against the Defendant, Coca-

Cola. A joint action against the Defendant, Coca-Cola, Civil Action File

No. 1:01-CV-2525 was filed September 21, 2001. Shortly after,

the Court issued an ORDER severing plaintiffs Mangum, Everson, Starks and Graham

October 25, 2001 [DOC.4] and, subsequently, Civil Action File No. 1:01-CV-2866 was

filed October 25, 2001.

A second complaint by Plaintiff, Civil Action File No.

1:03-CV-00223 against the Defendant, Coca-Cola was filed January 27, 2003 [DOC .

1], and was consolidated with Civil Action File No. 1:01-CV-2866 April 17, 2003

[DOC. 8] by CONSENT ORDER of

this Court.

June 25, 2003, amid allegations of fraud and racketeering filedwiththeFloridaBar Association (See   Goodman, Mangum et. al. vs. Gary, et. al., Civil Action File No. 1:03-CV-3387 [DOC. 47]), the Gary Firm filed a MOTION TO WITHDRAW   [DOC. 53] as Plaintiffs counsel, which was granted by this Court and an ORDER issued July 15, 2003 [DOC. 54]. Subsequently, Plaintiff filed a MOTION FOR ADMISSION to appear in PROPRIA PERSONA September 9, 2003 (Doc. 60].

August 18, 2003, Plaintiff filed a joint complaint against the Defendant, Coca-Cola, Civil Action File No. 03-CV-73797 in the Superior Court of Fulton County, for fraud and racketeering allegations against the Defendant, Coca-Cola resulting in Plaintiff's wrongful firing March 15, 2003. September 12, 2003 the Defendant, Coca-Cola, filed a NOTICE OF REMOVAL with COMPLAINT [DOC. 1] in this Court, and subsequently the case was transferred, Civil Action File No. 1:03-CV-2739.

November 18, 2003 Plaintiff entered into her second contractual agreement for legal representation with Breedlove & Lassiter, attorney Levi Breedlove. March 16, 2004, amid allegations of fraud [DOC. 80, 83], Breedlove & Lassiter filed a MOTION TO WITHDRAW [DOC. 74] as Plaintiffs counsel, which was granted by this Court and an ORDER issued April 14, 2004 [DOC. 79]. Subsequently, Plaintiff's second MOTION FOR ADMISSION to appear in PROPRIA PERSONA was filed May 5, 2004 [Doc. 84], and Plaintiff has represented herself since that time.

II . FACTS

1.   September 21, 2001 the Gary Firm filed a joint complaint, Civil Action

File No. 1:01-CV-2525 [DOC.1], for Plaintiff and three other individuals, Jacqueline

Everson, Wanda Starks and Tinlyn Graham.   On this exact date, CASE was

REFERRED to Magistrate Judge Joel M. Feldman (Herein Judge Feldman}.

    2.   October 15, 2001 an ORDER   [DOC. 3] issued by Judge Willis

B. Hunt, Jr. recusing himself and the case was reassigned to Judge Richard W. Story.

    3.   October 17, 2001 CASE REFERRED to Magistrate Judge E. Clayton

Scofield.

    a. Likewise in the highly profiled discrimination class action lawsuit, Abdalla
    et. al.,vs. Coca-Cola, Civil Action File No. 1:98-CV-3679, did Magistrate
    Judge John
    R. Strother, Jr. issue an ORDER January 11, 1999 [DOC. 3] to recuse
    himself and Magistrate Judge John E. Dougherty issue an ORDER January
    15, 1999 [DOC.4] to recuse himself as well.   Finally, on March 10, 1999 the
    case was REFERRED to Magistrate E. Clayton Scofield.

    b. Likewise in Tangela Gaines vs. Coca-Cola, Civil Action File No. 1:02-CV-
    2046 did Magistrate Judge Linda T. Walker issue an ORDER December 4,
    2002 [DOC.8] recusing herself and CASE REFERRED to Magistrate Judge E.
    Clayton Scofield.

    c. Likewise in Darryl Wallace vs. Coca-Cola, Civil Action File No. 1:03-CV-
    2590 did Magistrate Judge Janet F. King issue an ORDER October 30, 2003
    [DOC.11] GRANTING Defendant Coca-Cola's "motion for reassignment and
    transfer of case to District Judge Richard Story" and CASE REFERRED to
    Magistrate Judge E. Clayton Scofield.

    d. Likewise in Darryl Wallace and Sharron Mangum vs. Coca- Cola, Civil
    Action File No. 1:03-CV-2739 was removed from Superior Court of Fulton
    County (03-CV-73797) and on September 12, 2003 CASE REFERRED to
    Magistrate Judge E. Clayton Scofield.

    e. Likewise in Marietta Goodman, Sharron Mangum et. al., vs. Gary, et. al. Civil
    Action File No. 1:03-CV-3387 did
    District Court *Judge* Richard W. Story take assignment of
    this case through a CONSENT ORDER December 8, 2003 [DOC.

2] ·

i.   This action under the Racketeering Influenced and Corrupt Organizations Act ("RICO"), 18 U.S.C. § 1961, et seq, arose from an illegal scheme that was created, owned, operated, managed and controlled by Willie Gary (HereinGary) and their co-conspirators the Coca-Cola Company, wherein, twelve of the seventeen Coca-Cola individuals represented by Gary, were fraudulently induced into settling their claims with the Defendant, Coca-Cola.

ii.   Additionally, threeofthefour remaining individualsallegethat Garyandhisco- conspirators actedin amannertocommit: racketeering OCGA § 16-14-3(8&9);theftin violationofOCGA§ 16-8-1 *et seq.*; securities fraudinviolationofOCGA§ 10-5-24;mail fraudin violationof18U.S.C.§ 1341; obstructionof justiceinviolationof18 U.S.C.§ 1512; influencingwitnessesin violationofOCGA§ 16-10-93; tampering with evidence in violation of 16-10- 94; and extortion in violation of 18 U.S.C.§ 1951.

      a. See also Laosebikan vs. Coca-Cola, Civil Action File No. 1:01-CV-3040, Goodman vs. Coca-Cola, Civil Action File No. 1:01-CV-1774 and Everson vs. Coca-Cola 1:01-CV-2525.

4.   October 25, 2001 Judge Story entered an

ORDER SEVERING the claims of Plaintiff and three other

individuals, Jacqueline Everson, Wanda Starks and Tinlyn

Graham and DIRECTING the clerk to assign new and separate

civil case numbers [DOC.4].

    a. Likewise in joint Civil Action File No. 1:01-CV-

1336 against the Defendant, Coca-Cola, did Judge
Story issue an ORDER SERVERING the claims of
plaintiffs Motisola Abdallah, Ajibola Laosebikan,
and Gregory Clark November 13, 2001 [DOC. 23]
.and DIRECTING the clerk to assign new and
separate civil case numbers.

b. Likewise in joint Civil Action File No. 1:00-
CV-1774 (Originally filed in Superior Court of
Fulton County,
00-CV-6139.) against the Defendant, Coca-Cola did
Judge Story during a TELE-CONFERENCE
October 12, 2001 [DOC.
66] "raised concerns regarding case assignment" and
on October 22, 2001 [DOC. 68] issue an ORDER
SERVERING the claims of plaintiffs Marietta
Goodman, Kathy Fain, Dana Allen and Angela
Graham and DIRECTING the clerk to
assign new and separate civil case numbers.

c. Likewise in joint Civil Action File No. 1:01-CV-2105 against the Defendant,
Coca-Cola, did Judge Story issue an ORDER SERVERING the claims of
plaintiffs   Diletha
Waldon, Nicole Suddeth, Lesmer Morton Orr, Velma Thomas, Bonnita
Thomas, and V. Freeston Warner October 25, 2001 [DOC. 13] and
DIRECTING the clerk to assign new and separate civil case numbers

5.   Each of the aforementioned cases, whether joint or successive individual

complaints, as enumerated in paragraphs 3 and 4 above have been DISMISSED WITH

PREJUDICE with the exception of Laosebikan vs. Coca-Cola, Civil File No. 1:01-CV-

3040, Wallace vs. Coca-Cola, Civil File No. 1:03-CV-2590, Goodman and Mangum et. al.

vs. Gary, et. al, Civil Action File No. 1:03-CV-3387 (in which Coca-Cola stands accused

of collusion with the Gary Firm arising from the joint cases and their successive individual

cases as enumerated in paragraphs 3 and 4 above), and the above styled action. A total of

seventeen (17) cases against the Defendant, Coca-Cola, in which fraud has been alleged,

have come before this Court between 2001 and 2003 and were referred to Magistrate

Judge E. Clayton Scofield and District Court Judge Richard W. Story, and consequently dismissed in favor of the Defendant, Coca-Cola.

Fifteen of these individual cases were represented by prominent Stuart, Florida attorney, Willie Gary of Gary, Williams, Parenti, Finney, Lewis, McManus & Sperando. One case was represented by Decatur, Georgia attorney, Levi Breedlove, who has established ties to Willie Gary, and Gary's longtime friend, Jesse Jackson.

6.   April 22, 2004 [DOC. 82] Judge Scofield issued an ORDER DENYING Plaintiff's motion for leave to file third (3rd) amended complaint because Plaintiff did not exercise due diligence to assert any new matters when the case was initially filed or within the 30-day time period set forth in the rules, thus "Plaintiff has not shown good cause for modifying the scheduling order." On May 12, 2004 [DOC. 84] issued an ORDER STRIKING Plaintiff's amended complaint from the record.

7.   May 26, 2004, [DOC. 96] Plaintiff filed a MOTION for admission of her third amended complaint, wherein, Plaintiff seeks to add criminal claims:

a. Retaliation in violation of Title VII and Section 1981 and Title IX of the Civil Rights Act of 1964 (42 U.S.C § 2000h-2}

b. Slander and Defamation of Character in violation of Title VII and Section 1981 and in violation of Title IX of the Civil Rights Act of 1964 (42 U.S.C § 2000h-2)

c. Conspiracy to injure citizens in violation of 18 U.S.C.
§ 241 and Title IX of the Civil Rights Act of 1964
(42
U.S.C § 2000h-2)

It would have been impossible for Plaintiff to assert

any new matters when the case was initially filed October

25, 2001 or within the 30-day time period set forth in the

rules, because:

d. Plaintiff's wrongful firing did not occur until March 15, 2003 [DOC. 151].

e. Plaintiff's slander and defamation did not occur until May 17, 2003 [DOC 151].

f. Plaintiffs assertion that fraud was committed by her legal representation, the Gary Firm, wasnt until June 2003   [DOC. 144, 146 and 148].

g. Plaintiffs assertion that fraud was committed by her legal representation, Levi Breedlove, wasn't until April 2004 [DOC.78, 79,   80, 81 and 83].

8.   May 21, 2004 [DOC. 89 and 90] Plaintiffs filed NOTICE to take

deposition of Taneisha Dixon and Kerri Morse, two individuals Plaintiff alleged engaged

in criminal activity with Defendant Coca-Cola during her employment and were involved

in her wrongful firing March 15, 2003 (Civil Action File No. 1:03- CV-2739, which was

removed from Superior Court of Fulton County (03-CV-73797)).   Depositions were

scheduled to be held on June

3, 2003 and June 4, 2003.

9.   June 1, 2004   [DOC.99] Plaintiff received a telephone call from

Judge Scofields chamber informing her that an ORDER was issued staying discovery

"including all pending discovery" and requesting a fax number to which the ORDER could be sent.

        10.   Pursuant to F.R.C.P. 6(e), there is "three days" for mailing, therefore Plaintiff would not be held to Judge Scofield's ORDER [DOC. 99] until June 4, 2004, which would occur one day after Taneisha Dixon was deposed and possibly hours after Kerri Morse had been deposed.

        11.   Subsequently, Taneisha Dixon advised Plaintiff the morning of her deposition, June 3, 2004 [DOC. 89], that her attorney   (Michael Johnston, an attorney for the Defendant, Coca- Cola implied.)told her that she did not have to participant in anything, as indicated in the NOTICE Of Filing Notary's Certification Re Failure of Witness to Appear for the TakingofHerDeposition [DOC.   117)August 3, 2004.

        12.   June 5, 2004 Plaintiff received court documents from Michael Johnston, attorney for the Defendant, Coca-Cola, wherein Kerri Morse filed an OBJECTION June 3, 2004 [DOC . 100] to Plaintiff's notice to subpoena her for a deposition.

        13.   June 15, 2004 during a Motion HEARING before Judge Scofield [DOC. 105J, a VERBAL ORDER was issued "GRANTING [100-1] objection construed as a motion to quash by non-party Kerri [Morse]"despite neither Kerri Morse nor her

legal representation being present.

    14.   June 24, 2004 Judge Scofield issued an ORDER [DOC. 106) allowing Defendant, Coca-Cola to designate twelve witnesses[1] Plaintiff can depose despite:

> a. Plaintiffs request to present evidence to the Court of individuals having knowledge of the allegations outlined in her complaint.
>
> b. and Plaintiffs objections   *[DOC.* 110]pursuant to F.R.C.P. 30(a)(2)(A),where in it states, "that a party may depose anyone with discoverable information, party or non-party."
>
> c. Plaintiff was disallowed to depose Amanda Pace, Defendant Coca-Cola's Ombuds Director and Kerri Morse, President of M&S Specialty Welding.
>
> d. Additionally, Plaintiffs request third request to have her Third Amended Complaint added was denied.

    15.   August 19, 2004 Judge Story issued an ORDER [DOC.125] to concur "with the rulings and conclusions of Magistrate Judge and OVERRULES" Plaintiff's objection [DOC.110].

> a. Every litigant has the right to rely upon the rules as written, and it is the Court's duty to enforce the rules where an objection is made in reliance upon the language of the rule cited. *Continental Air Lines Inc. v. City and County of Denver,* 266P.2d 400, 129 Colo.1 (Colo.

01/18/1954).

[1] [DOC. 106] "These depositions are: Milagros Tomei, Marsha Holsombeck, Dianne Krantz, Deborah Haseley, Melissa Retminger, Dianna Haddon, Patricia Keener, James Garris, Peter Simpson, Bevin Newton, Tracy Koll and

b. The standard in Federal Court for amendment of pleadings is set forth in

Foman v. Davis 371 U.S. 178, 181-182-82 (1962)as follows: n[I]nthe

absence of..undue delay, bad faith or dilatory motive on the part of the

movant..undue prejudice to the opposing party...[or] futility of amendment,"

leave to amend pleadings should be allowed.

16. August 24, 2004 Judge Scofield issued ORDER

[126] scheduling a hearing on September 1, 2004 on several

pending motions three of which were Plaintiff's Motion to Compel discovery

responses from the Defendant, Coca-Cola, and, two subpoenas issued to non-party

M&S Specialty Welding and non- party Bashen Consulting.

17. September 3, 2004 Judge Scofield issued an ORDER [DOC. 128]

sustaining M&S Specialty Welding and Bashen Consulting's objection to subpoenas

despite neither non-party being present nor their legal representation being present at the

hearing September 1, 2003. Additionally, Plaintiff's Motion to Compel discovery

responses was DENIED, while Defendant's Motion to Compel was GRANTED,

Defendant's Motion for Sanctions ($14, 943.88) was GRANTED and Defendant's first

Motion to Dismiss was DENIED.

18. October 4, 2004 discovery closed in the above styled case as establish by the ORDER of Judge Scofield September 8, 2004 [DOC. 130].

19. October 19, 2004 Judge Scofield issued an ORDER [139] "extending the time for filing motions for summary judgment until twenty (20) days after this Court issues it Report and Recommendation on Defendant, Coca-Cola's Motion to Dismiss w/Prejudice [DOC. 138] filed October 8, 2004.

    a. February 23, 2004 Defendant Coca-Cola filed its third Motion to Dismiss w/Prejudice.

    b. March 1, 2004 Plaintiff filed a Default Summary Judgment in Response to Defendants Supplemental Motion to Dismiss based on an ORDER issued by Judge Scofield January 6, 2005 in which Plaintiff believed that the ORDER denied Defendants October 8, 2004 Motion to Dismiss [DOC. 138].

    c. Though mistaken unintentionally March 1, 2005, Plaintiff has come to realize that Judge Scofield had not ruled on the Defendant's Motion to Dismiss and the motion has been sitting on the docket for five (5) months.

20. October 28, 2004 Judge Scofield issued an ORDER [142J] requiring Plaintiff to pay to the Defendant within thirty (30) days $14, 943.88 awarded them in Sanctions [DOC. 128], and warning Plaintiff if she did not it could lead up to dismissal of this action. In response to this

ORDER Plaintiff filed a Proposed Settlement Agreement [DOC.125] January 25, 2004 wherein she states, "Plaintiff Mangum is financially destitute having no income to sustain the normal means of daily survival- food, clothing and shelter."

a.   In Newland v. Superior Court (1995)40 Cal.App.4th 608, Epstein wrote, "The time has come to reassert a well-established but apparently not well-known rule about monetary sanctions in discovery. The rule is that it is an abuse of discretion for a trial court to issue a terminating sanction for failure to pay the sanction."

21.   November 17, 2004 Plaintiff filed a Request to Charge the Defendant, Coca-Cola and several other named individuals with criminal charges pursuant to Title 18 §371, §1002, §1028,

§1031,§1111,§1113,§1506,§1509,§1621,§1622,§ 1623, §1512.

§1513 and OCGA § 16-14-4(a),(b),and (c).

a. Pursuant to the provisions of Criminal Justice Act of 1964 (18U.S.C.3006A) as amended by the Act of October
14, 1970 (PL. 91-447, 91st Cong.. 84 Stat. 916), and by
Title II of P.L. 98-473, 98 Stat. 1837, the Comprehensive Crime Control Act of 1984. the Judges of the United States District Court for the Northern District of Georgia have adopted, effective March 18, 1986, the following amended Plan for the adequate representation of any person, unable to obtain adequate representation:

i. who is a person for whom the Sixth Amendment to the Constitution requires the appointment of counsel or for whom, in a case in which he faces loss of liberty, any Federal law requires the appointment of counsel. Representation shall include counsel and investigative, expert, and other services necessary for an adequate defense and may request such services in an ex parte application submitted to a judge before whom the case is pending, or before a magistrate if the services are required in connection with a matter over which the magistrate has jurisdiction   (or if the judge otherwise refers such application to a magistrate for findings and report).

22.   Judge Scofield or Judge Story have not issued an order in this request nor have they appointed federal authorities to investigate these claims-leaving it on the docket unaddressed for four (4)months.

23.   Finally, it would be obvious to any reasonable law abiding citizen that a pattern exists across all the cases enumerated in paragraphs 3 and 4 above. A pattern of fraud, collusion, obstruction of justice, and so forth in which Plaintiff and the other named individuals have been deprived of their Due Process Rights under the Constitution of the United States.

24. Never during the course of this litigation and the other cases enwnerated in paragraphs 3 and 4 above, did Judge Scofield and Judge Story alert federal authorities to the systematic pattern of fraud and corruption (abandoningclaims, voluntary dismissal of claims, withholding evidence, creating false documents, etc.) committed by the Defendant, Coca-Cola and the attorneys for the plaintiffs: the Gary Firm, Levi Breedlove, Damien Turner, Howard Evans, Alan Garber and so many others, against the plaintiffs and this court. This truly is a travesty of justice.

III.LAW PURSUANT TO 28 U.S.C. §§144, 455

25. Plaintiff charges Judge Scofield and Judge Story with personal biases and prejudices against Plaintiff for various reasons, including, but not limited to, denying, depriving, and overlooking Plaintiffs Due Process Rights; violating the Constitutional Rights of Plaintiff to have Plaintiffsmotions heard and ruled upon in a timely manner, which denies Plaintiff meaningful access to the courts; manipulating hearings to deprive, and to deny, Plaintiff a meaningful hearing on the merits of Plaintiffs cause; issuing orders, which did not provide Plaintiff with any meaningful time to respond to the exhibits of the Defendant; violating

Plaintiff's duty to comply with the Supreme Law of the Land; and violating Plaintiff's duty to apply the Law even if the judge does not agree with the Law.

26.   This personal prejudice and bias evidenced by Judge Scofield and Judge Story is an extension of the prejudice and bias of the Georgia Federal District Courts and the Eleventh Circuit Court of Appeals towards non-represented litigants, as evidenced by case law from the time of **Haines v. Kerner**, 404 U.S. 520, 92 S.Ct. 594 (1972), to present.

27.   Judge Scofield and Judge Story violated their Oath to be a Judge, when they did not uphold the U.S. Constitution in this matter.   Judge Scofield and Judge story's actions in denying, depriving, and overlooking the Plaintiff's legal and constitutional rights were prejudicial against the Plaintiff pursuant to 28 U.S.C. §453.   Judge Scofield and Judge Story did not faithfully and impartially discharge and perform all the mandated duties incumbent upon them.

28.   Judge   Scofield   and   Judge   Story intentionally and effectively denied the Plaintiff's constitutional   right   to   effectively   "petition ..for a redress of grievances".

US. Constitution, Amendment I.

The Plaintiff has filed Motions with this court, which this court has refused to hear and rule on at a meaningful time.

The failure of these judges to promptly hear, in a meaningful manner and at a meaningful time, the
Motions of the Plaintiff does not satisfy the constitutional right to a redress of the Plaintiffs grievances. The failure of this court to hear at a meaningful time and in a meaningful manner the Motions of the Plaintiff deprives the Plaintiff of her legal and constitutional rights; it is prejudicial and
biased against the Plaintiff. Some of the Petitions- Motions include, but are not limited to, "Plaintiff s Motion to File Amended Complaint" , Plaintiff s Motion to Compel Defendants in Discovery Requests,

Plaintiff's Response to Defendant's Motion to

Dismiss" and"PlaintiffsMotionforaProposedSettlement

of Sanctions".

29. Judge Scofield and Judge Story effectively denied
Plaintiff of her rights of equal protection under the law under
Article VI of the U.S. Constitution. Judge Scofield and Judge
Story have been prejudicial and biased against Plaintiff, by
refusing to rule pursuant to the Supreme Law of the Land.

Judge Scofield and Judge Story have deprived
Plaintiff of the equal protection of the law, by not applying
the Supreme Law of the Land to the Plaintiff's position.

30. The United States Supreme Court stated,

"Chief Justice Marshall had long before observed in
Ross v. Himely, 4 Cranch 241, 269, 2 L.ed. 608,
617, that, upon principle, the operation of every
judgment must depend on the power of the court to
render that judgment. In **Williamson v. Berry**, 8
How. 495, 540, 12
L.ed. 1170, 1189, it was said to be well settled
that the jurisdiction of any court exercising
authority over a subject'may be inquired into in every other court whe
upon and brought before the latter by a party claiming
the benefit of such proceedings,' and the rule
prevails whether 'the decree or judgment has been
given, in a court of admiralty, chancery,
ecclesiastical court, or court of common law, or
whether the point ruled has arisen under the laws of
nations, the practice in chancery, or the municipal
laws of states.'" **Old Wayne Mut. L. Assoc. v.
McDonough**, 204 U·S· 8, 27 S.Ct. 236 (1907)·

By not complying with the law, Judge Scofield and
Judge Story have prejudiced this Plaintiff.

31. While this court has limited discretion, it must rule pursuant to law at all

times. The Seventh Circuit, Chief Justice Marshall state:

> "Courts are the mere instruments of the law, and can will nothing. When
> they are said to exercise a discretion, it is a mere legal discretion, a
> discretion to be exercised in discerning the course prescribed by law, and,
> when that is discerned, it is the **duty** of the court to follow it. Judicial
> power is never exercised for the purpose of giving effect to the will of the
> judge; always for the purpose of giving effect to the will of the legislature;
> or, in other words, to the will of the law." **Littleton v. Berbling,**
> 468 F.2d 389, 412 (7thCir. 1972), citing
> **Osborn v. Bank of the United States,** 9 Wheat (22 U.S.)
> 7381 866, 6 L.Ed 204 (1824); **U.S. v. Simpson,** 927 F.2d
> 1088 (9thCir. 1990).

While a judge **may** have **discretion** to make a ruling which may be

erroneous, he has a **duty** to rule on all valid issues, especially those issues which

deprive a party of his/hr constitutional rights, presented before the court.

Littleton, supra." Failure to rule on the issues presented to this court denies,

deprives, and overlooks this Plaintiffs constitutional rights. Judge Scofield and Judge

Story have repeatedly acted in a manner prejudicial and biased against Plaintiff.

32. Judge Scofield and Judge Story have manipulated the judicial process to

deny, deprive, and to overlook the rights of Plaintiff. Judge Scofield and Judge Story have

selected only those motions that they want to hear, mostly those of the Defendants. Judge

Scofield and Judge Story have intentionally selected only those specific demands of the

Plaintiffs motions that they desire to hear and to grant, while intentionally ignoring, not

considering, and not ruling on the other specific demands of the Plaintiffs motions that

they do not desire to grant. Such manipulation of the judicial process is prejudicial and

biased against the Plaintiff.

33. Judge Scofield and Judge Story must not be an advocate for either side; yet they have acted as an advocate for the Defendants.

34. Judge Scofield and Judge Story must give advice to a non-represented litigant, otherwise he has deprived and denied the non-represented litigant of his/her legal and constitutional rights. Judge Scofield and Judge Story must inform the non- represented Plaintiff at every stage of the proceedings of the Plaintiffs rights, whether Federal, State, or Local, in a timely manner and in a manner that the Plaintiff can understand. If the court fails to observe this free and natural person's rights in every respect, if the court denies, deprives, or overlooks any legal or Constitutional right of the Plaintiff, the court invalidates the judicial process. The failure of Judge Scofield and Judge Story to advise the non-represented litigant of all of her rights, as above, further evidences the prejudice and bias of the judge against this Plaintiff.

35. Judge Scofield and Judge Story must comply with the Federal Code of Judicial Conduct. Judge Scofield and Judge Story must comply with, among others, Canon 3.

They do not have discretion to pick and choose which Canon or Canons they will, or will not comply with. **Littleton,** supra.

36. By Judge Scofield and Judge Story's failure to comply with the mandatory requirement of reporting the misconduct of an attorney, **U.S. v. Anderson,** 798 F.2d 919 (7th Cir. 1986), Judge Scofield and Judge Story have acted prejudicially and biased against the Plaintiff.

37. The hearings scheduled and manipulated by Judge Scofield June 14, 2004 and September 1, 2004 is another "sham" hearing. If the purported non-party's have no valid claims against the Plaintiffs subpoenas for depositions and discovery, then the purported non-parties have no standing to bring a motion to be heard before this court, specifically if they do not appear. The validity of the purported claims against the Plaintiff, must be first heard in a meaningful manner.

38. Plaintiff states that it is unquestionable that a reasonable person would consider that Judge Scofield and Judge Story' actions were prejudicial and biased against the Plaintiff.

39. Though this court has set extensions of time and set dates for hearings, this court has not ruled in any substantive matters, and Plaintiff is entitled to disqualification of judge, pursuant to 28 U.S.C. §144.

40. Under Article VI, clause 3, of the U.S. Constitution, every judge or

government attorney takes an oath to support the U.S. Constitution. Whenever any judge or government attorney violates the Constitution in the course of performing his/her duties, then that judge or government attorney is acting without lawful authority, has defrauded not only the Defendant or the Plaintiff involved, but has also defrauded the government. The judge or the government attorney is paid to support the U.S. Constitution. By not supporting the Constitution, the judge or the government attorney is collecting monies for work not performed.

41. A judge is not the court. People v. Zajic, 88 Ill.App.3d 477, 410 N.E.2d 626 (1980).A judge is a state judicial officer, paid by the State to act impartially and lawfully. A judge is also an officer of the court, as well as are all attorneys.

42. Whenever any officer of the court commits fraud during a proceeding in the court, he/she is engaged in "fraud upon the court". In Bulloch v. United States, 763 F.2d 1115, 1121 (10th Cir. 1985), the court stated "Fraud upon the court is fraud which is directed to the judicial machinery itself and is not fraud between the parties or fraudulent documents, false statements or perjury.   It is where the court or a member is corrupted or influenced or influence is attempted or where the judge has not performed his judicial function --- thus where the impartial functions of the court have been directly corrupted.'

43.   "Fraud upon the court" has been defined by the 7th Circuit Court of Appeals to "embrace that species of fraud which does, or attempts to, defile the court itself, or is a fraud perpetrated by officers of the court so that the judicial machinery cannot perform in the usual manner its impartial task of adjudging cases that are

presented for adjudication." Kenner v. C.I.R., 387 F.3d 689 (1968); 7 Moore's Federal Practice, 2d ed., p. 512,   60.23. The 7th Circuit further stated "a decision produced by fraud upon the court is not in essence a decision at all, and never becomes final."

44.   It is also clear and well-settled Illinois law that any attempt to commit "fraud upon the court" vitiates the entire proceeding. The People of the State of Illinois v. Fred E. Sterling, 357 Ill. 354; 192 NE. 229 (1934) ("The maxim that fraud vitiates every transaction into which it enters applies to judgments as well as to contracts and other transactions."); Allen F. Moore v. Stanley F. Sievers, 336 Ill. 316; 168 NE. 259 (1929) ("The maxim that fraud vitiates every transaction into which it enters .."); In re Village of Willowbrook, 37 Ill.App.2d 393 (1962) ("It is axiomatic that fraud vitiates everything."); Dunham v. Dunham, 57 Ill.App. 475 (1894), affirmed 162 Ill. 589 (1896); Skelly Oil Co. v. Universal Oil Products Co., 338 Ill App. 79, 86 N.E.2d 875, 883-4 (1949); Thomas Stasel v. The American Home Security Corporation, 362 Ill. 350 ;   199 N .E . 798 (1935).

45.   Under Federal law, when any officer of the court has committed "fraud upon the court", the orders and judgment of that court are void, of no legal force or effect.

46.   Furthermore, pursuant to U.S.C. 28 sections 455(a) and (b) provide separate (though substantially overlapping) bases for recusal.   The former deals exclusively with the appearance of partiality in any circumstance, whereas the latter pertains to conflicts of interest in specific instances. Thus, the existence of the facts listed in section 455(b) requires recusal, even if the judge believes they do not create an

appearance of impropriety.11 Any circumstance in which a judge's impartiality might reasonably be questioned, whether or not touched on in section 455(b), requires recusal under section 455(a).1 2

47. Plaintiff believes that Judge Scofield and Judge Story have exhibited sufficient prejudice against Plaintiff that disqualification of Judge Scofield and Judge Story, pursuant to 28 U.S.C. §144 and §455, is appropriate.

48. Title VII of the Civil Right Act prevent challenges to a litigated or consent judgment or order on the ground that such judgment or order was obtained through collusion or fraud, or is transparently invalid or was entered by a court lacking subject matter jurisdiction; or authorize or permit the denial to any person of the due process of law required by the Constitution.

WHEREFORE, Plaintiff demands that the court suspend all proceedings until such an order can be issued that Judge Scofield and Judge Story be disqualified for, inter alia, their failure to perform their Constitutional duties in this cause, and for their prejudicial and biased actions against Plaintiff. That the Defendant, Coca-Cola be denied Summary Judgment based on collusion between Judge Scofield, Judge Story, and the Defendant, Coca-Cola. That Plaintiff be awarded all claims: equitable (including back pay and front pay) damages, compensatory damages, treble damages, and punitive damages, costs to include costs of investigation, attorney's fees, expenses and pre-judgment and post-judgment interest, and such other relief and benefits as the cause of justice may require.

Respectfully submitted this the   day of March 2005.

PLAINTIFF IN PROPRIA PERSONA

IN THE UNITED STATES DISTRICT
COURT FOR THE NORTHERN DISTRICT
OF GEORGIA ATLANTA DIVISION

SHARRON MANGUM   }
                                  }
                                  }
        Plaintiff,

                                  } CIVIL ACTION
                                  } FILE NO. 1:01-CV-2866
                                    (RWS)
                                  }
                                  }
                                  }
        Vs.   }

THE COCA-COLA

COMPANY

        Defendant.

CERTIFICATE OF SERVICE

I hereby certify that I have served a true and correct copy of the within and foregoing

PLAINTIFFS MOTION TO DISQUALIFY MAGISTRATE JUDGE E.CLAYTON

SCOFIELD AND DISTRICT COURT JUDGE RICHARD W.STORY PURSUANT

TO 28 US.C.§§144,455 AND MOTION FOR DEFAULT SUMMARY JUDGMENT

BASED ON COLLUSION by depositing same

in the US.Mail with sufficient postage thereon and addressed:

MICHAEL JOHNSTON

King & Spalding

191 Peachtree Street Atlanta, Georgia 30303

ELIZABETH FINN JOHNSON

The Coca-Cola Company One Coca-Cola Plaza Atlanta, Georgia
30313

Respectfully submitted this the _____ day of March 2005.

___Sharron Mangum

Appendix C

UNITED STATES DISTRICT
COURT EASTERN DISTRICT
OF MICHIGAN SOUTHERN
DIVISION

WENDY KUBIK, MICHELLE DeTOMASO, RITA DILLON, JANE DOE #1, JANE
DOE #2, JANE DOE #3, JUDITH FLENNA,
ELAINE KOLODZIEJ, PAMELA LINDSTROM, PAULINE MANIACI, MARY
RICHARDSON, JOAN RITCH, JANICE SANDORA,
MICHELE BOULTON, SUSAN SCHMALTZ, JUDY SPRADLEY, ELEANOR
TAYLOR, BEYERLY THOMAS, JUDITH THORNTON, MARY JO VAN TIEM,
RENEE WILLITS, REBECCA DITCH, SARA AGUINAGA, JOAN RAHILL, LISA
HADDIX,
BARBARA STEWART, PAT BOLONE, BONNIE BOUSSON, DONNA
VAUGHN, MARJORIE HARDER, CHRISTINA DIEM, KATHY DIEM, OSUIL
MAYO, CHRISTINE EWALD, PAM ROGERS,
BARBARA ARNOLD, GEORGINA GRAZAWI, PEGGY PRYZBYLSKI, JANET
BOTT, STEPHANIE HARBIN, DEBORAH PRESLEY, and THERESA GOULD,

        Plaintiffs,

v

WILLIE GARY, TRICIA HOFFLER, ROBERT PARENTI, SEKOU GARY, and
GARY, WILLIAMS, PARENTI, FINNEY, LEWIS, McMANUS, WATSON &
SPERANDO, P.C.,

        Defendants.

Civil Action No. 03-73350 Hon. Paul D. Borman
Mag. Judge Mona Majzoub

PLAINTIFFS' THIRD AMENDED COMPLAINT

DEMAND FOR JURY TRIAL

SCHWARTZ LAW FIRM, P.C.
By: Jay A. Schwartz
(P45268) Attorney for
Plaintiffs
37887 West Twelve Mile Road,
Suite A Farmington Hills, Michigan
48331 (248) 553-9400

WIGOD, FALZON, MCNEELY
& UNWIN, P.C.
By: Lawrence C. Falzon
(P30655) Attorney for Plaintiffs
29500 Telegraph Road, Suite 210
Southfield, Michigan 48034
(248) 356-3300

CLARK HILL PLC
By: Timothy D. Wittlinger
(P22490) Reginald M.
Turner, Jr. (P40543)
Attorney for Defendants
500 Woodward Avenue, Suite
3500
Detroit, Michigan 48226
(313) 965-8300

PLAINTIFFS' THIRD AMENDED
COMPLAINT

NOW COME Plaintiffs, Wendy Kubik, Michelle DeTomaso, Rita Dillon, Jane

Doe #1, Jane Doe #2, Jane Doe #3, Judith Flenna, Elaine Kolodziej, Pamela Lindstrom,

Pauline Maniaci, Mary Richardson, Joan Ritch, Janice Sandora, Michele Boulton, Susan

Schmaltz, Judy Spradley, Eleanor Taylor, Beverly Thomas, Judith Thornton, Mary Jo

Van Tiem, Renee Willits, Rebecca Ditch, Sara Aguinaga, Joan Rahill, Lisa Haddix,

Barbara Stewart, Pat Bolone, Bonnie Bousson, Donna Vaughn, Marjorie Harder,

Christina Diem, Kathy Diem, Osuil Mayo, Christine Ewald, Pam Rogers, Barbara Arnold,

Georgina Ghazawi, Peggy Pryzbylski, Janet Bott, Stephanie Harbin, Deborah Presley and

Theresa Gould (collectively hereinafter as "PLAINTIFFS"), by and through their

attorneys, Schwartz Law Firm, P.C. and Wigod, Falzon, McNeely & Unwin, P.C., and for

their Third Amended Complaint against Defendants, Willie Gary, Tricia Hoffler, Robert

Parenti, Sekou Gary, and Gary, Williams, Parenti, Finney, Lewis, McManus,

Watson & Sperando, P.C., jointly and severally, (collectively hereinafter

"DEFENDANTS/ATTORNEYS"), state as follows:

1.   Plaintiff, Wendy Kubik, formerly known as Wendy Curdie, is a

resident of the City of Fair Haven and a citizen of the State of Michigan.

2.   Plaintiff, Michelle DeTomaso, is a resident of the Township of

Shelby, County of Macomb and a citizen of the State of Michigan.

3.   Plaintiff, Rita Dillon, is a resident of the Township of Harrison,

County of Macomb and a citizen of the State of Michigan.

4.   Plaintiff, Jane Doe #1, is a citizen of, and resides by herself in, the State

of Michigan. She and Jane Doe #2 were represented by DEFENDANTS/ATTORNEYS, in part, as the only plaintiffs in a lawsuit filed in one of the state courts in Michigan. DEFENDANTS/ ATTORNEYS know the identity of Jane Doe #1. She is being designated as Jane Doe #1 to help preserve the confidentiality of the outcome of said prior litigation.

5. Plaintiff, Jane Doe #2, is a citizen of, and resides with her husband in, the State of Michigan. She and Jane Doe #1 were represented by DEFENDANTS/ATTORNEYS, in part, as the only plaintiffs in a lawsuit filed in one of the state courts in Michigan. DEFENDANTS/ ATTORNEYS know the identity of Jane Doe #2. She is being designated as Jane Doe #2 to help preserve the confidentiality of the outcome of said prior litigation.

6. Plaintiff, Jane Doe #3, is a citizen of the State of Michigan. She was represented by DEFENDANTS/ ATTORNEYS, in part, as the only plaintiff in a lawsuit filed in one of the state courts in Michigan. DEFENDANTS/ ATTORNEYS know the identity of Jane Doe #3. She is being designated as Jane Doe #3 to help preserve the confidentiality of the outcome of said prior litigation.

7. Plaintiff, Judith Flenna, is a resident of the Township of Chesterfield, County of Macomb and citizen of the State of Michigan.

8. Plaintiff, Elaine Kolodziej, is a resident of Grosse Pointe Park, County of Wayne and citizen of the State of Michigan.

9. Plaintiff, Pamela Lindstrom, is a resident of the Township of Columbus, County of Macomb and citizen of the State of Michigan.

10.   Plaintiff, Pauline Maniaci, is a resident of the Township of Clinton, County of Macomb and citizen of the State of Michigan.

11.   Plaintiff, Mary Richardson, is a resident of the Township of Macomb, County of Macomb and citizen of the State of Michigan.

12.   Plaintiff, Joan Ritch, is a resident in the City of Mt. Clemens, County of Macomb and citizen of the State of Michigan.

13.   Plaintiff, Janice Sandora, is a resident of the Township of Macomb, County of Macomb and citizen of the State of Michigan.

14.   Plaintiff, Michele Boulton, is a resident of the City of Romeo, County of Macomb and citizen of the State of Michigan.

15.   Plaintiff, Susan Schmaltz, is a resident of the Township of Armada, County of Macomb and citizen of the State of Michigan.

16.   Plaintiff, Judy Spradley, is a resident of the City of Detroit, County of Wayne and citizen of the State of Michigan.

17.   Plaintiff, Eleanor Taylor, is a resident of the Township of Shelby, County of Macomb and citizen of the State of Michigan. She was represented by DEFENDANTS/ ATTORNEYS, in part, in a lawsuit filed in one of the state courts in Michigan, which was also pending in the United States District Court for the Eastern District of Michigan, Case No. OO-CV-73161, before the Honorable Nancy Edmunds, at one point.

18.   Plaintiff, Beverly Thomas, is a resident of the City of Detroit, County of Wayne and citizen of the State of Michigan.

19.   Plaintiff, Judith Thornton, is a resident of the Township of Clinton, County of Macomb and citizen of the State of Michigan.

20. Plaintiff, Mary Jo Van Tiem, is a resident of the Township of Sylvan Lake, County of Oakland and citizen of the State of Michigan.

21. Plaintiff, Renee Willits, is a resident of the Township of Shelby, County of Macomb and citizen of the State of Michigan.

22. Plaintiff, Rebecca Ditch, is a resident of the Township of Casco, County of St. Clair, State of Michigan.

23. Plaintiff, Sara Aguinaga, is a resident of the Township of Washington, County of Macomb, State of Michigan.

24. Plaintiff, Joan Rahill, is a resident of the Township of Macomb, County of Macomb, State of Michigan.

25. Plaintiff, Lisa Haddix, is a resident of the City of Croswell, County of Sanilac, State of Michigan.

26. Plaintiff, Barbara Stewart, is a resident of the Township of Greenwood, County of St. Clair, State of Michigan.

27. Plaintiff, Pat Bolone, is a resident of the City of Auburn Hills, County of Oakland, State of Michigan.

28. Plaintiff, Bonnie Bousson, is a resident of the City of Capac, County of St. Clair, State of Michigan.

29. Plaintiff, Donna Vaughn, is a resident of the City of Woodhaven, County of Wayne, State of Michigan.

30. Plaintiff, Marjorie Harder, is a resident of the City of Mt. Clemens, County of Macomb, State of Michigan.

31. Plaintiff, Christina Diem, is a resident of the City of Warren, County of

Macomb, State of Michigan.

32.   Plaintiff, Kathy Diem, is a resident of the Township of Macomb, County of
Macomb, State of Michigan.

33.   Plaintiff, Osuil Mayo, is a resident of the City of Troy, County of Oakland,
State of Michigan.

34.   Plaintiff, Christine Ewald, is a resident of the Township of Harrison,
County of Macomb, State of Michigan.

35.   Plaintiff, Pam Rogers, is a resident of the City of New Haven, County of
Macomb, State of Michigan.

36.   Plaintiff, Barbara Arnold, is a resident of the Township of Brown City,
County of Sanilac, State of Michigan.

37.   Plaintiff, Georgina Ghazawi, is a resident of the City of Rochester Hills,
County of Oakland, State of Michigan.

38.   Plaintiff, Peggy Pryzbylski, is a resident of the Township of Utica,
County of Macomb, State of Michigan.

39.   Plaintiff, Janet Bott, is a resident of the Township of East Pointe, County of
Macomb, State of Michigan.

40.   Plaintiff, Stephanie Harbin, is a resident of the City of Southfield, County of
Oakland, State of Michigan.

41.   Plaintiff, Deborah Presley, is a resident of the City of Detroit, County of
Wayne, State of Michigan.

42.   Plaintiff, Theresa Gould, is a resident of the City of Detroit, County of
Wayne, State of Michigan.

43.   Upon information and belief, Defendant, Willie Gary, is a citizen of the state of Florida and is an attorney who at all times relevant herein was practicing his profession through the law firm of Defendant, Gary, Williams, Parenti, Finney, Lewis, McManus, Watson & Sperando, P.C., with a principal place of business in Stuart, Florida.

44.   Upon information and belief, Defendant, Tricia Hoffler, is a citizen of the State of Florida and is an attorney who at all times relevant herein was practicing her profession through the law firm of Defendant, Gary, Williams, Parenti, Finney, Lewis, McManus, Watson & Sperando, P.C., with a principal place of business in Stuart, Florida.

45.   Upon information and belief, Defendant, Robert Parenti, is a citizen of the State of Florida and is an attorney who at all times relevant herein was practicing his profession through the law firm of Defendant, Gary, Williams, Parenti, Finney, Lewis, McManus, Watson & Sperando, P.C., with a principal place of business in Stuart, Florida.

46.   Upon information and belief, Defendant, Sekou Gary, is a citizen of the State of Florida and is an attorney who at all times relevant herein was practicing his profession through the law firm of Defendant, Gary, Williams, Parenti, Finney, Lewis, McManus, Watson & Sperando, P.C., with a principal place of business in Stuart, Florida

47.   Upon information and belief, Defendant, Gary, Williams, Parenti, Finney, Lewis, McManus, Watson & Sperando, P.C., is a professional corporation incorporated under the laws of the State of Florida, with a principal place of business in the City of Stuart and at all times material herein, was responsible for the actions of its employees and/or agents.

48.   The matter in controversy exceeds the sum or value of $75,000.00,

exclusive of interest and costs.

49.   This Court has original jurisdiction of this civil action pursuant to 28 U.S.C. §1332(a)(l) and (c).

50.   Venue is appropriate in this judicial district pursuant to 28 U.S.C. §1391(c).

51.   In the spring of 2002, Plaintiff, Eleanor Taylor, had a pending lawsuit in a state court in Michigan against Company A. [1] Discovery and case evaluation had been completed. Company A's motion for summary disposition had been taken under advisement. The case was poised for trial. Her Michigan attorneys, Rundell & Nolan, LLP contracted with Defendant, Gary, Williams, Parenti, Finney, Lewis, McManus, Watson & Sperando, P.C. to serve as co-counsel for her in her claim against Company A. The terms of the contract were never disclosed to Plaintiff Taylor.

---

[1]The designation "Company A" is being utilized to help preserve the confidentiality of the outcome of said dispute. DEFENDANTS/ATTORNEYS know the identity of Company A.

52.   Concurrently in the spring of 2002, Jane Doe #1 and Jane Doe #2 had a pending lawsuit in a state court in Michigan against Company A and Company B. [2] The case was in the discovery phase. Jane Doe #1's and Jane Doe #2's Michigan counsel, Rundell and Nolan, LLP, contracted with Defendant, Gary, Williams, Parenti, Finney, Lewis, McManus, Watson & Sperando, P.C. to serve as co-counsel for Jane Doe #1 and Jane Doe #2 in their claims against Company A and Company B. The terms of the contract were never disclosed to Jane Doe #1 and Jane Doe #2.

53.   Also concurrently in the spring of 2002, Jane Doe #3 had a pending lawsuit in a state court in Michigan against Company A and Company B. The case was in the discovery phase. Jane Doe #3's Michigan counsel, Rundell and Nolan, LLP, contracted

with Defendant, Gary, Williams, Parenti, Finney, Lewis, McManus, Watson & Sperando, P.C. to serve as co-counsel for Jane Doe #3 in her claims against Company A and Company B. The terms of the contract were never disclosed to Jane Doe #3.

54.   After Defendant Gary, Williams, Parenti, Finney, Lewis, McManus, Watson & Sperando, P.C. contracted with Rundell and Nolan, LLP, DEFENDANTS/ATTORNEYS implemented a scheme designed to compel Company A and/or Company B to resolve the pending lawsuits and claims on terms extremely advantageous to DEFENDANTS/ATTORNEYS, including the securing of other women who were similarly situated to their existing clients with respect to claims against Company A and Company B so as to enhance the pool of claimants.

---

[2]The designations "Company A" and "Company B" are being utilized to help preserve the confidentiality of the outcome of said dispute. Company A in this paragraph is the same party as Company A in any prior or subsequent paragraph in this Complaint. Company B in this paragraph is the same party as Company B in any prior or subsequent paragraph in this Complaint. DEFENDANTS/ATTORNEYS know the identity of both Company A and Company B.

55.   Upon information and belief, Rundell and Nolan, LLP thereafter signed attorney/client representation agreements with 38 additional women (collectively with Plaintiffs Taylor, Jane Doe #1, Jane Doe #2 and Jane Doe #3 as the PLAINTIFFS) to pursue claims on their behalf against Company A and Company B.

56.   DEFENDANTS/ATTORNEYS never filed a lawsuit on behalf of any of these 38 other women against Company A or Company B.

57.   In May 2002 and July 2002, Company B made settlement offers to DEFENDANTS/ATTORNEYS for a global resolution of PLAINTIFFS' claims.

58.   DEFENDANTS/ATTORNEYS never presented these settlement offers to PLAINTIFFS.

59.   In July 2002, and without the knowledge and consent of PLAINTIFFS,
Company B and DEFENDANTS/ATTORNEYS entered into a global settlement of
PLAINTIFFS' claims, which settlement included, but is not limited to, $51.5 million
which would not be received by PLAINTIFFS, PLAINTIFFS permanently dropping their
claims against Company A and Company B, and DEFENDANTS/ATTORNEYS
agreeing never to sue in the future Company B and, in some circumstances, Company A

60.   PLAINTIFFS were never told of all of the details of total global settlement
       package.

61.   After reaching the global settlement, DEFENDANTS/ATTORNEYS
discovered they had never executed attorney/client representation agreements with any of the
42 individuals.

62.   DEFENDANTS/ ATTORNEYS immediately overnight mailed
PLAINTIFFS' contingency fee attorney/client representation agreements with
DEFENDANTS/ ATTORNEYS, whereby PLAINTIFFS each agreed to pay
DEFENDANTS/ATTORNEYS 33VJ% of their total recovery for their legal services
rendered.

63.   DEFENDANTS/ATTORNEYS instructed PLAINTIFFS to immediately
sign and return the contingency fee attorney/client representation agreements, not
informing their clients that the case was already settled.

64.   Within approximately one week of recelvmg the returned agreements,
DEFENDANTS/ ATTORNEYS scheduled meetings with each of the PLAINTIFFS to
discuss a settlement "offer" being made to them individually.

65.   During these meetings, DEFENDANTS/ATTORNEYS never divulged the

details of the global resolution to PLAINTIFFS and never advised that their claims were already settled.

66.   During these meetings, DEFENDANTS/ ATTORNEYS mislead PLAINTIFFS into believing that their claims were not yet settled.

67.   During these meetings, DEFENDANTS/ATTORNEYS never informed their clients that it was they (DEFENDANTS/ ATTORNEYS), not Company B, who decided how much out of the total settlement package each individual plaintiff would receive.

68.   DEFENDANTS/ ATTORNEY coerced PLAINTIFFS, through a variety of omissions, misrepresentations and other actions that constituted extreme duress, to accept the already agreed upon settlement package.

69.   As part of the settlement, DEFENDANTS/ATTORNEYS convinced PLAINTIFFS to permanently dismiss their claims against Company A without receiving any compensation from Company A.

70.   DEFENDANTS/ ATTORNEYS, without fully disclosing all of the elements of the global settlement package, and through intentional false, misleading and erroneous advice, induced PLAINTIFFS to sign various documents that permanently settled their claims against Company A and Company B.

71.   At the conclusion of the representation, DEFENDANTS/ATTORNEYS withheld monies substantially in excess of 33⅓% of each PLAINTIFF'S total recovery (the legal fees in excess of 33⅓% hereinafter called "ADDITIONAL LITIGATION PROCEEDS" [3]) as their purported legal fees, *exclusive* of the aforementioned $51.5 million.

72.   DEFENDANTS/ATTORNEYS represented that the ADDITIONAL

LITIGATION PROCEEDS were legal fees being paid by their new client Company B,

for other legal work performed for Company B, and that these monies had nothing to do

with their representation of PLAINTIFFS against Company B.

73.   Even if DEFENDANTS/ATTORNEYS' explanation were in fact true, which

PLAINTIFFS believe it is not, DEFENDANTS/ ATTORNEYS violated the Michigan

Rules of Professional Conduct by, among other things, entering into a blatant conflict of

interest arrangement for their own pecuniary advantage.

74.   Upon information and belief, the $51.5 million and the ADDITIONAL

LITIGATION PROCEEDS were monies Company A and/or Company B were willing

to pay to resolve PLAINTIFFS' claims.

75.   PLAINTIFFS have been harmed by DEFENDANTS/ATTORNEYS'

wrongful retention of monies belonging to PLAINTIFFS.

---

²The designation "ADDITIONAL LITIGATION PROCEEDS" is being utilized to help preserve the confidentiality of the outcome of said dispute. DEFENDANTS/ATTORNEYS know the specific sum being referenced.

COUNT I

LEGAL MALPRACTICE

76.   PLAINTIFFS repeat and reallege paragraphs 1 through 75 as

though each allegation was stated verbatim.

77.   At all times material herein, there was a lawyer/client

relationship between DEFENDANTS/ATTORNEYS who represented, advised

and counseled PLAINTIFFS.

78.   DEFENDANTS/ ATTORNEYS accepted responsibility in their

professional capacity as attorneys, agreeing to advise, consult and represent PLAINTIFFS, and pursue and protect PLAINTIFFS' interests against Company A and Company B, all within the applicable standard of care.

79.   At all times pertinent hereto, DEFENDANTS/ATTORNEYS owed PLAINTIFFS a duty to render and provide legal services in conformance with the acceptable standard of care required of lawyers in the community, in light of the facts of the case, and to refrain from acts of negligence and/or professional negligence and to further refrain from negligent omissions and to provide competent and accurate advice, service and legal representation to PLAINTIFFS and other duties which include, but are not limited to:

A   To use reasonable knowledge, skill, ability and care ordinarily possessed and exercised by attorneys in the State of Michigan, in representation of PLAINTIFFS;

B.   To act in a spirit of loyalty to PLAINTIFFS, assuming a position of the highest trust and confidence;

C.   To exert their best efforts while wholeheartedly advancing PLAINTIFFS' interests with complete fidelity and diligence;

D.   To familiarize themselves with the facts, the rules of the particular courts in which they practice and in the interpretation and construction said court's place upon the law in the State of Michigan and in the United States, including but not limited to common law, statutory law, and court rules;

E.   To enter into an agreement to retain and employ DEFENDANTS/ ATTORNEYS which conforms with the requirements of the Michigan Court Rules and/or the rules of the Florida State Bar;

F.   To comply with all duties imposed upon

DEFENDANTS/ATTORNEYS by the Michigan and/or Florida Rules of Professional Conduct, including but not limited to:

(i)   Competence;

(ii)   Diligence;

(iii)   Entering into a contingent fee agreement for representation of PLAINTIFFS only after providing to PLAINTIFFS a statement of client's rights and affording PLAINTIFFS complete opportunity to understand each of the rights set forth therein, and providing a copy of the statement to the PLAINTIFFS, signed by both PLAINTFFS and DEFENDANTS/ ATTORNEYS;

(iv)   Explaining matters to the extent reasonably necessary in order to permit PLAINTIFFS to make informed decisions regarding the representation;

(v)   Notifying PLAINTIFFS promptly of all settlement offers;

(vi)   Preserving the right of PLAINTIFFS to make the final decision regarding settlement of the case;

(vii)   Keeping PLAINTIFFS reasonably informed about the status of their matter and complying promptly with reasonable requests for information;

(viii) In conveying to PLAINTIFFS any settlement offer providing PLAINTIFFS with full disclosure of all payments of money and/or other consideration from Company A and/or Company B to PLAINTIFFS and/or to DEFENDANTS/ATTORNEYS, in order to permit PLAINTIFFS to make an informed decision regarding settlement;

(ix)   Upon conclusion of the contingent-fee matter, providing PLAINTIFFS with a written statement of the full outcome of the matter and the method used to determine PLAINTIFFS' portion of the monies they received;

(x)   Seeking of the lawful objectives of PLAINTIFFS against Company A and Company B through all reasonably available means permitted by law;

(xi)   Not entering into impermissible conflict of interest relationships;

(xii) Not participating in making an aggregate settlement of PLAINTIFFS' claims with Company A and/or Company B unless each PLAINTIFF consents after full consultation including explanation of the implications of the common representation of multiple clients and the DEFENDANTS/ATTORNEYS' own interests, and the advantages and risks involved, including disclosure of the existence and nature of all the claims involved and of the details of each person's participation in the settlement;

(xiii) Charging PLAINTIFFS a fee which is legal, reasonable, and not clearly excessive, considering, among other facts, the fee customarily charged in the locality for similar legal services and the maximum allowable fee for such legal services by rules of court and state bar regulation;

(xiv) Not acquiring a proprietary interest in the cause of action or subject matter of the litigation DEFENDANTS/ATTORNEYS were conducting for PLAINTIFFS, other than the contingency fee;

(xv) Not practicing law in the State of Michigan without a license to do so;

(xvi) Not participating in offering or making an agreement in which a restriction on DEFENDANTS/ ATTORNEYS' right to practice is part of the settlement of a controversy involving PLAINTIFFS; and

(xvii) Not soliciting employment from Company A or Company B when DEFENDANTS/ ATTORNEYS had no family or prior professional relationship with them and when a significant motive for DEFENDANTS/ATTORNEYS' doing so was DEFENDANTS/ ATTORNEYS' pecuniary gain.

G. Such other duties as are imposed by the Michigan and/or Florida Rules of Professional Conduct, Michigan Court Rules, Michigan Statutes, the common law of the State of Michigan and by the legal community in Michigan where the matter was pending.

80. DEFENDANTS/ATTORNEYS conducted themselves in a professionally negligent manner and breached their duties in rendering services to PLAINTIFFS within the

pendency of the attorney-client relationship, and that this professional negligence consisted of, but is not limited to, the following:

A.   Failing to inform PLAINTIFFS of the $51.5 million;

B.   Failing to take the necessary steps and use due diligence to pursue PLAINTIFFS' objectives against Company A and Company B;

C.   Failing to use reasonable knowledge, skill, ability and care ordinarily possessed and exercised by attorneys in the State of Michigan regarding settlement of disputes;

D.   Failing to act in a spirit of loyalty, with the highest trust and confidence, towards PLAINTIFFS;

E.   Failing to explain all matters to the extent reasonably necessary to permit PLAINTIFFS to make informed decisions regarding their claims against Company A and Company B;

F.   Failing to notifying PLAINTIFFS promptly of all settlement offers and the terms of all settlement offers;

G.   Failing to properly forward PLAINTIFFS their respective portion of their monies;

H.   Entering into impermissible conflict of interest relationships;

I.   Accepting compensation for representing PLAINTIFFS from Company A and/or Company B;

J.   Making an aggregate settlement of PLAINTIFFS' claims without informing each PLAINTIFF of all information needed to be known for them to make an informed decision;

K.   Making false statements and using egregious tactics to get PLAINTIFFS to make decisions about their case;

L.   Intentionally acquiring a proprietary interest in the PLAINITFFS' claims against Company A and/or Company B for their own pecuniary advantage;

M.   Entering into an agreement in which a restriction on DEFENDANTS/ ATTORNEYS' right to practice is part of the settlement;

N.   Failing in other ways to comply with the standard of practice and care, the Rules of Professional Responsibility, and ethical considerations applicable to attorneys in the State of Michigan and/or State of Florida;

O. Failing to enter into an agreement to retain and employ DEFENDANTS/ ATTORNEYS which conforms with the requirements of the Michigan Court Rules and the rules of the Florida State Bar;

P. Failing to preserve the right of PLAINTIFFS to make the final decision regarding settlement of their claims;

Q. Failing to convey to PLAINTIFFS settlement offers with full disclosure of all payments of money and/or other consideration from Company A and/or Company B so that PLAINTIFFS could make an informed decision regarding settlement;

R. Failing to inform PLAINTIFFS of the implication of the common representation of multiple clients, and the DEFENDANTS/ ATTORNEYS' own interests, and the advantages and risks involved;

S. Charging PLAINTIFFS a fee which is clearly excessive considering, among other facts, the fee customarily charged in the locality for similar legal services and the maximum allowable fee for such legal services by rules of court and/or state bar regulation;

T. Entering into a contingent fee agreement for representation of PLAINTIFFS without providing PLAINTIFFS a statement of client's rights and affording PLAINTIFFS a complete opportunity to understand each of the rights set for therein, and providing a copy of the statement of rights, signed by both PLAINTIFFS and DEFENDANTS /ATTORNEYS, to the PLAINTIFFS; and

U. Committing the acts set forth elsewhere in this Complaint.

81. As a direct and proximate result of DEFENDANTS/ATTORNEYS' breaches of duty to PLAINTIFFS, PLAINTIFFS have sustained substantial pecuniary damages.

WHEREFORE, Plaintiffs, Wendy Kubik, Michelle DeTomaso, Rita Dillon, Jane Doe #1, Jane Doe #2, Jane Doe #3, Judith Flenna, Elaine Kolodziej, Pamela Lindstrom,

Pauline Maniaci, Mary Richardson, Joan Ritch, Susan Schmaltz, Judy Spradley, Eleanor Taylor, Beverly Thomas, Judith Thornton, Mary Jo Van Tiem, Renee Willits, Rebecca Ditch, Sara Aguinaga, Joan Rahill, Lisa Haddix, Barbara Stewart, Pat Bolone, Bonnie Bousson, Donna Vaughn, Marjorie Harder, Christina Diem, Kathy Diem, Osuil Mayo, Christine Ewald, Pam Rogers, Barbara Arnold, Georgina Ghazawi, Peggy Pryzbylski, Janet Bott, Stephanie Harbin, Deborah Presley and Theresa Gould, respectfully request that this Honorable Court enter a Judgment in their favor, and against Willie Gary, Tricia Hoffler, Robert Parenti, Sekou Gary. and Gary. Williams, Parenti, Finney, Lewis, McManus, Watson & Sperando, P.C., jointly and severally, for an amount well in excess of Seventy-Five Thousand ($75,000.00) Dollars, for all pecuniary damages they have incurred, and provide such further relief as this Court deems just.

COUNT II CONVERSION

82.   PLAINTIFFS repeat and reallege the factual content only contained in paragraphs 1 through 81 as though factually each allegation was stated verbatim.

83.   DEFENDANTS/ATTORNEYS' retention of PLAINTIFFS' portion of the settlement package is a distinct act of dominion wrongfully exerted over PLAINTIFFS' personal property in denial of or inconsistent with their rights.

84.   As a direct and proximate result of DEFENDANTS/ATIORNEYS' actions, PLAINTIFFS have been severely harmed.

85.   DEFENDANTS/ATIORNEYS' actions were malicious, willful and wanton misconduct and indicated a reckless disregard of PLAINTIFFS' rights resulting in the

PLAINTIFFS suffering humiliation, a sense of outrage and indignity, such that they are entitled to exemplary damages.

WHEREFORE, Plaintiffs, Wendy Kubik, Michelle DeTomaso, Rita Dillon, Jane Doe #1, Jane Doe #2, Jane Doe #3, Judith Flenna, Elaine Kolodziej, Pamela Lindstrom, Pauline Maniaci, Mary Richardson, Joan Ritch, Susan Schmaltz, Judy Spradley, Eleanor Taylor, Beverly Thomas, Judith Thornton, Mary Jo Van Tiem, Renee Willits, Rebecca Ditch, Sara Aguinaga, Joan Rahill, Lisa Haddix, Barbara Stewart, Pat Bolone, Bonnie Bousson, Donna Vaughn, Marjorie Harder, Christina Diem, Kathy Diem, Osuil Mayo, Christine Ewald, Pam Rogers, Barbara Arnold, Georgina Ghazawi, Peggy Pryzbylski, Janet Bott, Stephanie Harbin, Deborah Presley and Theresa Gould, respectfully request that this Honorable Court enter a Judgment in their favor, and against Willie Gary, Tricia Hoffler, Robert Parenti, Sekou Gary, and Gary, Williams, Parenti, Finney, Lewis, McManus, Watson & Sperando, P.C., jointly and severally, for an amount well in excess of Seventy-Five Thousand ($75,000.00) Dollars, for all pecuniary damages they have incurred and exemplary damages.

COUNT III

BREACH OF FIDUCIARY DUTY

86.   PLAINTIFFS repeat and reallege the factual allegations only contained in paragraphs 1 through 85 as though each factual allegation was stated verbatim.

highest trust and confidence toward PLAINTIFFS.

88.   At all material times herein, PLAINTIFFS reposed their faith, confidence and trust in

DEFENDANTS/ATTORNEYS' judgment and advice.

89.   At all material times herein, DEFENDANTS/ATTORNEYS owed PLAINTIFFS a

        fiduciary duty that included, among other things, to act in their best interest and with

        unswerving loyalty.

90.   DEFENDANTS/ATTORNEYS breached their fiduciary obligations to PLAINTIFFS by,

        among other things:

        (i)   entering into an attorney/client relationship with
                Company B while representing PLAINTIFFS against
                Company B;

        (ii)   duping PLAINTIFFS into permanently releasing all
                claims they may possess against Company A so that
                ATTORNEYS could receive the ADDITIONAL
                LITIGATION PROCEEDS and additional
                compensation; and

        (iii)   misappropriating PLAINTIFFS' funds.

        91.   As a direct and proximate result of DEFENDANTS/ATTORNEYS'
                actions,

PLAINTIFFS have been severely harmed.

92.   DEFENDANTS/ATTORNEYS' actions were malicious, willful and wanton misconduct

        and indicated a reckless disregard of PLAINTIFFS' rights resulting in the PLAINTIFFS

        suffering humiliation, a sense of outrage and indignity, such that they are entitled to

        exemplary damages.

        WHEREFORE, Plaintiffs Wendy Kubik, Michelle DeTomaso, Rita

Dillon, Jane Doe #1, Jane Doe #2, Jane Doe #3, Judith Flenna, Elaine

Kolodziej, Pamela Lindstrom, Pauline Maniaci, Mary Richardson, Joan

Ritch, Susan Schmaltz, Judy Spradley, Eleanor Taylor, Beverly Thomas, Judith Thornton, Mary Jo Van Tiem, Renee Willits, Rebecca Ditch, Sara Aguinaga, Joan Rahill, Lisa Haddix, Barbara Stewart, Pat Bolone, Bonnie Bousson, Donna Vaughn, Marjorie Harder, Christina Diem, Kathy Diem, Osuil Mayo, Christine Ewald, Pam Rogers, Barbara Arnold, Georgina Ghazawi, Peggy Pryzbylski, Janet Bott, Stephanie Harbin, Deborah Presley and Theresa Gould, respectfully request that this Honorable Court enter a Judgment in their favor, and against Willie Gary, Tricia Hoffler, Robert Parenti, Sekou Gary, and Gary, Williams, Parenti, Finney, Lewis, McManus, Watson & Sperando, P.C., jointly and severally, for an amount well in excess of Seventy-Five Thousand ($75,000.00) Dollars, for all pecuniary damages they have incurred, and exemplary damages, and provide such further relief as this Court deems just.

COUNT IV

CONTRACT IN CONTRAVENTION OF PUBLIC
POLICY

93.   PLAINTIFFS repeat and reallege the factual allegations only contained in paragraphs 1 through 92 as though each factual allegation was stated verbatim.

94.   DEFENDANTS/ATTORNEYS entered into 113 contingency fee attorney/client representation agreements with PLAINTIFFS.

95.   DEFENDANTS/ATTORNEYS withheld monies from PLAINTIFFS in accordance with their attorney/client representation agreement, as legal fees.

96.   That the time DEFENDANTS/ATTORNEYS forwarded the Defendant

Gary, Williams, Parenti, Finney, Lewis, McManus, Watson & Sperando, P.C. contingency fee attorney/client representation agreement to PLAINTIFFS and instructed them to immediately sign it, the case was already settled so that there was nothing contingent about the outcome.

97.   Each attorney/client representation agreement DEFENDANTS/ATTORNEYS signed with PLAINTIFFS violates the Michigan Rules of Professional Conduct in the following particulars:

   (i)   Entering into an agreement for, charging, or collecting an illegal or clearly excessive fee;

   (ii)   Authorizing DEFENDANTS/ATTORNEYS to enter into an impermissible conflict of interest;

   (iii) Failing to explain the implications of common representation, and the advantages and risks involved, when seeking permission to enter in to a conflict of interest situation involving the representation of multiple clients;

   (iv)   Acquiring a proprietary interest in the cause of action or subject matter of litigation the lawyer is conducting for a client, other than the contingency fee; and

   (v)   Accepting compensation for representing a client from one other than the client without (1) the client consenting after full consultation; (2) there is no interference with the lawyer's independence of professional judgment or with the client-lawyer relationship; and (3) information relating to representation of a client is protected as required by MRPC 1.6.

98.   Attorney fee agreements that violate the Michigan Rules of Professional Conduct are unethical and unenforceable as a matter of law.

99.   As a direct and proximate result of DEFENDANTS/ATTORNEYS entering into arrangements with PLAINTIFFS, which contravene the Michigan Rules of Professional Conduct, PLAINTIFFS have been harmed.

WHEREFORE, Plaintiffs, Wendy Kubik, Michelle DeTomaso, Rita Dillon, Jane Doe #1, Jane Doe #2, Jane Doe #3, Judith Flenna, Elaine Kolodziej, Pamela Lindstrom, Pauline Maniaci, Mary Richardson, Joan Ritch, Susan Schmaltz, Judy Spradley, Eleanor Taylor, Beverly Thomas, Judith Thornton, Mary Jo Van Tiem, Renee Willits, Rebecca Ditch, Sara Aguinaga, Joan Rahill, Lisa Haddix, Barbara Stewart, Pat Bolone, Bonnie Bousson, Donna Vaughn, Marjorie Harder, Christina Diem, Kathy Diem, Osuil Mayo, Christine Ewald, Pam Rogers, Barbara Arnold, Georgina Ghazawi, Peggy Pryzbylski, Janet Bott, Stephanie Harbin, Deborah Presley and Theresa Gould, respectfully request that this Honorable Court order Defendants, Willie Gary, Tricia Hoffler, Robert Parenti, Sekou Gary, and Gary, Williams, Parenti, Finney, Lewis, McManus, Watson & Sperando, P.C., to disgorge all monies wrongfully received by Plaintiffs through their entering into arrangements that violate the Michigan Rules of Professional Conduct and Michigan Court Rules, and provide such further relief as this Court deems just.

COUNT Y

FRAUD

100. PLAINTIFFS repeat and reallege the factual allegations only contained in paragraphs 1through 99 as though each factual allegation was stated verbatim.

101. During the first two weeks of August 2002, at the law firm of Rundell & Nolan, LLP in Troy, Michigan , Defendants, Willie Gary, Robert Parenti, Sekou Gary, Curtis Rundell and Debra Nolan made numerous false representation to PLAINTIFFS about their claims such as that they did not have causes of action against Company A, that they could never prevail against Company A, that Company A "had nothing to do" with PLAINTIFFS' potential claims, that they could not be told what any of the other

PLAINTIFFS were being offered, that if they did not accept the settlement offer DEFENDANTS/ ATTORNEYS would not represent them any longer and they would have to pay back DEFENDANTS/ ATTORNEYS for all of the time they had spent so far, that some would have to give up their jobs, etc.

102.   Upon information, Defendant Tricia Holler participated in some of these meeting via telephone.

103.   During these discussions, DEFENDANTS/ATTORNEYS never informed PLAINTIFFS all of the details of the global settlement agreement they had reached with Company B.

104.   PLAINTIFFS made the ultimate decision regarding their claims against Company A and Company B, and signed documents in accordance therewith, without knowledge of all of the details of the global settlement, including the $51.5 million.

105.   DEFENDANTS/ATTORNEYS' representations and omissions were intentional, false and material.

106.   DEFENDANTS/ATTORNEYS' representations and omissions were made with the intention that PLAINTIFFS relied upon it.

107.   PLAINTIFFS acted in reliance upon DEFENDANTS/ATTORNEYS' actions.

108.   PLAINTIFFS have been severely harmed by their reliance upon DEFENDANTS/ATTORNEYS' fraudulent representations and omissions.

109.   DEFENDANTS/ATTORNEYS' actions were malicious, willful and wanton misconduct and indicated a reckless disregard of PLAINTIFFS' rights resulting in the PLAINTIFFS suffering humiliation, a sense of outrage and indignity, such that they are entitled to exemplary damages.

WHEREFORE, Plaintiffs, Wendy Kubik, Michelle DeTomaso, Rita Dillon, Jane Doe #1, Jane Doe #2, Jane Doe #3, Judith Flenna, Elaine Kolodziej, Pamela Lindstrom, Pauline Maniaci, Mary Richardson, Joan Ritch, Susan Schmaltz, Judy Spradley, Eleanor Taylor, Beverly Thomas, Judith Thornton, Mary Jo Van Tiem, Renee Willits, Rebecca Ditch, Sara Aguinaga, Joan Rahill, Lisa Haddix, Barbara Stewart, Pat Bolone, Bonnie Bousson, Donna Vaughn, Marjorie Harder, Christina Diem, Kathy Diem, Osuil Mayo, Christine Ewald, Pam Rogers, Barbara Arnold, Georgina Ghazawi, Peggy Pryzbylski, Janet Bott, Stephanie Harbin, Deborah Presley and Theresa Gould, respectfully request that this Honorable Court enter a Judgment in their favor, and against Willie Gary, Tricia Hoffler, Robert Parenti, Sekou Gary, and Gary, Williams, Parenti, Finney, Lewis, McManus, Watson & Sperando, P.C., for an amount well in excess of Seventy-Five Thousand ($75,000.00) Dollars, for all pecuniary damages they have incurred, and exemplary damages, and provide such further relief as this Court deems just.

COUNT VI

STATUTORY

CONVERSION

110. PLAINTIFFS repeat and reallege the factual allegations only contained in paragraphs 1 through 109 as though each factual allegation was stated verbatim.

111. Upon information and belief, the total global settlement monies were transferred from Company B to their attorney, Holland & Knight, to Defendant Gary, Williams, Parenti, Finney, Lewis, McManus, Watson & Sperando, P.C.

112. After Defendant Gary, Williams, Parenti, Finney, Lewis, McManus, Watson & Sperando, P.C. received the aggregate settlement amount, they disbursed PLAINTIFFS their net settlement monies.

113. Defendant Gary, Williams, Parenti, Finney, Lewis, McManus, Watson & Sperando, P.C. converted/embezzled THE ADDITIONAL LITIGATION PROCEEDS when they kept these funds and did not disburse them to PLAINTIFFS.

114. After converting/embezzling the ADDITIONAL LITIGATION PROCEEDS, upon information and belief, Defendant Gary, Williams, Parenti, Finney, Lewis, McManus, Watson & Sperando, P.C. transferred them to Defendants Willie Gary, Tricia Hoeffler, Robert Parenti and Sekou Gary.

115. Upon information and belief, Defendants Willie Gary, Tricia Hoeffler, Robert Parenti and Sekou Gary all received converted/embezzled property and knew the property had been converted/embezzled from PLAINTIFFS.

116. MCLA 600.2919a provides: "A person damaged as a result of another person's buying, receiving, or aiding in the concealment of any stolen, embezzled, or converted property when the person buying, receiving, or aiding in the concealment of any stolen, embezzled, or converted property knew that the property was stolen, embezzled, or converted may recover 3 times the amount of actual damages sustained, plus costs and reasonable attorney fees. This remedy shall be in addition to any other right or remedy the person may have at law or otherwise."

---

[4]Defendant Gary, Williams, Parenti, Finney, Lewis, McManus, Watson & Sperando, P.C determined PLAINTIFFS tax obligations on their settlements, withdrew these amounts from their gross award and, upon information and belief, eventually forwarded these monies to the tax authorities.

117.   Defendants Willie Gary, Tricia Hoffler, Robert Parenti and Sekou Gary, jointly and severally, have violated MCLA 600.2919a.

118.   As a direct and proximate result of their conduct, they are liable to PLAINTIFFS for 3 times the amount of actual damages they caused, plus reimbursement of PLAINTIFFS' costs and reasonable attorney fees.

119.   DEFENDANTS/ATTORNEYS' actions were malicious, willful and wanton misconduct and indicated a reckless disregard of PLAINTIFFS' rights resulting in the PLAINTIFFS suffering humiliation, a sense of outrage and indignity, such that they are entitled to exemplary damages.

WHEREFORE, Plaintiffs, Wendy Kubik, Michelle DeTomaso, Rita Dillon, Jane Doe #1, Jane Doe #2, Jane Doe #3, Judith Flenna, Elaine Kolodziej, Pamela Lindstrom, Pauline Maniaci, Mary Richardson, Joan Ritch, Susan Schmaltz, Judy Spradley, Eleanor Taylor, Beverly Thomas, Judith Thornton, Mary Jo Van Tiem, Renee Willits, Rebecca Ditch, Sara Aguinaga, Joan Rahill, Lisa Haddix, Barbara Stewart, Pat Bolone, Bonnie Bousson, Donna Vaughn, Marjorie Harder, Christina Diem, Kathy Diem, Osuil Mayo, Christine Ewald, Pam Rogers, Barbara Arnold, Georgina Ghazawi, Peggy Pryzbylski, Janet Bott, Stephanie Harbin, Deborah Presley and Theresa Gould, respectfully request that this Honorable Court enter a Judgment in their favor, and against Willie Gary, Tricia Hoffler, Robert Parenti, Sekou Gary, for an amount well in excess of Seventy-Five Thousand ($75,000.00) Dollars, for all pecuniary damages they have incurred, and exemplary damages, and provide such further relief as this Court deems just.

SCHWARTZ LAW FIRM, P.C.

By: _____
Jay A. Schwartz
Attorney for Plaintiffs

Dated: September 23,

2004

37887 West Twelve Mile Road, Suite A
Farmington Hills, Michigan 48331
(248) 553-9400

UNITED STATES DISTRICT COURT
EASTERN DISTRICT OF MICHIGAN SOUTHERN DIVISION

WENDY KUBIK, MICHELLE DeTOMASO, RITA DILLON, JANE DOE #1, JANE DOE #2, JANE DOE #3, JUDITH FLENNA, ELAINE KOLODZIEJ, PAMELA LINDSTROM, PAULINE MANIACI, MARY RICHARDSON, JOAN RITCH, JANICE SANDORA, MICHELE BOULTON, SUSAN SCHMALTZ, JUDY SPRADLEY, ELEANOR TAYLOR, BEYERLY THOMAS, JUDITH THORNTON, MARY JO VAN TIEM, RENEE WILLITS, REBECCA DITCH, SARA AGUINAGA, JOAN RAHILL, LISA HADDIX, BARBARA STEWART, PAT BOLONE, BONNIE BOUSSON, DONNA VAUGHN, MARJORIE HARDER, CHRISTINA DIEM, KATHY DIEM, OSUIL MAYO, CHRISTINE EWALD, PAM ROGERS, BARBARA ARNOLD, GEORGINA GHAZAWI, PEGGY PRYZBYLSKI, JANET BOTT, STEPHANIE HARBIN, DEBORAH PRESLEY, and THERESA GOULD,	Civil Action No. 03-73350 Hon. Paul D. Borman Mag. Judge Mona Majzoub PROOF OF SERVICE (re: Plaintiffs' Third Amended Complaint and Demand for Jury Trial)

Plaintiffs,

v

WILLIE GARY,
TRICIA HOFFLER,
ROBERT PARENTI,
SEKOU GARY, and
GARY, WILLIAMS,
PARENTI, FINNEY,
LEWIS, McMANUS,
WATSON &
SPERANDO, P.C.,

Defendants.

SCHWARTZ LAW FIRM, P.C.
By: Jay A. Schwartz (P45268)
Attorney for Plaintiffs
37887 West Twelve Mile Road,
Suite A Farmington Hills, Michigan
48331 (248) 553-9400

WIGOD, FALZON, MCNEELY

& UNWIN, P.C.

By: Lawrence C. Falzon
(P30655) Attorney for
Plaintiffs
29500 Telegraph Road, Suite 210

Southfield, Michigan 48034

(248) 356-3300

CLARK HILL PLC
By: Timothy D.
     Wittlinger
     (P22490)
     Reginald M.
     Turner, Jr.
     (P40543)
Attorney for
Defendants
500 Woodward Avenue, Suite 3500

Detroit, Michigan

48226

(313) 965-8300

PROOF OF SERVICE

STATE OF MICHIGAN   )

)

§ COUNTY OF
OAKLAND   )

       I, WENDY L. JONES, being first duly sworn, depose and state that I am employed by the Schwartz Law Firm and that on the 23rd day of September, 2004, I mailed a photocopy of Plaintiffs' Third Amended Complaint and Proof of Service to: Timothy D. Wittlinger, Esq., Suite 3500, 500 Woodward Avenue, Detroit, Michigan, 48226, by placing same in an envelope addressed as above and depositing same in a U.S. Mail receptacle located in Farmington Hills, Michigan. Further saith not.

Wendy J. Jones
JONES

Subscribed and sworn to before
me this 23rd day of September, 2004.

Linda Zarem
LINDA ZAREM, Notary Public
Wayne County, Michigan

My Commission Expires: *4/7105*
Acting in Oakland County, Michigan

Appendix D

4months,CLOSED,ECS,PROTO,TitleVII

U.S. District Court Northern District of Georgia (Atlanta)
CIVIL DOCKET FOR CASE #: 1:01-cv-03039-RWS

Clark v. Coca-Cola Company Assigned to: Judge Richard W. Story Demand: $0
Cause: 42:2000 Job Discrimination (Race)
Date Filed: 11/13/2001
Date Terminated: 08/06/2004 Jury Demand: Both
Nature of Suit: 442 Civil Rights: Jobs Jurisdiction: Federal Question

Plaintiff

Gregory Allen Clark	represented by **Adam J. Conti** Adam J. Conti, LLC

Suite 1250
1201 Peachtree Street
Atlanta, GA 30361
404-531-0701
Fax: 404-531-0082
Email: aconti@contilaw.com
LEAD ATTORNEY ATTORNEY TO BE NOTICED

Alan Howard Garber
The Garber Law Firm, P.C. Suite 14
4994 Lower Roswell Road, NE
Marietta, GA 30068
678-560-6685
Fax: 678-560-5067
Email: ahgarber@garberlaw.net
TERMINATED: 04/28/2003
LEAD ATTORNEY ATTORNEY TO BE NOTICED

F. Shields McManus
Gary Williams Parenti Finney
Lewis, et al.
221 East Osceola Street
Stuart, FL 34994
772-283-8260
Email: fsm@williegary.com *LEAD ATTORNEY ATTORNEY TO BE NOTICED*

Jerome A. Stone , Jr.
Gary Williams Parenti Finney Lewis,
et al.
221 East Osceola Street
Stuart, FL 34994
772-283-8260
LEAD ATTORNEY ATTORNEY TO BE NOTICED

V.

Secrets, Lies, and Betrayals
Defendant

Coca-Cola Company   represented by **Elizabeth Finn Johnson**
                                         The Coca-Cola Company
                                         P.O. Box 1734
                                         One Coca-Cola Plaza Atlanta, GA 30301
                                         404-676-3736
                                         Email:eljohnson@na.ko.com
                                         LEAD ATTORNEY ATTORNEY TO BE NOTICED

                                         Jeffrey Emery Tompkins
                                         Thomas Kennedy Sampson & Tompkins, LLP
                                         3355 Main Street
                                         Atlanta, GA 30337
                                         404-688-4503
                                         Email:j.tompkins@tkstlaw.com
                                         LEAD ATTORNEY ATTORNEY TO BE NOTICED

                                         Larry Dean Thompson
                                         King & Spalding
                                         191 Peachtree Street, N.E.
                                         Atlanta, GA 30303-1763
                                         404-572-4600
                                         LEAD ATTORNEY ATTORNEY TO BE NOTICED

                                         Michael Wayne Johnston
                                         King & Spalding, LLP-ATL 40
                                         40th Floor
                                         1180 Peachtree Street, NE
                                         Atlanta, GA 30309-3521
                                         404-572-4600
                                         Fax: 404-572-5135
                                         Email:MJohnston@KSlaw.com
                                         LEAD ATTORNEY ATTORNEY TO BE NOTICED

                                         R. Lawrence Ashe , Jr.
                                         Ashe Rafuse & Hill
                                         1355 Peachtree Street, NE Suite 500
                                         Atlanta, GA 30309-3232
                                         404-253-6001
                                         Email:rla@phrd.com *TERMINATED:08/14/2001*
                                         LEAD ATTORNEY ATTORNEY TO BE NOTICED

                                         Robert Allan Boas
                                         The Coca-Cola Company
                                         P.O. Box 1734
                                         One Coca-Cola Plaza
                                         Atlanta, GA 30301
                                         404-676-2121
                                         TERMINATED:08/14/2001
                                         LEAD ATTORNEY ATTORNEY TO BE NOTICED

                                         Samuel M. Matchett

King & Spalding, LLP
1180 Peachtree Street, N.E.
Atlanta, GA 30309-3521
404-572-4600
Fax: 404-572-5138
Email: smatchett@kslaw.com
LEAD ATTORNEY ATTORNEY TO BE NOTICED

Shelly Sharp Blews
Sheely Sharp Blews
2022 Ivy Ridge Rd.
Smyrna, GA 30080
770-319-1161
Email: shellyblews@gmail.com
LEAD ATTORNEY ATTORNEY TO BE NOTICED

Thomas G. Sampson
Thomas Kennedy Sampson & Tompkins, LLP
3355 Main Street
Atlanta, GA 30337
404-688-4503
Email: t.sampson@tkstlaw.com
LEAD ATTORNEY ATTORNEY TO BE NOTICED

William A. Clineburg , Jr.
Taylor English Duma LLP
Suite 400
1600 Parkwood Circle
Atlanta, GA 30339
678-336-7199
Email: bclineburg@taylorenglish.com
TERMINATED: 08/14/2001
LEAD ATTORNEY ATTORNEY TO BE NOTICED

Date Filed	#	Docket Text
05/24/2001	1	ORDER by Judge Richard W. Story establishing a civil action for only the individual claims of plas Abdallah, Clark, Laosebikan and Williams. The court will deem all claims to have been filed on the dates they were filed in 1:98-cv-3679. (cc) (fmm) (Entered: 05/29/2001)
05/24/2001		CASE REFERRED to Mag Judge E. C. Scofield III (Calendar sheets forwarded) (fmm) (Entered: 05/29/2001)
05/24/2001	2	AMENDED COMPLAINT by plaintiffs; jury demand (Filed on 4/22/99 in 1:98-CV-3679) (ck) (Entered: 06/11/2001)
05/24/2001		Added attorney for plaintiff: F. Shields McManus. (ck) (Entered: 07/25/2001)

05/24/2001	4	ANSWER to amended complaint [2-1] by Coca-Cola Company; jury demand (Filed 5/12/99 in 1:98-cv-3679-RWS) (ck) (Entered: 07/25/2001)
05/24/2001	5	ANSWER to second amended complaint [3-1] by Coca-Cola Company; jury demand (Filed on 2/4/00 in 1:98-cv-3679-RWS) (ck) (Entered: 07/25/2001)
05/24/2001	**6**	**ANSWER to second amended complaint [3-1] by Coca-Cola Company; jury demand (FILED UNDER SEAL) (Filed on 2/4/00 in 1:98-cv-3679) (ck) (Entered: 07/25/2001)**
07/24/2001	7	ORDER by Mag Judge E. C. Scofield III, DIRECTING parties to file a certificate of interested persons & proposed preliminary report within 15 days. [7-1] order to be submitted on 8/14/01 (cc by mag) (ck) (Entered: 07/25/2001)
07/25/2001		Added attorneys for defendant: William A. Clineburg Jr., Larry Dean Thompson, Michael Wayne Johnston, R. Lawrence Ashe Jr., Thomas G. Sampson, Jeffrey Emery Tompkins, Robert Allan Boas, Elizabeth Finn Johnson. (ck) (Entered: 07/25/2001)
08/07/2001	8	ORDER by Mag Judge E. C. Scofield III VACATING the deadlines set by the [7-1] order; plas are DIRECTED to file a motion to amend the complaint by 8/27/01. (cc by mag) (ck) (Entered: 08/09/2001)
08/08/2001	9	CONSENT MOTION by plaintiff for leave to file amended complaint with proposed order & proposed amended complaint in support. (ck) (Entered: 08/09/2001)
08/09/2001		SUBMITTED to Mag Judge E. C. Scofield III on [9-1] motion for leave to file amended complaint (ck) (Entered: 08/09/2001)
08/14/2001	10	Certification of Consent to Substitution of Counsel for defendant Coca-Cola Company. Samuel M. Matchett, Shelly Sharp Blews and Michael W. Johnston, Elizabeth Finn Johnson, Thomas G. Sampson, and Jeffrey E. Tompkins replacing attorneys Robert Allan Boas, R. Lawrence Ashe, and William A. Clineburg for Coca-Cola Company. (ck) Modified on 08/21/2001 (Entered: 08/15/2001)
08/21/2001	11	Response by defendant in support of [9-1] motion for leave to file amended complaint, with proposed order (ck) (Entered: 08/22/2001)
08/27/2001	12	ORDER by Mag Judge E. C. Scofield III GRANTING [9-1] motion for leave to file amended complaint. Plas have until 8/27/01 to file their Amended Complaint. Dft shall have 20 days following the date on which the Amended Complaint is served to file its Answer. The Joint Preliminary Report and Discovery Schedule & the Joint Certificate of Interested Persons will be due 15 days following the date on which dft files its Answer. (cc) (lme) (Entered: 08/29/2001)
08/27/2001		Terminated submissions. (lme) (Entered: 08/30/2001)
08/30/2001	13	AMENDED COMPLAINT; jury demand (fmm) Modified on 09/26/2001 (Entered: 09/24/2001)
08/30/2001	16	ORDER by Mag Judge E. C. Scofield III, amending [12-1] order; defendant's are to answer the amended complaint within 20 days of entry of this order (cc) (ck) (Entered: 09/26/2001)
09/05/2001	14	Attorney appearance for plaintiffs by Alan Howard Garber (lme) Modified on 09/24/2001 (Entered: 09/06/2001)

09/19/2001	15	ANSWER to amended complaint [13-1] by Coca-Cola Company; jury demand (fmm) (Entered: 09/24/2001)
10/23/2001	17	Joint Certificate of interested persons. (to judge & mag) (lme) (Entered: 10/24/2001)
10/23/2001	18	Preliminary Report and Discovery Schedule. (to mag) (lme) (Entered: 10/24/2001)
10/25/2001	19	ANSWERS TO INITIAL DISCLOSURES by defendant (lme) (Entered: 10/29/2001)
10/26/2001	20	ANSWERS TO INITIAL DISCLOSURES by plaintiffs. (lme) (Entered: 10/29/2001)
10/29/2001	21	Application for admission of Jerome A. Stone Jr. pro hac vice for plaintiffs. (To RWS) (lme) (Entered: 10/31/2001)
10/29/2001	22	ORDER by Mag Judge E. C. Scofield III APPROVING [18-1] preliminary statement, Discovery ends 4/19/02, pre-trial order due on 5/20/02, trial date shall be set following submission & approval of the consolidate pretrial order [22-1] order to be submitted on 5/21/02 (cc) (lme) (Entered: 10/31/2001)
11/06/2001		ENDORSED ORDER by Judge Richard W. Story GRANTING [21-1] pro hac vice application for Jerome A. Stone, Jr.. (cc) (lme) (Entered: 11/07/2001)
11/13/2001	23	ORDER by Judge Richard W. Story, DIRCTING that all the claims of the plas be severed. The clerk is DIRECTED to assign new and separate civil case numbers for plas Clark, Laosebikan and Williams. The clerk shall duplicate the record in this case for each of the new cases and the new cases shall proceed as if they were filed on the same date as this case. Pla Abdallah's case will proceed under civil action no. 1:01-cv-1336-RWS. W/in 20 days from entry, all pla's except the first named pla will be dismissed from this action w/out prejudice and are ORDERED to pay the proper filing fee to proceed in their individual cases. Should a pla fail to pay the fee, the clerk is DIRECTED to dismiss her suit w/ou prejudice. [23-1] order to be submitted on 12/7/01 (cc) (fmm) (Entered: 11/14/2001)
11/19/2001		Action duplicated from 1:01-cv-1336-RWS as required by [23-1] order (fmm) (Entered: 11/19/2001)
11/26/2001		Payment received $ 150.00 Receipt #: 480241 (ck) (Entered: 11/26/2001)
11/30/2001		Payment received $ 150.00 Receipt #: 480241 (lme) (Entered: 12/03/2001)
12/06/2001	24	ORDER by Mag Judge E. C. Scofield III, ORDERING parties to supply an original and duplicate of each filing for each captioned action. The Court DIRECTS that a courtesy copy of each future filing be supplied to the undersigned's chambers for each action captioned therein. (cc) (lme) (Entered: 12/10/2001)
01/04/2002	25	ORDER by Mag Judge E. C. Scofield III amending [24-1] order, directing that courtesy copy of only each motion and related brief, including responsive briefs and reply briefs, be supplied to the undersigned's chambers for each action captioned therein. Where the motions are identical in multiple cases, only one courtesy copy is required for chambers. (cc by mag) (lme) (Entered: 01/09/2002)
01/11/2002	26	MOTION by defendant for protective order with brief in support with proposed order. (lme) (Entered: 01/14/2002)
01/28/2002	27	REPLY by pla to [26-1] dft's motion for protective order (er) (Entered: 01/29/2002)

01/30/2002		SUBMITTED to Mag Judge E. C. Scofield III on [26-1] motion for protective order. (File in Chambers) (lme) (Entered: 01/30/2002)
02/07/2002	28	CONSENT MOTION to extend time for discovery period for 6 months after Court's ruling of [26-1] motion for protective order . (To ECS) (lme) (Entered: 02/08/2002)
02/11/2002	29	Reply brief to [26-1] motion for protective order by defendant. (lme) (Entered: 02/12/2002)
02/14/2002	30	SUPPLEMENTAL ANSWERS TO INITIAL DISCLOSURES by plaintiff (lme) (Entered: 02/19/2002)
02/28/2002		SUBMITTED to Mag Judge E. C. Scofield III on [28-1] motion to extend time for
		discovery period for 6 months after Court's ruling of [26-1] motion for protective order. (File in Chambers) (lme) (Entered: 02/28/2002)
03/18/2002	31	SECOND SUPPLEMENTAL RESPONSES TO INITIAL DISCLOSURES by plaintiff (lme) (Entered: 03/19/2002)
04/03/2002	32	ORDER by Mag Judge E. C. Scofield III GRANTING [28-1] motion to extend time for discovery period for 6 months after Court's ruling of [26-1] motion for protective order. (cc by mag) (lme) (Entered: 04/04/2002)
04/03/2002		Terminated submissions. (lme) (Entered: 04/04/2002)
04/04/2002	33	ORDER by Mag Judge E. C. Scofield III, motion hearing set for [26-1] motion for protective order on 5/1/02 at 10:00am . Each party is DIRECTED to submit a proposed proto, if they have not already done so, by 5/29/02. (cc by mag) (lme) (Entered: 04/08/2002)
04/22/2002	34	Notice to take deposition of Jeff Bramlett or Records Custodian by plaintiff (lme) (Entered: 04/23/2002)
05/03/2002	35	ORDER by Mag Judge E. C. Scofield III GRANTING [26-1] motion for protective order. (See order for specifics) (cc by mag) (lme) (Entered: 05/07/2002)
05/03/2002		Terminated submissions. (lme) (Entered: 05/07/2002)
05/06/2002	36	Oral argument/motion HEARING HELD on 5/1/02 before Mag Judge E. C. Scofield III on [26-1] motion for protective order. The Court will issue a pto. (cc by mag) (lme) (Entered: 05/09/2002)
05/29/2002		SUBMITTED to Mag Judge E. C. Scofield III on [22-1] order. (lme) (Entered: 05/29/2002)
06/03/2002		Terminated submissions. (lme) (Entered: 06/03/2002)
06/03/2002	37	ORDER by Mag Judge E. C. Scofield III, for leave of absence of MaryAnn Diaz for the periods of 5/31/02-6/5/02, 7/26/02-8/2/02, 8/19/02-8/22/02 and 9/3/02-9/20/02 (cc by mag) (lme) (Entered: 06/05/2002)
06/14/2002	38	Notice of service of subpoenas by defendant. (ck) (Entered: 06/17/2002)

11/01/2002	39	CONSENT MOTION to extend time thru 8/28/03 for discovery , and to amend scheduling order with brief in support and proposed order. (To ECS) (lme) Modified on 11/12/2002 (Entered: 11/04/2002)
11/08/2002	40	ORDER by Mag Judge E. C. Scofield III GRANTING [39-1] motion to extend time thru 8/28/03 for discovery, GRANTING [39-2] motion to amend scheduling order. Motions for sum jgm due on 9/23/03, Discovery ends 8/28/03 . (cc) (lme) (Entered: 11/12/2002)
11/12/2002	41	Notice of filing notice of service of subpoena by defendant. (lme) (Entered: 11/13/2002)
11/25/2002	42	MOTION by plaintiff to quash or modify subpoena , or, in the alternative, for protective order with brief in support. (ck) (Entered: 11/27/2002)
12/09/2002		Proposed Consent Order to extend time thru 12/17/02 for dft to respond to pla's [42-1] motion to quash or modify subpoena and [42-2] motion for protective order. (To ECS) (lme) (Entered: 12/10/2002)
12/09/2002	43	MOTION by pla for leave to file amend complaint with brief in support and proposed third amended complaint. (lme) (Entered: 12/10/2002)
12/12/2002	44	CONSENT ORDER by Mag Judge E. C. Scofield III, extending time thru 12/17/02 for dft
		to respond to [42-1] motion to quash or modify subpoena, [42-2] motion for protective order , [42-1] motion and [42-2] motion to be submitted on 12/18/02 (cc) (fmm) (Entered: 12/12/2002)
12/17/2002		Proposed consent order permitting the withdrawal of the [42-1] & [42-2] motion to quash or modify subpoena, or, in the alternative, for protective order; and ordering the production of documents sought in subpoenas directed at Hunter R. Hughes, III. (to ECS) (ck) (Entered: 12/18/2002)
12/17/2002		Withdrawal of [42-1] motion to quash or modify subpoena, [42-2] motion for protective order (ck) (Entered: 06/30/2003)
12/18/2002	45	MOTION by the Ingram Class to quash subpoenas , or for entry of a protective order , and for leave to file same with brief in support. (lme) (Entered: 12/19/2002)
12/19/2002		SUBMITTED to Mag Judge E. C. Scofield III on [42-1] motion to quash or modify subpoena, [42-2] motion for protective order. (lme) (Entered: 12/19/2002)
12/20/2002	46	ORDER by Mag Judge E. C. Scofield III GRANTING [43-1] motion for leave to file amend complaint. Pla may file his third amended complaint w/in 10 days from the entry of this order, [46-1] order to be submitted on 1/10/03 . (cc) (lme) Modified on 01/02/2003 (Entered: 12/24/2002)
12/30/2002		Proposed Consent Order to extend time thru 1/13/03 for dft to respond to [45-1] motion to quash subpoenas, [45-2] motion for entry of a protective order, and [45-3] motion for leave to file same. (To ECS) (lme) (Entered: 12/31/2002)
12/31/2002	47	Response by defendant to pla's [43-1] motion for leave to file amend complaint. (lme) (Entered: 01/06/2003)

01/02/2003	48	CONSENT ORDER by Mag Judge E. C. Scofield III, extending time thru 1/13/03 for dft to respond to pla's [45-1] motion to quash subpoenas, [45-2] motion for entry of a protective and [45-3] motion for leave to file same . {cc} (lme) (Entered: 01/06/2003)
01/02/2003	50	FOURTH AMENDED COMPLAINT by plaintiff. (lme) Modified on 01/21/2003 (Entered: 01/08/2003)
01/06/2003	49	Response by plaintiff in opposition to [45-1] motion to quash subpoenas, [45-2] motion for entry of a protective order, [45-3] motion for leave to file same. (lme) Modified on 01/16/2003 (Entered: 01/08/2003)
01/07/2003	51	ORDER by Mag Judge E. C. Scofield III, setting a hearing on 1/16/03 at 2:00pm . {cc by mag} (lme) (Entered: 01/09/2003)
01/13/2003	52	Response by defendant to [45-1] motion to quash subpoenas, [45-2] motion for entry of a protective order, [45-3] motion for leave to file same (ck) (Entered: 01/14/2003)
01/16/2003		SUBMITTED to Mag Judge E. C. Scofield III on [45-1] motion to quash subpoenas, [45-2] motion for entry of a protective order, [45-3] motion for leave to file same. (lme) (Entered: 01/16/2003)
01/17/2003	53	ORDER by Mag Judge E. C. Scofield III, AMENDING the caption of the [50-1] amended complaint to read "Fourth Amended Complaint" . The Clerk is DIRECTED to correct the docket and the first page of the amended complaint Doc. No. 50. {cc} (lme) (Entered: 01/21/2003)
01/21/2003	54	ANSWER by defendant to Fourth Amended Complaint [50-1]; jury demand. (lme) (Entered: 01/22/2003)
01/28/2003	55	Motion HEARING held before Mag Judge E. C. Scofield III on 1/16/03 re: [42-1] motion to quash or modify subpoena, [42-2] motion for protective order, [45-1] motion to quash subpoenas, [45-2] motion for entry of a protective order, [45-3]
		motion for leave to file same. Proposed consent order and motions taken under advisement. {cc by mag} (lme) (Entered: 01/31/2003)
01/31/2003	56	MOTION by pla for leave of absence of Jerome A. Stone, Jr. from 1/13/03 thru 1/14/04 for active duty with brief in support and declaration of F. Shields McManus. (To ECS) (lme) (Entered: 02/03/2003)
02/06/2003	57	ORDER by Mag Judge E. C. Scofield III GRANTING [56-1] motion for leave of absence of Jerome A. Stone, Jr. beginning 1/14/03 and extending through 1/13/04 for active duty. {cc} (lme) (Entered: 02/07/2003)
03/12/2003	58	CONSENT MOTION to extend time for expert disclosure with brief in support and proposed order. (To ECS) (lme) (Entered: 03/14/2003)
03/25/2003	59	ORDER by Mag Judge E. C. Scofield III GRANTING [58-1] motion to extend time for expert disclosure. {cc by mag} (lme) (Entered: 03/26/2003)

04/02/2003	60	ORDER by Mag Judge E. C. Scofield III GRANTING IN PART AND DENYING IN PART [45-1] motion to quash subpoenas, [45-2] motion for entry of a protective order and [45-3] motion for leave to file same. It is ORDERED that Mr. Hughes, the mediator, w/in 14 days, produce for inspection and copying to the dft and plas, pursuant to the subpoenas, all unredacted affidavits by all individuals, including the named plas herein, who are indentified by the plas in the pending actions as potential witnesses or as persons who may have knowledge or information re: the subject matter of these actions. Except as stated above, production of any other affidavits is quashed. Dft and plas shall confer re: the names of all individuals whose affidavits are so identified as subject production. Any dispute over these names may be submitted the Court for resolution, if necessary. (cc by mag) (lme) Modified on 06/30/2003 (Entered: 04/03/2003)
04/02/2003		Terminated submissions. (lme) (Entered: 04/03/2003)
04/16/2003	61	Notice of filing service of subpoenas by defendant. (lme) (Entered: 04/17/2003)
04/28/2003	62	Substitution of Counsel for pla. Adam J. Conti replacing attorney Alan Howard Garber for pla . (lme) (Entered: 05/08/2003)
07/02/2003	63	Notice of filing notice of serving 6th request for production to dfts by plaintiff. (lme) (Entered: 07/07/2003)
07/10/2003	64	CONSENT MOTION to extend time for discovery , and to amend scheduling order with brief in support and proposed order. (To ECS) (lme) (Entered: 07/11/2003)
07/16/2003	65	Notice of Withdrawal of [64-1] motion to extend time for discovery and [64-2] motion to amend scheduling order by parties. (lme) (Entered: 07/18/2003)
07/16/2003	66	Notice to take deposition of Diana Haddon by plaintiff. (lme) (Entered: 07/22/2003)
07/18/2003	67	Notice to take depositions of Jim Hush, Linda Bell, Steve Norman, Shannon Murray, Kelly Sanders, Tim Meadowns and Paul Markley by plaintiff. (lme) (Entered: 07/22/2003)
07/23/2003	68	AMENDED RESPONSES TO INITIAL DISCLOSURES by defendant. (lme) (Entered: 07/24/2003)
07/28/2003	69	Notice of filing notice of service of subpoenas by defendant. (lme) (Entered: 07/30/2003)
07/29/2003	70	Notice of filing notice of serving seventh request to produce by plaintiff. (lme) (Entered: 08/01/2003)
07/30/2003	71	AMENDED SUPPLEMENTAL ANSWERS TO INITIAL DISCLOSURES by plaintiff. (lme)
		(Entered: 08/04/2003)
07/30/2003	72	Objection to subpoena and MOTION by plaintiff to quash subpoena with brief in support. (lme) (Entered: 08/04/2003)
08/01/2003	73	MOTION by plaintiff for enlargement of number of depositions , and to extend time for 30 days for discovery with brief in support. (lme) (Entered: 08/05/2003)

08/01/2003	74	Notice to take depositions of Tara Goehring, Lisa Davis, Darlene Neely and Michelle Swearingen by plaintiff. (lme) (Entered: 08/05/2003)
08/04/2003	75	**MOTION by defendant to compel discovery from pla with brief in support and appendix of exhibits. (***FILED UNDER SEAL*** Brief in support and appendix of exhibits) (lme) (Entered: 08/05/2003)**
08/07/2003	76	Amended Notice to take deposition of Diana Haddon by plaintiff. (lme) (Entered: 08/11/2003)
08/08/2003	77	MOTION by plaintiff for leave to amend [50-1] 5th amended complaint with brief in support and proposed order and fifth amended complaint. (lme) Modified on 08/27/2003 (Entered: 08/12/2003)
08/08/2003	78	Pla's notice of withdrawal of objection to subpoena and the [72-1] motion to quash subpoena. (lme) (Entered: 08/12/2003)
08/18/2003	79	CONSENT MOTION to extend time thru 9/26/03 for discovery , to amend scheduling order with brief in support and proposed order. (To ECS) (lme) (Entered: 08/19/2003)
08/20/2003	80	Response by plaintiff to dft's [75-1] motion to compel discovery from pla. (lme) (Entered: 08/25/2003)
08/25/2003	81	Resposne by defendant to pla's [77-1] motion for leave to amend [50-1] 5th amended complaint. (lme) (Entered: 08/27/2003)
08/26/2003		SUBMITTED to Mag Judge E. C. Scofield III on [75-1] motion to compel discovery from pla. (lme) (Entered: 08/26/2003)
08/28/2003	82	ORDER by Mag Judge E. C. Scofield III GRANTING [77-1] motion for leave to amend [50-1] 5th amended complaint. Pla may file amended complaint w/in 10 days from the entry of this Order. (cc) (lme) (Entered: 08/28/2003)
08/28/2003	83	ORDER by Mag Judge E. C. Scofield III GRANTING [73-1] motion for enlargement of number of depositions, GRANTING [79-1] motion to extend time thru 9/26/03 for discovery, DENYING as moot the [73-2] motion to extend time for 30 days for discovery by Gregory Allen Clark, Discovery ends 9/26/03 . (cc) (lme) (Entered: 08/28/2003)
09/02/2003	84	Notice to take deposition of STEVE NORMAN & STEVE GRANT by plaintiff (ck) (Entered: 09/04/2003)
09/02/2003	85	Notice of serving answer to fourth interrogatories from defendant by plaintiff. (ck) (Entered: 09/04/2003)
09/04/2003	86	FIFTH AMENDED COMPLAINT by plaintiff; jury demand (lme) (Entered: 09/08/2003)
09/05/2003	87	Amended Notice to take deposition of Steve Grant by phone by plaintiff. (lme) (Entered: 09/08/2003)
09/05/2003	88	**Reply brief in support of [75-1] motion to compel discovery from pla by dft. (***FILED UNDER SEAL***) (lme) (Entered: 09/08/2003)**
09/08/2003	89	Second Amended Notice to take deposition by telephone of Steve Grant by pla. (lme) (Entered: 09/10/2003)

09/09/2003	90	Notice to take depositions of SILAS BROWN, DAVID CHEATHAM and TARA GOEHRING by plaintiff (lme) (Entered: 09/10/2003)
09/15/2003	91	Notice to take depositions of Charles Baker and Maurice Norman by plaintiff. (lme) (Entered: 09/16/2003)
09/19/2003	92	MOTION by defendant for extension of page limitation on dft's summary judgment briefs with brief in support and proposed order. (To ECS) (lme) (Entered: 09/23/2003)
09/22/2003	93	ANSWER by defendant to fifth amended complaint [86-1]; jury demand. (lme) (Entered: 09/23/2003)
09/22/2003	94	AMENDED SUPPLEMENTAL ANSWERS TO INITIAL DISCLOSURES by plaintiff. (lme) (Entered: 09/24/2003)
09/24/2003	95	First Re-Notice to take deposition of Charles Baker by plaintiff. (lme) (Entered: 09/29/2003)
09/29/2003	96	ORDER by Mag Judge E. C. Scofield III GRANTING [92-1] motion for extension of page limitation on dft's summary judgment briefs. (cc) (lme) (Entered: 09/30/2003)
09/30/2003	97	Notice to parties by Mag Judge E. C. Scofield III offering guidelines for filing motion for summary judgment. (cc) (lme) (Entered: 09/30/2003)
10/15/2003	98	CONSENT MOTION to extend time for filing their dispositive motions , and to exceed page limitation on dispositive motions with brief in support. (To ECS) (lme) (Entered: 10/16/2003)
10/16/2003	99	ORDER by Mag Judge E. C. Scofield III GRANTING [98-1] motion to extend time for filing their dispositive motions. Any motions for sum jgm must be filed by 10/24/03. Responses to motions for sjm jgm must be filed by 11/24/03 and replies must be filed by 12/12/03. GRANTING [98-2] motion to exceed page limitation on dispositive motions. (cc) (lme) (Entered: 10/17/2003)
10/17/2003		Terminated submission. (lme) (Entered: 10/28/2003)
10/24/2003	**100**	**MOTION by defendant for summary judgment with brief in support, statement of material facts and appendix of exhibits Vols I-III. (***FILED UNDER SEAL*** the brief in support, statement of material facts and appendix Vols I-III) (lme) Modified on 10/28/2003 (Entered: 10/28/2003)**
10/24/2003	101	Notice of filing original deposition transcript of Gregory Allen Clark by defendant. (lme) (Entered: 10/28/2003)
10/24/2003	102	Deposition of GREGORY ALLEN CLARK taken for defendant. (3 Vols) (lme) Modified on 10/28/2003 (Entered: 10/28/2003)
10/24/2003	103	Notice of filing request for filing original depos by defendant. (lme) (Entered: 10/28/2003)
10/24/2003	104	Notice of filing documents under seal by defendant. (lme) (Entered: 10/28/2003)
10/27/2003	105	Supplemental Notice of filing original depo of Gregory Allen Clark by defendant. (lme) (Entered: 10/28/2003)

10/27/2003	106	Videotape Deposition of GREGORY ALLEN CLARK taken for defendant. (lme) (Entered: 10/28/2003)
10/27/2003	107	ORDER by Mag Judge E. C. Scofield III GRANTING [75-1] motion to compel discovery from pla. Pla is ORDERED to produce the manuscript or narrative statement of any books, articles or treatieses as sought in dft's request for production No. 31, including a copy of the manuscript referred to in the depo as having been given to
		pla's editor. Production should be made w/in 20 days of entry of this Order. Production of this document may be made the subject of the consent protective order already entered in this case, at pla's election. Dft may submit an affidavit or any other material in support of an award of atty's fees under Rule 37(a)(4), also w/in 20 days of entry of this order. (cc) (lme) (Entered: 10/28/2003)
11/07/2003	108	Notice of filing affidavit of Michael W. Johnston by defendant. (lme) (Entered: 11/10/2003)
11/21/2003	109	Notice of filing under seal pla's response to motion for sum jgm. (lme) (Entered: 11/24/2003)
11/21/2003	110	Response by plaintiff to dft's [100-1] motion for summary judgment with statement of material facts and appendix of exhibits. (***FILED UNDER SEAL, Memorandum in support, statement of material facts and appendix***) (lme)
11/21/2003	111	Notice of filing under seal original discovery by plaintiff. (lme) (Entered: 11/24/2003)
11/21/2003	112	Deposition of CHARLES BAKER taken for plaintiff. (***FILED UNDER SEAL***) (lme) (Entered: 11/24/2003)
11/21/2003	113	Deposition of STEVE GRANT taken for plaintiff. (***FILED UNDER SEAL***) (lme) (Entered: 11/24/2003)
11/21/2003	114	Deposition of STEPHEN NORMAN taken for plaintiff. (***FILED UNDER SEAL***) (lme) (Entered: 11/24/2003)
11/21/2003	115	Deposition of CARL WARE taken for plaintiff. (***FILED UNDER SEAL***) (lme) (Entered: 11/24/2003)
11/24/2003	116	Supplement to appendix to plaintiff's [110-1] memorandum of law in response to motion for summary judgment. (***FILED UNDER SEAL***) (lme) (Entered: 11/25/2003)
11/24/2003	117	Notice of filing under seal original depositions of James Hush, Linda Bell, Silas Brown, Maurice Norman, Timothy Meadows and Tara Goehring by plaintiff. (lme) Modified on 11/25/2003 (Entered: 11/25/2003)
11/24/2003	118	Deposition of JAMES HUSH taken for plaintiff. (***FILED UNDER SEAL***) (lme) (Entered: 11/25/2003)
11/24/2003	119	Deposition of LINDA BELL taken for plaintiff. (***FILED UNDER SEAL***) (lme) (Entered: 11/25/2003)
11/24/2003	120	Deposition of SILAS BROWN taken for plaintiff. (***FILED UNDER SEAL***) (lme) (Entered: 11/25/2003)

11/24/2003	121	Deposition of MAURICE NORMAN taken for plaintiff. (***FILED UNDER SEAL***) (lme) (Entered: 11/25/2003)
11/24/2003	122	Deposition of TIMOTHY MEADOWS taken for plaintiff. (***FILED UNDER SEAL***) (lme) (Entered: 11/25/2003)
11/24/2003	123	Deposition of TARA GOEHRING taken for plaintiff. (***FILED UNDER SEAL***) (lme) (Entered: 11/25/2003)
11/28/2003	124	Notice of filing original deposition under seal by plaintiff. (lme) (Entered: 12/01/2003)
11/28/2003	125	Deposition of PAUL MARKLEY taken for plaintiff. (***FILED UNDER SEAL***) (lme) (Entered: 12/01/2003)
12/08/2003		SUBMITTED to Mag Judge E. C. Scofield III on [100-1] motion for summary judgment.
		(lme) (Entered: 12/08/2003)
12/12/2003	126	Reply brief in support of dft's [100-1] motion for summary judgment with appendix. (***FILED UNDER SEAL***) (lme) (Entered: 12/15/2003)
02/11/2004	127	Notice of original deposition under seal by plaintiff. (tcc) (Entered: 02/12/2004)
02/11/2004	128	Deposition of LESLIE ANN DAVIS taken for plaintiff. (***FILED UNDER SEAL***) (tcc) (Entered: 02/12/2004)
02/11/2004	129	Deposition of DARLENE M. NEELY taken for plaintiff. (***FILED UNDER SEAL***) (tcc) (Entered: 02/12/2004)
02/11/2004	130	Deposition of DIANNA HADDON taken for plaintiff. (***FILED UNDER SEAL***) (tcc) (Entered: 02/12/2004)
02/11/2004	131	Certificate of service of Notice of Filing Original Deposition Transcripts under Seal as to defendant Coca-Cola Company. (tcc) (Entered: 02/12/2004)
05/26/2004	132	FINAL REPORT AND RECOMMENDATION by Mag Judge E. C. Scofield III RECOMMEND GRANTING [100-1] motion for summary judgment by Coca-Cola Company with order for service (Submission of RR due 6/12/04) (jdb) (Entered: 05/26/2004)
05/26/2004		Terminated submissions. (jdb) (Entered: 05/26/2004)
05/26/2004		Completed referral to Mag Judge E. C. Scofield III (jdb) (Entered: 05/26/2004)
06/23/2004		SUBMITTED to Judge Richard W. Story on [132-1] report & recommendation, [100-1] motion for summary judgment (epm) (Entered: 06/23/2004)
08/06/2004	133	ORDER adopting 132 report and recommendation as the order of the court and granting 100 Motion for Summary Judgment . Signed by Judge Richard W. Story on 8/6/04. (fmm) (Entered: 08/10/2004)
08/06/2004	134	CLERK'S JUDGMENT ENTERED in favor of defendant against plaintiff for costs of action (fmm) (Entered: 08/10/2004)

08/18/2004	Mail Returned as Undeliverable. (Re: 133 Order on Motion for Summary Judgment; 134 Clerk's Judgment) Mail sent to Jerome A. Stone, Jr.; F. Shields McManus; Robert A. Boas; and Elizabeth F. Johnson (epm) {Entered: 08/20/2004}

Appendix E

SETTLEMENT AGREEMENT AND MUTUAL GENERAL RELEASE

This Settlement Agreement and Mutual General Release ("Agreement") is made and entered into between Gregory A. Clark (referred to herein as "Clark") on the one hand, and The Coca-Cola Company (referred to herein as "Coca-Cola"), on the other hand.

By means of this Agreement, Clark intends to fully and unconditionally release all claims relating to or arising from his employment or the termination of his employment with Coca-Cola, that he, his heirs, administrators, executors, personal representatives, beneficiaries, and assigns may have against Coca-Cola and each of its affiliates, predecessors, successors, parents, subsidiaries, divisions, assigns, officers, directors, shareholders, representatives, employees, former employees, attorneys, and agents (collectively referred to as "Releasees"), the remaining terms of which Agreement are now fully set forth below.

1.   Consideration.

On May 26, 2004, Magistrate Judge Scofield of the U.S. District Court for the Northern District of Georgia entered a Report & Recommendation ("the R&R") in Gregory Clark v. The Coca-Cola Company, Civil Action No. 1:01-CV- 3039-RWS (the "Lawsuit").

In the R&R, Judge Scofield recommended that all of Clark's claims against Coca-Cola in the Lawsuit be dismissed. If the District Court adopts the R&R, which the parties acknowledge and agree is a substantial possibility, the parties acknowledge and agree that Coca-Cola would be entitled to and would seek its litigation costs

- 12 -

against Clark, which are substantial. In consideration of Coca-Cola's waiver of its rights to seek those litigation costs against Clark as set forth in this Agreement, and the release of Clark by Coca-Cola provided in Paragraphs 8, 9 and 10 below, Clark gives the releases, covenants, representations, and warranties stated herein.

2.   Clark's Agreement Not to Object To Or Appeal The R&R.

Clark hereby knowingly and voluntarily agrees that he will not (1) file objections to the R&R pursuant to Fed. R. Civ. P. 72, or any other rule or statutory provision; or (2) appeal the decision of the District Court in the Lawsuit if the District Court adopts the R&R or otherwise dismisses all of Clark's claims. If, however, the District Court does not adopt the R&R or otherwise dismiss all of Clark's claims in the Lawsuit, Clark agrees to voluntarily dismiss the Lawsuit with prejudice pursuant to Fed. R. Civ. P. 41.

3.   General Release By Clark.

(a)   Clark hereby knowingly and voluntarily releases and forever discharges the Releasees, collectively, separately, and severally, from any and all state or federal claims, causes of action, liabilities, and judgments of every type and description whatsoever, including, but not limited to, claims asserted in the Lawsuit, claims asserted in or related to Clark's Charge of Discrimination with the U.S. Equal Employment Opportunity Commission dated March 9, 2004, and claims arising under the Civil Rights Act of 1964, as amended, 42 U.S.C. §

1981, the Rehabilitation Act of 1973, as amended, the Employee Retirement

Income Security Act of 1974, as amended, the Fair Labor Standards Act of

1938, as amended, the Family and Medical Leave Act, the Americans with

Disabilities Act of 1991, and any and all other claims for any other types of

discrimination, harassment, retaliation, personal injury, emotional distress,

additional compensation or fringe benefits, claims for continued employment,

including attorneys' fees or costs that he, his heirs, administrators, executors,

personal representatives, beneficiaries, and assigns have or may have against

Releasees arising from, or relating to, Clark's employment or termination of

employment with Coca-Cola for compensatory or punitive damages or other

legal or equitable relief of any type or description.

      (b)   The claims, causes of action, security interests, liabilities, and

judgments released in Paragraph 3(a) above shall be referred to collectively

herein as the "Clark Released Claims."

      (c)   Clark hereby covenants and agrees that he will forever refrain and

forebear from commencing, instituting, or prosecuting any lawsuit, action, or other

proceeding against any of the Releasees, individually or collectively, based on, arising out

of, or connected with any of the Clark Released Claims.

      (d)   Clark understands and agrees that this Agreement shall be binding

upon him in his individual capacity as well as upon his heirs, administrators, executors, personal representatives, beneficiaries, and assignees.

4.   Release Includes Unknown Claims.

(a)   Clark understands and agrees that the Clark Released Claims are intended to and do include any and all claims of every nature and kind whatsoever (whether known, unknown, suspected, or unsuspected) arising from or relating to Clark's employment or termination of employment with Coca-Cola, which he has or may have against the Releasees, individually or collectively, to the extent permitted by law.

(b)   Clark further acknowledges that he may hereafter discover facts different from or in addition to those which he now knows or believes to be true with respect to the Clark Released Claims and agrees that, in such event, this Agreement shall nevertheless be and remain effective in all respects, notwithstanding such different or additional facts, or the discovery thereof.

(c)   Clark represents and acknowledges (i) that he and his attorneys have conducted whatever investigation was deemed necessary by him and his attorneys to ascertain all facts and matters related to this Agreement; (ii) that he has consulted with and received advice from legal counsel concerning this Agreement; and (iii) that he is not relying in any way on any statement or representation by the Coca-Cola or its attorneys, except as expressly stated herein, in reaching his decision to enter into this Agreement.

5.   No Assignment or Transfer of Clark Released Claims.

Clark represents and warrants that as of the day on which this Agreement is signed by Clark or by or on behalf of Coca-Cola, whichever is later, Clark has not assigned, transferred, or hypothecated, or purported to assign, transfer, or hypothecate, to any person, firm,

corporation, association, or entity whatsoever any of the Clark Released Claims. Clark

hereby agrees to indemnify and hold harmless Releasees against, without limitation, any and

all rights, claims, warranties, demands, debts, obligations, liabilities, costs, expenses

(including attorneys' fees), causes of action, and judgments based on, arising out of, or

connected with any such transfer, assignment, or hypothecation, or purported transfer,

assignment, or hypothecation.

6.   Indemnification for Loss of Consortium Claims Against Coca-Cola.

If there is any claim for loss of consortium, or any other similar claim,

arising out of or related to Clark's termination of employment with Coca-Cola,

Clark will indemnify and hold Coca-Cola harmless from any liability, including

costs and expenses (as well as reasonable attorneys' fees) incurred by Coca-Cola

as a result of any such claim.

7.   No Admission of Liability by Coca-Cola.

Clark understands and agrees that this Agreement is a release of disputed

claims and does not constitute an admission of liability on the part of Coca-Cola as

to any matters whatsoever and that Coca-Cola merely intends by this Agreement to

avoid further litigation and buy its peace.

8.   General Release by Coca-Cola.

(a)   Coca-Cola hereby knowingly and voluntarily releases and

forever discharges Clark from any and all state or federal claims, causes of action, liabilities, and judgments of every type and description whatsoever, including attorneys' fees or costs, that it has or may have against Clark arising from, or relating to the Lawsuit or Clark's employment or termination of employment with Coca-Cola, for compensatory or punitive damages or other legal or equitable relief of any type or description.

(b)   The claims, causes of action, security interests, liabilities, and judgments released in Paragraph 8(a) above shall be referred to collectively herein as the "Coca-Cola Released Claims."

(c)   Coca-Cola hereby covenants and agrees that it will forever refrain and forebear from commencing, instituting, or prosecuting any lawsuit, action, or other proceeding against Clark based on, arising out of, or connected with any of the Coca-Cola Released Claims.

9.   Release Includes Unknown Claims.

(a)   Coca-Cola understands and agrees that the Coca-Cola Released Claims are intended to and do include any and all claims of every nature and kind whatsoever (whether known, unknown, suspected, or unsuspected) arising from or relating to Clark's employment or termination of employment with Coca-Cola, which it has or may have against Clark, to the extent permitted by law.

(b)   Coca-Cola further acknowledges that it may hereafter discover facts different from or in addition to those which it now knows or believes to be true with respect to the Coca-Cola Released Claims and agrees that, in such event, this Agreement shall nevertheless be and remain effective in all respects, notwithstanding such different or additional facts, or the discovery thereof.

(c)   Coca-Cola represents and acknowledges (i) that it and its attorneys have conducted whatever investigation was deemed necessary by it and its attorneys to ascertain all facts and matters related to this Agreement; (ii) that it has consulted with and received advice from legal counsel concerning this Agreement; and (iii) that it is not relying in any way on any statement or representation by Clark or his attorneys, except as expressly stated herein, in reaching its decision to enter into this Agreement.

10.   No Assignment or Transfer of Coca-Cola Released Claims. Coca-Cola represents and warrants that as of the day on which this Agreement is signed by Clark or by or on behalf of Coca-Cola, whichever is later, Coca-Cola has not assigned, transferred, or hypothecated, or purported to assign, transfer, or hypothecate, to any person, firm, corporation, association, or entity whatsoever any of the Coca-Cola Released Claims. Coca-Cola hereby agrees to indemnify and hold harmless Clark against, without limitation, any and all rights, claims, warranties, demands, debts, obligations, liabilities, costs, expenses (including attorneys' fees), causes of action, and judgments based on, arising out of, or connected with any such transfer, assignment, or hypothecation, or purported transfer, assignment, or hypothecation.

11.   Future Legal Actions.

In the event that any party to this Agreement commences an action, at law or in equity, to enforce any right under any provision of this Agreement or to compel compliance with any provision of this Agreement, Clark and Coca-Cola covenant and agree that the

- 12 -

prevailing party in any such action shall be entitled to recover all reasonable attorneys' fees and costs incurred in connection with such action.

12. No Future Employment.

Clark covenants and agrees that he will not, at any time or in any place, seek, apply for or accept employment with The Coca-Cola Company or any of its subsidiaries or any bottler of Coca-Cola products, including without limitation, Coca-Cola Enterprises or The Atlanta Coca-Cola Bottling Company, and hereby waives any claim he has or could have as a result of her inability to seek employment with Defendant or any of its subsidiaries or any bottler of Coca-Cola products.

13. Modification.

No provision of this Agreement may be changed, altered, modified or waived except in writing signed by Clark and a duly authorized representative of Coca-Cola, which writing shall specifically reference this Agreement and the provision which the parties intend to waive or modify.

14. Severability.

In the event any provision of this Agreement should be held to be unenforceable, each and all of the other provisions of this Agreement shall remain in full force and effect.

15. Attorneys' Fees, Costs and Expenses.

Clark understands and agrees that his release of Coca-Cola as set forth in this Agreement includes and encompass therein any and all claims with respect to attorneys' fees, costs, and expenses for or by any and all attorneys who have represented him or with

whom he has consulted or who have done anything in connection with the Clark Released
Claims.

16.   Entire Agreement.

The parties hereto acknowledge that this Agreement constitutes a full, final, and
complete settlement of the Clark Released Claims and the Coca-Cola Released Claims and
supersedes and replaces any and all other written or oral exchanges, agreements,
understandings, arrangements, or negotiations between or among them relating to the subject
matter hereof, and affirmatively state that there are no other prior or contemporaneous
agreements, exchanges, representations, arrangements,
or understandings, written or oral, between or among them relating to the subject matter
hereof other than that as set forth herein, and that this Agreement contains the sole and entire
Agreement between them with respect to the subject matter hereof. The parties hereto further
acknowledge and agree that language proposed for, deleted from, or otherwise changed in the
various drafts of this Agreement but not included herein shall not be considered in any way
in the interpretation and application of this Agreement and shall not in any way affect the
rights and obligations of the parties hereto.

17.   Understanding.

Clark acknowledges and represents that he has read this Agreement in full and, with
advice of counsel, understands and voluntarily consents and agrees to each and every
provision contained herein.

18.   Applicable Law and Mutual Submission to Georgia Jurisdiction.

This Agreement shall be construed and enforced according to the laws of the State of
Georgia. Clark agrees to submit any and all disputes arising out of or based on this

- 12 -

Agreement to the jurisdiction of the state or federal courts located in Fulton County, Georgia.

    19.   Counterparts Acceptable.

This Agreement may be executed in two or more counterparts, each of which shall be deemed to be an original but all of which together shall constitute one and the same instrument.

IN WITNESS WHEREOF, the undersigned have executed this Agreement on the date shown below.

GREGORY ALLEN CLARK

_____   Date
Gregory Allen Clark

THE COCA-COLA COMPANY

Made in the USA
Charleston, SC
23 February 2014